MASSACHUSETTS QUILTS

MASSACHUSETTS QUILTS

Our Common Wealth

Lynne Zacek Bassett, editor

UNIVERSITY PRESS OF NEW ENGLAND

HANOVER AND LONDON

Published by University Press of New England,
One Court Street, Lebanon, NH 03766
www.upne.com
© 2009 by The Massachusetts Quilt Documentation Project
Printed in China

5   4   3   2   1

Library of Congress Cataloging-in-Publication Data
Massachusetts quilts : our common wealth / Lynne Zacek
Bassett, editor. — 1st ed.
    p. cm.
  Includes bibliographical references and index.
  ISBN 978-1-58465-745-3 (cloth : alk. paper)
  1. Quilts—Massachusetts. 2. Quiltmakers—Massachusetts.
I. Bassett, Lynne Z., 1961–
  NK9112.M365 2009
   746.4609744—dc22   2008025016

In the varied patchwork of our individual

character let us put only strong fabricks and

lasting colors, lest, thro' the "wear & tear"

of life, we prove but a shabby coverlet

to wrap an immortal soul in.

Inscribed on a friendship quilt made for the
Reverend Thomas Treadwell Stone (1801–1895)
of Salem, 1847–1848, MassQuilt 3092.

CONTENTS

FOREWORD

One of my most cherished possessions is a large "Texas Star" quilt passed down to me by my grandmother, and made by her aunt, Ella Rath. Aunt Ella was born in October 1900 in Ithaca, Wisconsin; her father emigrated from Mecklenberg, Germany, in the 1870s; her mother was the daughter of a Civil War veteran. A teacher known across Richland County for more than forty years, Ella never married, choosing instead to help support her brother and sister, Leo and Emma, who also had remained single. After Ella died in 1972, another sister—my grandmother—Esther Edith Arneson (the only sister to marry), set the quilt aside for me. The quilt is spectacular—certainly to me and I think to anyone who sees the concentric bursts of red, orange, and yellow, which have a way of lighting the whole room. I was four years old when she died, so I never really knew Aunt Ella, but her quilt—beautiful in its own right—helps me remember the hardworking, intelligent woman whom my own mother recalls so fondly.

I have another quilt, too, just as dear to me, though in other ways. A double wedding ring quilt, it was sewn by a Mrs. Baxter as a going-away present for my father's family in 1935 when they moved from Beloit, Wisconsin (where my grandfather, Clayton Miller, had been working in a knife factory), to LaValle, where they were able to buy their own farm. (While the Great Depression meant disaster for so many, for my grandparents on both sides of the family, the low land prices allowed them to purchase farms they might not otherwise have been able to afford.) My aunt Jeannette, who was ten at the time, can still remember Mrs. Baxter sewing

the whole thing on her front porch. I was given the quilt after my father's mother, Fern Gibeaut Miller, died, and for me the quilt is more an artifact of her than of the maker, whose connection with my family was severed thirty years before I was born. Fern was a strong woman—tough, even hard—but when that quilt is on the bed, what I remember most is my six-year-old self lying in her lap on the green sofa in the living room of the town home they retired to, benefiting from the backrubs only those strong, loving hands could give. Or the hours she spent teaching us how to play cards. Or the unparalleled quality of her apple pie, the product of a secret recipe now lost. She had a twinkly little smile, perhaps made particularly appealing by its comparative rarity.

Those two quilts always make me proud of my Midwestern upbringing, and the women who shaped it. In them I can see resolve, affection, a love of beauty, a devotion to family. They are not the documents that historians like myself typically seek out—not the letters or diaries, ledgers or memoirs that are the usual stuff of history writing—but they capture something about the past just the same. That my relationship with the actual quilters is fairly tangential is evidence in itself of the powerful ability some artifacts hold to acquire meanings well beyond those predicted by their makers and users. Some stories are obvious to a quilt's beholder, preserved outright in the cloth and stitches; others can be known only if a given thread of oral history remains intact over generations. Quilts are vast repositories, capable of holding many things, overt and tacit.

Look a little closer, and with a more curatorial eye, and quilts like these can tell still more about the time and place where they were made, and the people who made and used them—something that the volunteers behind MassQuilts and the book before you will affirm. Since its inception in 1994, the Massachusetts Quilt Documentation Project has recorded and photographed almost six thousand pre-1950 quilts that were made, used, or are owned currently in Massachusetts. These volunteers have explored the collections of nearly one hundred historical societies and small museums and examined quilts brought to the "documentation days" across the state by hundreds of private owners. Along the way, the project volunteers have both amassed and shared an ever-larger store of knowledge about a form of needlework that has been important to Massachusetts communities since the seventeenth century. Quilts, to be sure, are artifacts of sentiment; they are mediums for nostalgia, affection, and veneration across generations. But they are also texts of historical insight, and, to the right reader, just as telling as the narrative sources that we see more often in the footnotes of scholarly work. In the choice of fabrics, the patterns quilted, the arrangement of shapes or application of ornament, evidence is embedded that can tell us something distinctive about the history of American families, of American industry, of social change.

Massachusetts Quilts: Our Common Wealth brings together for the first time a large and diverse sampling of quilts from private, public, and family collections that together show how important these artifacts are to the history of the Commonwealth. In the quilts assembled here are hundreds of stories—about individual women's lives to be sure, but also about the vast social, economic, cultural, and political changes that shaped them. Just as my family quilts cue stories about enlarging careers for women in the early twentieth century, or migrations from factories to farms in Depression-era Wisconsin, through the quilts in this volume we can hear a wide array of Massachusetts stories, about religious radicals who rejected the corruption they believed plagued the Church of England while continuing to embrace the aesthetic values of the British empire; about reform-minded women eager to put their

skills with the needle to work on behalf of the social justice movements that animated the nineteenth-century Commonwealth; and about factory operatives whose access to both the innovation and the detritus of the textile industry shaped the quilts they made for themselves and their loved ones. Through the arrangement of color and pattern, we track the history of design from the lush fields of color celebrated in the whole-cloth quilts of the Georgian era, to the visual cacophony of Victorian "crazy" quilts, to the soft pastel floral prints of the Depression era. The materials of the quilts themselves contain a history of cloth production from its artisanal origins to the apex of the industry in New England, and through the wrenches of de-industrialization that continue to transform the Massachusetts economy.

The pages that follow are a celebration of Massachusetts quilts and quiltmakers. The product of years of effort and thousands of hours of volunteer labor among quilt specialists from around the region, these images and their accompanying essays offer a whole that is far greater than the sum of their parts, a history of the Commonwealth as seen through the accumulated choices of over one hundred Massachusetts quiltmakers, whose decisions about materials and design each reveal something to us about the world they lived in—and the world they strove to make for themselves. After looking closely at the range of artifacts the authors have brought together here, it will be impossible to look at any quilt, or really any product of needle arts, in your own home without wondering: Who made this, when and why? What technologies made it possible? Or, what social or cultural forces shaped the maker's choice of materials, or pattern, or construction?

Ella, Fern, and Mrs. Baxter never knew the women whose work is gathered here, but they would have understood their efforts and artistry. And just as I appreciate the legacy contained in my Wisconsin quilts, through these pages, citizens of the Commonwealth can appreciate the legacy contained in the quilts today preserved in private and public collections across Massachusetts. The MassQuilts project, in going from community to community in an effort to document these rich artifacts, to help families better preserve them for posterity, and to help their owners, curators, and regional museum-goers appreciate them as unique sources of historical insight, has made an invaluable and lasting contribution to public humanities in the Commonwealth. The book they have produced augments that effort, and gives it tangible form.

Marla R. Miller
Hadley, Massachusetts

ACKNOWLEDGMENTS

After documenting nearly six thousand quilts, the number of private quilt owners, historical societies, and museums who have allowed us to examine their quilts is too large to mention individually here. However, this project clearly never would have happened without their cooperation. We thank the individual quilt owners who brought their quilts to our documentations. Their excitement during the documentation process energized the MassQuilts team, and we wish that we could have included all of their quilts in this book. Every single historical society we worked with was exceptional in their enthusiasm and helpfulness—some even gave our documentation team a free lunch! These local history museums are goldmines of important and interesting objects and information; it is hoped that this book helps at least in a small way to give them the recognition they deserve for their dedication to preserving this Commonwealth's history.

The generosity of several museums deserves special recognition. First, of course, is the New England Quilt Museum, which gave MassQuilts a home and has provided many and various forms of support for years. We cannot thank the staff and trustees of the New England Quilt Museum enough. Old Sturbridge Village, Historic Northampton, and Orchard House–Home of the Alcotts allowed us to use not only their quilts, but supplementary illustrative material free of charge. The Peabody Essex Museum and the Museum of Fine Arts, Boston, provided photographs at greatly reduced charges, and allowed members of their curatorial staff to work on this book on company time. Having the support of these important museums helped to open doors for Mass-Quilts and to keep us within budget, and we are deeply grateful.

David Stansbury's care and attention in photographing many of the quilts for this book is sincerely appreciated. His good humor and patience make him a joy to work with. We sincerely appreciate the advocacy of Ellen Wicklum, our editor at the University Press of New England, and her guidance in bringing this book to fruition.

As book editor, I am deeply grateful to the MassQuilts steering committee members: Barbara Bell (eastern Mass. co-chair), Marjorie Childers, Julie Crossland (documentation coordinator), Jane Crutchfield (western Mass. co-chair), the late Helen Ewer, Anne Gallo (past president), Laura Lane (secretary), Carolyn Millard (photo management), Joan Neisser (data entry), the late Florence Purcell (fundraising), Vivien Lee Sayre (past president), Martha Supnik (volunteer coordinator and website designer), and Cheryl Williams (treasurer). They all have been wonderfully enthusiastic and helpful. In addition to this extra work, all of these talented women have volunteered during documentation days, made quilts for raffles, and in other ways worked to raise money for the project.

My appreciation for the dedication and work of the volunteer authors of this book is beyond my ability to express. Anita Loscalzo provided valuable assistance as our copyeditor. Dr. Marla Miller, professor of history at the University of Massachusetts at Amherst, also volunteered her guidance as our historical advisor. We could not have asked for a more thoughtful and knowledgeable scholar to assist us. The friendship of all of these wonderful women has been my rock throughout this process.

Of course, none of this would have been possible without the dedication of the MassQuilts documentation day volunteers, who have given thousands of hours to this project. Because the Massachusetts Quilt Documentation Project has been of such long-standing duration—having begun in 1994—volunteers have come and gone over the years. We are grateful to them all. In addition to those already mentioned, the volunteers have included:

MassQuilts East: Sandy Anderson-Besecher, Ruth Ashton, Genie Barnes, Lance Bibbins, Carol Bikofsky, Maryanne Boberg, Ann Bonsett, Marian Bressel, Robin Brisson, Lynne Champion, Michele Chapais, Judy Clark, Ardi Cochran, Dalia Dainora, Carol DeBold, Mary Ann Dunn, Heidi Fieldston, Anne Gallo, Dawn Gauthier, Jenny Gilbert, Marcia Grey, Nancy Halpern, Beth Hayes, Peg Johnson, Glenda Jones, Barbara Kampas, Sandy Keller, Susan Wellnitz Krantz, Marcia Learmonth, Linda Lemire, Mary Leonard, Bebe Lewis, Jill C. Lillie, Sally Lingner, Karen McGarity, Anne Messier, John Messier, Wendy Moore, Sandra Muncey, Penny Myles, Ann Penn, Nancy Phillips, Enid Sackin Reddick, Deborah Rich, Carol Sabia, Ed Sayre, Marianne Schwers, Susan Spears, Bob Supnik, Ann F. Takvorian, Sheila Toomey, Carol Tyler, Cynthia Vanaria, Mary Walter, Alice Wiggin, Kermit Williams, Pam Worthen, and Meg Young.

MassQuilts West: Faith Banas, Helen Bardwell, Lynne Bassett, Susan Burns, Marion Carlson, Jean DeMers, Jan Drechsler, Suzanne Flynt, Janet Hale, Sydney Henthorn, Judi King, Irene Marsh, Aimee Newell, Lois Palmer, JoAnne Parisi, Samantha Ulen, Marilyn White, Judi Wilson, and Edna Zamachaj.

The gratitude MassQuilts feels for the Coby Foundation of New York is as deep as Boston Harbor. We sincerely thank the Coby Foundation board members and director Ward Mintz for the very generous grant that made this book possible, and for their faith in the MassQuilts team. The Massachusetts Foundation for the Humanities, an affiliate of the National Endowment for the Humanities,

also showed great faith in our project, and gave us an important grant to help us pay for professional photography, for which we are very grateful. The National Quilting Association provided financial support several times over the years to help us purchase necessary supplies and photographs.

Quilt guilds across Massachusetts gave us wonderful support, by allowing MassQuilts to set up information tables at their guild shows, by hosting our promotional Powerpoint lecture, and by financial contributions large and small, depending on their capabilities. We are very grateful to the following quilt guilds: Bayberry Quilters of Cape Cod, who meet in South Dennis; Berkshire Quilters Guild of Great Barrington; the Cape Cod Holly Berry Quilters of Falmouth; the Concord Piecemakers; Crosstown Quilters of Weymouth; Garden City Quilters Guild of Beverly; Granville Quilt & Needlework Guild; Hammersmith Quilters Guild of Saugus; Hands Across the Valley Quilt Guild of Amherst; Linsey-Woolsey Quilt Guild of Attleboro; Material Girls Quilt Guild of Leominster; Merrimack Valley Quilters Guild of Plaistow, New Hampshire; Pioneer Valley Quilters Guild of Agawam; Quilters' Connection of Watertown; Schoolhouse Quilters of Shrewsbury; Squanicook Colonial Quilt Guild of Townsend; Thimble Pleasures Quilt Guild of Mendon; Thimbles and Friends of Abington; Wayside Quilters Guild of Sudbury; Yankee Pride Quilter's Guild of Pittsfield; and the 100th Town Quilt Guild of Westboro. The International Quilt Association also contributed toward photography for this book.

Community organizations and businesses also made financial donations to MassQuilts, and we sincerely appreciate their interest in our project: Bank of America branches in Westford, Acton, and Ware; Bear Hollow Antiques and Collectables in Williamsburg; DeWolf Realtors; Friends of the Keep Homestead Museum in Monson; Heartbeat Quilts of Hyannis; and the Mary Mattoon Chapter Daughters of the American Revolution in Amherst. We wish to express special thanks to Country Curtains, Cranston Print Works, and P & B Textiles for their generous support.

The donations of individuals were critical to the

success of MassQuilts. We are especially grateful to Anne and John Messier, who gave a leadership gift in the beginning of the book project, allowing us to get photography underway. Their gift was presented in memory of Blanche Peloquin Messier and Yvonne Beaudet Provost. MassQuilts also thanks the following individuals for their generous contributions: Eleanor L. Atherton, Janice Bakey (in memory of her grandmothers, mother, aunts, and sister), Lynne Z. Bassett, Patti Benoit, "Bobbie" (in memory of Kathleen Weinheimer and Gail Lane), Gerard and Denise Boiselle, Mary Lee Breault, Susan Luttrell Burns, James and Donna Bussard, Pauline C. Cabana (in memory of her aunt, Zelia Chabotte), Camille M. Chilorio-Laliberte, Reverend Susan E. Christian, Nancy Clover (in honor of her grandmother, Leona Theberge), Lila Coyle, Jane Crutchfield (in memory of her mother, Grace Hildreth), Karen Cullen, Carol DeBold, Kathy Virginia DiOrio, Sylvia Einstein, Phyllis Farnsworth, Sandra Fenrick, Beverly Fine, Lorraine Gallagher-Rae, Emily Gallivan, Janet Garfield, JoAnne Garland, Pat Gouin, Liz Granger (in memory of her mother, Jean A. Ford), Gary S. Green (in honor of Mildred B. Remsen), Ann Gurley, Hands Across the Valley Quilters Round Robin II (Barbara Aiken, Norma Bassett, Jane Carnes, Carolyn Croteau, Susan Eastman, Gloria Fox, Lyn Heady, Nancy Kalin, Jane Lane, Cynthia Shepard, and Charlotte Smith), Donald and Jessica Leger, Martha Liddy, Anita and Joseph Loscalzo, Robin McElheny, Jo Ann Mills, Joan C. Neisser, Helen Matthews Plassmann, the late Deborah Pulliam, Joy Reece, Allene Rizzolo (in memory of Heather Erika Scholwin), Carol Rosa Sabia, Carolyn C. Saleski, Carol Siegel, Stacey Smith, Margaret A. Stancer, Helen V. Sullivan (in honor of Mary C. Andrew and Helen L. Bergstrom), Natalie Thomas (in memory of her grandmother, Nina Ide Dickinson), Marion Vaitkus (in honor of the Caira quilting family), Holly A. Van Orman, Shirley Weinberg, Marilyn Wessman, Kathy West (in celebration of Ann Hollis Davison and Laura May West), Connie White (in honor of Madeline Harrington), Marilyn White, Alice Wiggin, Elizabeth A. Wilhelmsen (in memory of her Wilkinson, Smith, and Kelly family members), Meg Young, Edna Zamachaj, and Geraldine Zecco.

Lynne Zacek Bassett
Palmer, Massachusetts

INTRODUCTION

Massachusetts is one of four states (also including Virginia, Pennsylvania, and Kentucky) that calls itself a "commonwealth." Such a term seems to belong to centuries past, and indeed, it does. Meaning public welfare and prosperity ("commonweal") or a government of the people, according to the *Oxford English Dictionary* its common usage goes back to sixteenth-century England. "Commonwealth" is a word that resonates with history, but in truth, its meaning is no different from "state" in the context of Massachusetts' position within the United States.

Though small in size, the role of Massachusetts in the history of the United States is very large. The quilts in this book provide a window through which to view that history—a window particularly into the lives of the women who helped to build this commonwealth and this nation: Englishwomen who toiled at their kitchen hearths and in their gardens, but whose needlework gave an air of gentility to their colonial households; women who no longer saw themselves as English, but as American and helped to establish the United States of America as an independent country; women who worked to free the slaves and gave comfort to Union soldiers in the Civil War; women who broke the social barriers of their sex and created independent livelihoods for themselves; women who came to Massachusetts from Canada and Europe to work in the textile mills and provide a better life for their families; and, of course, women who nurtured their children and kept them warm. They are famous women, women known only to their families, and anonymous women. Together, they are a crucial but often overlooked part of the history of the Bay State. The quilts they have left to posterity are, indeed, our common wealth.

The Massachusetts Quilt Documentation Project was formed in 1994 by Vivien Lee Sayre, with the goal of preserving the wealth of quilts and the history of quiltmaking in this state. Massachusetts was a bit late in joining the quilt documentation bandwagon, which began in 1981 with Kentucky. The late start was for a good reason, however—the effort of regional quilt lovers had for some years gone into establishing the New England Quilt Museum in Lowell, which opened its doors in 1987. After some years of meeting in MassQuilts members' livingrooms, the project was given office and meeting space at the quilt museum, which moved to its present building in 1993. All quilt documentation data is now stored at the museum. Realizing that the majority of MassQuilts members lived in the eastern part of the state and that western Massachusetts quilts were not proportionately represented in the database, Jane Crutchfield, with the help of Marjorie Childers, formed MassQuilts West in 2000. Overall, since 1994, MassQuilts has documented approximately six thousand quilts in private and museum collections across the Commonwealth. Countless hours by dozens of devoted volunteers have made this project possible.

The topics that the MassQuilts team desired to cover in this book were myriad. After creating a list of over twenty subjects that possibly could be explored, it was decided to group them by theme to provide an overall structure to the book. Thus, this book is divided into three parts: "History," "Community," and "Memory." Chapters within these three sections examine quilts in specific contexts. The History section first discusses the early history of silk, wool, and cotton quilts in Massachusetts, and then examines quilts of the Commonwealth geographically, beginning along the eastern shore and ending in the west, in the Berkshire Mountains. The Industrial Revolution and its impact on the economy and on quiltmaking are discussed in the last chapter of the History section. The theme of Community explores how quilts represent geo-graphical, ideological, familial, and ethnic groups. Finally, quilts within the theme of Memory reveal their use purposefully or unconsciously to document people, events, and periods within our history. These quilts were sometimes made with an eye to a public audience, or they were very private. *Massachusetts Quilts: Our Common Wealth* ends with a discussion of a quilt collector—a woman who, like us, recognized not only the beauty of these textile objects and the talent of their makers, but the interesting history that quilts could tell.

PART I

HISTORY

Chapter 1

Early Quilts and Quilted Clothing

The first permanent English settlement in America was established in Jamestown, Virginia, in 1607; the next two English colonies were founded in Massachusetts—Plymouth Colony in 1620, and Massachusetts Bay Colony in 1630. In this commonwealth, then, we can expect to find some of America's earliest quilting, in bed quilts and garments.

Research on early American quilts in the last thirty years has debunked the cherished chestnut that pieced quilts were commonly found in the first colonial homes.[1] In fact, the earliest quilts were whole-cloth—of silk, wool, or cotton—and were laid upon the beds of the wealthy as items of prestige. No documented seventeenth-century quilted item survives from Massachusetts, but references to quilts in this early period appear occasionally in probate records.[2] The 1633 estate inventory of Samuel Fuller of Plymouth Colony includes the earliest reference to a bed quilt in New England.[3] In reviewing the probate inventories of Essex County from 1635 to 1674, George Francis Dow found a paucity of bed quilts: "coverlets are mentioned 142 times and rugs 157 times while quilts are listed only four times."[4] In her analysis of Suffolk County inventories from 1650 to 1695, Linda Baumgarten found slightly more quilts, probably because she was working with the estates of merchants, who typically were among the wealthiest of New England colonists. Still, she found only a few: thirteen, to be exact, compared to 153 bed rugs.[5] Baumgarten notes that these quilts are "described as calico, painted calico, and East India, indicating an Indian origin. Other quilts were silk. No references to pieced quilts were found."[6]

A study of probate inventories in the Connecticut River Valley town of Deerfield, established in 1673, uncovered no quilts at all until 1729, when the estate of the Reverend John Williams was evaluated. In total, only four bed quilts in three Deerfield inventories appeared among forty-seven inventories dating prior to 1750.[7] Considering the very small number of bed quilts owned in early colonial Massachusetts, then, it comes as no surprise that the earliest surviving examples do not date before the second quarter of the eighteenth century.

The bed quilts, cradle quilt, quilted petticoats, and pieced silk handscreen examined in this chapter reveal the importance of imported textiles to the colonial Massachusetts household. Boston was America's most important port until the mid-eighteenth century. Even after its preeminence was eclipsed by Philadelphia and New York, hundreds of ships docked each year in Boston Harbor, their holds filled with goods from around the world—including wools, silks, linens, and cottons from England, France, Holland, India, and many other countries. Account books of merchants and weavers, along with import records, make it clear that at no time in its history was Massachusetts entirely self-sufficient in textile production—always, the importation of textiles far outstripped domestic production.[8]

The early Boston newspapers printed the advertisements of merchants offering textiles imported from England and the Continent:

> To be sold by Mr. Thomas Perkins at his Warehouse no. A near Mr. Henry Caswell's in Kingstreet, Boston, All sorts of European Goods,

Consisting of Broad-cloths, Saggatees, Drug-
gets, Curtain & Vallions of the Newest Fashions,
Feather-Beds, Ruggs, Quilts, Blankets, Wadings,
Whitney-Shaggs, Buttons, Mohair, Threds, Ribbons. . . . By whole Sale or Retail at a very Reasonable Rate, being in a short Time bound for
Great Britain.[9]

Wealthy colonists were able to purchase from merchants like Mr. Perkins professionally made British
or Indian quilts. The British East India Company
imported quilts made of shiny silk, closely stitched
with exotic scenes such as hunting parties amidst
bizarre foliage, as well as cotton quilts, vibrantly
painted and printed. Colonists also could purchase
English whole-cloth quilts in silk or wool, made in
the upholstery trade, and stitched with framed center-medallion designs.

It is not known when Massachusetts women
began to make their own bed quilts, but teachers
of needlework advertising in Boston papers from
the early 1700s offered instruction in quilting in the
English and French styles (see fig. 20/MQ 4960 and
fig. 24/MQ 5073). Examination of surviving quilts
suggests that by about the mid-eighteenth century,
women in the Massachusetts Bay Colony had established their own style of quilting and broken away
from the rigid framed center-medallion designs of
British whole-cloth quilts. Using glossy worsteds
(such as calamanco or tammy) imported from England for the face, Massachusetts quilters created bed
covers with designs that related perfectly to the baroque and rococo curves and fantastic foliate motifs
seen in the furniture, ceramics, metalwares, printed
textiles, and laces of their homes and wardrobes.[10]

Bed covers, however, were not the primary item
to be quilted in colonial Massachusetts. Diary references, along with probate inventories, indicate that
New England women quilted petticoats more often
than bed covers in the eighteenth century.[11] And
petticoats were only one category among many garment types that women frequently quilted. Museum
collections across the Commonwealth hold quilted
bonnets and hoods, pockets, coat linings, corsets,
pelisses, even baby shoes, from the eighteenth and
early nineteenth centuries. Like bed covers and pet-

ticoats, these items could be simple, or they could
be elegantly quilted with floral vines and feather
designs.

With the ascendance of cotton fabrics beginning in the late 1700s, quiltmaking in Massachusetts
began to change. Pieced bed quilts are mentioned
with increasing frequency in diaries and probate
inventories, and extant examples—such as the
Spaulding family quilt from Townsend (fig. 17/
MQ 4999)—reveal not only the change in preferred
fiber, but in decorative art design. The neoclassical
style superseded the mid-eighteenth-century cur-
vilinear rococo, bringing in a fashion for geometric
patterns. The decorative arts of the early nineteenth
century also delighted in mixing colors and patterns, leading to the popularity of the pieced calico
quilt, as we see in the Lynde family hexagon quilt
from Salem (fig. 18/MQ 2798).

The three major fibers, cotton, wool, and silk, di-
vide this first chapter in its exploration of the early
history of quilts and quiltmakers in Massachusetts,
both in bed covers and in petticoats.   —LZB

MARY COOPER CRIB QUILT
(FIG. 1)

Contemporary newspaper advertisements attest
to the abundance of bed quilts imported into
Boston in the eighteenth century. While "callico"
and "India quilts" appear on lists of sales and were
coveted luxury items, the preponderance of quilts
imported into the colonies were silk and wool (calamanco) whole-cloth quilts made in England by pro-
fessionals associated with the upholstery trades.[12]
Most merchants advertised their imports simply as
"bed quilts"; Boston merchant William Greenleaf,
however, made particular note of his "callaman-
coe and silk quilts" in the extensive list of items imported from London and Bristol that he published in
the *Boston Weekly News-Letter* in December 1760.

One English quilt that might have been included
in a colonial merchant's advertisement is this yellow satin crib quilt, made about 1744. The quilt
is backed with cream silk woven in a shiny, plain

FIGURE 1. Whole cloth crib quilt, English import, owned by Mary
Cooper (c. 1744–?) of Boston, c. 1744. Silk with wool batting (48"
× 38¾"). Collection of the Museum of Fine Arts, Boston (45.779).
Photograph © 2007 Museum of Fine Arts, Boston. MQ 2479.

FIGURE 2. Embroidered dais cover, North India (or Decca), early eighteenth century. Cotton, with silk and metal-wrapped yarns, quilted with silk yarns (128¾" × 99"). Collection of the Museum of Fine Arts, Boston, Gift of John Goelet (66.862). *Photograph © 2007 Museum of Fine Arts, Boston.*

weave commonly referred to as "lutestring" in the period.[13] It is filled with wool fleece. The quilt is an excellent example of a framed center-medallion design. Flanking the central medallion are four quarter-medallions that fan out from the corners inside a wide outer border.

While the center-medallion composition commonly appears in English needlework of the early eighteenth century, its source is clearly Eastern. Indian textiles and floor coverings, including embroideries from Gugerat and Cambay and printed cottons from the Coromondal Coast, were imported in great numbers into England by the British East India Company and became important stylistic influences on English traditional needlework during this period. The close relationship between English textiles and Indian embroideries can be seen in the striking similarity between the silk whole-cloth crib quilt and an embroidered Indian

dais cover made in Decca or North India in the early eighteenth century (fig. 2). The central medallion composition appears frequently on dais and floor coverings, revealing its roots in carpet design from Persia (now Iran). Some scholars have traced the center-medallion composition even further, pointing out its stylistic origins in fifteenth-century Persian book covers.[14] The central medallion and quarter-medallion composition later developed into a standard design for Persian carpets in the sixteenth century, which had a profound influence on art of the Muslim Mughal court of India in the seventeenth century.[15]

This yellow silk crib quilt also features traditional English quilting patterns, making it a fusion of East and West. Surrounding the central medallion and within the outer border are repeated geometric designs—fans, diamonds, and chevrons—that typically appear in this period on English quilted furnishing textiles and costume accessories, such as petticoats.

The crib quilt was donated to the Museum of Fine Arts by Katherine Homans, a descendant of the Amory family, who settled in Boston in the early eighteenth century. Accession records note that according to the donor, the quilt "probably belonged to Mary Cooper, born in Boston in 1744." Mary Cooper was the daughter of Mary (Foye) and the Reverend William Cooper, noted pastor of the Brattle Street Church. Mary Cooper's birth date is not recorded; however, her baptism took place at the Brattle Street Church on March 4, 1744. Mary's father died before she was born, so officiating at her baptism was the Reverend Samuel Cooper, her stepbrother from Rev. William Cooper's first marriage to Judith Sewell. In 1766, Mary married Dr. Samuel Gardner, a physician in Milton, Massachusetts. The connection to the Amory family was formed when their daughter, Sarah Gardner, married John Amory of Boston in 1794.[16] The quilt descended through the Amory family until it reached Katherine Homans, who donated it to the Museum of Fine Arts in 1945.

While family lore can be suspect at times, in this case, the history of the crib quilt appears to be accurate. As the only child of a socially prominent family, Mary Cooper likely would have been the recipient of an expensive, luxury import item such as this quilt. Stylistically, the quilt dates to the first half of the eighteenth century, thus making it possible that it even belonged to her mother, Mary (Foye) Cooper. Mary Foye was born in Boston in 1721 to Elizabeth (Campbell) and William Foye. Her father served as Treasurer of the Province from 1736 to 1759, and was a successful merchant in Boston prior to this appointment.[17] Mary Foye and Mary Cooper both belonged to families with enough wealth and prestige to afford this prized, imported silk quilt.

—LW

DEBORAH HOBART CLARK HANDSCREEN

(FIG. 3)

Made by Deborah Hobart Clark of Danvers, probably in the period between 1730 and 1750, this handscreen is the earliest example of American-made patchwork yet discovered. A passage from Jonathan Swift, the English satirist and author of *Gulliver's Travels*, points to the popularity of fashioning such handscreens in the early eighteenth century. In *Directions to Servants* from 1726,

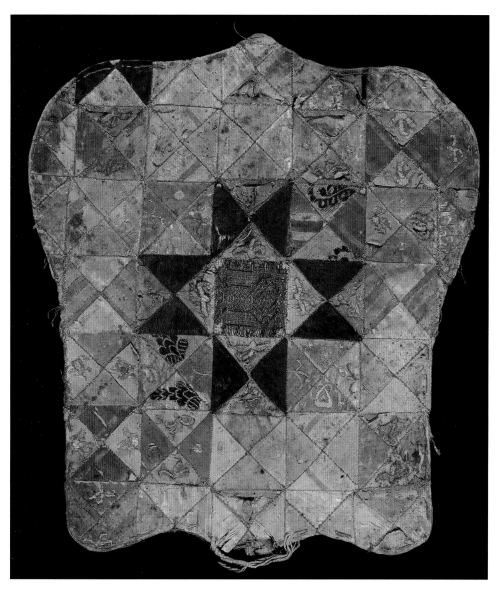

FIGURE 3. Pieced handscreen, made by Deborah Hobart Clark (c. 1702–1765) of Danvers, c. 1730–1750. Silk, metallic threads, paper, cardboard (11¾" × 10¼"). Collection of the Danvers Historical Society, Danvers, Mass. (1893.49.1). *Photograph courtesy of The Finer Image Photo Lab, Danvers, Mass.* MQ 5067.

FIGURE 4. Deborah Hobart Clark handscreen, back view, showing marbleized paper. *Photograph courtesy of The Finer Image Photo Lab, Danvers, Mass.*

Swift berates the practice of cutting up clothing to make "patchwork for screens, stools, cushions, and the like."[18] Deborah Hobart's handscreen features an elegant curved outline distinctive of the Queen Anne style, in fashion in colonial America from about 1730 to the 1760s.[19]

Deborah basted small triangles of silk fabrics over paper templates and then stitched them together in a pattern today called "Hourglass" or "Yankee Puzzle." (Unfortunately, the fragility of the handscreen prohibits close inspection of the paper templates for clues to the precise age of this item; however, most of the papers appear to be unmarked.) Surviving American pieced bed quilts from later in the eighteenth century, such as the Saltonstall quilt at the Peabody Essex Museum (fig. 5/MQ 2756), the 1785 Anna Tuels quilt in the collection of the Wadsworth Atheneum, and the Abercrombie quilt in the collection of Historic New England, also feature this simple patchwork pattern, along with the remains of their paper templates.[20] The handscreen's hourglass piecing provides the background for a central eight-pointed star. An interior lining of cardboard stiffens the handscreen, while marbleized paper covers the back (fig. 4/MQ 5067). A narrow tape, probably of silk, once edged the item, but stitch holes and remnants of sewing thread are virtually all that remain. The original turned wooden handle is now missing, and a cotton string loop was added to what originally would have been the bottom so that the screen could be hung for display.

Though merely a battered ghost now, the handscreen once declared its owner's wealth and social status. The square of elegant silver brocade pieced into the star's center sparkled in the firelight when Deborah held up the screen to shield her face from the heat. Its prominent placement suggests that it held some significance to Deborah, perhaps as a piece of a garment from a special occasion or beloved family member. Certainly, it was a very valuable fabric, being woven of silver threads—which alone would warrant its featured placement. Unfortunately, the bits of silk in the rest of the screen are too small to allow specific identification of the fabric designs, but what is evident is consistent with a date from the first half of the eighteenth century. Besides the silver brocade, there is a silk brocade in a stylized floral pattern, several woven stripes, satin, and plain weaves. Many of the silk fabric pieces are embroidered in silk threads with small leafy sprays and other figures. The embroidery is worked through the paper templates.

A native of Braintree, Deborah Hobart married the Reverend Peter Clark (1692–1768) of Watertown in 1719 when she was seventeen years old. The Reverend Clark, a Harvard graduate, had taken the pulpit in Salem Village (now Danvers) not long before and undoubtedly felt the need of a wife to assist him in his pastoral duties.[21] According to his biographer, Clark was "a shrewd bargainer . . . [who] after nearly a year of negotiation, obtained good terms: a salary of £90 a year, £90 in settlement money, and the parsonage."[22]

The parsonage previously belonged to the Reverend Samuel Parris, the minister at the center of the

Salem witchcraft hysteria of 1692 to 1693. Folklore would have it that the hysteria began at the parsonage's kitchen hearth, with the terrifying stories of witches and evil spells told by Parris's slave Tituba to his nine-year-old daughter Betty and eleven-year-old niece Abigail Williams. Historians have relieved Tituba of this burden, however, finding no evidence to support the myth.[23] A number of social and cultural factors that influenced the hysteria have been posited, including tension between Salem and Salem Village, anxiety over the place of women in the community, and fears generated by ongoing warfare with natives. Historians Paul Boyer and Stephen Nissenbaum suggest that the root of the witchcraft hysteria was acrimonious dissension within the village over the ministry of the Reverend Parris, pitting one family against another, and actuated by stressed adolescent girls.[24] Whatever the cause, by the end of the hysteria, scores of men and women had been accused of consorting with the devil; nineteen were hanged, one man was crushed to death under stones, and several more died in jail. Despite the intervening ministry of the Reverend John Green, the division of the community continued into the next generation. The townspeople still had not healed completely by the time the Reverend Peter Clark agreed to be their minister in 1717. (Not until 2001 were all of the accused finally exonerated.)

Clark's biographer wondered if the minister's parsonage "was haunted by the victims of the Reverend Samuel Parris. Sorcery was by no means dead in Salem Village, for under Mr. Clark the church had to take steps against members of the congregation who consulted witches and fortune-tellers."[25] Clark worked hard to provide loving guidance to his flock; his obituary in 1768 noted that "He delighted to promote Harmony among divided Christians, and was much made use of to this End. . . ."[26] He was a firm Calvinist, although he did allow that babies who died before baptism did not necessarily burn in the fires of Hell.[27] Perhaps it was his own experience as a father that gave him this gentler perspective. Clark was remembered as "tender and affectionate" to his children, and "endearing and kind" to his wife.[28] He and Deborah had six daugh-

ters and seven sons; only eight of their offspring were still living at the time of his death.

The Reverend Peter Clark died after serving his congregation for fifty-one years. In truth, he served longer than desired, as his declining health often forced him to sit down and rest in the middle of a sermon, or even caused him to "swoon away in his Pulpit," causing the one criticism in his obituary that his "fervent Desires of doing Good while he lived, [were] carried to an Excess." Nevertheless, his "bereaved Flock" "deplore[d] his Loss."[29]

The community of Salem Village remembered Deborah fondly, also. Her obituary in 1765 stated that she was "a Gentlewoman possessed of many excellent Qualities, with regard to which she was very much esteemed."[30] Born into wealth, she undoubtedly received instruction while a young girl in fine needlework, probably in Boston.[31] She would have been aware of the latest fancywork fashions, including patchwork. This handscreen, pieced of silk and silver fabrics, is testimony to her sophistication and wealth in a period when most colonial Massachusetts families lived in one- or two-room houses, tilled the rocky soil of their farms, feared their Indian neighbors, and in their heart of hearts, still believed in witches.

—LZB

SALTONSTALL FAMILY QUILT
(FIG. 5)

The Saltonstall family quilt is one of only four quilts made of silk patchwork with American provenance that survive from the eighteenth or early nineteenth century.[32] It is significant for its diverse array of imported textiles, including examples from Europe and Asia—evidence of the surprising range of fabric available in the colonies. While the Saltonstall quilt has been published and studied by a number of textile scholars, its history and attribution remain puzzling, as well as fascinating.

Small triangular pieces arranged into square blocks create a pattern called variously "Yankee Puzzle," "Bow Ties," or "Hourglass." The blocks are arranged in rows interspersed with narrow bands

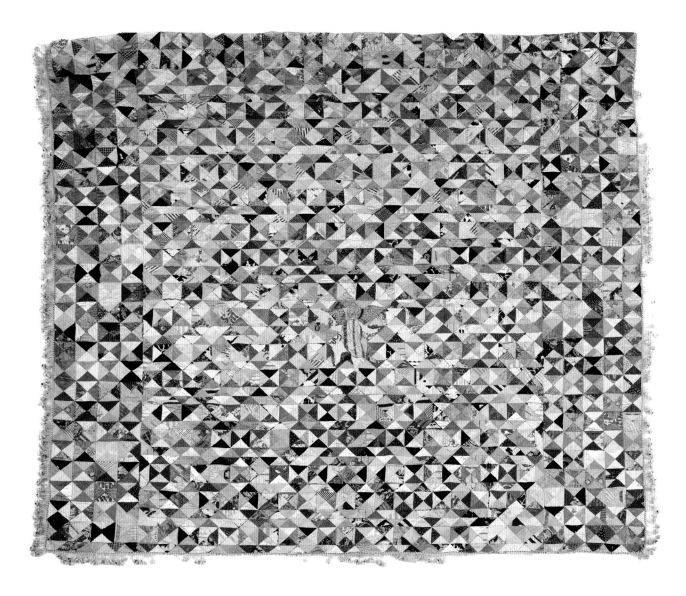

FIGURE 5. Pieced and appliquéd quilt, associated with the Leverett and Saltonstall families of Massachusetts, eighteenth century with later alterations. Silk, cotton, paper, metallic thread, wool (81 ½" × 83"). Collection of the Peabody Essex Museum, Salem, Mass., gift of the Honorable Leverett Saltonstall, 1978 (134358). *Photograph courtesy of the Peabody Essex Museum.* MQ 2756.

comprised of single or double rows of triangles to form a framed-center quilt. (The small fabric triangles, contrasting colors, and intricate, kaleidoscopic arrangement of the blocks make the organization of the quilt pattern difficult to discern.) The maker formed the silk triangles over paper templates, and at the center of the quilt she appliquéd an angel or winged figure embellished with silver metallic thread and hand-painted details (fig. 6/MQ 2756). A white-and-red wool ball-fringe edges the quilt.

The quilt features an extraordinary array of fabrics, including damask, brocade, velvet, satin, and striped, embroidered, and plain-woven silks. A small number of pieces, including resist-dyed and hand-painted silks, may be of Asian origin. A tiny white satin triangle features a hand-drawn embroidery pattern of leaves and possibly a caterpillar in a style of embroidery typical of seventeenth-century England (fig. 7/MQ 2756). Examples of similar embroidery by members of the Leverett family in the seventeenth century include the embroidered cabinet worked by daughters of Governor John Leverett, now in the collection of the Peabody Essex Museum, and a dressing glass and frame made of raised and padded embroidery in the collection of the Museum of Fine Arts, Boston.[33]

Many of the triangular paper templates, which measure about two and a half by one and three-quarters inches, were removed from the quilt in the 1930s, probably at the same time that the current backing fabric was added. A group of paper templates were carefully saved and now reside in the Saltonstall Family papers at the Massachusetts Historical Society. The paper templates include fragments of handwritten documents, the *London Gazette*, a printed document in Dutch, and purported copies of the Harvard College catalogue of 1701. Some paper templates feature handwritten inscriptions in an unidentified language, possibly a kind of shorthand (fig. 8/MQ 2756). Silk fibers and basting stitches remain attached to many of the paper templates. A number of the templates are also still visible embedded within the quilt and can be seen through an opening made for the purpose in the quilt lining.[34]

A hand-written paper label sewn to the back identifies its maker as the wife of Governor John Leverett (1616–1679) of the Massachusetts Bay Colony. Governor Leverett was married twice and his second wife, Sarah Sedgwick (born 1629), died in 1704/1705. When the quilt was first published in books such as Lenice Ingraham Bacon's *American Patchwork Quilts* (1973), Sarah Sedgwick Leverett and her daughter Elizabeth Leverett Cooke (1651–1717) were credited as the makers. Elizabeth's granddaughter, Mary Leverett Cooke, married Judge Richard Saltonstall (1703–1756), connecting these two prominent and influential Massachusetts families. The quilt descended in the Saltonstall family until 1978 when the Honorable Leverett Saltonstall

FIGURE 6. Detail of central appliqué figure of a cherub. *Photograph courtesy of the Peabody Essex Museum.*

FIGURE 7. Detail of silk patch showing embroidery pattern. *Photograph courtesy of the Peabody Essex Museum.*

FIGURE 8. Detail of paper template with inked inscription, possibly a form of shorthand. *Photograph courtesy of the Peabody Essex Museum.*

(1892–1979), donated it to the Essex Institute, now the Peabody Essex Museum.[35]

The date of the quilt has been debated over many years by quilt and textile scholars. While a few of the fabrics used to construct the quilt may date to the seventeenth century, the majority of the textiles are of eighteenth century origin and indicate that the quilt was made later than originally thought. Although outside of the scope of this essay, further research to analyze and document the origins and dates of individual fabrics and to transcribe and translate the handwritten and printed inscriptions on the templates may yield additional information for future textile scholars. This quilt and the seventeenth-century embroideries associated with the Leverett family are among the earliest and most historically significant textiles to survive from colonial Massachusetts. These textiles demonstrate the artistic accomplishments, skill, and sophisticated tastes of women from this distinguished New England family. —PBR

MARY ABBOTT BRIDGES QUILT
(FIG. 9)

The earliest bed quilt believed to have been made in Massachusetts is a greenish-brown worsted whole-cloth quilt. Much used by its family, it has been cut down and patched here and there, and is today a rather ragged survivor. Nevertheless, its elegant quilting pattern, stitched in blue worsted thread, remains evident. A combination of English tradition and New England design innovation supports the assertion of the quilt's early date. Typical of English framed center-medallion design, a central quatrefoil motif—framed by feathered vines terminating in opposing curves at the corners—is surrounded by closely worked vines blooming in an impossible array of stylized flowers, leaves, and fruit. A variety of feathered borders provides structure to this wild arrangement. Eventually, overall designs interpreting baroque and rococo floral, foliate, and vine motifs, without the structure of multiple borders, would come to dominate New England's whole-cloth quilt design.

FIGURE 9. Drawing of a whole-cloth quilt, made by Mary Abbot (1701–1774) of North Andover, c. 1738. Wool (86½" × 65"). Collection of the McCord Museum, Montreal, Canada (M971.109). *Drawing © 2004 by Lynne Z. Bassett.* MQ 5071.

Mary Abbot of North Andover made this quilt, probably around 1738, at the time of her marriage to James Bridges. In the previous century, the town of Andover (which at the time included North Andover) had been home to another creative woman, poet Anne Bradstreet (1612–1672). Famous for her lines,

> I am obnoxious to each carping tongue
> Who says my hand a needle better fits . . .

Anne Bradstreet well knew that society generally did not give women credit for their intelligence. Needlework offered the most acceptable outlet for a woman's talent. The quilt made by Mary Abbot Bridges is a testament to her skill with a needle and to her industry. It is also evidence of her desire to bring elegance to her new home.

The Abbots and Bridges were among the "more prosperous families" of North Andover, who fre-

quently intermarried in order to sustain local political and economic power.[36] James Bridges was a
representative to the General Court in Boston, a
man "of great influence and considerable wealth,"
who owned several slaves.[37] Mary Abbot undoubtedly needed the help of servants, as she became step-
mother to five children ranging in age from five to
fifteen when she married widower James. She soon
added three more children to the family. Wealth
and power could not save her husband from a terrible end, unfortunately. Fifty-one-year-old James
". . . melted to death / By extreme heat" in 1747, according to his gravestone.[38]

Mary's quilt was handed down to her youngest daughter, Chloe Bridges, who married Timothy Osgood, an Andover carpenter, in 1765. At
that time, it was still the height of fashion to have a
whole-cloth quilt on the most important bed in the
house, and certainly Chloe welcomed the gift. The
quilt passed next to Chloe and Timothy's son John
Osgood (b. 1773), who married Betsy Fuller. John
and Betsy's daughter Harriot (b. 1812) brought the
quilt with her to Canada when she married Ralph
Rugg of Quebec in 1836. Mary Abbot's quilt now
resides at the McCord Museum in Montreal.[39]

—LZB

REVEREND JONATHAN LIVERMORE QUILT

(FIG. 10)

The Reverend Jonathan Livermore and his sister
Abigail Livermore Keyes combined their talents
to make this brilliant pink glazed-worsted quilt in
1769 for the minister's marriage to Elizabeth Kidder (1743–1822) of Billerica, Massachusetts. Jonathan and Abigail, named for their parents, Jonathan
and Abigail (Ball) Livermore, were raised in North-
boro, Massachusetts, along with nine other siblings.
The elder Jonathan "possessed uncommon learning
for his time, was an accurate surveyor and an excellent penman." Added to his many accomplishments
as a leader in the town and in the Congregational
Church was his remarkable ability at the age of one

hundred to still ride a horse without fatigue.[40] The
Reverend Jonathan inherited his father's artistic
abilities, as family tradition states that he drew the
design for this quilt.

He also inherited his father's hunger for an education. Jonathan tried his hand at a trade for some
years before finally resolving to enter Harvard College and become a minister. At the age of twenty-
one, he began his studies. After graduating from
Harvard in 1760, he traveled a little north of the
Massachusetts border to settle in the town of Wilton, New Hampshire, where he was ordained in
1763. Tragedy struck the town ten years later when
the frame of the new church collapsed as it was
being raised, killing five men and severely injuring
many more. (Cooperative labor parties, even church
raisings, were often an opportunity for excessive
consumption of rum and hard cider, which seems to
have played a part in this calamity.) The Reverend
Jonathan Livermore's ministerial style is evident in
his sermon dedicating the completed church in 1775:

> And surely He has remarkably smiled upon us
> while we have been building this house. . . . It is
> true, we met with a most grievous disaster in erect-
> ing the frame which we ought never to forget;
> but whether we ought to consider it as a rebuke of
> Providence is matter of inquiry. So much mercy
> was displayed in the midst of the judgment that it
> evidently appears that we suffered far less than we
> deserved for our careless and presumptuous neglect
> of the proper means of safety.[41]

Jonathan preached the mercy of God to the Wilton
congregation until 1777, when he asked to be dismissed, possibly due to political differences with his
congregation. He continued to live in Wilton for
the rest of his life, running a sawmill and preaching
occasionally in surrounding towns.[42] He and Elizabeth raised eight surviving children.

Jonathan apparently enjoyed a close relationship with his older sister Abigail, who married John
Keyes of Shrewsbury in 1741. Amazingly, she found
the time to stitch this quilt according to Jonathan's
design, even while caring for nine children at home.
Using yellow worsted thread, she quilted seven
stitches to the inch through the bright pink, twill-

FIGURE 10. Whole-cloth quilt, designed by the Reverend Jonathan
Livermore (1729–1809) of Wilton, N.H., and made by his sister,
Abigail Keyes (1724–1801) of Shrewsbury, Mass., c. 1769. Wool (104"
× 98"). Collection of the Shelburne Museum, Shelburne, Vermont.
Photograph © Shelburne Museum, Shelburne, Vermont. MQ 5068.

woven, glazed worsted of the front, the wool batting, and the pale pink twill-woven worsted of the back.

The design Jonathan created is rooted in seventeenth-century baroque bizarre florals and eighteenth-century rococo undulating lines (fig. 12/MQ 5068).[43] Such designs were used for decorative arts of all sorts in this period. Jonathan had only to look around at his furniture, silver, laces, ceramics, and even the gravestones in his church's burying ground to find inspiration. Textiles, especially, lent themselves to surfaces covered with curling vines and stylized irises, pomegranates, and roses; note the similarity of this quilt's design with the crewel embroidery of the Fifield quilt (fig. 13/MQ 2510).

This glossy, fuschia pink quilt made an impressive gift to Jonathan's bride, as quilts in the colonial period were luxury items made from expensive

FIGURE 11. The Reverend Jonathan Livermore, from *The Livermore Family in America* (Boston: W. B. Clarke Company, 1902). *Photograph courtesy of the American Antiquarian Society, Worcester, Mass.*

FIGURE 12. Drawing of Livermore quilt. *Drawing by Lynne Z. Bassett, courtesy of Old Sturbridge Village, Sturbridge, Mass.*

imported cloth. Throughout the seventeenth and eighteenth centuries, the best bed of the house was displayed in the parlor where its elegant textiles could impress visitors. Almost certainly, this beautiful quilt was familiar to parishioners entertained in the Livermore's parlor. —LZB

FIFIELD FAMILY QUILT
(FIG. 13)

An interesting eighteenth-century bed quilt in the collection of the Museum of Fine Arts, Boston, is made of embroidery worked by the mother and grandmother of revolutionary patriot, Samuel Adams. Originally part of a set of crewel-work bed hangings for a four-poster bed, the embroideries were divided by descendants and stitched into four separate bed quilts, two of which now reside in the collection of the Museum of Fine Arts.

The larger of the two quilts, featured here, is pieced from two full curtains of linen and cotton twill weave (known as fustian) and worked with lightly twisted polychrome wool yarns. Narrower panels, probably originally valances, are pieced along the top and one side. Notched square cutouts at the bottom of the quilt allow for the bed posts.

The main panels feature bold, large-scale flowering trees sprouting from rocky mounds, with sharply twisting branches and exotic curling foliage. This exuberant branching tree design is typical of English needlework of the late seventeenth and early eighteenth centuries, the result of reciprocal influences between the East and West. During the seventeenth century, the East India companies brought to England rare and expensive Chinese and Indian goods, such as lacquer ware, ceramics, and painted and embroidered textiles. The East India companies, in turn, sent patterns from England to Indian embroiderers and cotton painters, to create designs more suited to English taste. The resulting exotic mix of Indian, Persian, and Chinese motifs (seen in the strange rock formations in this quilt), had a major impact on English embroidery of the seventeenth century, evolving into a distinctly English

design of stylized hillocks and branching trees with huge, fanciful exotic foliage, seen on numerous bed hangings of the period.[44]

An inscription, handwritten in ink on linen and stitched to the back of this quilt, reads "Wrought by Mrs. Mary Fifield of Boston Mass, about the year 1714, assisted by her daughter Mary, mother of the late Samuel Adams, Governor of Massachusetts." Letters written by two descendants provide more details as to the origins of the bed hangings. Both letters note that Richard Fifield (the husband and father of the two Marys) was a sea captain. However, Mrs. J. W. (Mary Irene) Fifield added in 1887 that "during his absence from home, his wife and daughter, not having pressing labors, he brought one time for them from France the cloth with the patterns marked on it and the crewels to work them."[45] Given the distinctly English style of the curtains, it is more likely that the cloth was purchased in England. In the seventeenth century, London boasted many artisans producing fabric with pre-drawn patterns. Boston newspapers also contained advertisements by local merchants for bed hangings "drawn in London," so the assertion that Captain Richard Fifield bought pre-patterned cloth is feasible.[46]

The original bed hangings probably were worked by Richard's second wife, Mary (Drew) Fifield (1672–1713) and his daughter, Mary Fifield (1694–1748), who married Boston brew master Samuel Adams in 1713.[47] According to family tradition, the bed hangings were then inherited by successive generations of daughters named Mary. Mary Adams gave the bed hangings to her daughter, Mary (sister of the revolutionary patriot, Governor Samuel Adams) who married James Allen in 1742. Mary Allen (born 1717), in turn, bequeathed them to her daughter Mary, who married the Reverend Joseph Avery of Holden, Massachusetts.[48] At some later date, Mary Avery (1754–1842) divided the set of bed hangings among her four daughters, who lined and quilted them into four separate bed quilts. These quilts subsequently were passed along to the descendants of the four Avery girls.

In 1928, this bed quilt entered the collection of the Museum of Fine Arts (MFA), Boston, as a loan; it was made a gift in 1972 by Mrs. E. Emerson Evans

FIGURE 13. Quilt pieced of embroidered bed hangings, from the
Fifield family of Boston, embroidery c. 1712, quilting late 1700s. Linen
and cotton, with wool embroidery (82¼" × 84⅝"). Collection of the
Museum of Fine Arts, Boston (1972.910). *Photograph © 2007 Museum of
Fine Arts, Boston.* MQ 2510.

of Framingham, who could trace her lineage back to the first Avery daughter, Mary.[49] The MFA's other Fifield bed quilt was lined and quilted by the second Avery daughter, Bethiah, and descended through the Grosvenor, then Manning families. It was donated to the MFA by Mrs. Joseph Avery Manning of Brookline in 1931.[50] The third bed quilt is in the collection of the Worcester Art Museum, Worcester, Massachusetts. The location of the fourth quilt remains unknown today.   —LW

CLEVELAND FAMILY QUILT
(FIG. 14)

International maritime trade profoundly influenced commerce, consumer goods, and material culture in Massachusetts from the seventeenth through the nineteenth centuries. Under the auspices of the British East India Company, the British government maintained tight control over trade in colonial Massachusetts. Freed from the East India Company's monopoly on international commerce after the Revolutionary War, American merchants and mariners were able to trade directly with Asia and other ports around the world. The first American vessel, the *United States*, from Philadelphia, reached India in 1785, and the *Empress of China* from New York returned from China that same year. Quickly taking advantage of new opportunities, forty American ships traded in Asian waters by 1789. During a three-month residency in Calcutta in the winter of 1799–1800, Salem captain Richard Jeffrey Cleveland recalled, "twelve ships were laden with the produce and manufactures of Hindustan for the United States, whose cargoes would average about two hundred thousand dollars each."[51]

Among the most desirable and lucrative goods that American merchants imported from India were cotton and silk textiles. American ships returned with cargoes of sugar, spices, and textiles called by exotic names such as chintz, baftas, and bandannas. Cotton textiles were particularly popular—inexpensive plain goods for clothing and domestic use, and also fine white cotton mulls and muslins, and

brightly colored printed cottons. Merchant families and their customers acquired palampores, bed covers made of printed and painted cotton that often featured floral patterns known as the "Tree of Life."

The name "palampore" can be traced to the Persian and Hindi "palangposh" or bed cover. Techniques used to create the elaborate designs included painting and resist dyeing with vegetable dyes set by a mordant. This was a complex and time-consuming process that required repeated washings, rinsing, and manipulation of the fabric, sometimes involving weeks of labor by multiple craftspeople. The large-scale pattern of a tree with undulating branches growing out of a rocky hillock drew inspiration from a mixture of sources, including Indo-Persian, Chinese, and European artistic traditions. Exported to Europe since the seventeenth century, design motifs on palampores (particularly later examples) also catered to Western taste, as demonstrated by the border pattern of floral garlands or swags tied with ribbons in this example.[52] Close examination of the palampore reveals small animals and exotic birds gamboling at the base and in the branches (fig. 15/MQ 2779).

Palampores came in a variety of sizes and could be fashioned into window or bed curtains, coverlets, and other domestic furnishing textiles. In the Cleveland family quilted palamore, the wide border of floral swags has been cut in two corners to fit a tall-post bed. Piecing indicates that the top of the quilt was constructed from two different palampore panels, with the extra fabric used as lining on the back of the quilt. The lining also includes a rectangular block-printed cotton panel from India typically used as a floor covering (fig. 16/MQ 2779). Brown-and-beige striped woven tape binds the edges of the quilt and forms ties to secure the sides around the bed posts.

Sisters Mary Saunders Cleveland (born 1849) and Lucy Hiller Cleveland (born 1846) donated the quilted palampore to the Peabody Essex Museum in 1918. They were descendants of a prominent seafaring family involved in international maritime trade in the late eighteenth and early nineteenth centuries. The sisters' grandfather was William Cleveland (1777–1842), a shipmaster and merchant who traded

FIGURE 14. Quilted palampore, from the Cleveland family of Salem,
1825–1850. Cotton (117½" × 112"). Collection of the Peabody Essex
Museum, Salem, Mass., gift of Mary S. and Lucy H. Cleveland, 1918
(106358). *Photograph courtesy of the Peabody Essex Museum.* MQ 2779.

FIGURE 15. Cleveland family palampore, detail of bird design. *Photograph courtesy of the Peabody Essex Museum.*

FIGURE 16. Cleveland family palampore, back view. *Photograph courtesy of the Peabody Essex Museum.*

in the East Indies and China. William's brother, Richard Jeffrey Cleveland (1773–1860), was an enterprising navigator who traded in Asia, India, and Europe and authored an important book that chronicled the international trading ventures of American ship masters and mariners during the early nineteenth century. The donor's step-grandmother, Lucy Cleveland (1780–1866), was a children's book author and textile artist whose work
 is featured in this book (fig. 131/MQ 5075). Another of her sculptural vignettes, "The Sick Chamber," features a miniature palampore as a bed covering, indicating that this type of imported textile was well known within the Cleveland family.[53]   —PBR

SPAULDING FAMILY QUILT

(FIG. 17)

During the late eighteenth and early nineteenth centuries, textile manufacturers in France and Britain tempted their customers with wonderful toile and chintz furnishing print designs, including pastoral genre scenes, images taken from historical events and exotic locales, beautiful florals, cavorting animals, and elegant birds.[54] Wealthy homes in Europe and America boasted fine wall coverings, window draperies, bed coverings, and hangings of these large-scale designs; after they had served their initial purpose, these valued textiles often found their way into quilts.[55]

Pictorial quilts that incorporate these elegant furnishing prints often elicit a sense of awe from the viewer. This is certainly the case with the Spaulding family quilt top. The individual who made this top had an excellent eye for detail and was also a very accomplished needlewoman. She arranged designs cut from fine toile and chintz fabrics into pictorial assemblages, framed by octagonal sashing. The octagonal frame was not a new concept. Following the neoclassical fashion for geometric designs, this pattern was widely used in architecture, painting, sculpture, wallpaper, and printed textiles as a means of highlighting the interior pattern.[56]

The twenty octagonal blocks, sixteen square blocks, and fourteen triangular blocks of this quilt top were all appliquéd with human figures (allegorical, historical, and contemporary), flowers and fruit, or game birds and domestic fowl. One block commemorates the capture of Gibraltar in 1782 by the British, while others depict children "Playing at Marbles" and "Spinning Top."[57] The cock and hen toile in red is a mirror image of the plate-printed fabric by Bromley Hall, circa 1765 to 1775, also in red.[58] The floral display above the cock's head is a clever cutting and rearranging of the grape vine and flowers from the same print. The maker also used the fruit motifs from that fabric in two other squares. Yet another block is a mirror image of the pheasant in the pheasant and mandarin duck fabric printed by Talwin & Foster, circa 1775 to 1785.[59] Again, by careful cutting and placement of the bird, tree trunk, leaves, and vines, the maker created a striking and unique pictorial block.

This quilt has been attributed to various female ancestors of Rolland Harty Spaulding (1873–1942), sixty-third governor of New Hampshire. The probable maker is either his great-great-grandmother Mary (Heald) Spaulding (1745–1826), wife of Lieutenant Benjamin Spaulding (1743–1832), or his great-grandmother, Sibyl (Sanders) Spaulding (c. 1772–1818), who became the second wife of Benjamin Spaulding (1767–1842) in 1797.[60] Lieutenant Benjamin Spaulding was the first person in town to own a four-wheel carriage, indicating that his wealth and interest in elegant accoutrements certainly could have encompassed the expensive toile fabrics that went into the making of this quilt top.[61]

One of Townsend's oldest families, the Spaulding (or Spalding) family was prominent in Townsend Harbor, also known as East Townsend. Like their neighbors, they were farmers until the Civil War era, when Jonas and Waldo Spaulding, Rolland's father and uncle, developed or renovated a number of mills to plane wood, saw lumber, and process grain. However, it was the manufacturing of leatherboard that brought the greatest financial success to the family. The Spaulding brothers—and later Jonas Spaulding's sons—supplied leatherboard counters for shoe heels to markets in France, England, and Russia, in addition to the United States. Even-

FIGURE 17. Appliquéd quilt top, "Octagon Frame with Figures," from the Spaulding family of Townsend, c. 1782–1800. Cotton and linen (83" × 96"). Collection of the Shelburne Museum, Shelburne, Vermont (1957–533). *Photograph © Shelburne Museum, Shelburne, Vermont.* MQ 4999.

tually, they expanded their manufacturing empire to New York, Missouri, and New Hampshire. By 1900, Rolland and his brother Huntley had moved to New Hampshire, where they both became prominent in politics as well as business. Rolland Harty Spaulding served one term as governor of New Hampshire beginning in 1915; his brother also was elected governor in 1927.[62] This wonderful quilt top was inherited by Rolland and passed down through his branch of the Spaulding family until it entered the collection of the Shelburne Museum in Vermont.　　　　　　　　　　—VLS and LZB

LYNDE FAMILY QUILT

(FIG. 18)

The template-pieced quilt pattern known as "Hexagon" or "Honeycomb" was the earliest type of patchwork identified in an American publication. First published by Eliza Leslie in *The American Girl's Book* in 1831, a description and illustration of the pattern were later reprinted in 1835 by *The Lady's Book* as the article, "Fancy Needlework."[63] This periodical, subsequently renamed *Godey's Lady's Book*, was the earliest magazine for American women that attained national readership and significance. Although examples of hexagon-pieced quilts survive from the eighteenth century, the taste for hexagonal and intricate geometric patterns in quilt making expanded in the early nineteenth century, in part as a manifestation of the aesthetic style known as "Fancy." Colorful and boldly patterned furnishings became fashionable following the introduction of the kaleidoscope to America in 1818. The intricate geometric patterns produced by kaleidoscopes influenced textile design and production, including carpets and some quilts.[64]

The flower-like medallions composed of hexagonal pieces suggest the name commonly used for this pattern today, "Grandmother's Flower Garden." Made of printed cotton dress fabrics, the pieced medallions were composed in rows set into a pieced white cotton ground also made of hexagons. A thoughtful approach to color placement was advocated in *The Lady's Book* article. In composing rings of colored hexagons on the white ground, the author advised, "Let each ring consist of the same sort of calico, or at least of the same colour. For instance, one ring may be blue, another pink, a third yellow, & c."[65] The maker of this quilt heeded this advice and made concentric hexagonal rings of color. Some of the textiles were "fussy cut," a fabric-cutting technique in which material is cut to accentuate certain design elements, thus requiring extra fabric (fig. 19/MQ 2798).

During the early nineteenth century, textile production was noted for experimentation and innovation with dyeing and printing technologies. Likely of British manufacture, the cotton fabrics in this quilt demonstrate the fine printing achieved by various industrial techniques: roller printing, block printing, and copperplate printing. The small scale of the patterns suggests that the textiles were meant for use as dress or clothing fabrics, although they also could be used for other purposes. The quilt is lined with a glazed cotton fabric printed with leaves overlaying a trellis pattern; the edges of the quilt are bound with striped "Trenton" tape.[66]

Interestingly, several textiles in this quilt bear ink inscriptions with numbers, possibly pricing notations recorded by wholesale or retail merchants. During this time period, British fabrics passed through multiple vendors between the time the goods left the manufacturer and ultimately arrived in the hands of the consumer. The Peabody Essex Museum owns a merchant's sample book containing swatches of printed cotton fabrics similar to those found in the quilt. Comparing the two sources has helped to establish the approximate date of the quilt. The unidentified merchant's ledger recorded lists of goods purchased from New York and Philadelphia merchants and auctioneers with dates of transactions ranging between 1828 and 1834. Margin notes indicate that many of these fabrics were of British origin, although a small number of samples were of French or domestic production. This comparison documents the complex nature of early nineteenth-century international trade between the United States and Europe, which supplied fabrics used for quilt making and clothing.[67]

When the Peabody Essex Museum acquired the quilt in 1939, the donor recorded the family tradition that it had been made for Benjamin Lynde, Jr. (1700–1781), and used at his homes in Salem or Castle Hill. The donor also suggested that its fine state of preservation indicated use as a "best marriage quilt." Genealogical research confirms that the donor was a direct descendant of Benjamin Lynde, Jr. However, the textiles and construction techniques imply a date later than his lifetime and call the family tradition into question. A more likely provenance is descent through members of the Lynde, Walter, and McCleary families of Massachusetts.[68]　　　　—PBR

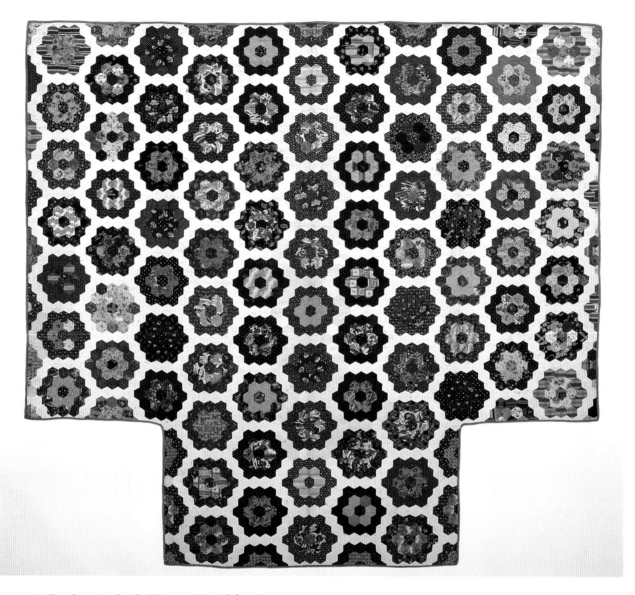

FIGURE 18. Template-pieced quilt, "Hexagon Mosaic," from the Lynde family of Salem, c. 1830. Cotton (75" × 107¾"). Collection of the Peabody Essex Museum, Salem, Mass., gift of Helen C. McCleary, 1939 (PEM 123834). *Photograph courtesy of the Peabody Essex Museum.* MQ 2798.

FIGURE 19. Lynde family quilt, detail of calicoes. *Photograph courtesy of the Peabody Essex Museum.*

REBECCA KINGSBURY PETTICOAT

(FIG. 20)

Throughout the eighteenth century, quilted petticoats were worn by women, often underneath a type of dress known as an "open robe," which was open across the center front of the skirt to show a decorative or matching petticoat. Many New England women purchased their quilted petticoats ready-made, imported from England by merchants like Mr. Ambrose Vincent, who offered a new shipment of imported textiles to the residents of Boston in 1720:

> To be sold by Publick Vendue at the Crown Coffee House On Thursday Afternoon the 14th Currant, . . . Scots Plaids, Blanketing, and Flannel, India Muzling, White and Brown Hollands, Quilted Silk Petticoats . . . to be seen daily at Mr. William Wilson's Warehouse in Merchants Row, Boston.[69]

At this time, quilting was a fancywork technique practiced by young women from elite New England families, many of whom learned from schoolmistresses. For example, the wife of George Brownell advertised in the *Boston News-Letter* on March 2, 1712:

> At the House of Mr. George Brownell in Wings-Lane Boston is Taught, Writing, Cyphering, Dancing, Treble Viol, Flute, Spinnet &c. Also English and French Quilting, Imbroidery, Florishing, Plain Work, marking in several sorts of Stitches, and several other works, where Scholars may board.

It is likely that, throughout the first half of the eighteenth century, quilted petticoats were closely modeled after the geometric aesthetic of English quilting styles, so that it is difficult to distinguish the earliest American quilting from imported examples. Such is the case with the petticoat of Rebecca Kingsbury, with its typically English motifs of arching feathers, scrolls, circles, simple leaves, and flowers. The manner in which Rebecca packed together the individual motifs, however, is unusual in ready-made English petticoats, which typically are organized into clearly defined bands of patterns and are not so heavily quilted.

Family history states that Rebecca made this petticoat when she was teaching school in Sharon, sometime before her marriage to Lieutenant Nathaniel Gay (1711–1776) in 1740. Rebecca was the seventh of nine children born to innkeeper Nathaniel and Abigail (Baker) Kingsbury of West Dedham. Her father was a substantial landowner, with a number of luxury items, including books, listed in his probate inventory.[70] He could afford a good education for his daughter; probably, Rebecca learned to quilt in the English style while a schoolgirl.

For Rebecca to leave her hometown to teach was unusual in the eighteenth century. Generally, women taught summer session only, as all available men were needed for haying and other farm work. Perhaps Rebecca taught needlework skills in a school such as that offered by Mrs. George Brownell. After their marriage, Rebecca and Nathaniel Gay settled in Walpole and had six children, four of whom survived to adulthood. —LZB

FIGURE 20. Quilted petticoat, made by Rebecca Kingsbury
(1713–1807) of Sharon, c. 1730–1740. Silk and glazed worsted with
wool batting (length 37½"). Collection of Historic Deerfield,
Deerfield, Mass. (2000.72.3). *Photograph by Penny Leveritt, courtesy
of Historic Deerfield.* MQ 4960.

COFFIN FAMILY PETTICOAT

(FIG. 21)

The histories of Nantucket and the Coffin family are inextricably entwined. Tristram Coffyn (1605–1681), a native of Devonshire in England, emigrated to the American colonies in 1642 with his family. In 1659, Coffyn (as he spelled his last name) organized a company of Massachusetts Bay colonists to purchase Nantucket, which at that time was under the jurisdiction of New York. The following year, Coffyn moved his family to the island, joining others whose names would become forever associated with Nantucket, including the Macy and Starbuck families. They all came to the windswept island with a desire to improve their fortunes through farming.[71]

The ultimate success of the Coffin family on Nantucket is embodied in this elegant quilted silk petticoat, worn by at least three generations of Coffin women on their wedding days. The petticoat, a gift to the Nantucket Historical Association from Coffin family descendants in 2000, has an old muslin label written by Eliza Coffin (1811–1903) stitched to the inside, which reads: "Elizabeth Ramsdell married Levi Starbuck 1793 and was the 5th person married in this skirt her mother & all her ancestors having worn it before . . ."[72] (see fig. 68/MQ 1007). According to family tradition, the maker of this petticoat and the first to wear it was Damaris Gayer (born 1673), who married Nathaniel Coffin (1671–1721), a grandson of Tristram Coffyn, in 1692.[73]

The skirt of a fashionable dress in the late seventeenth century was drawn up to reveal an elegant petticoat, which at the time was considered to be outerwear, not underwear as in the nineteenth century. Englishwoman Mary Evelyn wrote a satirical poem in 1690 describing the wardrobe necessary for a voyage to Maryland, in which the emigrating

FIGURE 21. Quilted petticoat, from the Coffin family, Nantucket, eighteenth century. Silk, linen, and wool, with wool batting (length 37"). Collection of the Nantucket Historical Association, Nantucket, Mass. (2000.86.1). *Photograph by Jeffrey Allen, courtesy of the Nantucket Historical Association.* MQ 5074.

gentleman's wife requires a short petticoat "quilted White and Red."[74] Thus, quilted petticoats clearly were worn at the time that Damaris Gayer married Nathaniel Coffin. However, the Coffin petticoat's quilting design is inconsistent with such an early date. Compare its stylized floral vine border with the geometric design of Rebecca Kingsbury's yellow silk petticoat (fig. 20/MQ 4960). A late seventeenth-century quilted petticoat would have been based on English design tradition, like Rebecca's petticoat, as were quilted bed covers. New Englanders did not develop quilting designs like that seen in the Coffin petticoat until the rococo style, with its airy vines, curving feathers, and stylized shell motifs, came into fashion in the second quarter of the eighteenth century.

Oral history states that the skirt was worn by several women who married into the Coffin family, and then was passed to Elizabeth Ramsdell, who was in a different branch of the Coffin family.[75]

This awkward scenario of passing the petticoat from daughter-in-law to daughter-in-law is not typical for eighteenth-century families, who tended to pass such items as petticoats and household textiles through direct female lines, from mother to daughter or granddaughter, or from aunt to niece in the case of a childless woman.

A more probable history of the petticoat is that it was first worn by Damaris's daughter, Catherine Coffin Gardner, who married in 1736. Next, it was most likely used by Catherine's three daughters, Deborah (born 1737), Catherine (born 1747), and Ruth (born 1752), when they married. Ruth's only daughter Elizabeth Ramsdell then wore the skirt when she married in 1793, as noted by Eliza Coffin's label. This scenario would account for Eliza's claim that five brides wore the skirt.[76]

The quilted skirt has a lovely blue silk satin face. Striped tan and blue domestically produced cloth, probably linen, was used for the backing in the quilted areas, while the upper area of the petticoat around the waist is pieced of plain-woven brown worsted and deep blue calamanco. The quilter used blue silk thread to create her pattern of stylized floral vines around the lower half, bordering the vines with a line of paired feather fronds and then filling in the rest with a simple diamond grid design. A silk tape binds the bottom edge. The waist of the petticoat has been altered; it probably was originally a drawstring waist, but at some point in time the fullness was pleated into a linen waistband that fastens with a nineteenth-century porcelain button. The design of the Coffin petticoat, like scores of other eighteenth-century New England quilted petticoats, bears a close relationship to the designs of the region's wool whole-cloth bed quilts.

Despite the fact that the petticoat dates later than family tradition would have it, its significance is considerable. It has an irrefutable connection to an important Nantucket family, and is a gorgeous and well-preserved document of eighteenth-century American quilting.   —LZB

STODDARD FAMILY PETTICOAT
(FIG. 23)

The gentry families of the Connecticut River Valley of Massachusetts in the seventeenth and eighteenth centuries were called the "River Gods." In their positions as leaders in the law, the military, and in religion, members of the Stoddard, Williams, Ashley, Dwight, Partridge, Porter, and Pynchon families controlled the region from the court and from the pulpit.[77] As successful merchants and wealthy farmers, they also controlled large tracts of land.

This pink silk petticoat was worn by either Prudence Chester Stoddard or her daughter, Esther. The closely quilted petticoat is worked with a simple border pattern of scallops arranged in points, and a diamond grid above. The backing fabric is a block-printed red and white striped cotton. The petticoat has been stitched to a new waistband, but its width indicates that it was meant to be worn over the wide

hoops (or "panniers") that were fashionable from about 1740 to 1780. In its original form, it probably had a drawstring waist. A pocket slit, bound in pink silk tape, appears over each hip.

The diary of Elizabeth Porter Phelps in neighboring Hadley reveals that women of the local social elite frequently gathered together to quilt petticoats in the eighteenth century. In fact, these gatherings of women were important to the social cohesion of the River God families, offering contacts for prospective business and marital partners.[78] While it is possible that the Stoddard petticoat was imported, the fineness of the stitching suggests that it was probably made at one of these quilting parties.[79]

Prudence Chester of Wethersfield, Connecticut, married Col. John Stoddard of Northampton in 1731. The Chesters were one of the ruling families of Connecticut, (called the "Standing Order" in that region). Alliances through marriage with the River God families of Massachusetts were very common and consolidated political and economic power within those few ruling families. Col. John Stoddard was the son of Northampton's minister Solomon Stoddard and uncle of the famed Reverend Jonathan Edwards, who was a leader of the religious revival called the "Great Awakening" in the late 1730s and 1740s. John Stoddard was a military man; he built forts and fought Indians (proposing the use of dogs to terrorize the natives and thus defend white settlements). It was he who negotiated the return of captives who had been marched to Canada following the 1704 attack on Deerfield. He was also a very wealthy man who married well and enjoyed a comfortable home furnished with many luxuries. The Stoddard house, called "the Manse," still stands on Prospect Street, and silver and fine linens from the family are in the collection of Historic Northampton. The Stoddards are said to be the first family in Northampton to enjoy the drinking of tea.[80]

John Stoddard's wife, Prudence Chester, was noted in the History of Ancient Wethersfield as being a "noble and accomplished" woman. Yale College president Timothy Dwight, Esq., as an old man in the nineteenth century, reminisced that "when a boy in Northampton, if in his walks, he saw Madam

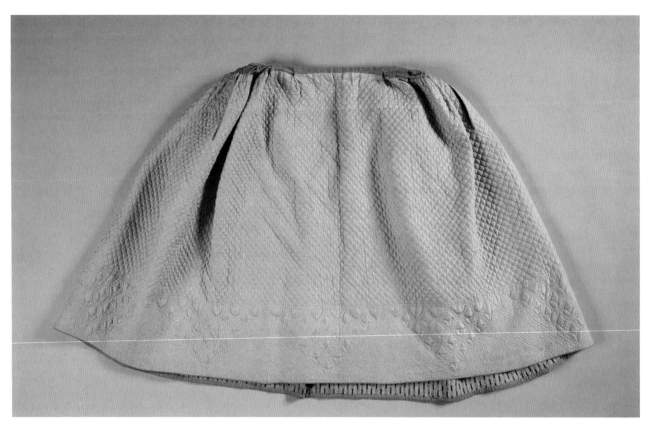

FIGURE 23. Quilted petticoat, worn by either Prudence Chester Stoddard (1699–1780) or her daughter Esther Stoddard (1738–1816) of Northampton, c. 1740–1780. Silk and cotton with wool batting (length 36½"). Collection of Historic Northampton, Northampton, Mass. (66.686). *Photograph by David Stansbury.* MQ 3941.

Stoddard approaching from a distance, he began at once to straighten up and put on the best possible appearance and manner, that he might gain favor in the eyes of so dignified and elegant a woman."[81]

Prudence taught her daughters the elegance for which she was herself noted. Her daughter and namesake Prudence, who married Ezekiel Williams of Wethersfield, was described in a letter by a family friend as a "lady of great strength of character, and uncommon dignity of deportment." Another admirer wrote that she was "a woman of remarkable excellence, intelligent and lovely."[82] Of daughter Esther, we can only surmise that she too was elegant in her deportment. Esther died unmarried, and is therefore not discussed in the history and genealogy books, a common oversight much regretted by the modern researcher.

Education was a priority in the Stoddard family, for the girls as well as the boys. James Russell Trum-

bull wrote in *The History of Northampton* that Col. John Stoddard's daughters were educated in Boston, "their teacher being a man by the name of Turner. They would ride to Boston on horseback, sometimes on a pillion behind their father or some other person, and occasionally on a side-saddle."[83] Their education in Boston would have included reading, writing, some math, and probably French. It was unusual but not unheard of for some privileged girls also to learn the classics in Greek and Latin. The knowledge that was valued above all others for wealthy and accomplished young ladies, though, was needlework. The Stoddard girls would not have learned this skill from their teacher Mr. Turner, but from the female proprietress of a young ladies' school. Esther Stoddard's "Reclining Shepherdess" canvaswork picture and metal thread embroidery of the Stoddard coat of arms is preserved in the collection of Historic Northampton. —LZB

WORTHINGTON FAMILY PETTICOAT

(FIG. 24)

The 1740s witnessed the development of a weaving technique that imitated hand quilting. Specifically, the inventors wished to duplicate the appearance of Marseilles quilting (or "French" quilting as it was sometimes called in colonial newspaper advertisements), which was distinctive for its fine corded and stuffed designs, generally worked on white cotton. Hand-stitched Marseilles quilting was sold commonly as finished garments (such as men's waistcoats and women's unboned corsets, called "jumps"), layette sets, or yard goods. Perfecting the machine-woven imitation took the better part of two decades. "Quilted in the loom" Marseilles petticoats began to be advertised in London newspapers in 1770, and soon became popular exports to America.[84]

Family history states that this petticoat and its English Spitalfields silk gown were worn by at least three generations of Worthington women for their weddings, beginning with Hannah Hopkins when she married John Worthington (1719–1806), a lawyer from Springfield, in 1759. While this history may be possible because machine-made Marseilles was invented prior to this date, it is unlikely, as Marseilles fabric did not become common until the later 1760s and 1770s. Thus, this may be one of the earliest surviving examples of a Marseilles petticoat in America, or it actually was worn first by Hannah Hopkins Worthington's daughter and namesake, Hannah Worthington Dwight (1761–1833). Two other silk Marseilles petticoats of this same pattern are preserved at the Webb-Deane-Stevens Museum in Wethersfield, Connecticut, and at the Museum of the City of New York. The coincidence of three surviving examples suggests the date of the petticoat is later rather than earlier.

Hannah Hopkins was born in 1731, the daughter of Samuel and Esther (Edwards) Hopkins, of Hartford County, Connecticut. Her mother, Esther Edwards, was a granddaughter of Northampton's minister, Solomon Stoddard, and sister of the

FIGURE 24. Quilted petticoat, worn by Hannah Hopkins Worthington (1731–1766), c.1759 or by her daughter, Hannah Worthington Dwight (1761–1833), of Springfield, c. 1790. Machine-woven Marseilles quilting, silk (length 39"). Collection of Historic Deerfield, Deerfield, Mass. (F.495A). *Photograph by Penny Leveritt, courtesy of Historic Deerfield.* MQ 5073.

Reverend Jonathan Edwards—thus, Hannah enjoyed the benefits of belonging to the Connecticut River Valley's ruling gentry. Unfortunately, she did not enjoy the benefits for long, dying after only seven years of marriage, during which she produced six children. Keeping to the Connecticut Valley's rather incestuous tradition of intermarriage among the River God families, John Worthington's second wife was Mary Stoddard, the daughter of Colonel John and Prudence Stoddard (see fig. 23/MQ 3941) of Northampton—Hannah Hopkin's cousin once removed.

Hannah Worthington wore the petticoat and her mother's silk brocade gown when she married Thomas Dwight (another River God family member) of Springfield in 1791. It was worn next by her daughter Elizabeth ("Betsy") Dwight (1801–1855), who married Charles Howard in 1824.[85] Betsy altered the gown to make the skirt narrower, as was the fashion in the early 1820s.[86]   —LZB

MARY WOODBURY DUDLEY PETTICOAT

(FIG. 25)

Mary Woodbury, known to her family and friends as "Polly," probably wore this ensemble of quilted petticoat, pumpkin hood, and bag as part of her wedding outfit when she married John Dudley (1793–1880) in 1840. The Woodburys and Dudleys were both farming families in Sutton, a town in south-central Massachusetts along the Blackstone River. While Sutton proper continued to focus on agriculture in the nineteenth century, the town's outlying villages developed their industrial potential. In fact, the Blackstone River Valley, which runs between Worcester, Massachusetts, and Providence, Rhode Island, was America's first industrialized corridor, beginning with the establishment of Samuel Slater's cotton-spinning mill in Pawtucket, Rhode Island, in the early 1790s. Two sections of Sutton, Wilkonsville and Manchaug, became significant textile mill villages, including a mill that turned out "Fruit of the Loom" fabrics.[87]

Mary, the daughter of Benjamin and Sarah (Carriel) Woodbury, had five surviving siblings. Sarah, or "Sally," her two-year-older sister, married widower Joshua Armsby in 1823 and became mother to his two boys. She promptly began having children of her own, producing six little ones within the first twelve years of her marriage. As it was a common practice in this period for an unmarried sister to help in a sibling's household, it can be surmised that Mary delayed her own marriage in order to assist Sarah with housekeeping and childcare chores.[88]

When Mary did finally marry at the age of thirty-eight, she used fabric from her sister Sarah's wedding dress to make this quilted petticoat and matching hood and bag. The fabric is a shot silk, with blue threads in one direction of the weave, and reddish purple in the other, giving it a shimmering violet appearance. The petticoat is lined with brown glazed cotton, and the bottom edge is bound with brown wool twill tape, called "brush braid." Both of these features begin to appear commonly in women's clothing in the 1840s. The shoulder straps that help carry the weight of the heavy petticoat are also seen frequently in 1840s quilted petticoats.

Nineteenth-century quilted petticoats can be distinguished from their eighteenth-century counterparts not only by the different fabrics used, but by the quilting designs. Nineteenth-century quilting designs for petticoats tend to be large-scale undulating feathers and other simple designs, without the stylized florals or compact geometrics of earlier examples. There is overall less quilting in later petticoats.

Mary and John Dudley prospered as farmers in Sutton.[89] They had two children, a boy and a girl named for themselves, born in 1840 and 1844. Census records show them still farming and "keeping house," with the children assisting them, in 1870. The 1880 census notes that John, a widower, died in March of that year of "old age."   —LZB

FIGURE 25. Quilted petticoat, pumpkin hood, and bag, worn by Mary Woodbury Dudley (1801–c. 1875) of Sutton, c. 1840. Silk and cotton (length 38"). Collection of the Worcester Historical Museum, Worcester, Mass. (1988.620 a-c). *Photograph by David Stansbury.* MQ 2038.

Chapter 2

Northeastern Massachusetts: The Crucible

Northeastern Massachusetts encompasses Norfolk, Suffolk, Middlesex, and Essex counties and contains some of the state's best-known historic sites. Geographically reaching from the Atlantic west to Worcester County, the region abuts New Hampshire to the north, and Bristol and Plymouth counties to the south. Here one finds the state capital of Boston, major shipping ports, Revolutionary War sites, literary shrines, and the legacy of industrial giants.

In 1630, when John Winthrop and company landed in what is now Boston, they were delighted to find a well-situated harbor, allowing them in a short time to make the Massachusetts Bay Colony one of the most influential in British America. From the seventeenth century to the mid-eighteenth century, Boston was North America's most important seaport in terms of volume.[1] With the growth of the mid-Atlantic region, the ports of Philadelphia and New York began to eclipse that of Boston; in response, the city's merchants and ship captains developed a "far-flung foreign trading network, bringing wealth, culture and influence" to the region.[2] Starting in the mid-nineteenth century, convenient access to railroads and nearby factories and farms also aided in keeping Boston one of the country's top international ports.[3] The city's prosperity attracted Yankee farmers as well as European, Canadian, and West Indian immigrants.

The North Shore, stretching north of Boston to New Hampshire, became a wealthy summer retreat during the late nineteenth and early twentieth centuries; large mansions still stud the shore. The North Shore also includes the fishing towns of Cape Ann, the tanneries and shoe factories of Lynn, and the commercial centers of Newburyport and Salem. Although best remembered for the infamous seventeenth-century witch trials, by the time Deborah Hobart Clark pieced her silk handscreen (fig. 3/MQ 5067) in the mid-eighteenth century, Salem was well on its way to becoming one of the busiest ports in America and the wealthiest city per capita. Trade with China, Europe, the West Indies, and Africa brought incredible prosperity to Salem merchants and investors, and Salem artisans flourished in the culturally rich environment. Seafaring extended to women, too, as evidenced by Alice G. Brown of Newburyport, who learned to sew as she sailed with her sea captain father (fig. 50/MQ 2354).

Further inland, Concord and Lexington contain Revolutionary War battlefields, the path of Paul Revere's ride, and the homes of Transcendental reformers Margaret Fuller, Bronson Alcott, and Ralph Waldo Emerson, and writers Louisa May Alcott, Henry David Thoreau, and Nathaniel Hawthorne. Massachusetts' role as a center of reform and literature is explored through the Alcott family quilts (fig. 33/MQ 4692 and fig. 35/MQ 4697).

In the 1820s, the Merrimack River began powering the mills of Lowell and Lawrence. Factories were found throughout the state, and while Fall River to the south became the single-largest cotton manufacturing city in the United States, most of the industries were concentrated around Boston and its railroads. By the late nineteenth century, Massachusetts was the most industrial state in the nation and the northeast corner contained the most manufactories.[4] Women participated in and benefited from the

FIGURE 26. *Boston Common*, lithograph by James Kidder, 1820, published by Abel Bowen of Boston, Mass. Established in 1634 for the grazing of cattle and other livestock, the Boston Common became a public park after the cattle were banished in 1830. The Commonwealth of Massachusetts is still governed from the Boston State House, overlooking the Common; it was designed by Charles Bulfinch and built in the 1790s. *Photograph courtesy of the Boston Atheneum, Boston, Mass. (B B64B6 P.b. [no.2])*

new industries, working in the mills and purchasing factory-made fabric.[5]

Norfolk, the southernmost of the four northeastern counties, calls itself the "County of Presidents"; it is also home to revolutionary women—perhaps most notably Abigail Adams. During the Revolution, the future First Lady kept the family farm in Braintree, and advised husband John to ". . . remember the ladies" as he helped create America's new legal framework. The Peabody Essex Museum owns one of her quilted petticoats (fig. 27/MQ 3099).

Northeastern Massachusetts is a land of traditions and innovations, as are its quilts. This is the home of Paul Revere's ride—and Revereware. Here slavery was an important source of revenue for merchants and manufacturers, and here abolitionist William Lloyd Garrison printed *The Liberator*. It is the birthplace of presidents and the last land seen by "those that go down to the sea in ships."[6] It is the site of desperate city slums and sprawling mansions. The quilts featured in this section, ranging from expensive eighteenth-century imports to utilitarian cotton patchwork, reflect the region's complexity.   —DCA

The famed Yankee trading ships brought silks from China and cottons from India, as well as wools, cottons, and linens from Europe. But not all trade was so benign. In the infamous "triangle trade," Boston merchants also imported sugar and molasses from the West Indies, which was made into rum in Boston distilleries, and then traded for slaves in Africa—who were then sold in the West Indies, southern states, and Massachusetts. Massachusetts ended slavery in the 1780s and banned its residents from participating in the slave trade in 1788, but slave labor provided the cotton that fueled Massachusetts' textile industry and made Massachusetts a financial partner in slavery.

Source: http://www.massport.com/ports/about_histo.html. See also http://www.medfordhistorical.org/slavetradeletters.php for actual letters describing the slave trade, conducted by merchants of Medford, Massachusetts, in the mid-eighteenth century.

ABIGAIL ADAMS PETTICOAT

(FIG. 27)

In October of 1818, upon learning of the death of Abigail Smith Adams, wife of President John Adams, the Reverend William Bentley of Salem recorded recollections of meeting her years before. His remembrance included a description of her physical appearance and dress:

> She was in appearance of middle size, in the dress of the matrons who were in New England in my youth. The black bonnet, the short cloak, the gown open before, & quilted petticoat, & the high heeled shoe, as worn universally in that day. Everything the best but nothing different from our wealthy & modest citizens.[7]

A pale blue, quilted silk satin petticoat entered the Peabody Essex Museum's collection with a history of association with Abigail Adams. The shimmering aquamarine satin is quilted with designs of flowers and leaves that emerge from a scalloped pattern encircling the hem. The fabric's reflective surface emphasizes the stitching lines to create a bold decorative effect. The petticoat is lined with plain-woven

FIGURE 27. Quilted petticoat, associated with Abigail Smith Adams (1744–1818) of Quincy, c. 1765–1785. Silk, wool, cotton (length 37"). Collection of the Peabody Essex Museum, Salem, Mass., gift of Mrs. H. A. Cook, 1921 (112448). *Photograph courtesy of the Peabody Essex Museum.* MQ 3099.

white worsted, and wool provides the batting. A white cotton waistband is a later alteration.

Quilted petticoats, whether ready-made or domestically produced, seem to have found particular favor among English and American women. While accompanying her husband on a diplomatic mission to the court of France in 1785, Abigail Adams corresponded with a friend at home who asked for information about French women. Abigail noted that quilted petticoats were not worn at all by French women, implying that they were no longer in fashion in that country.[8]

Abigail Adams's life and that of her family became closely intertwined with public life during this formative period in the nation's history. John Adams's political appointments during and after the American Revolution resulted in long years of separation for the couple during the war, followed by extended periods of travel in Europe in the years immediately after the end of the conflict. As she accompanied her husband on diplomatic missions in the 1780s, Abigail experienced and observed the royal courts of both England and France. Her letters from this period reveal her dilemmas about how to select fitting attire for elite social engagements that also would convey the identity and values of American citizenry to those in aristocratic circles at the most powerful courts of Europe. Her voluminous correspondence with family members and friends recorded insightful, witty, and sometimes critical observations about fashionable attire in London and Paris. However, these experiences shaped her ideas about appropriate dress for wives and families of public leaders that she later used during the first two presidential administrations of the newly formed United States government.[9]

Very few examples of clothing associated with Abigail Adams survive. In 1921, Mrs. H. A. (Elizabeth Osgood) Cook of Salem donated this petticoat "owned by Mrs. John Adams (Abigail Smith)" to the Essex Institute, now the Peabody Essex Museum. Genealogical research has revealed a line of possible descent from Abigail Adams's niece, Abigail Adams Shaw (1790–1859), who married Joseph Barlow Felt (1789–1869) of Salem, a prominent historian and antiquarian. The couple had no children. Felt's sister, Elizabeth Curtis Felt (1792–1864), married into the Osgood family of Salem and was the grandmother of the donor.[10] Abigail Adams's letters and also a will that she drafted in 1816, reveal that she gave garments to various family members including Abigail Adams Shaw, although the petticoat apparently was not recorded.[11]   —PBR

GOVERNOR INCREASE SUMNER QUILT

(FIG. 29)

A second silk, whole-cloth quilt in the collection of the Museum of Fine Arts, Boston, features a center-medallion design similar to that of the Mary Cooper crib quilt (figure 1/MQ 2479), but in a significantly more complex form. Here, the central medallion is embellished with additional shapes—triangles and circles—that extend as far as the quarter medallions in each of the four corners of the field. These elements, as well as the two outer borders, are filled with extremely fine stitching in floral, wave, and grid motifs. The overall effect is one of dense geometry and reflects the neoclassical taste that emerged in the late eighteenth century.

The most distinctive feature of this quilt, however, is its striking pinkish-red color. Scientific analysis of several fiber samples reveal that this color was produced by cochineal, a dyestuff prepared from the dried insect, *Dactylopius coccus*, which feeds on cacti in Central America. The test also showed traces of aluminum and sulfur, indicating that an alum mordant was likely used to fix the dye to the silk fibers.[12] Cochineal was discovered by the Spanish when they entered Mexico in the early sixteenth century, and became a major dye stuff, along with madder, by the eighteenth century.[13] Combinations of dyes and mordants were carefully controlled to produce particular shades. The pinkish-red produced by cochineal seems to have become popular in the 1790s, and the Boston Museum of Fine Arts collection contains several items from this period featuring variations of the pink-red tone.[14]

The quality of the stitching and complexity of the composition suggest professional production, probably English. Unlike wool calamanco quilts, which waned in popularity at the end of the eighteenth century, silk whole-cloth quilts continued to be fashionable items, and were imported in quantity in Boston, even after the Revolution. Several merchant notices of the period list silk quilts imported from Europe, and in 1787, Boston merchant Thomas Brewer included "Pink, blue, and white sarsnet and satin quilts" in his advertisement for recently imported "European goods."[15]

The steep prices garnered by imported European goods would not have posed any problems for the illustrious owner of this quilt, Increase Sumner. Born in Roxbury on November 27, 1746, to a wealthy farmer of the same name, the younger Increase attended Harvard College until 1767, opened a prosperous law practice, and was later chosen to be a representative to the General Court from 1776 to 1779, a senator in 1782, and finally, associate justice to the Supreme Court of Massachusetts, where he served for many years. In 1797, Sumner was elected governor of Massachusetts.[16]

This silk whole-cloth quilt has a particularly interesting connection to Increase Sumner's tenure as governor of Massachusetts. Georgiana Welles, the donor (and great-granddaughter of Increase Sumner), recorded the family lore surrounding the quilt, noting that it had been "used by Increase Sumner at the Oath of Office in 1799."[17] This curious application has engendered much speculation over the years. However, contemporary accounts indicate that in April of 1799, Increase Sumner was re-elected unanimously as governor of Massachusetts, but quickly declined in health and, by May, was on his deathbed. Concerned with ensuring the official transition of executive power to the attorney general, members of the legislature convened at Sumner's house in Roxbury to exact an acceptance of the office before he passed away. Eyewitness Daniel Davis related the events of the day in a letter to Increase Sumner's son-in-law, Colonel Benjamin Welles, in 1829:

> When we arrived at the Governor's mansion in Roxbury, Dr. Warren . . . told us we might proceed. We entered the chamber and the scene that immediately followed can neither be described nor conceived. The Governor was raised in his bed and received the committee in his usual kind and polite manner. . . . The late Col. Davis, who was the chairman of the committee, immediately delivered the message in a very dignified and emphatic manner. I shall never forget the words of the Governor's answer. They were these: "Gentlemen, I am

FIGURE 29. Whole-cloth quilt, English, belonged to Governor
Increase Sumner (1746–1799) of Boston, c. 1790s. Silk (123" × 108").
Collection of the Museum of Fine Arts, Boston (49.886). *Photograph ©
2007 Museum of Fine Arts, Boston.* MQ 2509.

extremely grateful to the people of the Commonwealth for the honor they have conferred upon me
by electing me to the office of their Governor; I
now declare to you my acceptance of the office,
and will wait upon the Legislature to take the oaths
of office, as soon as my health will permit." As he
pronounced the last words, he was much affected
and fell back upon his pillow, from which, I pre-
sume, his venerable head was never again raised.[18]

This lovely imported quilt thus witnessed an important moment in the history of Massachusetts, as
it elegantly covered the governor while he received
guests in bed.   —LW

MOLLY HOWARD RICHARDSON QUILT

(FIG. 30)

Mary Howard was born in 1773, the daughter
of Samuel and Mary (Snow) Howard; she
was their eighth and penultimate child. Her family
called her "Molly," possibly to differentiate her from
an older sister who had died in 1764 at the age of
three. Molly's family was a prospering and patriotic
farming family, active in the Revolutionary War,
and respected in the Congregational Church and in
town politics.[19] In 1800, Molly Howard married Elijah Richardson, who was born in 1767, the seventh
of eight children to Zachariah and Sarah (Warren)
Richardson of Chelmsford. Elijah was a farmer, and
had served in the milita to put down Shays' Rebellion in 1786 to 1787.[20]

The quilt was probably made in anticipation of
Molly and Elijah's marriage. The front is an elegant,
dark blue, twill-woven, glazed worsted fabric most
likely imported from England. The back is plain-
woven wool, with an even 30/30 count in the warp
and weft, dyed a rich golden color (the color most
typically used for wool quilt backings in New England). The backing fabric was probably spun and
woven domestically, perhaps even by Molly herself.
Inside is a batting of plain white wool. The quilting is done with dark blue worsted thread, generally

at seven to nine stitches per inch. The rather uneven
stitching across the quilt suggests that it is the product of a quilting party, with a number of experienced hands lending assistance.

Like most whole-cloth quilts made in eastern
Massachusetts, the design of Molly's quilt is closely
packed with a wide variety of fantastic floral and foliate motifs derived from a traditional design vocabulary developed in the renaissance era.[21] A central
stem of imaginative and bizarre floral and shell
forms, emanating from a small mound of scallops,
is flanked by undulating vines bearing bunches of
grapes, abstracted roses and pomegranates, and curling leaves.

Molly and Elijah did not have such a large family as they grew up in themselves; they had four
children, three of whom lived to adulthood. They
continued to farm in Chelmsford into the mid-
nineteenth century. Molly and Elijah were of the
last generation of Massachusetts residents to experience in their youth and young adulthood the agricultural economy of New England. Founded in the
mid-1600s, Chelmsford was a farming town, with
only a few small industries, including manufactories
for producing lime, window glass, gun powder, and
wool flannels, along with a granite quarry.[22] Tremendous change to the area came quickly, though,
when the farms of East Chelmsford were purchased
in order to create the textile mill town of Lowell,
incorporated in 1826. The population exploded, and
suddenly the local economy was driven by industry,
not agriculture. Canals and trains were as likely as
horses and wagons to take the produce of farms to
the factory towns.

Molly's blue wool quilt, no longer fashionable
once the printed cottons of the factory became
common, remained a valued family heirloom. It
was passed down in the family, probably to her only
daughter, Mary (b. 1809). Eventually, it came to descendant William Fulton, who sold the quilt to another member of the extended family (connected
through the Warren line), who then donated the
quilt to the Chelmsford Historical Society.[23]   —LZB

FIGURE 30. Drawing of a whole-cloth quilt, made by Molly Howard
(1773–1851) of Chelmsford, c. 1800. Wool (96¼" × 89¼"). Collection
of the Chelmsford Historical Society (72.4.3). *Drawing © 2006 by Lynne
Z. Bassett.* MQ 5001.

HARRIS FAMILY QUILT

(FIG. 31)

In nineteenth-century America, women who spent a significant portion of their time and labor supplying textiles and clothing for their families and homes also used sewing as a creative and expressive medium, producing needlework now recognized as extraordinary works of art. While working within the prescribed format of traditional pieced designs, women experimented with the use of color, pattern, and fine craftsmanship to create unique and visually appealing quilts.

The pattern of this quilt is known by a variety of names, including "Mariner's Compass," "Chips and Whetstones," and "Sunburst."[24] Its maker achieved a bold design through the selection of vibrant red, blue, and brown patterned fabrics, and through expert piecing in a radiating circular motif, appliquéd onto a white cotton background.[25] Each of the thirty circular motifs is composed of thirty-three

FIGURE 31. Pieced quilt, "Mariner's Compass," from the Harris family of Marblehead, c. 1840–1850. Cotton (85" × 82"). Collection of the Peabody Essex Museum, Salem, Mass., gift of Miss Bessom Harris, 1969 (131932). *Photograph courtesy of the Peabody Essex Museum.* MQ 2770.

THEY THAT GO
DOWN TO THE SEA
IN SHIPS
1623 – 1923

individual pieces of richly colored, mid-nineteenth-century dress calicoes printed in dotted, striped, floral, and abstract patterns.

The person who donated this quilt to the Peabody Essex Museum recorded the maker's identity as "Aunt Libby," her grandfather's sister. According to family records, she was in her eighties when she made this quilt and made it "without glasses." The donor, Bessom S. Harris (1894–1969), was descended from several Marblehead families including the Bessoms and the Frosts. Her paternal grandfather, James A. Harris (b. 1840), was born in Nova Scotia and later immigrated to Marblehead, where he married in 1863. One notation suggests that "Aunt Libby" may be associated with the Nova Scotia line of the family, although her identity remains unknown.

An historic Massachusetts seaport, Marblehead is known for its maritime heritage, especially fishing and yachting. Several Massachusetts communities, including Marblehead, had ties with the Canadian Maritime Provinces because of the fishing industry that lured American vessels to the Grand Banks off Newfoundland. One local historian summarized the occupations in Marblehead in the mid-nineteenth century as consisting of "two chief occupations— shoe manufacturing and sailoring, either to the Banks as a fisherman or on merchant ships."[26] In acknowledgment of fishing's centrality in the local economy and culture, the Marblehead town seal features a fisherman in a dory. Similarly, this "Mariner's Compass" quilt symbolizes the importance of maritime industry—not only to Marblehead, but to the entire Massachusetts coast.   —PBR

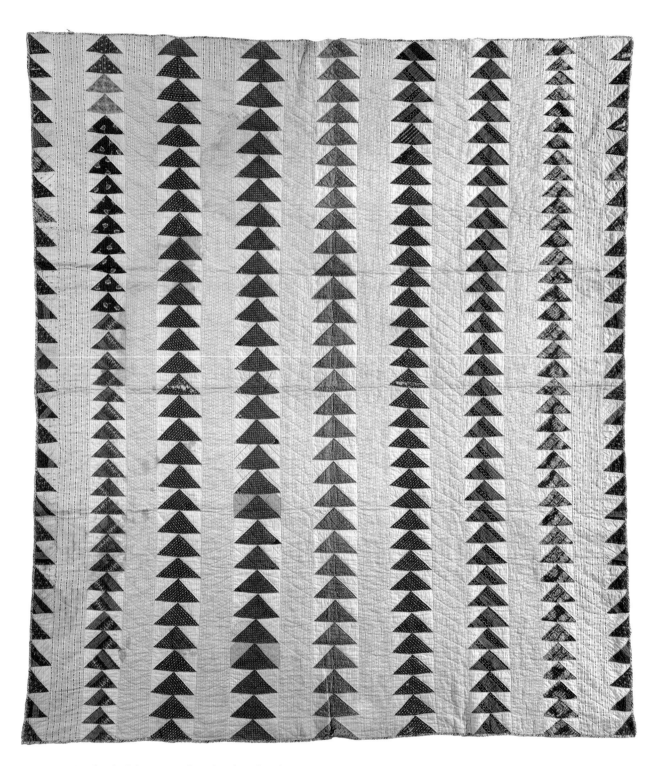

FIGURE 33. Pieced quilt, "Flying Geese," attributed to Abigail May
Alcott (1800–1877) of Concord, c. 1850. Cotton and wool (81½" ×
71"). Collection of Orchard House—Home of the Alcotts, Concord,
Mass. *Photograph by David Stansbury.* MQ 4692.

Alcott Family Quilts

"FLYING GEESE" QUILT
(FIG. 33)

Louisa May Alcott's *Little Women* is one of the most familiar stories in American literature. Written for girls and presenting an idealized version of the Alcott family's life in Concord, it conveys a strong message of the value of hard work, charity, modesty, and sisterly love. The lofty values and financial struggles characterizing both the Alcott family and the fictional March family of *Little Women* are embodied in the Alcott family quilts featured here.

Abigail (Abby) May Alcott and Amos Bronson Alcott married in 1830. They had four daughters as well as a son who died shortly after birth. Neither of the couple received a formal education, but they shared an interest in progressive schools, and met as teachers at the Boston Charity Infant School. They both devoted themselves to the anti-slavery movement. Bronson Alcott, Abby's brother Samuel May, and William Lloyd Garrison, editor of the *Liberator*, were founding members of the first antislavery society in Boston. Abby and her friend Lydia Maria Child attended the meetings, and the Alcotts' commitment to this movement included not only speeches but also sheltering a runaway slave in their home during the 1850s.[27]

Bronson Alcott put his personal philosophy into action in his several schools, which emphasized Socratic dialogue and liberal politics. Unfortunately, they all failed due to controversies over curriculum, and—in at least one case—the admission of a Black student. Although he did not belong to a denomination, Quaker and Unitarian beliefs strongly influenced Alcott. He participated in the intellectual discussion groups of Concord, especially later in life, and made a number of lecture tours spreading the ideas of Transcendentalism, progressive education, and abolition.

These tours often were undertaken when the family was without money. In addition to the failed schools, Alcott also was unsuccessful at farming, first in the Concord area, and—in 1843 to 1844—

at Fruitlands, a utopian farm experiment in Harvard, Massachusetts (see fig. 35/MQ 4697). Abby, later aided by her daughters, took in sewing to make ends meet several times during her marriage. In the late 1840s and early 1850s, she worked as a secular missionary (a sort of social worker), who provided food and clothing to the poorest in Boston, and subsequently ran an employment agency for young women. Her valuable and practical skill as a seamstress helped to pay the family's bills and provided clothing and bedding for household use. While no direct evidence links her to quilts or other items sold at anti-slavery fairs (see, for example, Lydia Maria Child's cradle quilt, fig. 133/MQ 4961), the association of the Alcott women with sewing and with social reform is very strong.

This scrap quilt, probably made for everyday use, is constructed in strips of pieced triangles all pointing in the same direction and alternating plain strips of cloth. The overall color scheme is tan, red, and brown—the madder shades popular in the nineteenth century—although the triangles incorporate a number of different fabrics. While most of the strips are composed of dark triangles of one fabric set with a light background, the strip next to the left edge uses at least four different dark fabrics. Some of the plain strips are also pieced, using similar-colored fabrics. The strips of "geese" along the outer edges use smaller triangles than those in the rest of the top. A border of half-square triangles appears on each side. This economical use of scraps strongly

FIGURE 34. Abigail May Alcott, c. 1850. *Photograph courtesy of Orchard House— Home of the Alcotts.*

suggests both good design sense and economy on the part of the maker.

Quilting follows the shape of the triangles in the pieced strips but is stitched in diagonal parallel lines in the plain strips. The batting is wool, again suggesting utility and warmth. This quilt is displayed frequently on the bed in Abby and Bronson Alcott's bedroom at Orchard House. —MC

"GARDEN PATH" QUILT
(FIG. 35)

The intricacy of the cut-out corners of this quilt, with an unusual perpendicular slash at the top of the cut, suggests that it was made for a particular four-posted bed that probably had slender, square foot-posts. The collection of fabrics used in this quilt appear to have come from a stash of cotton dress goods produced in Europe as well as the United States prior to 1840. There are chintz as well as plain prints and plaids, including early madders, Prussian blues, and other colorations and printing styles such as picotage dotted backgrounds. The choice of fabrics creates an overall appearance of delicacy, despite its construction from scraps.

The design of the quilt is a combination of plain and pieced strips. The pieced strips use random four-patch blocks set on point. The plain strips between the pieced strips are in some cases pieced, using similar-colored fabrics to achieve the length needed. The center plain strip is a ribbon print (with some piecing at one end). Yet another light printed stripe is used for the side borders. Quilting is utilitarian rather than a design in itself, stitched in straight lines—horizontal in the pieced strips and diagonal in the plain. The back is pieced of at least a dozen different fabrics, mostly of the brown prints. The binding is also pieced of a variety of fabrics. The frugal use of materials to achieve a pleasing product is in keeping with the Alcott family's values and history.

In the early 1840s, when this quilt is believed to have been made, the Alcott family was particularly destitute. Bronson Alcott's schools had failed and his attempt to write for a Transcendentalist periodical was rejected. Friend and neighbor Ralph Waldo Emerson came to the family's aid, financing a trip to England for Bronson to meet with like-minded educators and philosophers. Bronson returned six months later with several of his new friends and together they established a utopian farm, Fruitlands, in Harvard, a northern Worcester County town. This experiment in communal living was based on Transcendentalist ideals of spiritual growth through self-reflection, made radical by the desire to separate from society and to live literally on the fruits of the land, with no assistance—or sustenance—from animals. An entirely vegan diet was eaten, and not even wool for quilt batting was allowed, for, according to their beliefs, wool belonged to the sheep, not man. Members of the community, not oxen (except in desperate need), pulled the plows. Unfortunately, because the male members were often out lecturing and philosophizing with other Transcendentalists, the work generally fell on the shoulders of Abby May Alcott and her daughters. Willing to put up with her husband's self-absorption over spiritual and intellectual matters, but not with the endless, backbreaking labor of the farm, nor especially his divisive friends, Abby threatened to take the children and leave—with or without him. The "new Eden" of Fruitlands, which already had lost most of its members, came to an end in early 1844 and the family, with Bronson, moved back to Concord the following year.[28] —MC and LZB

FIGURE 35. Pieced quilt, "Garden Path" variation, attributed to
Abigail May Alcott (1800–1877) of Concord, c. 1840–1845. Cotton
(85" × 79"). Collection of Orchard House—Home of the Alcotts,
Concord, Mass. *Photograph by David Stansbury.* MQ 4697.

FIGURE 36. The Alcott family at Orchard House, Concord, c. 1865. *Photograph courtesy of Orchard House—Home of the Alcotts.*

FIGURE 37. Louisa May Alcott, 1858. *Photograph courtesy of Orchard House—Home of the Alcotts.*

"LITTLE WOMEN" QUILT
(FIG. 38)

The mid-twentieth-century "Little Women" quilt completes the picture, romanticized as it may be, of the Alcotts and quiltmaking.

Marion Cheever Whiteside Newton designed and sold through her company, Story Book Quilts, about fifty different designs for appliqué during the 1940s and 1950s.[29] The appliqué designs were available as patterns, kits, and completed quilts. The appearance of the "Little Women" design coincided with the 1949 release of one of several film versions of this story, which may have boosted the quilt's popularity.

This quilt has alternating plain and appliquéd blocks. The maker, Mildred Remsen, a homemaker who lived most of her life in Needham, chose to place her appliquéd figures on a pink background, suggesting that she used the pattern rather than a kit, as other known examples of this quilt use other colorations. The colors used are reminiscent of the

FIGURE 38. Appliquéd quilt, "Little Women," made by Mildred
Remsen of Needham, c. 1950, from a commercial pattern produced
by Story Book Quilts of New York, designed by Marion Cheever
Whiteside Newton. Cotton (96" × 79"). Private collection. *Photograph
by David Stansbury.* MQ 4118.

FIGURE 39. Detail of the "Little Women" quilt: the March girls under a tree with Laurie. *Photograph by David Stansbury.*

"Garden Path" quilt attributed to Abigail May Alcott (fig. 35/MQ 4697).

Pictured on the quilt are major events from the novel: Beth at her piano, Jo and the Professor courting under an umbrella, Meg's wedding, and two scenes in which the girls are sewing (while also talking and hearing a letter from their father).

While *Little Women* is a work of fiction, it does use many events and characters that can be traced to the Alcotts' family life: the four sisters, the idealized parents who are poor but principled, and especially the parallels between Jo and Louisa in personality and childhood experiences. The romances in *Little Women* are only partly traceable to real life, but the tensions between the themes of sisterly devotion and rivalry are present in both the novel and in journals from the family. This ambivalence raises the novel from a children's story to a more complex relationship-based novel.[30] Since its publication in 1867, and with its translation into many languages, the story has become very real to its millions of readers and serves as an icon of women's coming of age. —MC

MUNROE FAMILY QUILT

(FIG. 40)

The donors of this quilt to the New England Quilt Museum stated that it descended in the family of Wesley W. Munroe (1896–1964) of Lynnfield. Research reveals that the quilt almost certainly was made by Wesley's grandmother, Emily L. (Wiley) Munroe, the only daughter of Robert and Rosetta Wiley. Emily married Luther Simonds Munroe (1823–1885) in 1851, and together they had three daughters and three sons. As farmers in Lynnfield, the Wileys and Munroes supplied the nearby cities of Boston and Salem, as well as surrounding manufacturing towns, with eggs, milk, cheese, fresh produce, and hay.[31] Luther owned land valued at $2,000 in the 1850 federal census—considerably more than his neighbors. Members of the family also were involved with the manufacturing of shoes, the largest industry in the state.[32]

Emily recycled the everyday, coarse wools and cottons of a farmer's wardrobe for use in her extraordinary folk art bedcover. The backgrounds of the fifty-four blocks consist of twill- and plain-woven wool and wool/cotton mixed fabrics in shades of brown, black, gray-blue, tan, and beige. Many of the fabrics are pieced to make them large enough for the squares, and they show signs of their original wearing, such as shininess from the seat of woolen trousers. Emily chose particularly coarse white wool for the horse and dog in the center block to give them a visual texture, as if they were embroidered with French knots. She made the "clay" flower pots of coarsely woven pumpkin-colored wool—a fabric commonly found on the back of New England's whole-cloth wool quilts. She appliquéd the leaves of the flowers of green baize, probably cut from the lining of an old coat or cloak, or from a worn-out table cover, and she used cotton tape to embellish the horse saddles. With an extra touch of artistry and attention to detail, Emily often twisted yarns of two different colors to outline her motifs and used couching stitches to keep them in place. Each block of the quilt is worked on a foundation of denim, striped ticking, or plain cotton.

FIGURE 40. Pieced, appliquéd, and embroidered summer quilt, original pattern attributed to Emily L. (Wiley) Munroe (1823–1894) of Lynnfield, c. 1865. Wool and cotton (69" × 68½"). Collection of the New England Quilt Museum (2000.02). *Photograph by David Stansbury.* MQ 1538.

FIGURE 41. Emily Munroe appliqué quilt, detail. *Photograph by David Stansbury.*

FIGURE 42. Emily Munroe appliqué quilt, detail. *Photograph by David Stansbury.*

FIGURE 43. Emily Munroe quilt, back, showing individually finished blocks. *Photograph by David Stansbury.*

FIGURE 44. Emily Munroe appliqué quilt, detail of block with house, horse, and dog. *Photograph by David Stansbury.*

Emily turned the edges of each eight-and-a-half-inch-square block back and under, then whip-stitched the blocks together. There is no further finish around the outer edges, and no backing on the quilt.

The fabrics are consistent with the donor's belief that this quilt was made around the time of the Civil War. The connection to the war is found on Emily's side of the family. Four of her six brothers enlisted: Daniel and Joseph joined together on 13 June 1861, and served in the same regiment; Charles volunteered for duty in 1864; and baby brother Zachary Taylor Wiley lied about his age, declaring himself to be twenty-one, in order to enlist in 1864 when he was actually only sixteen.[33]

No war in American history cost more lives—over 600,000 men were dead by the time the end came in the spring of 1865. Emily must have anxiously scanned the lists of dead and wounded in the newspapers at every opportunity, not only for her brothers, but for the scores of other Lynnfield men who served with the federal troops. With what distress did she greet the news that Joseph had been wounded at the Battle of Gettysburg, or when Daniel was wounded a year later? Was she thinking of Charles and young Zachary, who both served in the cavalry, when she appliquéd the horses on her quilt? They were all her younger brothers, and as the only sister and older sibling, she must have provided much of their care when they were little. Her concern was not just sisterly, but motherly. Did the quilt offer some distraction and comfort from her worry? Was she thinking of happier days as she embellished with embroidery the white house in the center—their childhood home?—and surrounded it with designs of apple trees, pet cats, dogs, horses, and baskets of flowers? Or perhaps the quilt was made in celebration once they all returned home safely. Emily's brothers were more fortunate than George W. Wiley of Lynnfield—undoubtedly a relative—who died of disease while serving in Maryland in 1864.

The exact motivations for the creation of this bed cover are no longer known, but clearly it reflects the life and loves of the family and was treasured by them. Emily's son, Harry Wingate Munroe,

was probably the one who inherited the quilt. It next passed to his son, Wesley Wingate Munroe, who married local school teacher and widow Bernice Lang Ayers. Wesley and Bernice did not have children together, so the quilt passed to Bernice's daughter-in-law, who donated it to the New England Quilt Museum.   —LZB

HARRIET WEBSTER HAYNES QUILT
(FIG. 45)

Harriet Webster Haynes's life spanned most of the nineteenth century—all of it spent in the town of Haverhill. Called "Aunt Moses" by friends and family for her husband Moses Haynes (b. 1799), whom she married in 1825, Harriet undoubtedly made many quilts to keep her family warm. She and Moses were both of Yankee heritage with family histories going back generations in Haverhill. They had six children, five of whom survived to become adults.

Harriet and Moses lived in Ayer's Village, west of Haverhill's town center. Moses was a shoemaker, undoubtedly in one of the nine shoe manufactories located in Ayer's Village. The Haverhill economy was almost entirely dependent on the making of shoes in the nineteenth century. In a promotional publication for the town written in 1889, the Board of Trade boasts,

> Some faint idea of how the business has grown may be gleaned from the statement that in 1832 there were twenty-eight firms engaged in the manufacture of shoes in Haverhill; in 1837, forty-two; while at the present time there are fully two hundred firms, giving employment to fifteen thousand operatives, distributing annually more than $2,000,000 in wages, and shipping each year over two hundred thousand cases, the shipment the past year reaching the enormous total of 256,338 cases.[34]

Each case contained fifty-five pairs of shoes, meaning that in 1888, Haverhill produced fourteen million pairs of shoes! The Board of Trade claimed that

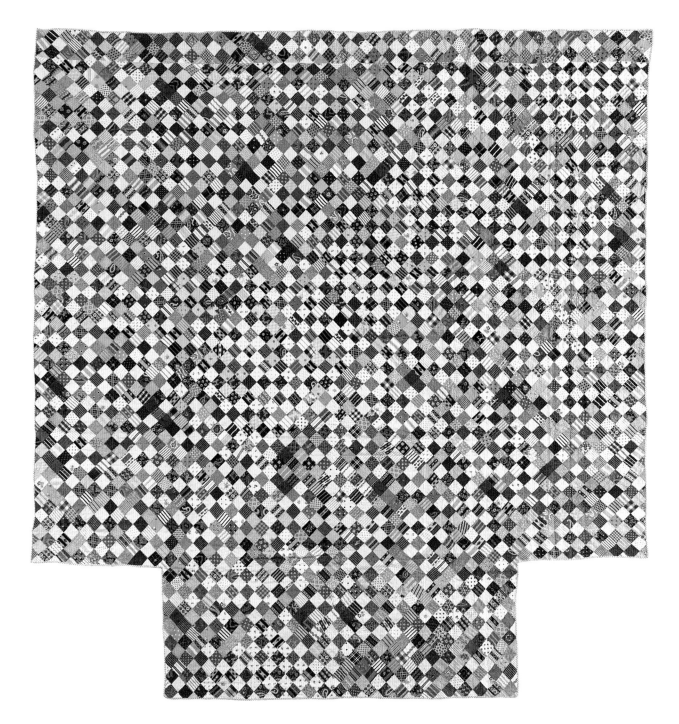

FIGURE 45. Pieced quilt, "One Patch," made by Harriet Webster
Haynes (1803–1894) of Haverhill, c. 1876. Cotton (104" × 98"). Private
collection. *Photograph by David Stansbury.* MQ 1802.

FIGURE 46. Harriet Webster Haynes, c. 1865. *Photograph courtesy of Roberta Hoffman.*

itants. We believe that not only is every business man in the place a native of the immediate vicinity, but they are all more or less intimately connected by the ties of consanguinity."[37] The Haynes family, along with the Webster family, was very numerous in Haverhill; certainly there was a "tie of consanguinity" between factory owner Phineas Haynes and Moses Haynes, but the exact relationship is not known.

This one-patch quilt is evidence of the deep scrapbag that Harriet accumulated through decades of sewing for her family. Hand-pieced over a ten-year period after the Civil War, the one-and-a-half-inch-square calico patches of madder reds and browns, shirtings, double pinks, mourning prints, and at least one 1876 Centennial print, undoubtedly reminded Harriet of her old dresses and the garments worn by her much-loved family members. The quilt has no batting; the backing is plain, white cotton, and the edges are bound with a narrow strip of checked cotton cut on the bias. It remains in the family.   —LZB

Haverhill produced more shoes than any other town in the world.[35]

The shoe-making industry supported scores of ancillary local industries, including leather tanning, making and repairing machinery for the shoe factories, and even producing the cardboard boxes in which the shoes were packaged. "In fact, Haverhill is one vast shoe manufactory, its very life, existence, and prosperity dependent on the trade which has made it what it is," the Board of Trade wrote.[36] The growth of the shoe industry in Massachusetts was made possible by the invention of the sewing machine. In addition to a few hat manufacturers and wool mills that supplemented the shoe factories, Haverhill also manufactured the Pentucket Variable Stitch Sewing Machine.

In Ayer's Village, the principal shoe manufacturers were Phineas Haynes and Amos Hazeltine. The author of *The History of Haverhill*, published in 1860, noted that "A pleasant, as well as somewhat remarkable fact connected with this thriving village, is found in the close relationship of its inhab-

MIDDLEMAS FAMILY QUILT
(FIG. 47)

This unusual and striking quilt combines two trends of the late 1800s—a blue and white color scheme and the use of pieced letters to form the quilt's top. Its maker pieced the words of the Lord's Prayer into her top using indigo blue fabrics to form the letters against a white ground fabric. The letters are hand-pieced and the strips are machine-sewn together. The quilt has a thin cotton batting and is hand-quilted only in the sashing with a pattern of diagonal lines.

In part due to a resurgence of interest in colonial American history surrounding the 1876 United States Centennial celebrations, blue and white quilts became especially popular during the last quarter of the 1800s, probably inspired by blue and white overshot and Jacquard coverlets made earlier in the century. The similarity of the lettering style used in this quilt to the appearance of cross-stitched letters on

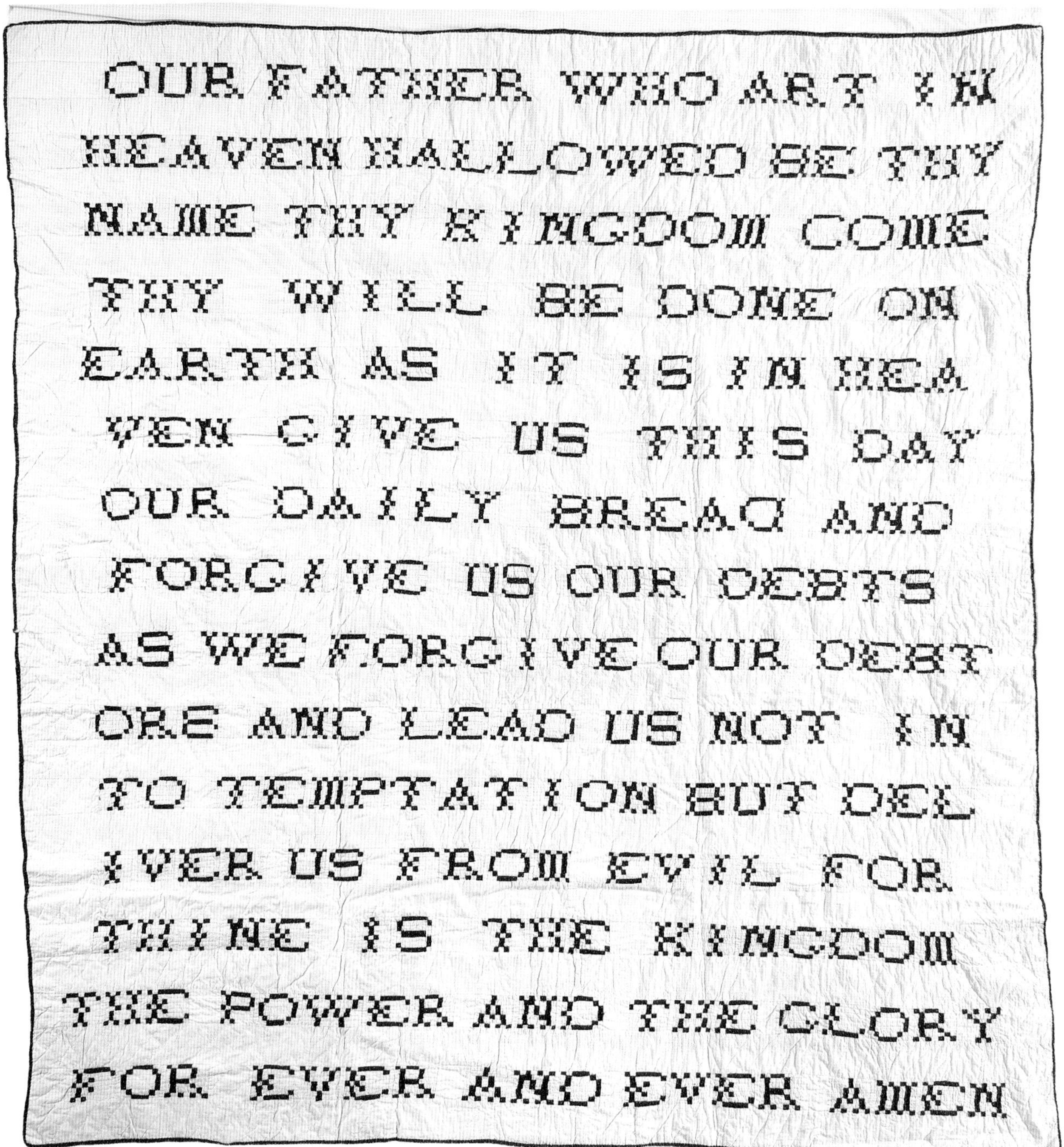

FIGURE 47. Pieced Quilt, "The Lord's Prayer," attributed to the Middlemas Family of Brighton and Natick, c. 1880–1900. Cotton (90" × 83"). Collection of the Natick Historical Society, Natick, Mass. *Photograph by David Stansbury.* MQ 866.

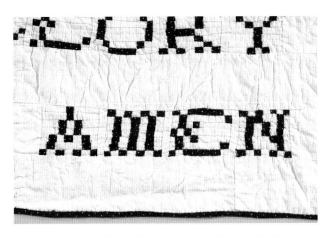

FIGURE 48. Detail, "AMEN," from the Lord's Prayer quilt. *Photograph by David Stansbury.*

FIGURE 49. Detail, "GLORY," from the Lord's Prayer quilt. *Photograph by David Stansbury.*

early American samplers also suggests an interest in the colonial past.

Quilts with pieced lettering are rare, but several documented examples dating from 1807 to the 1890s originating in New York, Connecticut, and New Jersey have been published.[38] Another Massachusetts quilt made with pieced letters forming a religious message, in the collection of the Pocumtuck Valley Memorial Association in Deerfield, was documented by MassQuilts (MQ 3242). These known examples suggest that this type of quilt was particularly popular in the Northeast, but not during a specific decade or era.[39] American Folk Art Museum curator Stacy Hollander suggests that "the lettering device combined with the religious texts creates an emotional link to the long history of female application in the needle arts, the preparation from childhood to assume adult responsibility for providing domestic textiles, and a woman's role as her family's moral and religious center."[40] In addition, "writing" words across a quilt allowed the maker a voice in a society that prohibited her from voting and disapproved of women speaking publicly.

Recent work by quilt historians puts behind us the idea that quilts were simply practical, functional household objects. This quilt, and others like it with pieced lettering, follows from the tradition of friendship quilts made in the 1840s and 1850s, offering women a way to communicate their opinions and feelings in a socially approved way—using those most feminine of tools, a needle and thread.

Growing evidence indicates that many women made some of their quilts primarily to maintain connections between themselves and friends or family. As quilt historian Laurel Horton suggests, quilts could represent "a repository of personal capital, reflecting the commerce of women's mutual obligations and relationships."[41] Around the same time that this quilt was made, other women were making quilts to express political opinions (see fig. 146/MQ 5617) or to draw attention to any number of reform efforts such as abolition (see fig. 133/MQ 2028 and fig. 135/MQ 4961), temperance, and women's suffrage.

Unfortunately, the identity of this quilt's maker is not certain. It was presented to the Natick Historical Society in 1978 by Arthur Middlemas (1896–1987) and his wife, and is believed to have come from the Middlemas family. Perhaps it was made by Arthur's mother, Emma, a native of Nova Scotia, who immigrated to Massachusetts in 1890 at the age of twenty.[42] Arthur's father, Judson A. Middlemas, was also a native of Nova Scotia, who came to the United States in 1880. The 1900 U.S. census lists him as a carriage maker in Boston, but by 1920, he was a truck farmer (meaning that he grew a variety of vegetables that were sold in nearby cities). Arthur and his younger brother George followed in their father's footsteps, growing vegetables in nearby Natick to sell at their farmstand in the Brighton section of Boston, where they grew up.[43] The Massachusetts Audubon Society acquired their Natick farm as a wildlife sanctuary in 1973.   —AEN

ALICE GRAY BROWN QUILT

(FIG. 50)

This elegant crazy quilt has the ironic history of being made in a most inelegant situation—on board ship during a long sea voyage. Alice Gray Brown was born in 1863, the daughter of Captain Lawrence W. Brown (1831–1903) and Jane Wormstead (1839–1871). A Newburyport mariner, her father sailed on and commanded numerous voyages during his career. Seafaring was in the family's blood: Captain Brown's father, John Pike Brown, was also a ship captain out of Newburyport, who died at sea when Lawrence was only four years old. Alice's uncle, John E. Brown, also made his living as a mariner. Her own family participated in business related to seafaring: Alice's maternal grandfather, Michael Wormstead, was a ropemaker in Newbury.

Newburyport was first settled in 1635 as part of Newbury. It was set off and incorporated as a town in 1764. In 1840, the town was notable as "the smallest in its territorial limits of any in the commonwealth," composed of only 647 acres. However, at least one visitor was impressed by the town, despite its size, "By whatever avenue it is approached, its appearance never fails to impress the mind of the visitor with pleasurable sensations."[44] At that time, Newburyport's economy was almost totally dependent on the sea, with 128 vessels employing 1,000 people in the cod and mackerel fishery, along with 4 vessels and 120 people employed in the whale fishery. Back on dry land, the community produced $113,173 worth of boots and shoes in 1837 through the work of 206 men and 114 women.[45] Newburyport continued to grow throughout the nineteenth century, becoming a city in 1851.

Lawrence Brown and Jane Wormstead married in the early 1860s. Their listing on the 1870 U.S. census in Newburyport notes that Lawrence owned a personal estate worth $5,000, and the household included Jane, who was "keeping house"; their daughters, Agnes (b. 1862) and quiltmaker Alice; Jane's mother, Mary Wormstead, aged fifty; Jane's sister, Hannah, aged twenty-two; and a domestic servant, Amy Lambert from England. Jane died in 1871 and

Lawrence Brown married his second wife, Abbie Ingalls Orne (1841–1910) on January 19, 1875.

At the time of the 1880 census, Alice Brown lived in Newburyport with her aunt, Elizabeth Brown (1826–1923). Her father's absence from the 1880 U.S. census suggests that he was away at sea and left Alice with his sister in Newburyport. The dangers inherent in ocean travel and trade are documented dramatically in one of Captain Lawrence Brown's more notable trips: In 1863, Captain Brown commanded the ship *Sonora*, which sailed from Hong Kong in November with a cargo of rice for India. In December, the *Sonora* was captured and burned by the *Alabama*. Built in England in 1862 for the Confederate States Navy, the *Alabama* never laid anchor in a Southern port. Instead, the ship served as a commerce raider, attacking Union merchant and naval ships in the East Indies, the North Atlantic, and points in between. Between 1862 and its sinking in 1864, the *Alabama* claimed more than sixty prizes valued at almost $6 million, including the *Sonora*. The officers and crew of that ship were set adrift with no provisions. Fortunately, they were rescued and lived to tell the tale.[46]

Despite the dangers, Captain Brown did sometimes take his family on his voyages. Alice accompanied her father on at least six voyages between 1878 and 1888. She went along on three voyages of the ship *Elcano*, including one when she celebrated both her fifteenth and sixteenth birthdays aboard ship. Alice's diaries and letters record many challenges faced during the trips. In a letter written after she married, she summarized the contents of one of her shipboard diaries,

> I tell of lovely days spent on the *Elcano* of which my Father was Master and my mother and I passengers. Ships passed and spoken, whales, sharks, flying fishes, porpoises, pilot fish, and others seen. Mostly fine weather spent. But also Rain, Heavy seas, calms. Shooting stars, wonderful sunsets and my Father reading many books aloud to us . . . We played cards—I painted. Had lessons. Did fancy work, plain sewing . . . Listened to Papas stories that I wish I could remember. Sundays always a sermon + service.[47]

FIGURE 50. Foundation-pieced crazy quilt top, made by Alice Gray
Brown (1863–1956) of Newburyport, c. 1880–1885. Silk (58" × 56¼").
Collection of the Newburyport Maritime Society, Newburyport,
Mass. *Photograph by Patricia Bashford, courtesy of the Newburyport Maritime
Society.* MQ 2354.

FIGURE 51. Detail of Alice Brown crazy quilt showing painted landscape and stork. *Photograph by Patricia Bashford, courtesy of the Newburyport Maritime Society.*

She also took three voyages on the ship *Mary L. Cushing* while her father commanded it between 1884 and 1888. Launched in 1883, the *Mary L. Cushing* is said to be the last square-rigged vessel built in Massachusetts.[48] The captain's quarters were fitted out for the Browns' comfort, including "red plush upholstery" and an "upright piano" in the cabin.[49]

Alice's diary entries suggest that painting was her true passion. In August 1879, she noted "I learned a Geography lesson this morning and have spent the afternoon in painting." A few days later, she recorded "I have been busy all the morning sewing. I made a catcher for the bird cage and hemmed the bottom of my new garments. I intend to spend two hours every day painting."[50]

To pass the time on at least one of these voyages, Alice combined her painting with her requisite sewing time and made the quilt top shown here. In the well-known crazy quilt style, the top is hand-

pieced. The quilt does not have uniform blocks, but is composed of five vertical rows that are each eleven and a half inches wide. She used a variety of plain and patterned silks in the top, including plain weaves, twill weaves, satin weaves, and pile fabrics (such as velvet). A number of the blocks are made with a pieced fan design, while others have detailed painted images of houses, flowers, and leaves. Many blocks have decorative embroidery along the seams. A friend of Alice's granddaughter, to whom the quilt descended, put a backing on the quilt in the early 1980s to help protect it and allow it to be displayed.

Alice married Merrill Draper Brigham (b. 1863) of Worcester in October 1889. By the time of the 1900 Census, the couple was settled in Worcester. They had five children: Lawrence Whitney (b. 1890), Ruth Montague (b. 1892), Harold Kingsbury (b. 1894), Eleanor Agnes (b. 1895), and Margaret

Woodbury (b. 1897). In August of 1900, Alden In-galls, their sixth child, arrived. The 1900 census also lists a housekeeper in the Brigham home, Mabel E. Cady, aged twenty-five. Over the next thirty years, the Brigham family remained in Worcester, where Merrill worked as a bookkeeper at a farm imple-ments business and as a "credit man" at an "install-ment house," while Alice looked after their home and children. In 1930, the U.S. census lists Merrill and Alice living at home with their thirty-seven-year-old daughter Ruth, who was a public school teacher, and their thirty-six-year-old son Harold, who was a physician in private practice. Alice lived a long life, dying in Worcester in 1956 at the age of ninety-three. —AEN

FRANCES CLARKE WESTERGREN QUILT
(FIG. 52)

After the Civil War, women began making signifi-cant strides in expanding their career oppor-tunities. More and more colleges were open to women, offering them better educations. Still, few ventured outside of the most socially acceptable roles of being a teacher, missionary, shop girl, millworker, or office worker.

> It is only a few years since the idea of a woman en-tering the profession of medicine and graduating as a doctor was something so quixotic, if not actually absurd, that any girl who alluded to such a vocation was reasoned with and talked to as if she has con-templated suicide.[51]

Female physicians were very rare, but Massachu-setts led the way in opening that career path. The world's first college for women doctors, the Boston Female Medical College (soon renamed the New England Female Medical College), opened in 1848 with twelve students. Almost one hundred medical degrees had been granted to women by 1874, when the school merged with Boston University Medical School.[52] Ironically, although Massachusetts took a very advanced view of women's education, its most

venerated medical school was remarkably slow to accept women. Harvard Medical School began to allow female students to matriculate in 1945, almost a hundred years after the founding of Boston Female Medical College. The profession in general dragged its heels in welcoming women to its ranks, finally admitting women into the American Medical Asso-ciation in 1915.

The maker of this quilt, Frances E. Clarke Westergren, is therefore particularly remarkable for achieving a career in medicine in the nineteenth century. Born in Mansfield Center, Connecticut, "Fannie" Elizabeth Clarke graduated from Boston University School of Medicine in 1892 at the age of thirty-one. Her graduation thesis was entitled *Al-cohol: Its Abuses and Uses*.[53] Fannie, a pretty woman with fashionable curly bangs, looks confident in a photographic portrait taken around the time of her graduation. She practiced homeopathy, a medical career path that was especially popular with women. Homeopathy is based on an idea that arose in the early nineteenth century that to cure an ailment, one must treat it with small doses of a drug that in large quantities would create the same symptoms as those being suffered (a principal known as the "Law of Similars"). Its rejection of "heroic" medi-cine, which advised balancing the body's "humors" by the extremely unpleasant practices of bleeding, blistering, and purging, made homeopathy attractive to many people, including Boston's upper classes, re-formers, and abolitionists. Boston City Directories show that Dr. Westergren moved her office several times to different locations on Huntington Avenue and Massachusetts Avenue beginning in 1898; by 1917 she was practicing at 5 Hamilton Street, New-ton Lower Falls, south of Boston.

Fannie Westergren was also an artist. This quilt's owner, Fannie's great-granddaughter, owns a num-ber of Fannie's paintings, along with more quilts. Fannie's husband, Andreas Magnus Westergren (1844–1936), a Swedish immigrant, combined an interest in the natural world and art to create his career; the 1910 U.S. census lists Andreas as a natu-ralist at an unspecified college. He traveled to places such as the Galapagos Islands in order to paint flow-ers and wildlife. Either because their careers did not

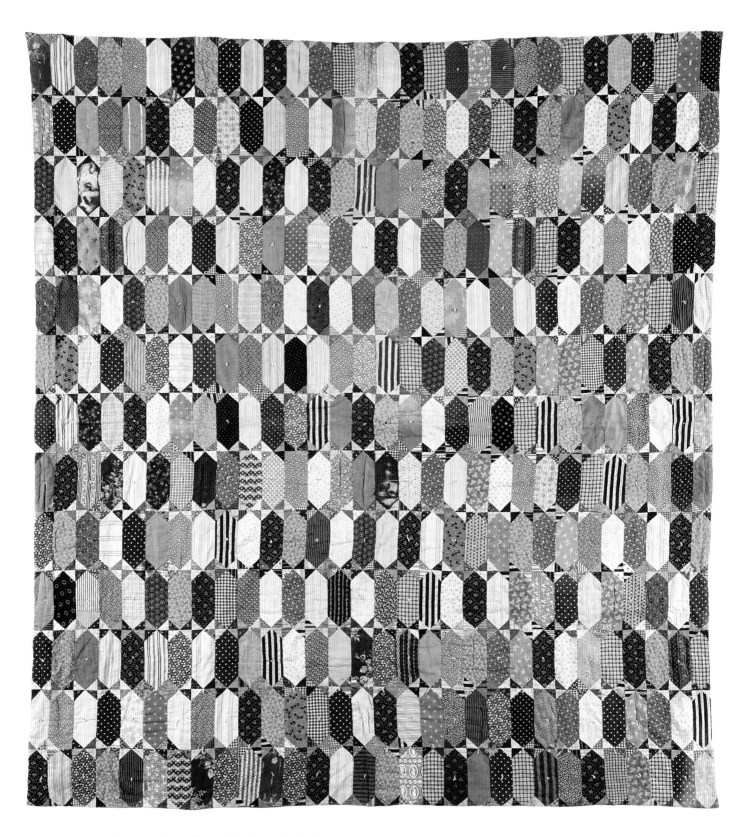

FIGURE 52. Pieced comforter, "Stained Glass," made by Dr. Frances
Clarke Westergren (1861–1936) of Boston, c. 1890. Cotton (89½" ×
81½"). Private collection. *Photograph by David Stansbury.* MQ 3858.

provide sufficient income, or because they liked the company, the couple took in boarders as they became elderly. The 1920 census shows four boarders living with them, including a milliner, a dressmaker, a salesman, and a railroad employee. Fannie died of a heart attack in July of 1936 and is buried in her home state of Connecticut.[54]

The top of Fannie's comforter, pieced by hand in lozenge shapes, contains a multitude of colorful late-nineteenth-century calicoes, including mourning prints. Small triangles pieced at the points of the lozenges form a secondary hourglass pattern. The backing fabric consists of a printed patchwork simulating triangular piecing with paisley, checked, and floral prints. The medium-weight cotton batting is held in place with cotton ties, while a knife edge (in which the edges of the fabric are turned to the inside) finishes the comforter.   —HE and LZB

FIGURE 53. Dr. Frances Clark Westergren, c. 1890. *Photograph courtesy of Frances Collinson.*

FIGURE 54. Detail, printed patchwork backing fabric of Frances Westergren's quilt. *Photograph by David Stansbury.*

ALICE LYNWOOD DOWD FORD QUILT

(FIG. 55)

FIGURE 56. Alice Lynwood Dowd Ford, c. 1930.
Photograph courtesy of Deborah Brunetto.

Patterns specifically for children's quilts started to appear in women's periodicals in the 1880s. Outline embroidery and appliqué techniques have dominated designs for children's quilts from that time. The appeal of these quilts increased throughout the end of the nineteenth century and into the beginning of the twentieth century; by the time this quilt was made around 1936, children's quilts were all the rage.[55]

The pastel palette that most quilters identify with the 1930s actually was inspired by post–World War I improvements in synthetic dyes.[56] The maker of this charming quilt, Alice Lynwood Dowd Ford, used black embroidery in a blanket stitch to outline the pastel ducks. Alice was a watercolor artist and embroiderer; she only made two quilts as gifts for her children. Her needlework skill and artist's eye are evident in this quilt, which uses both to make a small quilt visually appealing.

The block pattern with a duck wearing a sunbonnet is a variation on innumerable animal motifs used throughout the early 1900s. In addition, this pattern probably was inspired by the multitude of "Sunbonnet Children" designs that proliferated during the early 1900s. The sunbonnet patterns evolved from illustrations by Bertha Corbett, who in turn was inspired by Kate Greenaway's illustrations of children. While Corbett's books appeared in 1900 and patterns were adapted for outline embroidery soon after, the "Sunbonnet Children" patterns did not become popular until the late 1920s and 1930s, around the time this quilt was made.[57]

Quiltmaker Alice Lynwood Dowd was born in Osterville, Massachusetts, in 1909. She married Edward John Ford in 1935 and the couple lived in Boston, where Edward was an insurance agent. They had three children, two of whom lived to adulthood. Their oldest child, Deborah, was born in Boston in 1936. Their youngest child, Edward, was born in Medford in 1942. At retirement, Alice and Edward Ford moved to Florida, where Alice exhibited some of her paintings. She died in Tampa in 1994.

The twelve blocks are ten inches square and are machine-stitched together. The quilt has only two layers—top and backing—and has been tied at the corners of the blocks to hold the layers together. The lack of a batting in between technically makes this a summer coverlet or spread rather than a quilt.

—AEN

FIGURE 55. Appliquéd and pieced summer spread, "Sunbonnet Duck," made by Alice Lynwood Dowd Ford (1909–1994) of Boston, c. 1936. Cotton (55" × 42"). Private collection. *Photograph by David Stansbury.* MQ 2898.

Chapter 3

Southeastern Massachusetts: From Pilgrims to Poplins

The southeastern region of Massachusetts begins at the Atlantic Ocean and extends west to Worcester County. Norfolk County marks its northern border, and Rhode Island and Buzzards Bay delineate the southern. Technically, the area includes Barnstable, Nantucket, and Dukes counties, which Bay Staters refer to as "the Cape and Islands," but those counties are discussed elsewhere, leaving Plymouth and Bristol counties to be explored here.

The Wampanoags greeted Massachusetts' first permanent European colonists in 1620 when the *Mayflower* Separatists, better known as the Pilgrims, established Plymouth Colony. Within a year of their arrival, other Puritans followed, creating numerous communities up and down the coast by 1650. The Massachusetts Bay Colony, centered in Boston, quickly dominated them all. Plymouth and the Massachusetts Bay colonies, nevertheless, retained separate governments until 1685, when King James II revoked all charters and consolidated New England and New York into the Dominion of New England under Sir Edmund Andros. The Dominion itself ended in the Revolution of 1688 that placed William and Mary on the English throne. Although new charters returned many former rights to individual colonies, Plymouth and the Massachusetts Bay colonies were officially merged in 1689.[1]

Most of the first colonists relied on agriculture for subsistence, even in coastal settlements. The development of industrial and urban centers in New England in the nineteenth century led farmers to concentrate more on commercial, rather than subsistence agriculture, for the residents of the new cities needed to be fed. The most successful farmers specialized to supply new markets. Today such agricultural traditions are found in the crimson cranberry bogs of Plymouth County and such works as Carver cranberry grower Cora Appling's Depression-era quilts (figures 64/MQ 3678 and 213/MQ 3680).

Southeastern Massachusetts' two largest cities are Fall River and New Bedford. During the late nineteenth and early twentieth centuries, Fall River was the largest cotton-manufacturing city in the United States, and ranked among the wealthiest communities in America. Weekly cotton fabric production in the late 1880s exceeded 450 million yards of cloth. The cloth found its way into many quilts, while the money generated by the mills was evidenced in the mansions on the city's hills. Among those houses was the home of Lizzie Borden, who was tried for the sensational ax murders of her father and step-mother in 1892. Although press coverage compared to that of the Lindbergh kidnapping or the O. J. Simpson trial, historically, Borden's acquittal illustrated society's reluctance to challenge prescribed gender and class roles.[2] The circa 1830 "Star of Lemoyne" quilt made by a Borden family member pre-dates the infamous Lizzie (see figure 59/MQ 2329).

New Bedford's affluence derived from its role as one of the East Coast's largest whaling ports. Established in 1652, New Bedford did not flourish until after the Revolutionary War, when Quaker whalers arrived in the port city, bringing both their business acumen and their social justice. By the early 1800s, the city became the vibrant seaport described in the opening passages of *Moby Dick* and home to

a growing and diverse population. Free Blacks and those escaping slavery found New Bedford filled with maritime economic opportunities and a less restrictive environment. New Bedford became an active anti-slavery center, and home to the abolitionist and orator Frederick Douglass. As the nineteenth century progressed, Irish, French Canadians, and Portuguese all claimed New Bedford as home and added to the complexity of the city. The Lemieux embroidered redwork quilt is evidence of such contributions (see fig. 61/MQ 2312).

Today, southeastern Massachusetts is home to numerous colleges, beaches, vineyards, and farms, and is a revitalized tourist destination filled with historic and cultural treasures. —DCA

BORDEN FAMILY QUILT
(FIG. 59)

This visually stunning quilt is associated with the family that also produced one of America's most notorious murder defendants: Lizzie Borden (1860–1927). In a sensational 1893 trial, Lizzie was acquitted of murdering her father and step-mother with a hatchet.[3] Succeeding generations of American children have grown up chanting the gruesome rhyme,

> Lizzie Borden took an ax
> And gave her mother forty whacks
> When she saw what she had done
> She gave her father forty-one.

Found in the Fall River home of Lizzie's great-uncle, Cook Borden (1810–1880), this quilt may have been made by his wife, Mary A. Bessey (1810–1894) at the time of their marriage in 1832. Cook Borden started his own lumber business, Cook, Borden and Company, in the 1830s or early 1840s, and became wealthy by supplying the burgeoning mills of the area with boards, molding, and shingles.[4] Between April 1863 and April 1867 alone, the company sold $445,000 worth of lumber.[5]

Located on the Taunton River, Fall River established itself as a manufacturing center during the early 1800s. The town had ten mills by 1837 and the industry grew rapidly from there; eventually Fall River became one of the textile capitals of the nation and adopted the moniker, the "Queen City of Cotton."[6]

The maker of this "Star of LeMoyne" quilt utilized early cotton prints, toiles, and a particularly striking pillar print in its top.[7] Pillar print chintzes were extremely popular in the United States during the 1820s and 1830s. Archeological discoveries in Greece and Italy during the late 1700s and early 1800s drew attention to the architecture and design of those ancient democracies. As Americans created their own new democracy, they viewed pillars as a symbol of their government and political independence. Yet, ironically, most pillar prints were manufactured in England and exported to this country.[8]

Six to seven stitches per inch are quilted in an outline pattern, parallel lines, and a series of circles often called "teacup quilting" because it employed a teacup (or other round household object) as a template. Several colors of thread (cream, tan, indigo, black, and brown) blend the stitches into the quilt.
—AEN

FIGURE 59. Pieced quilt, "Star of LeMoyne," attributed to the Borden family of Fall River, c. 1825–1835. Cotton (104" × 109"). Collection of the New England Quilt Museum (1996.07). *Photograph by David Stansbury.* MQ 2329.

CLARA CHASE QUILT
(FIG. 60)

Family history states that Clara G. Chase of Mansfield probably made this striking quilt. The diverse fabrics date it to the last quarter of the nineteenth century, suggesting that Clara stitched it as a child or young woman, probably using her father's shirting fabrics and the calicoes of her own and her sisters' dresses from the family's scrapbag.

Clara used one of the many variations on the "Log Cabin" block for her quilt, but gave it an interesting design twist. Instead of letting the red centers of each block dominate visually, as is common, she finished each block with a strip of bright orange and a strip of red, arranging them to create a secondary pattern, like a square grid laid over the diagonal log cabin blocks.

During the late 1800s, "Log Cabin" quilts were often pieced using the foundation method or "pressed patchwork" technique. The maker cut her "foundation" from a piece of fabric in the dimensions of the finished block and stitched her pattern pieces to the foundation; the completed blocks were then sewn to each other.[9] Clara Chase's quilt is foundation-pieced and is composed of 144 blocks that are six and a half inches square. Many "Log Cabin" quilts are tied rather than quilted, because the extra foundation layer makes quilting difficult. However, this quilt is hand-quilted "in the ditch" (along the piecing seams) with six stitches to the inch. The quilt has a thin cotton batting and is backed with an off-white cotton fabric.

Scant details about Clara found in official records sketch only the basic outlines of her life. Her family is listed on the federal census throughout the late 1800s and early 1900s in the Bristol County town of Mansfield. Incorporated in 1775, Mansfield was home to a wide variety of industries during Clara's lifetime, including several cotton mills, shoemakers, straw hat makers, foundries, jewelry manufacturers, soap makers, and a knife business.[10] These industries attracted many workers, causing the town's population to jump over 50 percent between 1900 and 1920, from slightly over 4,000 to 6,255.

Clara was the second of four daughters born to Albert Chase, a blacksmith, and his wife Harriet. By the time of the 1910 census, Clara, who never married, was head of her household; her younger sister, Alice, who worked as the "forelady" in a jewelry shop, lived with her. Data from the 1920 census shows that Clara worked as a clerk in the Mansfield post office. She still lived with Alice and with a middle-aged boarder, Grace M. Cassiday. By pooling their resources and taking in a boarder, Clara and Alice were able to make ends meet, probably with some degree of comfort since they had no children to support.

The job opportunities for women in this period, while still limited, were expanding. With education, women became doctors, lawyers, and college professors. Most working women, however, continued to hold more traditionally female jobs. Clerking, whether for a store or a post office, was a common, though low-paid position for women. Advice literature of the period for women who wished to pursue an occupation did not find it unjust that women systematically were paid less than men: "Both men and women earn, as a rule, just what they are worth. . . . Sentimental forces have no place in the business world, and nothing is more certain than that woman is fairly treated."[11] In 1920, Clara could finally cast a vote, but she had no hope of earning pay equal to a man.   —AEN and LZB

LUMINA AND ROSE LEMIEUX QUILT
(FIG. 61)

Sisters Lumina and Rose Lemieux were workers in the cotton mills of New Bedford when they collaborated on this exceptional redwork quilt. It features forty-four blocks of embroidered squares alternating with plain blocks in each row. Each of the plain blocks is quilted in red thread with a stylized floral design. The embroidered squares depict children participating in various seasonal activities, many with titles such as "A Mid-Summer Shower," "Icicles For Sale!," "School Day Pals," and "Skating

FIGURE 60. Foundation-pieced quilt, "Log Cabin," attributed to
Clara Chase (c. 1876–1956) of Mansfield, c. 1885–1900. Cotton (80" ×
78"). Private collection. *Photograph by David Stansbury.* MQ 3705.

Weather." The holidays of the year are represented in the blocks titled "Merry Christmas!," "Happy New Year!," "For My Valentine," "The Cherry Tree" (Washington's Birthday), "Easter Greetings," "Columbus Tells Her" (Columbus Day), "For Thanksgiving Day Cheer," and even "Arbor Day." The thirty-one titled blocks are supplemented with thirteen untitled blocks depicting children of various ethnicities, including Chinese, Japanese, Dutch, Mexican, Russian, and (presumably) American, along with several more generic juvenile designs.

Outline embroidery became very popular on household linens, such as aprons, pillowcases, and towels, during the late nineteenth century.[12] Because makers of these pieces favored Turkey red thread for its colorfastness, the outline embroidery of this period came to be known as "redwork." Late nineteenth- and early twentieth-century ladies' magazines, such as *Ladies Home Journal*, advertised sources for outline embroidery patterns; many magazines and sewing-supply businesses offered full kits, with all the supplies necessary to transfer a design onto a piece of cloth. In the early twentieth century, perforated or pre-stamped patterns were developed specifically for quilt squares. While other examples have not been found of redwork incorporating the same delightful patterns seen in the Lemieux sisters' quilt, Rose and Lumina appear to have used patterns from two or possibly three different commercially available design series.[13]

Rose and Lumina were second-generation French Canadians, whose parents were drawn to Massachusetts in the late nineteenth century by employment opportunities in the New Bedford textile mills. The 1900 U.S. census finds their father, Raphael Lemieux, working as a "third hand" in one of the cotton mills, while their mother, Adele, worked as a warper, even though two-year-old Rose was at home. The census lists two other Lemieux families living on their street, so Adele probably had babysitting help from a relative at this early time in her

marriage. By 1930, Raphael had worked his way up to become a cotton mill overseer—probably in the same mill that employed his son Alfred as a section hand, as well as his daughters. Neither Rose nor Lumina ever married, but they were active in the community as musicians. Rose was a singer, and Lumina played the piano in local clubs and for private parties. They also were skilled needlewomen and left many examples of embroidery and quilts, which are still in the family.[14]   —HE and LZB

FIGURE 62. Detail, "A Mid-Summer Shower," embroidered block from Lemieux redwork quilt. *Photograph by David Stansbury.*

FIGURE 63. Detail, "Icicles for Sale," embroidered block from Lemieux redwork quilt. *Photograph by David Stansbury.*

FIGURE 61. Embroidered redwork quilt, made by Lumina Lemieux (1908–1991) and Rose Lemieux (1898–1981) of New Bedford, c. 1925–1930. Cotton (79" × 60"). Private collection. *Photograph by David Stansbury.* MQ 2312.

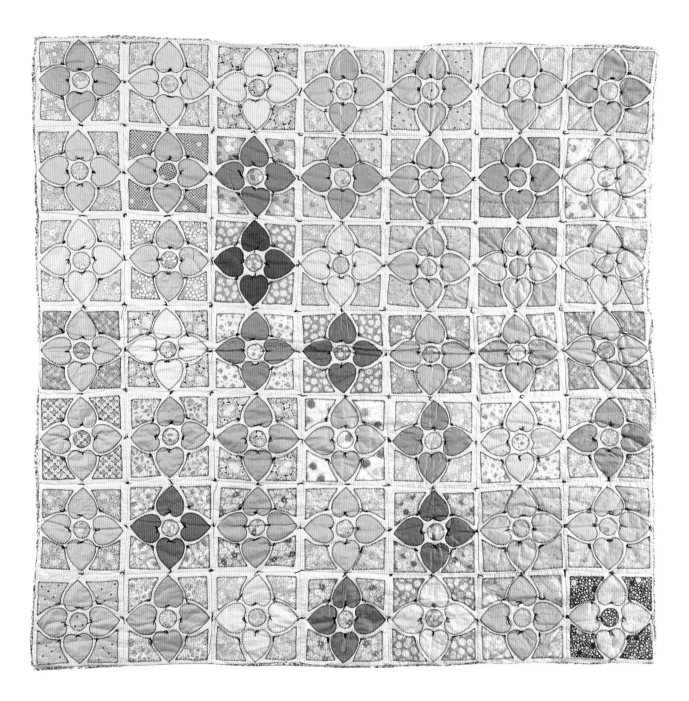

FIGURE 64. Appliquéd comforter, "Sweetheart," made by Cora
(Bruce) Appling (1879–1969) of North Carver, c. 1930–1950. Cotton
(78" × 76"). Private collection. *Photograph by David Stansbury.* MQ 3678.

FIGURE 65. *Harvest*, by John Austin, poster paint on board, 1985.
Cranberries, floating on the water of the bog where they grow, are
pushed toward a conveyor belt in the harvesting process. *Photograph
courtesy of the Nantucket Historical Association, Nantucket, Mass.*

CORA BRUCE APPLING QUILT

(FIG. 64)

Quiltmaker Cora Bruce Appling was of English-Canadian heritage, born in Nova Scotia. She came to Massachusetts as a child in the 1880s and by 1900, she had married Henry Appling (1868–1956) of Carver, in Plymouth County.[15] Cora's granddaughter, the current owner of her quilts, states that Cora was assisted in making these bed covers by a group of friends from the North Carver Congregational Church and the North Carver Grange; they used both venues for their quilting activities.[16] (This book features another of Cora's quilts, figure 213, in the discussion of the Colonial Revival.)

The solid pastel colors that dominate Cora's quilts are typical of the 1930s. Another common feature of the period, the black blanket-stitch embroidery that outlines each appliquéd piece of the "Sweetheart" comforter, creates a particularly eye-catching effect similar to stained glass. Quilt scholar Barbara Brackman notes that the "Sweetheart" appliqué pattern was first published in *Capper's Weekly*, a newspaper out of Topeka, Kansas.[17] As Cora was unlikely to be reading a Kansas newspaper, she probably saw the pattern when it was offered by mail order under syndication as Famous Features, based in New York City.[18]

By 1910, Cora and Henry owned their own cran-berry bog—a widespread agricultural pursuit in Plymouth County. Cranberries originally grew wild along the coastlines of the Carolinas up to the Maritime Provinces of Canada. Native Americans taught European settlers the nutritional and medicinal properties of this unfamiliar fruit. The colonists found cranberries to be excellent protection against scurvy, blood disorders, stomach ailments, and other diseases. In the early nineteenth century, Lydia Maria Child offered yet another use for cranberries in her advice book, *The American Frugal Housewife*: "A corn may be extracted from the foot by binding on half a raw cranberry, with the cut side of the fruit upon the foot. I have known a very old and troublesome corn drawn out in this way, in the course of a few nights."[19] Effective or not, at least this was one "cure" that did no harm. Her recipe for cranberry jelly perhaps proved more useful.

An attempt at large-scale cultivation began around 1816 on Cape Cod, near Dennis, which offered the necessary acidic peat soil, coarse sand, a water supply and a moderately frost-free growing season. The Cape Cod industry thrived during the 1850s and 1860s, dominating the market and providing cranberries to Union soldiers during the Civil War. Serious cultivation began in Plymouth County in 1856 in the vicinity of Carver. By 1895, Carver had become the new center of the cranberry industry. Initially, cranberry picking was a family affair,

with husband, wife, and children gathering at the nearest swamp or bog to collect the berries using fingered wooden scoops. As late as 1927, permits were given out to schoolchildren allowing them to miss school so they could work in the bogs during cranberry picking time in September and October.[20] Cora helped during the cranberry harvest by standing at a conveyor belt screening out the bad cranberries. As the cranberry industry grew, the workforce expanded to include more community members and, eventually, migrant workers.

Today, the cranberry continues to symbolize the success of the Pilgrims and Plymouth Colony, which we celebrate every November at Thanksgiving. And the nutritional benefits of cranberries has been proven scientifically—though testing remains to be done on the fruit's effectiveness in removing corns.

—HE and LZB

Chapter 4

Cape Cod, Nantucket, and Martha's Vineyard: Quilting by the Sea

Cape Cod's ocean vistas have inspired countless authors and artists over the centuries, including Henry David Thoreau, who wrote this elegant description:

> Cape Cod is the bared and bended arm of Massachusetts behind which the state stands on her guard, with her back to the Green Mountains, and her feet planted on the floor of the ocean, like an athlete protecting her Bay . . .[1]

The easternmost part of Massachusetts, Cape Cod extends into the Atlantic Ocean and, with the nearby islands of Nantucket and Martha's Vineyard, is known for its seafaring history. Both islands and the Cape have miles of sandy beaches with scrub vegetation and many ponds and lakes (over 360 in Barnstable County alone). While Plymouth is commonly remembered as the site of the state's first European settlement, the *Mayflower* first cast anchor on Cape Cod in November 1620 in what is now Provincetown Harbor and the Pilgrims first made landfall on Eastham's First Encounter Beach in early December 1620, *before* the famous Plymouth landing.[2]

Although the Pilgrims moved on from Cape Cod in 1620, it did not take long for the Europeans to come back and establish a settlement. The first settlement, in Sandwich, took root in 1637. Within two years, Yarmouth, Dennis, and Barnstable were also founded. Barnstable County, consisting of the entire Cape Cod peninsula, was established in 1685 when Plymouth County was split into three separate counties. Barnstable County currently has fifteen towns and over 550 miles of shoreline.

The homeland of the Wampanoag tribe, the islands of Nantucket and Martha's Vineyard were discovered by Europeans when Bartholomew Gosnold explored the area in 1602 and were settled by Thomas Mayhew in the mid-1600s. The first European settlement on Martha's Vineyard was established in 1642, while Nantucket was not inhabited by Europeans until 1659. Initially part of New York, both islands were considered part of Dukes County in that state when it was established in 1683. Eight years later, in 1691, the islands were transferred to Massachusetts and split into two counties, Nantucket County for the island of the same name and Dukes County for the Vineyard.

All three counties experienced a similar pattern of development, shifting from an agrarian to a maritime economy, and finally to tourism. When the land proved difficult to farm, Cape and Islands residents turned to raising sheep. By the early 1700s, Nantucket was one of the chief sheep-raising districts in the colonies. Eventually, the call of the sea, teeming with fish and whales, proved too difficult to ignore and all three counties developed maritime economies. Initially, the residents could make a living by shore whaling (processing whales that stranded on the beaches) and fishing near the coast. However, as the population grew and more and more men turned to the sea, the ships were forced to sail further and further from home to make a living and find enough whales and fish. Eventually, whaling voyages set sail halfway around the world to the South Pacific in search of the prized sperm whales with their valuable oil. Nantucket, with a large Quaker population, became the pre-eminent

FIGURE 66. *Old Mill*, by Anne Ramsdell Congdon, oil on canvas, 1940. Wind-powered mills for grinding grain once dotted the landscape of Cape Cod and the islands of Nantucket and Martha's Vineyard. *Photograph courtesy of the Nantucket Historical Association, Nantucket, Mass.*

whaling port in the world from the 1820s through the 1840s. A devastating fire in 1846 and the gradual silting in of the harbor spelled doom for the island's whaling industry; whalers headed for the deeper port of New Bedford, which was also close to railroad lines for distribution. When the first successful drilling for petroleum in Pennsylvania took place in 1859, any chance for Nantucket to recover its whaling business was over. Petroleum offered a better product for fuel and illumination. In addition, drilling for oil on land was more efficient than sending crews and ships away on multiple-year voyages in the hope that they would find a sufficient number of sperm whales.[3]

Martha's Vineyard, despite a head start on shore whaling in the 1650s before Nantucket was settled, was quickly overshadowed by Nantucket's success in the whaling industry. The Vineyard provided personnel for whaleships setting sail from its own harbor, as well as Nantucket's and, later, New Bedford's. In addition, the towns of the Vineyard pursued a variety of supplemental industries including farming, milling, and saltworks. Prior to mechanical refrigeration, salt was important for storing food, for improving its flavor, and for packing fish for export. By 1807, salt manufacturing was the second largest industry on the Vineyard.[4]

As the nineteenth-century fishing and whaling trades declined, many residents of the Cape and Islands moved further west, seeking new opportunities and greater financial stability. As a result, during the late 1800s, the area did not industrialize or urbanize like other areas of the state. The Cape and Islands were re-discovered during the last half of the 1800s and prized for their "quaint" villages, fresh ocean air, and picturesque beaches. Nantucket became especially popular for artists and writers, such as the painter Eastman Johnson, while the Vineyard received a boost from religious camp meetings that started to gather on the island. Likewise, the Cape experienced annual visitation from city residents looking for a restful vacation spot.

The quilts in this section span the period from Nantucket's whaling peak to Cape Cod's resurgence as a tourist destination. The earlier quilts employ high-quality imported fabrics, probably brought home by the many locally based merchant vessels. Although Nantucket, the Vineyard, and the Cape appear isolated geographically, throughout the eighteenth and nineteenth centuries they were anything but isolated economically. Harbors and ports of all three counties experienced constant comings and goings, with cargoes of whale oil and merchant goods arriving and crews of sailors departing. The twentieth-century quilts continue the story of the Cape's history, perhaps inspired by the vibrant colors of ocean sunsets, and made from saved scraps and recycled garments, as the maritime economy continued to decline. —AEN

MAYHEW FAMILY QUILT
(FIG. 67)

In the majority of its pieced blocks, this quilt employs a large-scale chintz similar to that seen in the whole-cloth chintz quilt attributed to the Coffin family of Nantucket (fig. 68/MQ 1007). Both examples of chintz probably originated in France or England. The quilt top is hand-pieced with nine-patch blocks in the "Ohio Star" pattern, placed on point. The alternating solid blocks are made from bright yellow printed cotton. The quilt is framed by its outer row of blocks, where pieced Ohio Stars alternate in the blue chintz and an additional rusty-red printed cotton. As a whole, the quilt top is a dynamic mix of primary colors and would have brightened a Vineyard room on the island's many foggy mornings.

The batting is a thin cotton flannel sheet, and the quilt is backed with off-white cotton. The straight-applied binding is machine-sewn, an early example of the use of the sewing machine by quilt makers. The quilt is hand-quilted with five colors of thread at five stitches to the inch. Quilting patterns vary across the top and include diamonds, chevrons, and pumpkin-seed motifs.

A handwritten note attached to the quilt provides its history:

The patchwork for this quilt was made and pieced together by Miss Susan P. Mayhew of Chil-

FIGURE 67. Pieced quilt, "Ohio Star," pieced c. 1830 by Susan P.
Mayhew (1811–1834) of Chilmark and quilted by Phoebe Parnall
(dates unknown) and Carolyn Lambert (1814–1895) of West Tisbury,
Martha's Vineyard. Cotton (106" × 94½"). Collection of the Martha's
Vineyard Museum, Edgartown, Mass. (1969.13.1). *Photograph by Robert
Schellhammer, courtesy of the Martha's Vineyard Museum.* MQ 1508.

mark who died 1835. She was the daughter of Mr. Ephraim & Mrs. Susan Mayhew and the sister of Mrs. Herman Vincent and Mr. Ephraim Mayhew Jr. It was given to me by my grandmother in 1850 and quilted in 1856 by the Misses Phoebe Parnall and Carolyn Lambert. Susan Mayhew Johnson of West Tisbury.

The note provides family information and provenance for the quilt, although Susan P. Mayhew actually died in 1834. Exact information on Phoebe Parnall has proven elusive; her relationship and that of Carolyn Lambert to the Mayhew family remain a mystery.[5]

As the note explains, the quilt was initially pieced by Susan Pease Mayhew, who was born in Chilmark on Martha's Vineyard on March 15, 1811. Her father, Ephraim Mayhew (1778–1857), was a farmer and a descendant of the island's original proprietor, Thomas Mayhew (1620–1657). Ephraim Mayhew married Susanna Pease (1780–1856) on February 13, 1805.[6] Two of Ephraim and Susanna Mayhew's daughters, quiltmaker Susan and her younger sister, Sophronia (1815–1828), died young. Susan may have been working on this quilt at the time of her death, explaining why it was quilted later.

Susan Mayhew (Vincent) Johnson (b. 1836), who wrote the note about the quilt's history, was the daughter of quiltmaker Susan Pease Mayhew's sister, Louisa Mayhew (b. circa 1806), who married Herman Vincent (b. circa 1806). The note explains that Susan Mayhew Johnson's grandmother gave the quilt to her in 1850. Her grandmother was Susanna (Pease) Mayhew (mother of quiltmaker Susan Pease Mayhew), who lived near the Johnson family in Chilmark, according to the 1850 census. Perhaps the gift was made because young Susan shared a name with both her grandmother and the quilt's initial maker (her aunt). In turn, Susan Mayhew (Vincent) Johnson's daughter, Sarah (Johnson) Burt gave the quilt to the Martha's Vineyard Historical Society, where it remains today.   —AEN

COFFIN FAMILY QUILT

(FIG. 68)

Although an island located thirty miles off the coast of Massachusetts, Nantucket was far from isolated during the 1700s and 1800s. Islanders traveled around the globe, opening whaling grounds in the South Pacific and Asia, and returned home with fascinating stories and souvenirs. As Herman Melville wrote in *Moby-Dick*, "Thus have these . . . Nantucketers . . . issuing from their anthill in the sea, overrun and conquered the watery world like so many Alexanders." This elegant whole-cloth chintz quilt reveals that islanders kept up with current fashions and enjoyed access to dry goods from all over the world.

The quilt's glazed chintz, printed with floral sprays and pink roses on a blue ground, probably came from France or England. The same fabric is used on top and back, the lengths seamed together without matching the pattern. The quilting is done with dark green thread in parallel diagonal lines with crosshatching and an "X" motif at the corners; Trenton tape binds its edges.

The quilt is associated with one of the island's founding families, the Coffin family. An old label found with the quilt reads, "Made on Eliza Coffin's quilting bars, 75 Main Street Nantucket for her granddaughter, Lydia Coffin Everett when she married." Eliza Starbuck Coffin (1811–1903) was the daughter of Levi Starbuck and his wife Elizabeth (see fig. 21/MQ 5074). She married Henry Coffin (1807–1900), one of the richest men on Nantucket. A whaling ship owner, merchant, and candle manufacturer, Coffin built the house at 75 Main Street in 1833, the year that he and Eliza married.[7]

Henry, with his brother Charles G. Coffin, inherited his father's whale oil and candlemaking business in 1828. The brothers established their own firm, Charles G. and Henry Coffin, and set about improving their father's business. They owned more than ten whaling ships, allowing them to make a profit from the whale oil and associated products that their captains and crews brought home. Best known is their ship *Charles and Henry*, on which Herman

Melville served as a crew member during its 1840 to 1845 voyage. He later described his experiences in his novel *Omoo* (1847). Nantucket's whaling industry peaked around 1830 and started to decline throughout the 1830s and 1840s as the harbor silted in; a fire that scorched the downtown and wharf area in 1846 caused further devastation to this long-standing industry. Despite these setbacks, the Coffin brothers remained successful by selling or refitting their ships for trading and by relying on a natural talent for business affairs.[8]

Henry and Eliza Coffin had nine children, six of whom survived to adulthood. Their daughter, Lydia (born 1836), was actually the recipient of this quilt, not Eliza's granddaughter, as the old label found with the quilt states—a signature in brown ink, "L.C. Everett / 1856," appears along one edge of the quilt. Lydia married Richard Boardman Everett of Cambridge in 1856, after which the couple took up residence in Boston. The quilt was passed down in the family until it was given to the Nantucket Historical Association in 1981.   —AEN

ELIZABETH GROSS PETERSON QUILT

(FIG. 69)

Elizabeth Gross Lombard Peterson pieced her "Log Cabin" quilt with thought and precision to create a visually striking bed cover. By connecting the dark or "shadow" sides of each group of four adjoining blocks, the light or "sunshine" sections recede into the background, creating a checkerboard arrangement. As a native of Cape Cod, perhaps Elizabeth drew on the natural colors of the beach and its beautiful sunrises and sunsets to create her quilt.

The quilt is composed of one hundred blocks that are eight and one-half inches square. The blocks are whip-stitched by hand to their foundation, a popular means of making "Log Cabin" or template-pieced quilts during the late 1800s. The maker then simply bound the edges of the quilt with a straight-applied pink fabric to finish her work. With no batting or backing, this is technically a "summer spread," or throw.

Elizabeth Gross was born in 1794 in Truro, on Cape Cod, the eldest daughter of Jaazaniah Gross (1770–1816) and Anna Lombard (1772–1856). Truro is a small town, incorporated in 1709, and located just below Provincetown on the long "arm" of Cape Cod. A visitor to Truro in the late 1830s remarked, "The face of the township is composed of sandhills and narrow valleys between them . . . the inhabitants here, who derive their principal subsistence from the sea, are as 'well off' as any people in the commonwealth."[9] In 1837, 512 people were employed on sixty-three vessels involved in the cod and mackerel fishery. In addition, there were thirty-nine establishments in town that made salt—a maritime-related pursuit, but one that is less well-known than the Cape's fishing and whaling activities.[10]

Elizabeth Gross experienced both the ups and downs of fishery life. In 1813, at age nineteen, she married Thomas Lombard (1786–1819). Six years later he was lost at sea, leaving Elizabeth with three small daughters: Sally (b. 1814), Betsey (b. 1816), and Anna (b. 1818). The life of a widow during the early 1800s was often a struggle. Many women mar-

ried again in order to support themselves and their families. In 1821, Elizabeth married John Peterson (1800–1872), a carpenter, who had come to Truro from Boston. Presumably, she made her choice carefully, picking someone who made his living on land, rather than on the dangerous waters offshore.

Despite choosing a husband who worked on land, Elizabeth experienced another loss to the sea when her son, John William Peterson (b. 1824), died during a gale in October 1841. Just seventeen years old, John William was working on the *General Harrison,* which was fishing for mackerel well off the coast of Truro in the Atlantic Ocean. Five other crew members on board also were lost, along with fifty-two Truro men from six other ships.[11]

Elizabeth and Thomas Peterson remained married for fifty-one years. After Thomas's death in 1872, Elizabeth moved to Somerville to live with her daughter Anna Lombard Davis. Prior to Thomas's death and her move, Elizabeth made this quilt as a wedding gift for Joanna Rust Allen, who married Elizabeth's grandson Solomon Davis in 1869 in Truro. The quilt has since been passed down in the family and remains a treasured family heirloom.   —AEN

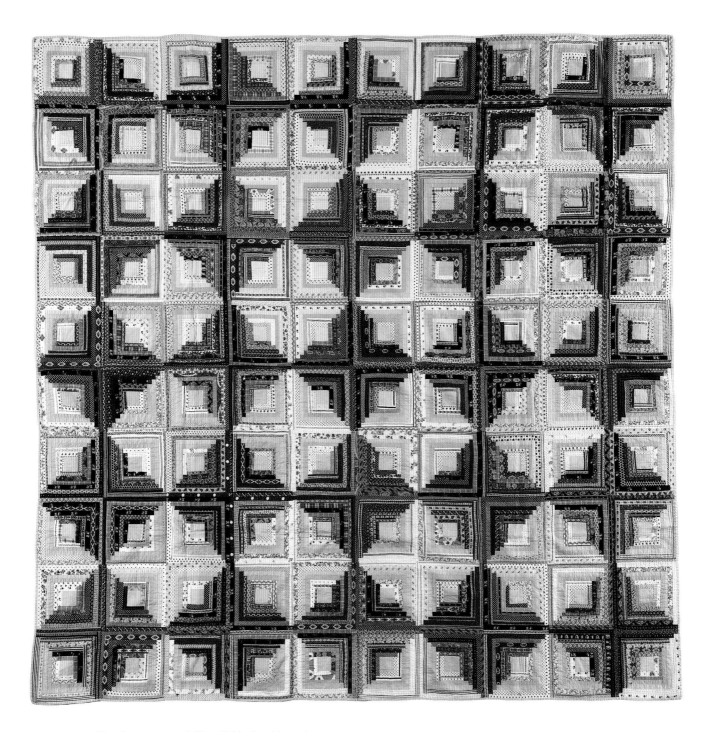

FIGURE 69. Pieced summer spread, "Log Cabin, Sunshine and
Shadow variation," made by Elizabeth (Gross) Lombard Peterson
(1794–1873) of Truro and Somerville, 1872. Cotton (84" × 80").
Private collection. *Photograph by David Stansbury.* MQ 4487.

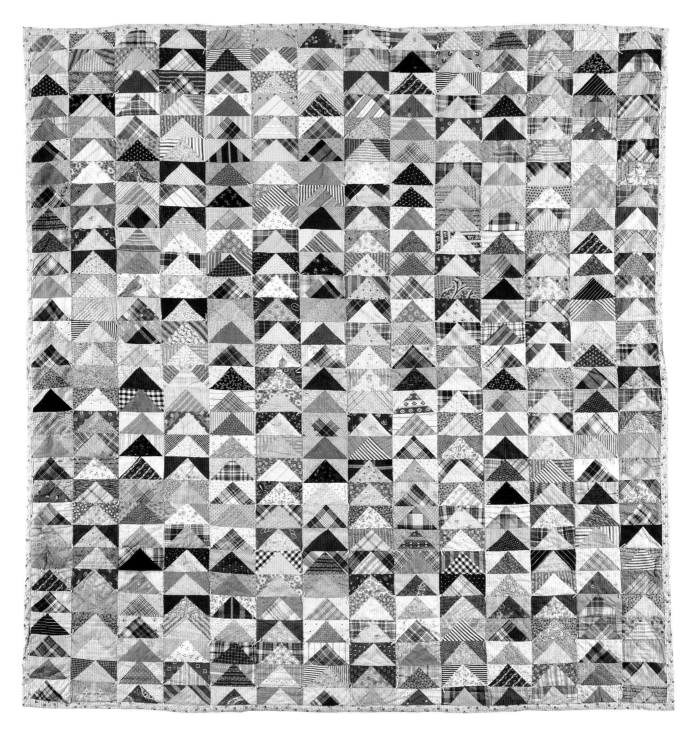

FIGURE 70. Pieced comforter, "Flying Geese," made by sisters Mary
Kelleher (1861–1934) and Nell Kelleher (1867–1952) of Sandwich, c.
1890; finished c. 1930s. Cotton (86" × 82"). Collection of the New
England Quilt Museum (2006.12). *Photograph by David Stansbury.*
MQ 200.

MARY AND NELL KELLEHER QUILT

(FIG. 70)

Founded in 1637, Sandwich is the oldest town on Cape Cod. While the rest of the Cape developed an economy based on fishing and whaling, Sandwich, without a deep ocean harbor, remained a farming community until Deming Jarves arrived in town. A former agent of the New England Glass Company in Cambridge, Jarves chose Sandwich to establish a new factory, the Boston & Sandwich Glass Company, in 1825. Ample wood for firing fur-

naces grew in the surrounding forests, marsh hay provided excellent packing material, and the distribution center of Boston was only fifty miles away.[12] Unfortunately, Cape Cod sand was too impure for glassmaking, which Jarves already knew, so sand was imported from New Jersey and the Berkshire Mountains of western Massachusetts. Jarves also imported his first glassblowers from Great Britain, or lured them away from the New England Glass Company. The old families of Sandwich did not welcome the immigrants, particularly the Irish Catholics, who came to work in the glass factory. The clash of industrial and agricultural cultures aggravated the tensions.

FIGURE 71. Women decorators at the Boston & Sandwich Glass Factory, 1885. Seated first on the left in the front row is Nell Kelleher; Mary Kelleher is seated third on the left in the same row. *Photograph courtesy of the Sandwich Glass Museum, Sandwich, Mass.*

Eventually, the sons and daughters of Jarvesville, the area of town where the factory workers lived, inherited much of the factory work. Sisters Mary and Ellen ("Nell") Kelleher, the second generation of an Irish glassmaking family in Sandwich, made this "Flying Geese" comforter. Mary and Nell joined their brothers at the glass factory, working as decorators, one of the most prestigious positions in the industry. They skillfully painted landscapes, birds, and flowers on kerosene lamps, vases, and plates, according to the direction of the department supervisor, Mr. Swann. While Nell is remembered as the "more artistic and meticulous of the two," the delicate coloration of a long-legged finch painted on a plate by Mary is clear evidence that she also was very talented.[13]

As decorators, they had the potential to earn a good wage. They were paid by the piece, and depending on how fast they could work and how much work was available, they might earn as much as $15 or $16 a week.[14] Some years later, a Sandwich resident remembered that "The decorators were the best dressed women in town. We all envied their beautiful gowns."[15] Indeed, an 1885 photograph of women decorators at the Boston & Sandwich Glass Factory, including Nell and Mary Kelleher, shows a group of fashionably coiffed and garbed young women.

The Boston & Sandwich Glass Company, which produced pressed, mold-blown, cut, and painted glass products, thrived until cheaper glass from midwestern states such as Ohio began to dominate the market in the years after the Civil War. While this first of Sandwich's glass companies closed its doors in 1888, others were started by former Boston & Sandwich Glass Company employees. Mary and Nell Kelleher continued to have work as decorators with one or another of these companies at least through 1900, according to town directories.

Federal census records through 1930 find them

FIGURE 72. Plaque decorated with a long-legged finch, attributed to Mary Kelleher. *Photograph by Don Parkinson, courtesy of the Sandwich Glass Museum, Sandwich, Mass.*

living with their older brother John, a former glassblower turned hardware store owner; none of the siblings ever married. Mary and Nell both worked as pickers for antiques dealers interested in acquiring Sandwich glass, which became a popular collectible in the early twentieth century's Colonial Revival.[16] Certainly, their connections to the industry and the families who worked in it gave them extraordinary access to these items. Sadly, Nell was struck with a debilitating disease, probably polio, and was confined to a wheelchair during her later years—but she kept her hands busy, making quilts and other useful items for the household. This comforter is said to be the combined effort of Mary and Nell. The fabrics of the front are a range of late nineteenth-century dress calicoes, plaids, and shirting fabrics, while the backing material is a 1930s calico. The colorful triangles of the "geese" are thoughtfully arranged for visual balance, as one would expect from two experienced artists.   —LZB

Chapter 5

Worcester County: The Heart of the Commonwealth

The largest county in the state in terms of area, Worcester County extends from north to south straight through the middle of the commonwealth. Established in 1731 with fourteen towns, the county currently has a total area of 1,579 square miles with sixty towns and cities. Due to the county's large size, many attempts were made during the 1800s to split it in two, but these efforts did not succeed.

The county offers many picturesque landscape features, from hills—like Mount Wachusett—to the shores of the Blackstone River and Lake Quinsigamond. As one county historian described, "Several of the towns of Worcester County are stretches of pastoral loveliness; others charm with their gentle lines of hill and dale; while some become majestic in the rugged outline of mountain crags, and are enchanting in their rocky glens."[1]

Initially, the county was attractive for its fertile farm land, as early settlers slowly moved west from the easternmost coastline. Farming remained a major means of making a living through the early 1900s, with dairy farms dotting many county towns. But, Worcester County was also one of the earliest parts of the state to industrialize. Its rivers offered sufficient power for a variety of mills and factories. Residents quickly adapted to early toll roads to Stafford, Connecticut, and Boston, and the completion of the Blackstone Canal in 1828. Soon after, in 1835, the railroad arrived, speeding up travel between Worcester and Boston for residents and their goods, whether those goods were from the earth or from the factory.[2] County seat Worcester became the second-largest city in the state and by 1880 was the twenty-eighth-largest city in the United States.[3]

By 1924, Worcester County was known as "the world's greatest textile machinery center."[4] One of the early pioneers in this field was Pliny Earle (1762–1832) an inventor who pioneered advances in wool and cotton card cloth and carding machines.[5] Eli Whitney (1765–1825), the inventor of the cotton gin, was born in Westborough. Elias Howe (1819–1867), holder of the first United States patent for a sewing machine, was also a Worcester County native, born in Spencer.

County industry was not limited to the textile field. Almost from the beginning of factory production, Worcester County diversified with cotton and woolen mills, shoemaking, machine shops for cutlery and edge tools, paper milling, foundries and coachmaking, among other industries.[6] Southbridge, known as "the eye of the Commonwealth," was home to the American Optical Company, making spectacles by the thousands. And, into the 1920s, Gardner was "the largest chair town in the world . . . [producing] as many as 4,000,000 chairs in a year."[7] Leominster produced celluloid combs and household accessories. Additionally, the famed Willard clockmaking family got its start in Grafton.

While Worcester County produced numerous consumer products, it also produced notable residents, many with a strong social conscience. John Chapman (1774–1847), better known as "Johnny Appleseed," was born in Leominster, and Clara Barton (1821–1912) of Red Cross fame was a native of North Oxford (figure 189/MQ 3487). Worcester County holds a vital spot in the history of women's rights.

FIGURE 73. *Haying Scene in Auburn, Massachusetts,* artist unknown, oil on canvas, c. 1860–1870. While the Blackstone River Valley— running from the city of Worcester to Providence, Rhode Island—became the nation's first industrial corridor, much of Worcester County's economy remained agricultural throughout the nineteenth century. *Photograph by Henry Peach, courtesy of Old Sturbridge Village, Sturbridge, Mass.*

Not only was suffragist Lucy Stone (1818–1893) born and raised in West Brookfield, but the first national Women's Rights convention met in Worcester in 1850. For every woman that attended the convention, countless more stayed at home raising their children, working their farms and making quilts. The quilts in this section span the centuries and the county, but they pull together the threads of history from the heart of the state.   —AEN

BIGELOW FAMILY QUILTED PELISSE

(FIG. 74)

Family history identifies Hannah (Gardner) Bigelow (1780–1857) as the owner of this quilted coat with matching detachable double cape-style collar.[8] The style of the coat suggests that it was made about 1830. The coat follows fashionable lines so that it could be worn comfortably over dresses with large puffed sleeves and wide skirts. It is fully lined with beige silk. While primarily quilted in a pattern of parallel vertical lines, along the opening edges, cuffs, and collar, the coat is quilted in a pattern of triangles resembling vandyke points. This zigzag edge pattern was popular during the Romantic Era of the 1820s to 1840s, which looked back to Renaissance styles for design inspiration, such as the pointed-edge lace collars—called "vandykes" after the famed painter Sir Anthony van Dyke—depicted in sixteenth- and seventeenth-century portraits.

Quilted or wadded coats, often known as "pelisses," were worn by women from the early 1800s through the 1830s. In 1821, Salem Towne of Charlton, Massachusetts, wrote to his wife Sally from Boston explaining the fashionable way to make her pelisse: "your Pelise should be wadded round bottom up & down forward + collar . . ." An 1823 advertisement in Boston's *Columbian Centinel* newspaper offered eider down "suitable for Hoods, Counterpanes . . . and Ladies' Pelisses." Dark colors, such as black, gray, and the deep blue-green of this example, seem to have been popular. In 1805, Ruth Henshaw Bascom of Leicester wrote in her diary, "Sally Flint & I sewed on my plumb colored lutstring police [pelisse]."[9]

The word "pelisse" came from France, where it was often associated with a coat with a fur lining.

FIGURE 74. Quilted coat from the Bigelow family of Worcester, c. 1830. Silk (length 54¾"). Collection of the Worcester Historical Museum (1976.787). *Photograph by David Stansbury.* MQ 5443.

This European fashion of the early 1800s quickly made its way to the rural New England countryside and was embraced by the provincial class. High-style examples are illustrated throughout the early 1800s in fashion magazines like *Ackermann's Repository* and *Godey's Lady's Book*. An 1827 issue of *Ackermann's Repository* shows a pelisse in a similar style, described as follows: "The pelisse fastens in front with hooks and eyes, and is decorated with bows . . . the sleeves are en gigot, and have broad . . . bands."[10]

The Bigelow family undoubtedly followed the current styles. Hannah Gardner was born in Leominster and married Abijah Bigelow (1775–1860) of Worcester in 1804. Abijah graduated from Dartmouth College in 1795 and was admitted to the bar in 1798. He opened a law office in Leominster where he also became active in town government, serving as town clerk and representing the town in the general court. In 1811, he was elected to Congress and served two terms. Around 1817, he and Hannah moved their family to Worcester. Abijah served as Clerk of the Courts there from 1817 to 1833. The couple had seven children between 1805 and 1817; six survived to adulthood.[11]

After Hannah Bigelow died in 1857, the coat was passed down in her family for three generations before Hannah's great-granddaughter Anne Bigelow Henshaw donated it to the Worcester Historical Museum. A note accompanying the coat read, "In as much as Mrs. A. Bigelow was a slight lady, this could have been one of her gowns." Fashionable and warm, the coat combines functionality for a New England winter with style to illustrate how quickly European fashions traveled to rural New England, as well as the pervasiveness of the Romantic aesthetic.

—AEN

MATILDA FISKE QUILT

(FIG. 75)

Passed down in the Fiske family, this quilt was donated to Old Sturbridge Village with the information that it was made by Matilda Fiske.[12] The printed cotton fabrics in the top suggest that it was made around 1830, when she was in her forties. Matilda, who lived in Sturbridge her entire life, was somewhat unusual for her generation as she never married; nevertheless, she eventually owned her own home.

Sturbridge began as a farming settlement, although it was not long before the power of the Quinebaug River was harnessed for milling lumber. From a population of 965 in 1765, the town grew to 1,740 people in 1790. In 1810, the population reached 1,927, but declined during the 1810s and 1820s, dropping to 1,688 in 1830, around the time when Matilda Fiske made this quilt. By 1837, there were six cotton mills on the river, manufacturing 829,749 yards of cotton goods annually and employing 117 women and 71 men.[13] Several of the mills were owned by members of the extended Fiske family (though none directly related to Matilda). They produced both cotton yarn and cotton cloth, which was then sold to printers to be colored and patterned. Some of the mills also produced woolen yarn and cloth, but in far less quantity than the cotton. By 1855, the number of textile mills in Sturbridge was slightly reduced: three cotton mills produced yarn, cloth, and batting, and one woolen mill produced yarn and satinet, a coarse fabric with a cotton warp and wool weft.[14]

Matilda's grandfather, Henry Fiske, and her great-uncle, Daniel Fiske of Watertown, were among the first proprietors of Sturbridge, settling there in 1731. The Fiske brothers established their farms on a rise of land that would come to be known as Fiske Hill. Family history attributed "great taste and sound judgment" to the Fiske brothers in choosing this location. As one town history explained, "Fisk Hill is the most beautiful swell of land in the town, possessing fertility, and commanding an extensive and delightful view in every direction." When the town of Sturbridge was incorporated in 1738, both Henry and Daniel were elected selectmen, and Daniel was also the first town clerk. Over the next two centuries, the family would continue to serve the town and their neighbors, holding many positions in local government.[15]

Matilda's father, Henry Fiske, Jr. (1745–1815), was

FIGURE 75. Pieced quilt, "Melon Patch," made by Matilda Fiske
(1784–1880) of Sturbridge, c. 1830. Cotton (83" × 91"). Collection
of Old Sturbridge Village, Sturbridge, Massachusetts (26.23.181).
Photograph by David Stansbury. MQ 4597.

one of the wealthiest men in Sturbridge. According to the 1798 federal direct tax records, he owned 433 acres; his land and two houses were worth almost $7,000, placing him in the top five of Sturbridge's 215 propertied households that year.[16] It is unclear whether Matilda inherited her house and land from her father or whether she purchased them by other means. However, tax records from 1820 and 1830 list her name with real estate valued around $2,000. In 1830, in addition to the land she owned, she also was listed as part-owner of a sawmill with her brother-in-law. Federal census data from the early 1800s shows that Matilda sometimes lived with her sister Amy and Amy's husband Daniel, and sometimes lived in her own home, with one of her great-nieces for companionship and assistance.[17]

Matilda's quilt has cut-out corners along the bottom edge so that it will fall easily around the bedposts. The quilting is done in an echo pattern with approximately six stitches to the inch. The block pattern, with four ovals on a square ground, is known as "Melon Patch" or "Orange Peel." Most of the block names that we use today come from the latter half of the 1800s. However, there is evidence to suggest that some block names date to the early 1800s, or even to the late 1700s. A weaving draft (or pattern) in the museum's collection that was used by Peace and Patience Kirby of Dartmouth, Massachusetts, to weave overshot coverlets between 1790 and 1820 includes a handwritten notation titling the design, "orring [Orange] Peal." This draft produces a woven design with ovals within a square that is very similar to this pieced quilt pattern.[18] Not only does this suggest that the "Orange Peel" quilt block was one of the few quilt block patterns known by name in the early 1800s, but it also demonstrates how designs and motifs were used interchangeably by Massachusetts women whether weaving, embroidering, sewing, or quilting.

Indeed, a large collection of Fiske family artifacts also in the museum's collection shows us that Matilda and her female relatives were masters of many needle arts. In addition to this quilt, two tablecloths, a towel, four pillowcases, and a charming yarn-sewn footstool cover are attributed to Matilda.

She lived a long life, dying on July 15, 1880, at the age of ninety-six. —AEN

SARAH CLARKE ELLIS IDE QUILT
(FIG. 76)

Sarah Clark Ide's mosaic quilt, made with over two thousand hexagons, is part of a long mosaic patchwork tradition in Massachusetts. To keep the thousands of geometric shapes for mosaic patchwork uniform in shape and size, quiltmakers basted their fabric pieces over paper templates, a technique adopted from England. The practice continued to be common for mosaic-style quilts throughout the nineteenth century, although the vogue for block-style quilts—pieced without templates—took precedence around the second quarter of the century. Sarah Ide's quilt top retains some of its paper templates attached to the hexagons. Sometimes these quilts were intended solely as tops or summer spreads, as quilting through the multitude of seams between thousands of small pieces could be a challenge.[19] While this quilt could be interpreted as an unfinished piece, it is also possible that the maker did not plan to line, back, and quilt it, though that would limit its use to special occasions.

This top has a center section of hexagon-shaped "flowers" set off by a double row of light-colored borders. Sometimes Sarah "fussy-cut" her fabric to include a specific motif in the center of the hexagon; other fabrics she cut more freely. Sarah added a large-scale yellow, brown, and off-white floral chintz on all sides, creating a 20-inch drop at the bottom and sides with cut-out corners so it would drape smoothly around the bedposts.

Sarah Clark (Ellis) Ide was born in Milford in 1822. Sarah probably made her beautiful hexagon-pieced quilt top around the time of her marriage to Timothy Ide, Jr. (1814–1912), in 1842. Sarah and Timothy had six children between 1843 and 1859. According to the 1860 United States census, Timothy and Sarah lived in Milford, where he worked as a blacksmith. Timothy's real estate at that time

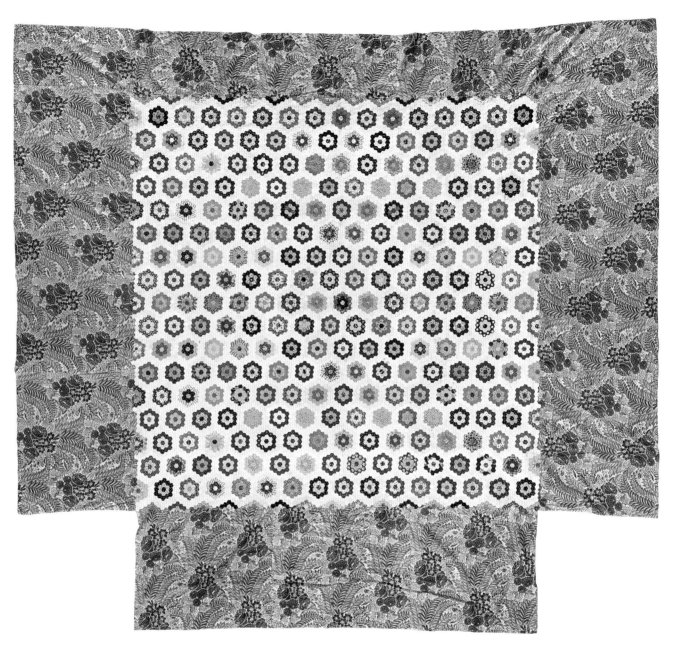

FIGURE 76. Pieced quilt top, "Hexagon Mosaic," made by Sarah Clark (Ellis) Ide (1822–1902) of Milford, c. 1845. Cotton (68" × 72"). Private Collection. *Photograph by David Stansbury.* MQ 1372.

was assessed at a value of $1,400 and his personal estate at $300—enough for him to be able to afford a live-in servant to help Sarah with the housework, cooking, and childcare. Nineteen-year-old Hannah O'Brien, who was born in Ireland, is listed in the census as living in the Ide household; she probably served as Sarah's domestic help. By 1880, Timothy

and Sarah had moved to Medway, but Timothy still earned a living as a blacksmith. Several of the couple's children had married and started homes of their own, but the two youngest children, Lizzie Mann Ide (b. 1855) and Alton W. Ide (b. 1859) still lived at home.

In 1899, three years before her death, Sarah pre-

FIGURE 77. Detail of calicoes in Sarah Clark Ide quilt. *Photograph by David Stansbury.*

sented the quilt to her granddaughter, Nina Frances Ide, as a gift for her marriage to Charles Edwin Dickinson. At some point, Nina attached a tag to the quilt with the information, "This quilt is over 100 years old." The tag remains on the quilt, which is now owned by Nina's granddaughter (Sarah Ide's great-great-granddaughter). —AEN

REBECCA CORDELIA AYERS MACK HEYWOOD QUILT

(FIG. 78)

Rebecca Cordelia Ayers was born in 1798, one of thirteen children of Deacon George and Hannah (True) Ayers of Goshen, New Hampshire. In 1805, the family moved to Plainfield, Vermont. Here, Rebecca grew up and in 1818 married Daniel

Miner Mack, the son of David and Sarah (Rogers) Mack of Woodstock, Vermont. Daniel died in 1833, leaving Rebecca destitute and with no choice but to place her three young sons and two daughters with relatives in Vermont. She moved to Winchendon, in north central Massachusetts, to support herself by working in the recently established textile mills.[20]

Winchendon, incorporated as a town in 1764, had a fulling mill for finishing locally produced woolen cloth by 1793. In the early nineteenth century, a mill for spinning and weaving wool was built, powered by the appropriately named Millers River. It prospered despite repeated setbacks from fires (a constant worry for the early textile mill owners). By 1849, the Winchendon Manufacturing Corporation employed "15 male and 13 female hands" and produced about 200,000 yards of twill flannels, valued at $50,000.[21] The manufacturing of woolen goods continued under various proprietors until the mill

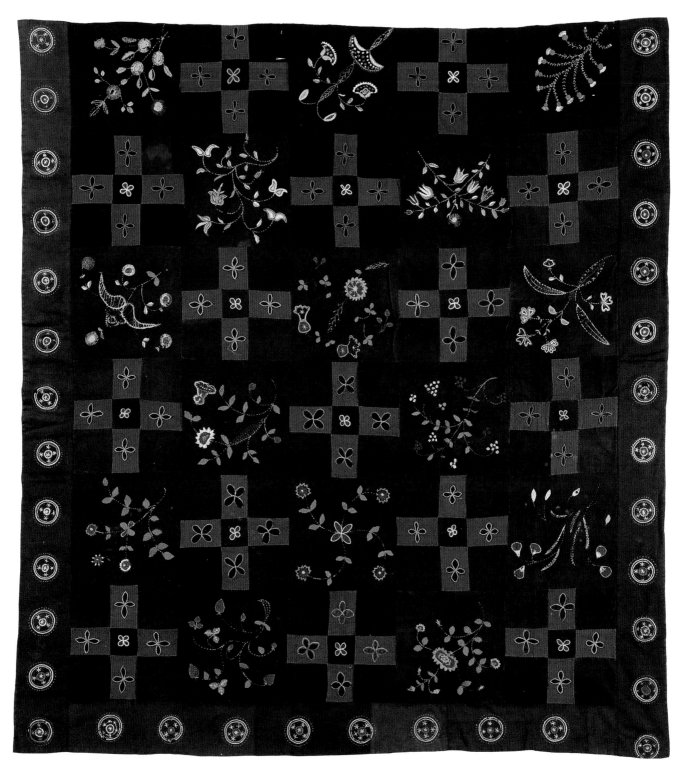

FIGURE 78. Pieced, appliquéd, and embroidered summer spread,
original pattern, made by Rebecca C. Ayers Mack Heywood (1798–
1868) of Winchendon, c. 1850. Wool and cotton (78" × 71"). Private
collection. *Photograph by David Stansbury.* MQ 3564.

FIGURE 79. Detail of embroidery on Rebecca Heywood summer spread. *Photograph by David Stansbury.*

in 1839. She embroidered multicolored baskets and bouquets of flowers and fruit, sashed by floral garlands, on black wool broadcloth. The design was Rebecca's own, marked out with tailor's chalk directly onto the wool. Unfortunately, the location of this quilt is not known, but a photograph, revealing a 1954 Eastern States Exposition blue ribbon, documents its stunning beauty.

Rebecca's great-great-granddaughter owns this similarly constructed but simpler quilt, made about 1850. This "everyday" quilt is pieced in a nine-patch design alternating with blocks appliquéd and embroidered in wool yarns with stylized floral bouquets. Satin stitch, outline stitch, chain stitch, and straight stitch are all employed to create the imaginative spriggy flowers, embellished circles, and quatrefoil designs. There is no batting, but the plain cotton backing is held in place with sparse quilting stitches following the pieced pattern. The quilt is finished with a knife edge.

In the thirty-five years that Rebecca lived in Winchendon, she witnessed tremendous changes in the town. In the early 1830s, industrialization was taking over the agricultural economy of New England, and scores of individuals and families moved to mill towns like Winchendon looking for employment. The population of Winchendon in 1840 was 1,679; only six years later, it had grown by over twenty percent to 2,020.[24] That decade also brought to town a revolutionary method of transportation, the railroad, enabling the efficient movement of the town's products to markets around the country. Industrialization fueled a growing disparity in income of New England's inhabitants: Textile mill owner John White's house, "Marchmont," a massive castle complete with crenellated towers, stood in contrast to the wooden, crowded, multi-family dwellings of the mill workers in nineteenth-century Winchendon. Events outside of the town also affected Rebecca's life: The Civil War drew away her son Daniel, who was a chaplain in a Massachusetts regiment. In 1867, Lemuel succumbed to the lung disease brought on by his vocation as a stonecutter. One year later, Rebecca passed away. They are buried beside each other in the Riverside Cemetery in Winchendon.   —LZB

burned down and was abandoned in 1859. By then, however, cotton dominated the town's textile industry, having been established north of the town center at Winchendon Springs in 1831. In 1860, encouraged by the railroad that came to town in 1847, Winchendon produced $300,000 worth of cotton fabrics.[22] Yet cotton was not even the primary industry of the town; it came in second to the production of woodenware—in fact, Winchendon was long called "Shingletown."

Several years after moving to Winchendon, at age thirty-eight, Rebecca defied convention and married Lemuel Alfred Heywood, sixteen years her junior. Rebecca gave birth in 1837 to a daughter, naming her Abigail Pearson after Lemuel's mother. The 1840 federal census reveals that Rebecca's children from her first marriage joined her in Winchendon: Laura (b. 1820), Rufus (b. 1823), Daniel (b. 1826), Cordelia (b. 1827), and George (b. ca. 1828). At least one daughter, Cordelia, went to work in the mills like her mother before her. Rebecca's son, Daniel, who became a Methodist minister, eventually founded two orphanages, one in Franklin, New Hampshire, and one at Lake Dennison in Winchendon, undoubtedly hoping to relieve others of the emotional and financial suffering that his own family had experienced.[23]

Rebecca took great pride in her quilts. Family history asserts that she was determined to make an "even better" quilt when her favorite was stolen

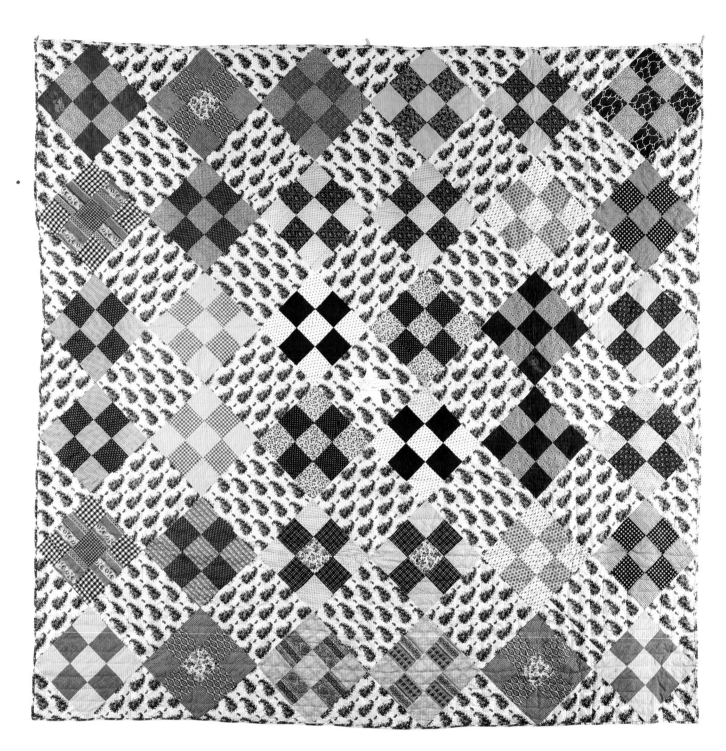

FIGURE 80. Pieced quilt, "Nine Patch," made by Ella Hapgood Ward (1854–1915) of Shrewsbury, 1859. Cotton (91" × 90"). Collection of the Artemas Ward Museum, Harvard Real Estate Services, Shrewsbury, Mass. *Photograph by David Stansbury.* MQ 5076.

ELLA HAPGOOD WARD QUILT

(FIG. 80)

In the center of this colorful pieced quilt is an appliquéd star with an ink inscription reading, "Commenced at 4. Completed at 5½ years old by Ella Hapgood Ward. Shrewsbury Sept. 9th 1859." Young Ella used the traditional nine-patch block to make her quilt, turning the blocks on point and incorporating a colorful floral paisley fabric for the alternating squares. Ella probably chose her solid, printed, plaid, and check fabrics from the family's scrap basket. The charming contrast of the juvenile stitching of the blocks with the accomplished quilting, at seven to eight stitches per inch, indicates that Ella was assisted by the experienced hands of her mother or other older relatives. The back of the quilt is made from seven pieces of two different fabrics; both are white with a small brown printed design. One of the backing fabrics shows signs of reuse—seams were taken out to maximize the size of the fabric piece.

Ella's quilt has the appearance of being treasured by the family. It is in excellent condition, indicating that it was not frequently used. In addition, there are several cream-colored linen tape loops along the top of the quilt, presumably used to hang it up at some point in the past, probably at a local agricultural fair. The annual Worcester County Agricultural Fair began in the 1810s. Newspaper accounts of the textile and fancy work section often called attention to items made by the very young and the very old.[25]

While the quilt has signs of being shown in public as an accomplishment, it also has the characteristics of a learning exercise—the scrap fabrics used in the top and the recycled backing fabric. All young girls learned basic sewing skills, which they would need later in life to make household textiles and clothing for their families. Several early nineteenth-century books directed at mothers and children praised the virtues of learning patchwork. For example, Lydia Maria Child explained in her 1831 publication, *The Mother's Book*, ". . . if a child is taught to fit [piecing] herself, it may be made really useful. If the corners are not fitted exactly, or the sewing done neatly, it should be taken to pieces

FIGURE 81. Detail of inscribed center star, Ella Hapgood Ward quilt. *Photograph by David Stansbury.*

and fitted again, for it is by inattention to these little things that habits of carelessness are formed."[26] It was not unusual for Ella Ward to learn to piece quilt blocks at the age of four, although it was unusual for her quilt to have the added inked inscription in the center of the quilt.

Ella Hapgood Ward lived her entire life in Shrewsbury, where her family was prominent. Her great-great-grandfather, Artemas Ward (1727–1800), was a major general in the Revolutionary War, second in command under George Washington of the Continental Army. Although poor health forced him to resign his military position in 1777, Ward continued to serve his country as a member of the Continental Congress in 1779. Ella's parents, Samuel Denny Ward (1826–1908) and Abigail Marion

Hapgood (1829–1917), were married in 1853. Samuel Denny Ward was a farmer in Shrewsbury and also served as president of the Shrewsbury Historical Society.

Ella was the oldest of three daughters. According to the published family history, she was "for many years assistant librarian, taking special interest in the children, particularly those whose home life gave no strong upward influence and encouragement."[27] The Shrewsbury Public Library dates to 1872 when town meeting voted to provide a room for the library in the Town House, expanding the resources and services of the town "Social Library" that had been established in 1792. By 1901, the library had grown so much that a new building was needed; it opened in 1903.

Ella and her sisters—Florence Grosvenor Ward (b. 1856) and Clara Denny Ward (b. 1857)—never married, continuing to live in the family home throughout their lives. The 1910 U.S. census, the last before Ella's death in 1915, still lists all three sisters living at home together.   —AEN

HARRIET LOMBARD RICHARDSON AND MARY RICHARDSON QUILT

(FIG. 82)

In the easily recognized "Tumbling Blocks" pattern (also known as "Box," "Baby Blocks," and "Building Blocks"), this quilt represents a popular quilt style of the mid- and late 1800s, often made as a gift for a new baby. Several women's magazines, including *Godey's Lady's Book* and *Peterson's Magazine*, included illustrations and descriptions of hexagon and box patterns. This particular pattern is found in an 1851 issue of *Godey's Lady's Book*. In June 1877, *Peterson's Magazine* noted that the "box pattern" was becoming fashionable again.[28]

The quilt was probably pieced using templates cut from paper, a technique that lends itself to a group project, as each quiltmaker could baste and stitch together many pieces of the quilt and later join their

work. This silk quilt is believed to have been made by two women working together. An inked label attached to the quilt identifies the makers as Harriet Lombard Richardson and Mary Richardson of Warren, the same town where Arthur Lewis Moore made his hexagon template-pieced quilt in 1882 (see fig. 85/MQ 4112). Harriet's father, Elijah Lombard, ran the Hitchcock Tavern in Warren and moved his family into the building in 1810. She married Nathan Richardson (1806–1892) of nearby Brookfield in 1835. Nathan worked in the Boston area during the early years of their marriage and the couple adopted a daughter, Anna, who was born in Boston in 1840.[29]

Nathan and Harriet Richardson returned to Warren in 1845, where they became leading citizens. Nathan was one of the founders of the Warren Public Library, served as town assessor and, in 1866, as representative to the state legislature. The Richardsons owned extensive real estate during the late 1800s, including at least two houses.[30] On the 1850 census, Nathan is listed as a "gentleman" with real estate valued at $5,000. Presumably, the notation of Nathan as a "gentleman" reflected both the significance of his assets as well as his involvement in town affairs. However, ten years later, in 1860, he is listed as a "farmer" with real estate valued at $15,000 and a personal estate of $13,000. And, in 1870, he is identified as "no occupation" with a yet larger estate, totaling $42,000. The variety of occupational listings for Nathan show that these terms varied according to time, place, situation—and the whim of the census taker. Regardless of how he was listed, Nathan was a well-to-do man with influence and authority in town.

In 1880, Nathan was once again listed on the census as a farmer. He and Harriet lived at that time with forty-four-year-old John M. Davis and thirty-three-year-old Mary J. Doherty. Davis is listed as a farm laborer and Doherty's occupation is listed as "housework." Nathan and Harriet certainly could afford to have paid help, and given their advanced age, along with the fact that they had no children at home, this assistance was undoubtedly essential to keep their house and farm running. This very same

FIGURE 82. Template-pieced quilt, "Tumbling Blocks," made by Harriet Lombard
Richardson (1811–1882) and Mary Richardson of Warren, circa 1880. Silk (65½"
× 56"). Collection of the New England Quilt Museum, Lowell, Massachusetts.
Photograph by David Stansbury. MQ 4258.

FIGURE 83. Harriet Richardson, c. 1885. *Photograph courtesy of Carol Andrews.*

FIGURE 84. Mary Richardson, c. 1885. *Photograph courtesy of Carol Andrews.*

assistance allowed Harriet to devote time to this elegant quilt. As many quilt historians have explained, silk quilts like this one were not made for practical reasons, but instead showed a woman's leisure time as well as her stitching skill.

Unfortunately, conclusive information about the identity of the Mary Richardson named on the label attached to the quilt has not been discovered. However, according to family history, Harriet had a niece named Mary M. Moore (1831–1913), who married another Nathan Richardson. When her Nathan died in 1859 in France (where he had studied music, writing a book on method for the pianoforte), Mary moved home to Warren. She is listed on the 1860, 1870, and 1880 United States censuses as living with her parents, in one case on the same page as Harriet and Nathan Richardson. She turned fifty in 1881 and could have assisted Harriet's seventy-year-old eyes with piecing and quilting this quilt. Mary's brother, Joseph Henry Moore (1833–1892), had a daughter, Charlotte, born in 1880; it is possible the quilt could have been made for her.[31]

The quilt has only two layers, without any batting between the top and backing. The top is composed of two-inch diamonds cut from a variety of elegant silk fabrics including plain weave, satin weave, and brocade, some solid-colored and some patterned. It is hand-quilted along the seams with an extremely proficient nine stitches to the inch. The edges are finished with cording rather than a more traditional fabric binding, and the back is made from a brown striped silk fabric. The quilt was passed down in the family and recently donated to the New England Quilt Museum. —AEN

ARTHUR LEWIS MOORE QUILT
(FIG. 85)

Family history states that Arthur Lewis Moore made this quilt at the age of twelve. The fabrics in the quilt date to the late 1800s, giving credence to the family story. He was a sickly child, and died of tubercular meningitis at the young age of thirty-five.

FIGURE 85. Template-pieced comforter, "Wheel of Life," made by
Arthur Lewis Moore (1870–1905), Warren, c. 1882. Wool and cotton
(83" × 83"). Collection of the Warren Public Library. *Photograph by
David Stansbury.* MQ 4112.

Like the "Tumbling Blocks" quilt made by Harriet and Mary Richardson of the same town in 1880 (see figure 82), this quilt probably was pieced using templates cut from paper.[32] The paper-piecing technique was brought over to America from England and enjoyed several revivals throughout the nineteenth century. The technique is easy to learn and provided a use for countless small scraps that most women had on hand. Popular writers Eliza Leslie and Lydia Maria Child extolled the value of patchwork for children in their 1830s books (which were reprinted frequently). Leslie specifically mentioned the appropriateness of template-pieced hexagonal designs, while Child wrote that little girls "often have . . . large remnants of time, which they don't know what to do with; and I think it is better for them to make cradle-quilts . . . than to be standing around, wishing they had something to do."[33] Arthur's mother may have been acting on this advice, learned from her own mother who was of the generation to read Leslie's and Child's books. Fifty years later, these authors' recommendations were still sound for Arthur's situation: sick in bed, template piecing would keep him occupied for hours.

An inked label attached to the quilt identifies the maker and the place where the quilt was made. The town of Warren was established in 1742 with the name Western; the town's name was changed in 1834. The Quaboag River runs through the center of town and was the power source for many textile mills during the 1800s. The Moore family was prominent in town. Arthur's grandfather, John (1802–1878), was town clerk and postmaster, and his brother, Isaac Walter (1876–1968), was town treasurer, tax collector, and Warren Public Library treasurer—all positions he held for over twenty years. Arthur's father, Isaac Elijah (1839–1921), manufactured ink with his father John. Excelsior School Writing Ink was sold nationally, no doubt including in John Moore's general store in Warren's Lower Village.[34]

In his twenties, Arthur used his artistic eye to become a photographer. Several images of Warren taken between 1897 and 1902 can be attributed to Arthur's lens. He was particularly fond of shooting trains that passed through the town.[35] The striking graphic nature of the quilt, with its bright orange "border" around the "blocks," is evidence of Arthur's future talent as a photographer.

The quilt is made from a wide variety of mostly worsted fabrics, both plain and patterned, and in plain and twill weaves. It is tied with a thick batting inside. The quilt is backed with a plain blue cotton fabric. A first place ribbon is attached to the quilt, but unfortunately, there is no information about where and when the prize was won. Treasured by the family, Arthur's quilt was passed down through the generations and given to the Warren Public Library by his grand-niece, Mary Anne (Damon) Jackson.

—AEN

SOUTH ROYALSTON QUILT

(FIG. 86)

The MassQuilts West documentation team encountered this quilt, dated 1885, in the collection of the Athol Historical Society. The only history available was that it had been donated by the Athol Grange. The search for its story began with a dead end, as it was soon discovered that the Athol Grange was not founded until 1887—two years after the date appliquéd on the quilt. No mention of any group in Athol making such a quilt appears in the local newspaper in 1885. There was more success, however, when some of the names that appear on the quilt were submitted to online genealogical searches, and the location of these individuals moved the place of its making to a town a few miles north of Athol—Royalston—particularly, South Royalston. While the story of why the quilt was made has not been discovered, information about two of the women whose names appear on the quilt has been found.

Especially fruitful was a search of the Royalston town directory, assembled in 1885.[36] It identified Belle Kendall, whose name appears on a coffee-pot in the lower section of the quilt, as a single woman about fifty years old who boarded with widower Albert Kendall (probably her brother) on the Baldwinville Road in South Royalston. An addi-

FIGURE 86. Foundation-pieced and appliquéd crazy quilt, "Country Scenes," various makers of South Royalston, c. 1885. Cotton (93" × 92"). Collection of the Athol Historical Society. *Photograph by David Stansbury.* MQ 4994.

FIGURE 87. Detail, block with man driving a pig, from "Country Scenes" crazy quilt. *Photograph by David Stansbury.*

FIGURE 88. Detail, block showing man with a jug and a pot of soup, from "County Scenes" crazy quilt. *Photograph by David Stansbury.*

tional name, Angeline Townsend, appears on the center block. The Townsend family was prominent in South Royalston, and their burial site in the Riverside Cemetery offered further information.[37] Angeline, whose first name was Julia, is buried there with her parents and brother, a Civil War casualty. Like Belle, Angeline was about fifty years old in 1885. Additional information from census data indicates that Angeline was living as the head of her household in 1880, and that her niece, Mary Baldwin, was living with her. Later census data report that Mary continued to live in this household after she married and had at least one child. Angeline died in 1925, and her name appears on one of the twelve stained glass windows installed in the Second Congregational Church in South Royalston. The church was built in 1906 after the original building burned in 1904, the same year that a devastating fire destroyed the woolen mill that had been the major business in South Royalston. It is probable that church records were lost in the fire; if the group who made the quilt was associated with the church, the tie can no longer be verified. Searches for "Mrs. Griffin," whose name is on the flag block, and a Mrs. H. P. (?) Day, on the center block, did not yield any information.

This folk art crazy quilt, a celebration of rural life, was likely a group effort. It is a modest and rustic version of the more-common silk and velvet embroidered crazy quilts fashionable at this time. Constructed by hand of twenty-five lattice-stripped blocks, each seventeen inches square, it is rich in figures, symbols, names, and initials. Many of the blocks use the foundation over-patch technique of crazy quilts, while a few combine a mix of traditional pieced blocks. Figures are both embroidered and appliquéd with embroidered embellishments. An American flag without stars and a house are prominent, as are farm animals and house pets. A man driving a pig with a whip, a coffee pot with the name "Belle Kendall," a cat with the name "Addie" (the cat's name or the owner's?), a sunflower, several chickens, a cow, all speak to the harmony, hospitality—and labor—of farm living. An especially interesting block features what appear to be doughnuts near a man who holds a jug with the word "sap"

FIGURE 89. Detail, first printed patchwork fabric used on back of "Country Scenes" crazy quilt. *Photograph by David Stansbury.*

FIGURE 90. Detail, second printed patchwork fabric used on back of "Country Scenes" crazy quilt. *Photograph by David Stansbury.*

in one hand and possibly a frying pan in the other, standing next to a pot labeled "SOUP." There are also pieced fans, crescent moons, and a grandfather clock that shows one o'clock. A number of printed motifs cut from a variety of fabrics have been used as appliqué pieces within the patches as well. The embroidery does not follow the lines of pieces, as was customary in the more elaborate crazy quilts.

The quilt is tied. Its makers used two different "cheater cloth" fabrics to construct the back: one is dark and gives the appearance of pieced work, while the other is lighter and printed to resemble "crazy" patch blocks. Small scraps of both of these fabrics are also found in the top.[38] —MC

Chapter 6

The Connecticut River Valley: A Rich Heritage

The Connecticut River, called "the Great River" by the early European settlers, provided an easy path for settlement into the western interior of the Massachusetts Bay Colony soon after Salem and Boston were established on the coast. The town of Springfield was founded as a place to carry on the fur trade in 1636. The flood plains of the river provided extraordinarily rich soil, and farming communities quickly followed to the north: Northampton in 1654, Hadley in 1659, and Deerfield in 1669.

Settlers had a strong religious disposition. Two of colonial America's most important theologians, the Reverend Solomon Stoddard and his grandson the Reverend Jonathan Edwards, preached in Northampton. "Sinners in the Hands of an Angry God," a sermon that famously left congregants shaking, weeping, and crying out for mercy, was delivered by Edwards in nearby Enfield in 1741.[1] His powerful Calvinist message was an important spark that fired the religious revival known as the "Great Awakening."

Wars with the Indians and the French in Canada kept the Connecticut River Valley of Massachusetts from achieving general prosperity until well into the eighteenth century; the violence took a terrible toll on all sides. In 1675, during King Philip's War, Deerfield was attacked and burned and had to be abandoned for several years. In 1704, during Queen Anne's War, Deerfield was again attacked, with half of its inhabitants killed or marched as captives to Canada. The last attack on a civilian population in the Valley occurred during the French and Indian War in the 1750s (see the Nims family quilt, figure 99/MQ 3311).

A distinctive regional identity developed due to the Valley's many years of relative isolation, its inland farming economy, and a consolidation of authority among certain leading families (called by their contemporaries, the "River Gods").[2] Timothy Dwight, president of Yale College and a Northampton native, noted in his *Travels in New England and New York* that "The inhabitants of this valley may be said in several respects to possess a common character, and in all the different states resemble each other more than their fellow citizens who live on the coast resemble them."[3] This regional identity was manifested in unique decorative art design, architecture, and even in personal appearance throughout the colonial period and into the nineteenth century.[4]

Originally, Hampshire County included the entire Connecticut River Valley of Massachusetts, dipping south of the modern state border of Connecticut, and reaching north to Vermont. In the early nineteenth century, Franklin County to the north and Hampden County to the south split off from Hampshire. Outside of its main community of Greenfield, Franklin County is largely rural, mixed with small mill towns. Hampden County, with the city of Springfield (once one of this country's most important commercial, financial, and manufacturing centers) is much more heavily urban and industrialized.

Timothy Dwight observed that Valley inhabitants emphasized the importance of education.[5] The legacy of this characteristic is seen particularly in

FIGURE 91. *View from Mount Holyoke*, attributed to Victor de Grailly, oil on canvas, c. 1845. *Photograph by Stan Sherer, courtesy of Historic Northampton.*

present-day Hampshire County. The towns of Amherst, Northampton, and South Hadley are home to the "Five Colleges": Amherst College, Hampshire College, the University of Massachusetts, Smith College, and Mount Holyoke College. Numerous private schools also thrive in the region. The intellectual culture of the entire Connecticut Valley has nurtured authors and poets for over three centuries, including the Reverend Edward Taylor (1642–1729) of Westfield; Noah Webster (1758–1843), Emily Dickinson (1830–1886), and Robert Frost (1874–1963) of Amherst; Theodor Geisel, a.k.a. "Dr. Seuss" (1904–1991) of Springfield; Archibald MacLeish (1892–1982) of Conway; and Tracy Kidder (1945–) of Williamsburg.

The rich soils of the valley and the numerous mills and factories that developed in the nineteenth century attracted thousands of immigrants to the region. First the Irish came to dig canals and build the railroads, then French Canadians joined the Irish in the factories after the Civil War. At the end of the nineteenth century and early twentieth century, Poles came to be farmers. Italians, Greeks, Portuguese, Russian Jews, Armenians, and African-Americans from the South came too. Today, the valley is a rich mixture of cultures, with a diverse economy based on industry, agriculture, education, the arts, and tourism. —LZB

FIGURE 92. Whole-cloth quilt, from the Clarke family of
Northampton, c. 1787. Wool (87½" × 83½"). Collection of Historic
Northampton, Northampton, Mass. (68.51). *Photograph by David
Stansbury.* MQ 4068.

CLARKE FAMILY QUILT

(FIG. 92)

Lydia Cook (1765–1815) probably made this dark blue calamanco quilt at the time of her marriage to Joseph O. Clarke of Northampton in 1787. The Cooks and Clarkes were well-established and affluent families in the Connecticut River Valley. Joseph Clarke was the nephew and adopted son of Major Joseph and Mercy (Lyman) Hawley. Major Joseph Hawley (1723–1788) was a Yale graduate, an ardent patriot and leader in the Revolution, influential in his work in the state government until he withdrew from public life because of mental illness. Like his father before him, he suffered from manic depression. (Major Joseph Hawley's father killed himself in a fit of religious despair in 1735.)

Fortunately, Joseph Clarke was the son of Mercy Lyman Hawley's sister and did not inherit the Hawley family curse of depression. He did inherit the family's patriotic fervor, and served for three years in the Revolutionary War. He became Joseph Hawley's law partner and served as town treasurer for many years. Lydia Cook, the daughter of Captain Joseph and Lydia (Miller) Cook, was his second wife. Joseph Cook served in the French and Indian War and was a patriot in the Revolutionary War, serving for the town of Northampton on the Committee of Correspondence, Inspection, and Safety (which had as its primary duty to rout Loyalists). The captain, an inn keeper as well as keeper of the jail, was one of the "prominent citizens" who supported, in 1784, the first school in town to admit girls along with boys.[6] The school may have been established too late for Lydia to attend, but clearly her father thought it was important for girls to be educated. Probably in another school, Lydia learned the reading, writing, spelling, arithmetic, grammar, geography, and French that was offered to Northampton girls at the new co-educational school supported by her father.

Lydia's quilt is made with a face of English twill-woven shalloon, while the back is made of plain-woven wool in a pattern of blue and white checks, probably domestically produced. The batting is natural black sheep's wool. Residents of the Connecticut River Valley had raised sheep since they first settled the area in the seventeenth century, but flocks did not grow to large numbers until the eighteenth century, once farms were better established and fears of attack by the Indians and French were alleviated.[7] Much spinning and weaving took place in Valley homes, but coarser fabrics that could be used for work clothing or traded for finer imported stuffs were the products of the looms. Dyeing blue with indigo was very common. Sylvester Judd noted in his *History of Hadley* that "the women made checks and stripes of wool, flax and cotton, for shirts, trowsers [sic], aprons, gowns, bedticks, &c."[8] It is likely that the blue-and-white checked pattern of the quilt backing is similar to the blue-and-white checked shirts with which Valley men were identified. Judd writes that "when Benjamin Tappan first attended meeting in Northampton in 1768, he was surprised to find that all the men in the meeting house, except five or six, wore checked shirts. Hadley shirts were equally checkered. The people of Worcester County wore white shirts, and they said they could tell a Connecticut River man by his checked shirt."[9]

Like the blue-and-white checked shirts of the

FIGURE 93. Drawing of the Clark family quilt. *Drawing © 2004 by Lynne Z. Bassett.*

men, or the distinctive scrolled pediment doorways that adorned the eighteenth-century mansion houses of the Connecticut River Valley elite, the quilting pattern of Lydia's bed cover is typical of this region of Massachusetts.[10] A reliance on large-scale feather patterns is seen in many early whole-cloth quilts throughout the river valley, up into Vermont. The abstracted shell and floral forms are typical of eighteenth-century rococo design, but they are made unique in this quilt by the large C-curved feathers flanking the motifs. As in most wool whole-cloth quilts, the background is filled with narrowly spaced diagonal lines, without which the design would be indistinguishable.   —LZB

ESTHER WHEAT QUILT
(FIG. 94)

Esther Wheat (1774–1847) of Conway undoubtedly went into her marriage with high hopes. She married Benjamin Lee (b. 1775) in 1799; he was the son of Eber and Bethiah Lee, whose estate, as estimated in the town tax records in 1788 and 1791, was valued twice as high as that of Esther's father, Benjamin, who apparently was struggling financially in comparison to his neighbors. Esther was marrying up considerably. Benjamin Lee first appears in the tax records in 1798, so he was just starting out as a tradesman or farmer when they married a year later. They did not stay in Conway for long; Benjamin disappears from the tax and voter lists by 1802.[11] His common name makes it difficult to track their movements in census records, which did not list a wife's name until 1850, but their great-great-granddaughter, who gave this quilt to the National Museum of American History, stated that Esther died in Canastota, New York, in 1847.[12] Canastota, which is in Madison County, was not established until 1810, so evidently they did not go directly there; a Benjamin Lee is listed in the census for the town of Sullivan in Madison County in 1830, but he is gone by 1840. The 1850 census finds a Benjamin Lee of the correct age, birth place, and marital status in Poland, Chatauqua County, New York. The surname of their great-great-granddaughter, Hurlburt, as well as the surname Lee appear in Chatauqua County records, so it is possible that Benjamin went to live with a married son or daughter after his wife's death.

The unrooted life that this research reveals suggests financial difficulty for Esther and Benjamin Lee, or perhaps just a feeling that the grass was greener a little farther west, a little farther west. Upstate New York attracted many Massachusetts natives in the early nineteenth century, who were getting more and more crowded on farms that had been divided over generations and could no longer support large families. Conway, established in 1767 as a southwestern section of Deerfield, was at the height of its population in 1790, when it numbered 2,092 inhabitants.[13] For the next two hundred years, this hilltown of the Berkshire Mountains steadily lost population as its young people left to find land and work elsewhere. The largest decline came in the 1830s, probably due to the opening of the Erie Canal in 1825. The canal runs through Madison County; it must have taken Benjamin and Esther Lee to that area as they sought land and employment.

The quilt was clearly a treasured item, carefully packed for each remove and then passed down through the generations. Considering her father's finances, it was a significant acquisition prior to Esther's marriage, as the dark blue calamanco was an expensive imported fabric. It must have been with some pride that Esther brought it to her new household, especially in light of the much more prosperous position of her husband's family. The backing is a golden yellow, plain-woven wool, probably spun from the wool of local or family-owned sheep, woven and dyed at home. It is filled with natural black sheep's wool and quilted with two-ply worsted thread. The pattern, with the large feathered designs preferred in the Connecticut River Valley, is surmounted by a feathered heart.[14]   —LZB

FIGURE 94. Drawing of a whole-cloth quilt, made by Esther Wheat
(1774–1847) of Conway, 1799. Wool (91" × 93¼"). Collection of the
National Museum of American History, Washington, D.C. (308057).
Drawing © 2003 by Lynne Z. Bassett. MQ 4959.

LYDIA BATCHELOR QUILT

(FIG. 95)

A comparison of the design of Esther Wheat's quilt (fig. 94/MQ 4959) with the dark blue calamanco quilt of Lydia Batchelor (fig. 96/MQ 4958) makes it clear that the patterns of both bed covers were drawn by the same hand. Lydia was also from Conway, the daughter of John and Lydia Batchelor, early settlers of the town. Who designed these two quilts? It could not have been Esther, for she had left town by the time Lydia's quilt was made. Was it Lydia? Most likely it was a talented neighbor who earned a little extra income by drawing quilting and embroidery patterns for the women in town. For example, in the New England tradition of exchanging labor, or "changing works" as it is called in documents of the period, Sarah Snell Bryant (1768–1863) of Cummington, a town south of Conway, noted in her diary in 1822 that she drew "a feather on a bedquilt" for her neighbor Mrs. Briggs (fig. 97).[15] Sarah, who was a prolific quilter and weaver herself, doodled designs resembling quilting patterns in her diary in 1805, including the feather pattern seen here. Such designs were drawn directly on the surface of the quilt, probably with chalk or pencil, depending on the color of the cloth. The discipline that enabled some women and men to draw perfectly measured feathers and flourishes without the use of a template can be seen in the repetitions of letters and scrolled ornament in copybooks and calligraphic documents from this period. These penmanship skills were part of both boys' and girls' education. Although the identity of the local artist who drew Esther's and Lydia's quilts probably will never be known, the quilts themselves are evidence of the many ways that women could contribute to the household economy: by spinning and weaving fabrics such as those used on the backs of the quilts, by designing quilts and embroideries if she was particularly artistic, or by doing the actual quilting. All of these skills could be exchanged for goods or labor in other forms.

Lydia Batchelor married Simon Dewolf (1776–1863) of Deerfield on December 1, 1803. Lydia quilted her initials and the year 1803 within a feathered heart in the center of her quilt. She came into her marriage effectively in the position of a stepmother: In 1802, Simon had taken in his toddling nephew Rufus, whose father had deserted Simon's sister Esther, leaving her "in Such low Circumstances" that she was unable to support her several children.[16] More family embarrassment was caused by Simon's older married brother Elisha, when he was named in a paternity suit by "singlewoman" Jemima Dodge in 1805.[17]

Simon was better behaved. He was a respected yeoman, serving as justice of the peace for the town in the 1820s. Simon's brother Joel married Lydia's sister Polly and they all lived in the neighborhood of town called "Mill Village," south of Deerfield Center. Lydia and Simon had only two children. It must have been a severe blow to lose their oldest, a daughter named Lyntha, at age twelve in 1816, but their son Almon raised his own family, inherited the family farm, became a selectman of Deerfield, and lived to the ripe old age of eighty.

Simon and Lydia's hard work greatly increased their estate. In the year of their marriage, Simon's real estate was valued at only $38 by the tax assessor. Thirty-five years later, the tax assessor appraised his land at $2,530, plus he had another $296 in animals, placing him solidly in the middle class. Their three cows gave them milk, butter, and cheese; in 1837, Simon wrote a testimonial to the superiority of the "Roberts Patent Churn" (although Lydia was undoubtedly the one who actually used it), saying "I have no hesitation in recommending it to the community as a Labor Saving Machine in good earnest."[18] The local country store owned by Walter and Orlando Ware accepted Simon and Lydia's farm products, including bushels of corn, in exchange for goods that they could not produce themselves. The merchants' account book shows Simon's purchases from 1811 to 1819 of yellow flannel, skeins of silk, indigo, ginger, Bohea tea, allspice, pepper, rice, sugar, nails and screws—and quite a lot of West India rum, though that appears to have been bought mostly during harvesting season, when Simon was

FIGURE 95. Whole-cloth quilt, made by Lydia Batchelor (1776–1847)
of Conway, 1803. Wool (103¼" × 108"). Collection of Historic New
England, Boston, Mass., gift of Bertram K. and Nina Fletcher Little
(1991.296). *Photograph by Peter Harholdt, courtesy of Historic New England
(digital ID 000224).* MQ 4958.

probably rewarding his helpers.[19] The six sheep owned by the Dewolfs in 1838 provided them with wool, which Lydia may have spun and knitted or woven to make everyday clothing for the family.

—LZB

FIGURE 96. Drawing of the Lydia Batchelor quilt. *Drawing © 2003 by Lynne Z. Bassett.*

FIGURE 97. Drawing of quilting pattern from the diary of Sarah Snell Bryant (1768–1847) of Cummington, 1805. *By permission of the Houghton Library, Harvard University, Cambridge, Mass.*

SUSANNAH ALLEN ANDERSON HOWARD QUILT

(FIG. 98)

Susannah Allen Anderson probably completed this impressive quilt around the time of her marriage to Emery Gustav Howard (1814–1863) in 1839. Composed of almost twelve thousand pieces, the quilt employs four-patch blocks, eight-point stars, and a center medallion of hexagons. The quilt includes a wide variety of cylinder-printed fabrics, many of which were likely scraps left over from family clothing and household textiles. It illustrates the rural vernacular style of the early 1800s and helps tell the story of a woman who left no diaries or letters.

Susannah Allen Anderson was born in Ware on September 16, 1813, the oldest child of four. Her younger sister died in 1822 at the age of six, and in 1825, when Susannah was eleven, her mother died. Inevitably, Susannah must have made a significant contribution to the household chores of sewing, cooking, cleaning, and looking after her younger brothers after the passing of her mother. When she was thirteen, in 1827, her father died, leaving Susannah and her brothers orphaned. The children were wards of their uncle but lived in their grandfather's household. Shortly after her father's death, one of Susannah's other uncles died, leaving six more orphans to care for on top of her two younger brothers. Her grandfather died a few years later, followed by her legal guardian, her Uncle Amasa, who passed away in 1836 when she was twenty-three, leaving Susannah as the guardian of her brothers.[20]

While almost every early nineteenth-century family experienced the untimely death of children or parents, Susannah experienced a larger than normal share of tragedy. By the time Susannah married Emery Howard in 1839, running a household must have been second nature. Susannah and Emery continued to live in Ware, farming the land and caring for their two daughters, Susan Adelaide and Madora.

According to one 1840 source, Ware was "a flourishing village," located on the Ware River in cen-

FIGURE 98. Miniature-pieced quilt, made by Susannah Allen (Anderson) Howard (1813–1891) of Ware, c. 1839. Cotton with wool batting (102" × 101¼"). Collection of Old Sturbridge Village, Sturbridge, Mass. (26.23.142). *Photograph by Thomas Neill, courtesy of Old Sturbridge Village.* MQ 4642.

tral Massachusetts with several active industrial pursuits. In 1837, there were two cotton mills, two woolen mills, along with boot, shoe, straw bonnet, palm-leaf hat, and auger industries.[21] Early nineteenth-century New Englanders embraced these manufactured goods, prizing their uniformity, affordability, and appearance. The cylinder-printed fabrics in Susannah's quilt were popular for the same reasons. The quilt is backed with a blue and white fabric with a printed leafy vine design. It is quilted in an outline pattern with seven stitches to the inch in white, red, and blue thread.

The riot of color and exuberance of pattern in Susannah's quilt represent the vernacular rural aesthetic of the early 1800s. Although urban tastemakers had begun to deride colorful pieced quilts in favor of elegant whitework quilts, rural New England women like Susannah continued to create bedcoverings from their scrap baskets, using both remnants from clothing and new printed cottons.[22] Susannah showed her quiltmaking talent and an understanding of late 1830s fashion by making another quilt that probably also dates to the time of her marriage in 1839. Her second quilt is the epitome of taste—a stylish whitework quilt with a center medallion, florals, feathers, and a diagonal grid—all quilted with eight stitches to the inch.

After Susannah passed away in 1891, her quilts were passed down to her daughters. The pieced quilt was given to Old Sturbridge Village by Susannah's grandson in 1980, while the whitework quilt was purchased by the museum in 1976.[23] —AEN

NIMS FAMILY QUILT
(FIG. 99)

Charlemont, where Elizabeth (Betsy) Rice was born in 1751, is one of the "hilltowns" of western Massachusetts. The hilltowns are scattered through the rugged terrain west of the fertile floodplain of the Connecticut River Valley and into the Berkshire Mountains. The current population of these communities averages between twelve hundred and two thousand—not much larger than in earlier times, and they are still governed by town meetings. Agriculture in these rocky, wooded hills proved to be challenging to settlers' efforts to clear and plow fields; large cash crops proved to be impossible by the latter part of the nineteenth century. Second-growth forest now shades old stone boundary walls, built using the materials that once obstructed the plows. While working dairy farms, orchards, and hayfields continue to exist, residents now more often earn their income by commuting to more urban employment, or through specialty agri-

cultural enterprises such as organic foods and high-end crafts.

Several members of the Rice family settled Charlemont during the 1740s. This was still the frontier, and four years after Betsy's birth, one of her relatives, Captain Moses Rice, the town's largest landowner, was scalped and died in an Indian attack while plowing a field.[24]

Betsy married John Nims III, a Revolutionary War veteran, in 1771. The Nims family had been instrumental in founding the older town of Deerfield, to the southeast of Charlemont. Betsy and John had a total of four sons and nine daughters; two boys and a girl who were the first born died as small children. The large Nims family and the children's spouses lived continuously in the area called Buckland, which separated from Charlemont in 1779. Seven of Betsy Rice Nims' daughters lived nearby at the time this quilt was made. Since she would have been in her eighties in the 1830s, probably one or more of them participated in its making, if Betsy herself was not responsible for its entire construction and quilting.

The quilt is made up of twenty-five blocks, each about eighteen inches square, set five across and five down. Each block has two diagonally crossed laurel branches with red "blossoms" in the corners that form a secondary pattern where the blocks meet. There is also a four-leaf cross in the center of each block. The quilting, at nine stitches per inch, echoes the appliqué pattern at quarter-inch intervals; a stylized daisy is quilted in the white space where block sides touch.

Very similar individual blocks and one contemporary quilt are pictured in *Quilts of Virginia 1607–1899*.[25] The Nims quilt is similar in size and layout, but the quilt from Virginia has an additional row of blocks. These "Laurel Leaves" blocks appear in album quilts of the 1840s and 1850s, some made by Quaker quilters. Clearly, the sharing of quilt-block patterns happened over long distances even before the wide circulation of published patchwork designs in ladies' magazines later in the nineteenth century.

Red and green quilts enjoyed great popularity between the 1830s and 1890. While we associate these colors today with Christmas, the combination

FIGURE 99. Appliquéd and pieced quilt, "Laurel Leaves," attributed to Betsy Rice Nims (1751–1842) of Buckland and/or her daughters, c. 1840. Cotton (90½" × 90¾"). Collection of Pocumtuck Valley Memorial Association, Memorial Hall Museum, Deerfield, Mass. (1987.29.500). *Photograph by David Stansbury.* MQ 3311.

has long been popular for all types of decoration. Red and green are considered "complementary" across the color wheel. More importantly for quilts, however, is the state of dye technology at this time, which helped make the physical survival of red and green quilts possible.

"Turkey" red, initially a dye process using the root of the madder plant, was perfected in the Ottoman empire of the eastern Mediterranean area. By the mid-eighteenth century, English and French textile printers used this multi-step technique to produce a fast color. While it tended to fade to a strawberry pink, it did not bleed onto other fabrics in a pieced design. After the Civil War, a chemical substitute for the natural dye was developed and red prints were increasingly produced in the United States.[26]

The color green presented more problems in printing fabrics. Greens that were used in pre–Civil War quilts often were produced in a two-step process—over-dyeing blue and yellow—using both mineral and vegetable sources. A fast synthetic green appeared around 1875, but the earlier green printed fabrics tended to fade to blue or tan.[27] The green used in this quilt appears to have stayed close to its original color.

While Betsy Nims may have appreciated the appliqué pattern of laurel or bay branches for its similarity to the June-blooming mountain laurel bushes common to the hilltowns, its roots as a decorative motif go deeper. The Classical Greek tradition of creating crowns and wreaths of laurel and bay branches for rewarding champion athletes and revered poets is a probable source for the design.[28]

—MC

SUSAN MONROE SHEPHERD QUILT

(FIG. 100)

The will of Thomas Shepherd (1856–1923) established the Shepherd family home, along with its myriad contents, as a museum memorializing the Shepherd family in Northampton. The house is now owned and operated by the local historical society. The Shepherd family—Thomas in particular—kept everything. Multiple archival boxes hold documents and photographs chronicling the Shepherd family members' business activities and daily home life, their travels, and their participation in the colonial revival movement.

This quilt probably was made by Thomas's mother, Susan Munroe Shepherd, the daughter of John Foye Munroe and Susan Lorinda Brigham Munroe of Boston. After graduating from the Arcade High School of Boston in 1836 at the age of fifteen, Susan was sent to the Gothic Seminary in Northampton, a prestigious ladies' academy. Ac-

cording to an 1836 catalogue of the school, Miss Margarette Dwight, proprietess, emphasized "the cultivation of traits of character that are estimable," eradicating bad habits, and preparing students for "future usefulness" by "the acquisition of general and practical knowledge."[29] Following this introduction to the goals of the school, Miss Dwight presented a long list of "standards" every pupil should strive to reach in her studies and in her behavior. Susan wrote these standards into her copybook, with the added notation that she had "not knowingly or intentionally violated them."[30] The Gothic Seminary, in accordance with its name and architecture, was a very religious school. Miss Dwight declared that "THE WORD OF GOD is considered, not only [as] the means of enlightening the conscience, and purifying the heart, but as the *basis* of *all* correct Education."[31]

Appropriately, for she was a religious woman, Susan chose for her quilt a design that has assumed a biblical name, "King David's Crown."[32] She probably made the quilt in preparation for her marriage to Henry Shepherd (1811–1900) of Northampton in 1851. The quilt is made of a variety of dress calicoes, including a bright orange wavy stripe that strikingly sets off the darker "crowns." Made in a T-shape, the quilt would fit nicely around the foot posts of a tall-post bed.

Because widower Henry had four children, Susan instantly became a mother when they married. In her diary, Susan related in discreet Victorian fashion her emotions on her wedding day: "My sensations upon assuming the responsible situation in life and not that alone but Mother also—I will draw a veil over such feelings, they are sacred and even I can not transcribe them."[33]

From generation to generation, the Shepherd family was active in Northampton business and farming. Henry's father, Thomas Shepherd, imported some of the first merino sheep to the United States and became a successful manufacturer of fine wool broadcloth. Henry chose farming over manufacturing or merchandising; to supplement his income, he became superintendent of what soon became the Western Union Company. He was remembered as "a frisky man," and a talented horse-

FIGURE 100. Pieced quilt, "King David's Crown," attributed to Susan Lorinda Brigham (Munroe) Shepherd (1821–1897) of Northampton, c. 1850. Cotton (75" × 93½"). Collection of Historic Northampton, Northampton, Mass. (68.9). *Photograph by David Stansbury.* MQ 3946.

man.[34] Susan and Henry's son, Thomas, became the most successful businessman of the family. He presented Northampton's citizens with a new wing for the local hospital, in addition to a number of other generous gifts.

— LZB

FIGURE 101. Susan Lorinda Brigham Munroe Shepherd, c. 1850. *Photograph courtesy of Historic Northampton.*

FIGURE 102. Engraved letterhead from stationery of The Gothic Seminary, Northampton, Mass. *Photograph courtesy of Historic Northampton.*

WILLIAMSBURG FRIENDSHIP QUILT

(FIG. 104)

The history of industrialization includes disasters and losses as well as triumphs and profits. Massachusetts industries were originally water-powered, first using the current of natural rivers, and later, man-made canals and dams that directed and increased the power of running water. The risk of accidents increased along with the profits of the mills. Fires were not uncommon, but floods were an even more dramatic consequence of the growth of manufacturing.

The Mill River Flood of 1874, which killed 154 people and destroyed mills and homes in the Hampshire County communities of Williamsburg, Haydenville, Skinnerville, Leeds, and Northampton, was the most deadly dam failure of its time. It occurred only three years after the Chicago Fire, which had killed over 300 people. It would be overshadowed by the Johnstown, Pennsylvania, flood of 1889, which killed over 2,000—but in this rural area of Hampshire County at this time, the emotional as well as economic losses were severe.[35]

Like the Johnstown Flood, the Triangle Shirtwaist Fire, and other disasters that cost many workers' lives, the Mill River Flood was the result of an attempt to cut costs by ignoring safety. Although

the dam held for eight years, keeping back the water in a reservoir that fed a brook leading to the Mill River, doubts about its adequacy had been quietly voiced since its construction.

In the early 1870s, the banks of the Mill River between Williamsburg and Leeds (in the northwest section of Northampton) supported woolen, cotton, and silk mills, a large brassworks, and many other factories producing buttons, sewing machines, brushes, firearms, tools, and paper. Hundreds of people were at work in these mills and more were beginning their day at home when the dam broke on a May morning. In forty-five minutes, the resulting flood destroyed more than $1 million in property and killed over 150 people.

It was a Saturday morning at breakfast-time when the reservoir overseer, who lived with his family on site, saw a large chunk of earth break off from the dam. Before the dam itself broke, he took off on his old horse for Williamsburg to sound the warning. The dam broke with a boom that was heard for miles, and the water began to rush down the brook, then the river, overwhelming the mill ponds and sweeping away trees and buildings. In Williamsburg, Collins Graves in his milk wagon took over spreading the alarm, driving as fast as his horse could take him through Skinnerville to Haydenville. Hundreds were saved by his alert. A wall of water estimated by eyewitnesses to be forty feet high swept through the villages, taking not just

FIGURE 103. Stereoscopic view of the ruins of Williamsburg, after the Mill River Flood, 1874. *Photograph courtesy of Historic Northampton.*

FIGURE 104. Template-pieced friendship quilt, made by the Ladies of Williamsburg,
1871. Cotton (84" × 76½"). Collection of the Williamsburg Historical Society,
Williamsburg, Mass. *Photograph by David Stansbury.* MQ 2535.

FIGURE 105. Stereoscopic view of the ruins of the Brass Mill in Haydenville, after the Mill River Flood, 1874. *Photograph courtesy of Historic Northampton.*

houses but the Haydenville Brassworks, an imposing brick structure three stories tall and 600 feet long.

The first victims were Sarah Bartlett and her little daughter Viola, whose house was a short distance above Williamsburg. Sarah's name is on the center block of this quilt top, made a few years before the flood and now in the collection of the Williamsburg Historical Society. Although stitched by a number of women in and around Williamsburg as a friendship project, it became a memorial piece after the disastrous Mill River flood. The "flowers" are pieced by hand, using a mix of many cotton prints from the third quarter of the nineteenth century.[36] The center of each block is white and has the inked name of a local woman. A pathway of red hexagons joins the pieced "flowers," which total over 130, plus about sixty partial blocks around the edges. The bright colors of this top are in contrast to its eventual role as a reminder of the disastrous Mill River Flood.

After the flood's devastation, many businesses and homes were rebuilt. The Skinner family chose to relocate to Holyoke, moving sections of their damaged home as well as their business

as silk manufacturers. They prospered in Holyoke, and their mansion, Wistariahurst, is now a museum. Many families, however, never recovered economically or personally. Fortunately, by the end of the nineteenth century, steam replaced water power and such a flood was no longer a common risk.

—MC

ROENA DRAPER QUILT
(FIG. 106)

Roena Draper's quilt top contains 7,200 one and one-half-inch triangles made from hundreds of scrap fabrics. Although similar to a charm quilt in which no two fabrics are the same, this quilt does incorporate some repeat fabrics—but the delightful effect of Roena's colorful array of multitudinous calicoes is not dampened. Charm quilts were popular during the late 1800s and first decade of the 1900s. They also are characterized by the use of a single pattern piece (such as the triangle in this quilt) and a multicolor palette. Charm quilts received little at-

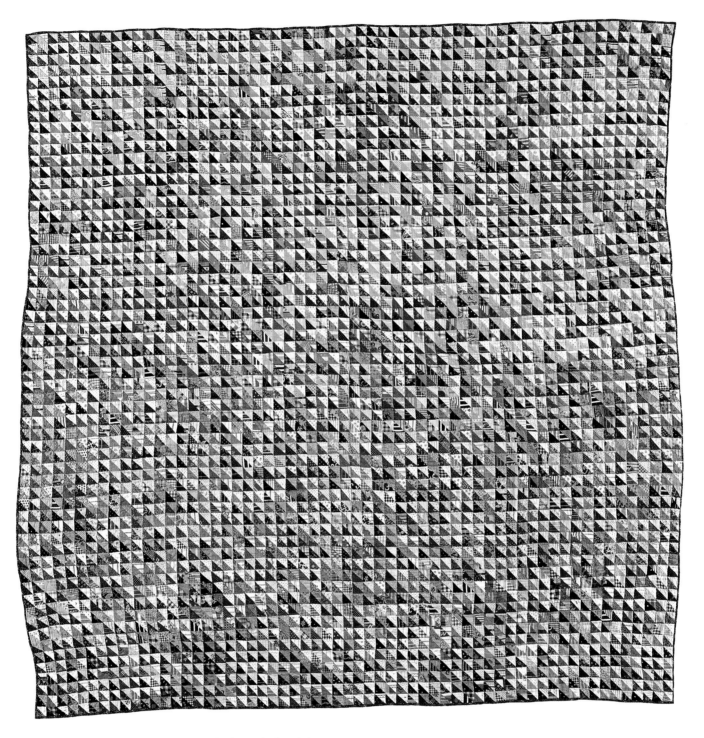

FIGURE 106. Pieced quilt top, "Thousands of Triangles," made by
Roena Draper (1836–1916) of Springfield, c. 1888. Cotton (81" ×
81½"). Private collection. *Photograph by David Stansbury.* MQ 3161.

FIGURE 107. Detail of calicoes, Roena Draper quilt. *Photograph by David Stansbury.*

tention in women's magazines of the period, but certainly must have brought local notice to their makers.[37]

Quilts with tops composed of thousands of small pieces were often noted in nineteenth-century accounts of regional agricultural fairs. In her study of Ohio state and county fairs, Virginia Gunn found that "judging committees, like newspaper reporters . . . seemed impressed by quilts made with extraordinary numbers of pieces."[38] Barbara Brackman discovered the same trend and attributed it to "the inarticulateness of the male reporters assigned to cover the ladies' exhibits."[39] These quilts were considered particularly noteworthy when made by the very young or the very old, or by those with handicaps like poor eyesight. Roena Draper was only about fifty-two when she made this quilt, not considered elderly at the time, but certainly an age at which she may have experienced diminished eye-

sight and have started to feel the aches and pains of getting older.

The quilt offers a vast array of fabrics from the late 1800s, including shirtings, conversation prints, double pinks, madders, mourning, and half-mourning prints. Most likely, many of these scraps were left over from years of making family clothing and other quilts and household textiles. The quilt top was a family gift and the fabrics contained within it may have strengthened its personal value for both the giver and the recipient.

Three generations of Springfield women are associated with the quilt. An accompanying hand-written note reads "Quilt Top Made by my Aunt Etta [Roena Draper] and given to me when I was a young girl. 80 x 80 Marion L. Converse." Marion L. Davis was born around 1890 to Charles and Anna Davis, so the quilt, dated by the current owner as 1888, may have been a gift for her birth.[40] Throughout the nineteenth century, quilts were given as gifts between family members to commemorate significant life events such as marriages and births. A recent study of thirty-three American quilts given as gifts between 1820 and 1860 found that the majority were given by women to female relatives.[41]

According to the current owner (Marion Converse's daughter), the quiltmaker learned to quilt as a young girl and the family used handmade quilts on their beds all the time. Marion Davis married Horatio L. Converse (b. 1883) and had three children—Howard, Robert, and Florence—between 1914 and 1918. According to the 1930 census, the family lived in Springfield, where Horatio worked as an inspector for the street department and Marion was listed as a saleslady. In addition to the couple's three children, the census also lists Marion's mother, Anna M. Davis, age seventy-five, as an occupant of the home. Seven years later, in 1937, Marion entrusted the quilt to her daughter's care to "keep it in the family."

—AEN

Springfield, located at the junction of the Agawam and the Connecticut Rivers, was established in 1636 by William Pynchon and six other men from Roxbury. Initially, they hoped to establish a trading and fur-collecting post. When Springfield was incorporated in 1641, it was named in honor of Pynchon's birthplace in England. From its beginnings as a trading post and agricultural area, Springfield developed its first industries during the late 1700s. The U.S. Armory was built in 1794, attracting many artisans, craftsmen, and merchants to the area. When railroad links to Boston, Hartford, and New York City came in the mid-1800s, Springfield flourished, officially becoming a city in 1852. By the time this quilt was made around 1888, Springfield was the region's retailing and financial capital.
Source: Richard D. Brown and Jack Tager, *Massachusetts: A Concise History* (Amherst: University of Massachusetts Press, 2000), 212–13.

CROSSMAN FAMILY QUILT
(FIG. 108)

The current owner rescued this quilt from a pile of household discards at the bottom of the cellar steps when she cleaned out her mother's house in Gardner. Her decision to save it provided the Massachusetts Quilt Documentation Project with one of the most visually exciting examples of scrap piecing found in almost fifteen years of documenting quilts.

The comforter is believed to be the work of Susan Elizabeth Crossman, the owner's great-grandmother, who lived in Shutesbury and later in nearby North Amherst. According to the United States census, Susan lived with her farmer husband, Newton D. Crossman, and their two children, Alice and Frank, in Shutesbury in 1880. In 1900, shortly after the probable date of the comforter's construction, forty-nine-year-old Susan still lived in Shutesbury with her husband, but her mother, Louisa T. Wood, and an elderly female boarder had joined the household. By 1910, the family was living in North Amherst, where Newton was the postmaster.

Susan intricately pieced the quilt top using a fabric foundation. Beginning in the center of each of the diamond and triangle shapes that make up the stars and border, Susan added successive strips in the manner of piecing a log cabin block, but without that pattern's uniformity. Instead, she incorporated odd-shaped small bits, sometimes triangles of red and/or white for her centers, then added strips of scrap fabrics around the center, creating the appearance of a swirl in each diamond point of the stars. Her technique is unlike traditional string piecing, which is all strips—often of uneven width—covering the foundation piece in a consistent orientation.

Tied at regular intervals with white heavy thread or string, the comforter is finished with a machine-stitched knife edge. Two strips of "cheater" cloth, the same as that used on the back of fig. 86/MQ 4994, are incorporated into the backing.

This quilt brings to mind the New England saying, known in several variations, that urges people to "Use it up, wear it out, make it do, or do with-

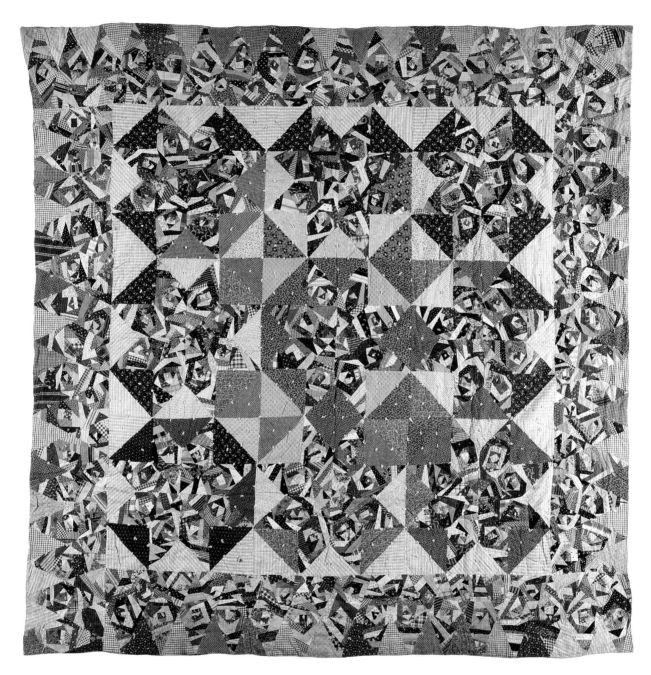

FIGURE 108. Pieced comforter, "Lemoyne Star" (string variation),
attributed to Susan Elizabeth Crossman (1851–?) of Shutesbury and
North Amherst, c. 1890. Cotton (88" × 88"). Private collection.
Photograph by David Stansbury. MQ 3454.

The eastern section of Hadley was given its independence as a district in 1759. In 1776, the year that the American colonies became a country, the eastern district of Hadley declared itself to be the town of Amherst. The town grew quickly, necessitating the establishment of a post office in North Amherst in 1834 and in South Amherst in 1841. Originally an agricultural community, Amherst's economy diversified at the end of the eighteenth century with a paper factory along the Mill River; its success inspired several other paper factories to establish themselves in town. Attempts to produce cotton and woolen goods were largely unsuccessful, but the production of palm-leaf hats proved to be a remunerative venture: "The business for the year 1871 amounted to about 100,000 dozen hats." Other nineteenth-century Amherst companies produced wire hoop skirts, rifles, woodworking tools, cook stoves, and carriages.

However, it was the organization of two edu-cational establishments in the nineteenth century that forever changed the character of the community. Amherst Academy (later Amherst College) was chartered in 1816; its beautiful campus, with many of its early buildings still in use, continues to dominate the center of town. The Massachusetts Agricultural College (now the University of Massachusetts at Amherst) accepted its first students in 1867. Today, the population of the town nearly doubles when the twenty-five thousand UMass students return to the sprawling North Amherst campus in the fall. As the North Amherst postmaster, Newton Crossman undoubtedly handed many care packages and letters through the post office window to homesick university students.

Source: The History of the Town of Amherst, Massachusetts (Amherst, Mass.: Press of Carpenter & Morehouse, 1896), 68, 333–34, 292.

out." The small bits of fabric were stitched together in a way that suggests shattered glass or another fragmented, yet cohesive, gathering of light and dark. Thus, the final product was frugal in its making, but dazzling in its effect. —MC

CHRISTIANA KING SHELLY QUILT
(FIG. 110)

When the colorful and ambitious British General John Burgoyne devised his plan to strand the American forces at Saratoga in 1777, surrender never entered his mind. Nor did he imagine that the subsequent American victory would be celebrated in a quilt pattern. Yet both occurred. This striking pieced and appliquéd quilt is a variant of the "Burgoyne Surrounded" pattern.[42] Quiltmaker Christiana King Shelley selected the pattern during the Colonial Revival movement, perhaps to commemorate the Shelley family's involvement in the Revolutionary War.[43]

Born in 1832, in Ellenville, New York, Christiana's earliest years remain elusive. Her mother was born in New York, but her father may have been a German immigrant.[44] In 1850, Christiana appeared in the industrial town of Chicopee, where she met her future husband, Edwin D. Shelley, a young mechanic boarding with a carriage maker.[45] Edwin and Christiana married around 1851; by 1860, they had settled in nearby Holyoke.

Located on the Connecticut River just north of Springfield, Holyoke's development was hampered by Hadley Falls, where the Connecticut River dropped nearly sixty feet.[46] In 1848, however, a group of Boston industrialists and investors—inspired by successes at Lowell and Lawrence—incorporated the Hadley Falls Company. Purchasing water rights and the surrounding 1,100 acres of land, the incorporators successfully dammed the river to control its hydropower and developed the planned community of Holyoke.[47]

Wide, straight avenues and boulevards crisscrossed the city, as opposed to the narrow, meandering streets typical of older communities. Nearby ponds fed a public water system; factories lined canals, while boardinghouses and public parks promised healthy living for workers. By 1890, the city population exceeded 28,000, and Holyoke's reality included overcrowded tenements and periodic health epidemics. But still, there was much to be proud of. The city contained seventeen grade schools, the Holyoke Business College, and two public libraries. More than a dozen church spires punctuated the city skyline, and an equal number of newspapers in various languages were sold on the streets.[48]

Like most New England mill towns, Holyoke initially focused on textile production, but by 1890, this self-proclaimed "Paper City of the World" housed twenty-four paper mills employing almost three thousand people and generated close to $7 million worth of goods.[49] Much of the success of those mills and others must be credited to the immigrants from Ireland, Canada, and Eastern Europe.

The Shelley household was busy and relatively prosperous. In 1860, thirty-three-year-old Edwin owned property worth $5,000. As a self-employed blacksmith, much of his worth was tied up in his shop, but he employed two apprentices, who (along with two other men) boarded with the family. The household also included Christiana and Edwin's one-year-old son, Frank (sadly, the family earlier had lost two children).[50] By 1870, the family owned real estate worth more than $15,000, and Edwin was a wagon maker. The number of boarders increased to seven, most of whom were young Irish men working as blacksmiths or in the wagon shop. A thirty-one-year-old female cotton mill worker, an eleven-year-old girl who may have been a niece, and Shelley sons Scott and Willie rounded out the household. Eventually, Christiana and Edwin would add two daughters to their family.[51]

Many works of the talented quiltmaker Christiana Shelly have survived (see also fig. 146/MQ 5617). She made this claret and white, pieced and appliquéd cotton quilt when she was in her late fifties or early sixties. "Burgoyne Surrounded" may be among the last quilts she produced as a Massachusetts resident, however. Still a resident of Holyoke in 1892, by 1900, Christiana, her husband Edwin, and

FIGURE 110. Pieced and appliquéd quilt, "Burgoyne Surrounded," made by Christiana King Shelley (1832–1919) of Holyoke, c. 1890–1900. Cotton (94" × 86"). Private collection. *Photograph by David Stansbury.* MQ 92.

their youngest daughter, twenty-five-year-old Ada, had left Holyoke for a small farm in Windsor, Connecticut.[52] Christiana died there in 1919 at the age of eighty-seven, leaving behind her many quilts.

—DCA

GALETSA ROBERTSON QUILT

(FIG. 111)

The silk and velvet crazy quilts of the late nineteenth century were made as show pieces, but during the first part of the twentieth century, New England needlewomen frequently produced a more practical version. Using wool scraps stitched onto a foundation, with backing and sometimes batting, quilters created a very warm cover. Many of the wool crazy quilts of the twentieth century discovered during the Massachusetts Quilt Documentation Project used scraps from men's suits and sometimes coats. These quilts tend to be dark, enlivened with decorative stitching—though often only somewhat so. Galetsa Robertson's quilt, however, uses bright and light-colored wool scraps as well as darks, and has several whimsical touches, including a decorative border of "petals" that extend out from the edge.

Galetsa and her husband Edward W. Robertson farmed near Readsboro in Bennington County, Vermont. They had four children: William, Minnie, Mary, and Ida. William (called "Willie" and born about 1864) died as a young man in an accident: As he crossed a bridge with a load of wood on a horse-drawn wagon, the bridge collapsed and he drowned.[53] In 1900, the United States Census lists Galetsa as a widow living with Minnie, her husband Bryon Stowe, and their son, Edward (born in 1897), in Readsboro. The family moved to Colrain, in northern Franklin County, around 1908. As it has always been since its founding in 1761, Colrain is a small, rural hilltown. Apple orchards and sheep provided the basis for its agricultural economy in the nineteenth and early twentieth centuries.[54]

Soon after the move to Colrain, Galetsa made this quilt for her grandson, Edward B. Stowe (1897–1980), as indicated by his initials, EBS, cross-stitched on the cotton flannel backing. The quilt is constructed in blocks set five across and six down. Elaborate embroidery in a variety of stitches appears on every seam; Galetsa also embroidered a small flower at the intersections of all the blocks. She appliquéd a red heart on one block near the center of the quilt—perhaps a special message from grandmother to grandson.[55] The edge finish is a unique feature of this quilt. Petals or tongues of assorted woolen scraps, two to two and half inches long, extend from all four sides to make a scalloped edge. They are secured by two rows of machine top-stitching. Each petal has a decorative line of embroidery following the curved edge.

Further evidence of Galetsa's needlework, a velvet cushion cover embroidered in the typical crazy quilt style of the late nineteenth century, is also in the collection of Memorial Hall.

—MC

FIGURE III. Crazy quilt, made by Galetsa Robertson (1834–1916) of Colrain, c. 1910. Wool and cotton (58½" × 50¼"). Collection of the Pocumtuck Valley Memorial Association, Memorial Hall Museum, Deerfield, Mass. (1985.20). *Photograph by David Stansbury.* MQ 3318.

Chapter 7

Berkshire County: Rising to the Challenge

Berkshire County spans the western end of Massachusetts, bordered on the south by Connecticut, on the west by New York, and on the north by Vermont. It is fairly narrow, averaging around 35 miles from west to east. The landscape is hilly to mountainous and is marked by north/south river valleys that have scant, if any, floodplains. Near the center of Berkshire County stands Mount Greylock, the highest point in Massachusetts at 3,491 feet. Settlement of the Berkshires followed a south-to-north pattern along the rivers during the eighteenth century, with the town of Sheffield founded in 1733, Stockbridge in 1739, Pittsfield in 1761, and Williamstown in 1785. Farming (mostly on a subsistence scale) and timber harvesting formed the original base of the county's economy. The heavily forested, rocky, uneven land made clearing, plowing, planting, and harvesting a challenge, to say nothing of the sparse population, which limited the availability of labor.

By 1800, however, industry began to use waterpower from the rivers, fueling gristmills, cotton spinning, and paper production. Cottage industries also added to the local economy; before Whitney's cotton gin, home-based cleaning of cotton bolls supported the earliest cotton fabric production. Workers at home also made shoes, hats, and household goods such as knives and crockery. Many fabrics were woven in the home before production moved into factories in the nineteenth century. Mechanization increased throughout that century; eventually, Berkshire County produced wool and cotton printed fabrics, shoes and other leather goods, iron, and paper (including the paper that is still used

for U.S. currency). In the twentieth century, the manufacturing of small electrical appliances and motors came—and went. The loss of this industry, along with the closing of the textile-printing mills, left the area in economic distress.

Beginning in the 1830s, the beauty of Berkshire County attracted the leisure classes of New York and Boston, who built "cottages" able to accommodate scores of guests, requiring the employment of local people as domestic staff. Summer homes and temporary residences were enjoyed also by the literary figures Nathaniel Hawthorne, Herman Melville, William Cullen Bryant (who returned to his family's homestead in Cummington after becoming a famous poet), Edith Wharton, and Henry James. Norman Rockwell, the illustrator, was a prominent resident of Stockbridge in the mid-twentieth century. Recreational and cultural activities such as skiing, hiking, music, dance, and theater continue to draw tourists and form a substantial part of the local economy.

Berkshire County claims several famous natives who reflect the combination of austerity, independence, and dedication fostered by this picturesque but rugged environment. Elizabeth Freeman, called "Mum Bett" (1742–1829), a slave in the household of John Ashley, successfully sued for her freedom in 1781 with the assistance of Stockbridge lawyer Theodore Sedgwick (1746–1813). Her court case led to the legal acknowledgment that under the new (1780) Massachusetts constitution, slavery was unallowable. Theodore Sedgwick's daughter, Catherine Maria Sedgwick (1789–1867) became one of America's first successful female authors and an advocate for the

rights of women, African Americans, and Native Americans. Susan B. Anthony (1820–1906), a pioneer in the women's rights movement, hailed from North Adams. Mum Bett's great-grandson, W. E. B. DuBois (1868–1963), from Great Barrington, became a sociologist and a leader of the movement to recognize the intellectual achievements of African Americans; the library of the University of Massachusetts, Amherst, is named in his honor. These five Americans illustrate a crusading spirit that may be traced to the challenging landscape and living conditions of the region.   —MC

KATHERINE MARIA BELDEN QUILT

(FIG. 113)

The "Chimney Sweep" is one of the most frequently used signature quilt blocks in New England. Typically, the maker sets the blocks as in this quilt: on point, providing a plain white center cross on which to ink names, dates, and places within a field of contrasting print fabric. Sashing of another print outlines the blocks. Partial blocks are pieced around the edges and corners; in Kath-

erine Belden's quilt, they do not bear any name or message. "Kate," as she was called by her family, hand-pieced her blocks primarily of brown, madder, tan, and pink prints, along with a few strategically placed greens—most notably, the center block, which draws the viewer's eye to its inscription, "My Mother Jane A. Belden Lenox 1861."

This quilt was created during the Civil War period: dates written in ink on the forty-one quilt blocks range from 1861 to 1866. Sixteen families are represented from the towns of Lenox and Pittsfield, which are adjacent within Berkshire County. Nine members of the Belden family (including quiltmaker Kate) and seven from the Mattoon clan account for half of the names on the quilt—Kate Belden's mother was a Mattoon. John and Kate Cook, whose names also appear on the quilt, were related by marriage to the Mattoons. The Bangs, Root, and Ingalls families also shared relatives among the Mattoons and Beldens.[1]

Kate Belden's family has a long history in Berkshire County. Around 1750, Gershom (dates unknown) and Bathsheba Nash Martindale (1729–1808) came to Stockbridge from Westfield to join her parents, Stephen and Elizabeth Smith Nash. (The Nashes came to the area in order to be near the Reverend Jonathan Edwards, who had just

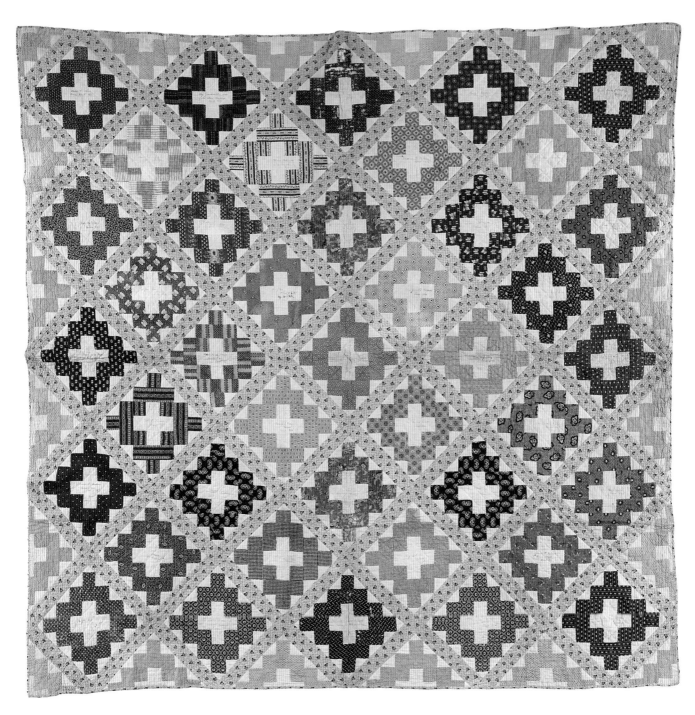

FIGURE 113. Pieced friendship quilt, attributed to Katherine Maria Belden (c. 1847–1894), Lenox, c. 1866. Cotton (84″ × 82″). Private collection. *Photograph by David Stansbury.* MQ 3571.

left his pulpit in Northampton.) The Martindale's daughter Frances ("Fannie"), born just before her parents left Westfield, married Charles Mattoon in 1769. Fannie and Charles's son, also named Charles, married Julia Ann Burnham in 1805. Kate Belden's mother, Abby Jane Mattoon Belden, was the daughter of Charles and Julia Ann Mattoon. The block bearing her name (in the top row, second block from the left) was inscribed by Kate: "My Grandmother's dress/Julia Ann Mattoon/August 1864."

One person whose name appears on the quilt but does not seem to have a blood connection to these families is Charles J. Wade, Second Lieutenant in the Massachusetts Infantry, who was born in Lansingburg, New York, in 1842. "Miss Lusie Wade" and "Mrs. Jacob Wade" from Lenox, probably his sister and mother, also have blocks. According to 1880 census records, Charles Wade lived with his wife and family in Lenox; he was a member of the Lee post of the Grand Army of the Republic.[2] The Wades were likely neighbors of the Beldens and Mattoons. No Beldens or Mattoons from the Lenox area were found in Civil War service records, but in earlier generations, men of the family were soldiers in the War of 1812 and in the Revolutionary War (while some family members were Tory sympathizers).

Kate Belden made her quilt at the same time that Jane Stickle, about thirty miles to the north in Bennington, Vermont, made her famous 225-block masterpiece. As Stickle wrote on her quilt, they were both made "in time of war" to provide comfort both emotional and physical.[3] The Beldens, Mattoons, their relatives, and friends gathered in Lenox to commemorate their ties during these stressful years and created a document of their lives, as well as a useful bed cover.   —MC

MINNIE BURDICK QUILT

(FIG. 114)

Among the rich quilt holdings of the Shelburne Museum in Vermont is a pictorial quilt, known as the "Centennial Album" quilt. Made of appliquéd and pieced plain and printed cottons, it consists of thirty-six different pictorial blocks arranged in six rows of six blocks. The most recognizable images—and the ones that give the quilt its name—are in two blocks illustrating buildings in the Centennial Exhibition, held in Philadelphia in 1876.[4] The widely published illustrations of this exhibition probably inspired these two blocks. An image of the Liberty Bell hangs over a grand building that resembles the Agricultural Building in the fifth block of the fourth row from the top. More intriguing is the inclusion of the Women's Pavilion in a block in the third row down and second in from the left. The brainchild of Elizabeth Duane Gillespie, the Women's Pavilion showcased the abilities and achievements of women in "all spheres of activity," including needlework, clothing, household items, and even industry—the latter category represented by inventions such as interlocking bricks, land pulverizers, and emergency flares.[5] In recognizing the potential and achievements of women, the Women's Pavilion was mildly controversial in its time, and its representation in this quilt is, therefore, of interest.

Two other blocks feature religious themes. In the second row from the top appears a block illustrating Baby Moses found among the bulrushes, while the last block in the second row from the bottom depicts Jonah and the Whale. (The unusual rendering of Jonah's boat looks like a Viking vessel.)

Some of the most striking blocks depict domestic scenes, carefully pieced with printed fabrics to realistically evoke Victorian parlors and chambers. Other blocks containing figures and handwritten captions, such as "Troublesome Tom," "My first Proposal," and "My Last Proposal," suggest subjects taken from illustrations published with contemporary ladies' magazine stories.[6]

Several blocks illustrate individual buildings and urban landscapes—perhaps mill buildings, smokestacks, and residences of North Adams. While most of the buildings are not specific and conform to building types found throughout New England, the structure appearing in the first block of the bottom row is noted by a local historian as possibly being "what in the 1970s was called the 'fish market.' It

FIGURE 114. Appliquéd and pieced quilt, "Centennial Album,"
attributed to Minnie Burdick (1857–1951) of North Adams, c. 1876–
1880. Cotton (78½" × 79¼"). Collection of the Shelburne Museum,
Shelburne, Vermont (1987-040). *Photograph © Shelburne Museum,
Shelburne, Vermont.* MQ 4997.

appears to have been a dwelling in the 1890s."[7] Other outdoor scenes include a woman watching her child ride a bicycle (of the type used before the rear wheel drive was introduced in 1885), and a policeman patting a child on the head.

A final group of blocks featuring animals and flowers is rendered in a simpler, more generic style, suggesting the hand of a different quilter. In 1997, the Shelburne Museum attributed the quilt to "a member of the Burdick-Childs family" of North Adams.[8] More recently, former Shelburne curator Henry Joyce attributed the Centennial Album quilt to Minnie Burdick of North Adams, and noted that the "quilt remained in the Burdick-Childs family until shortly before its purchase by Shelburne Museum."[9]

A related quilt may provide a key to the Shelburne's Centennial quilt maker. In the collection of the International Quilt Study Center (IQSC) at the University of Nebraska, Lincoln, is a quilt made for (or by) Hattie Burdick, about 1890. The "Tile Quilt" (as it is known) is composed of forty-two blocks made in a dense, pieced and appliquéd crazy-quilt format. In the center of the quilt appears the name "HATTIE BURDICK," silhouetted with stitches. While the "Tile Quilt" shares little stylistically with the Shelburne Centennial quilt, a giraffe that appears in a block in the top row appears to have been cut from the same template as a giraffe on the Shelburne quilt, found in the second to last block of the bottom row.[10] IQSC records note that "according to dealer information," the "Tile Quilt" was "made by Annie Adams McKee, Elvira Mixer, Minnie Burdick, and/or for Hattie Burdick."[11]

Minnie Melissa Burdick was born on December 27, 1857, in New London, Connecticut, the daughter of Christopher Columbus Burdick and Harriet Amanda Beebe. Her younger sister, Hattie (Harriet) E. Burdick, was born on June 2, 1861. In 1877, Minnie married Herbert Dwight Childs (born 1857) in North Adams, where they lived at least through 1893.[12] Hattie, whose name appears on the "Tile Quilt," never married and is conjectured to have moved to North Adams to be near her older, married sister. Whether alone or with the assistance of family and friends, the designer of the "Centennial Album" quilt produced an endearing and enduring vision of American society—of its values and interests—in the late nineteenth-century.   —LW

IDA MAE DAVIS WOOD QUILT

(FIG. 115)

The "Rail Fence" (or "Roman Stripe") is a simple quilt block that requires only straight seams to join strips of fabrics; setting the blocks in alternating orientations, as in this example, achieves a basket-weave effect. Ida Mae Wood, however, spared no effort in making her rail fence an object of fashionable late-Victorian taste and beauty, as she ornamented the seams, edges, and sometimes the strips themselves with embroidery that shows off her repertoire of stitches. While not as elaborate as many crazy quilts of this period with their symbols and figures, this quilt shares with them a destiny not of service in keeping a body warm, but as an object of admiration—for the workmanship, the aesthetics, and the time devoted to its making.

Contemporary sociologist and economist Thorstein Veblen coined the term "conspicuous consumption" to describe the ostentation of the new American middle class; he bemoaned their lifestyle, especially the circumscribed role of women of leisure.[13] The crazy quilt is proof that the makers did not have to be sewing in order to serve the family's survival needs. Needlework, especially embroidery, had been a skill taught to young ladies in private schools of nineteenth-century America, but it became almost a competitive sport in the 1880s, the high point of the parlor, the most decorated room of the Victorian house. No surface was without ornaments, and draperies—whether hung at the windows and doors or just thrown over pieces of furniture—were considered essential parts of the ensemble.[14]

Ida Mae Davis, born into a well-established Pittsfield family, was the wife of William Porter Wood (1853–1917), who became a businessman there. They married in 1873 and had two daughters and two sons. Wood was born in England but came to Pitts-

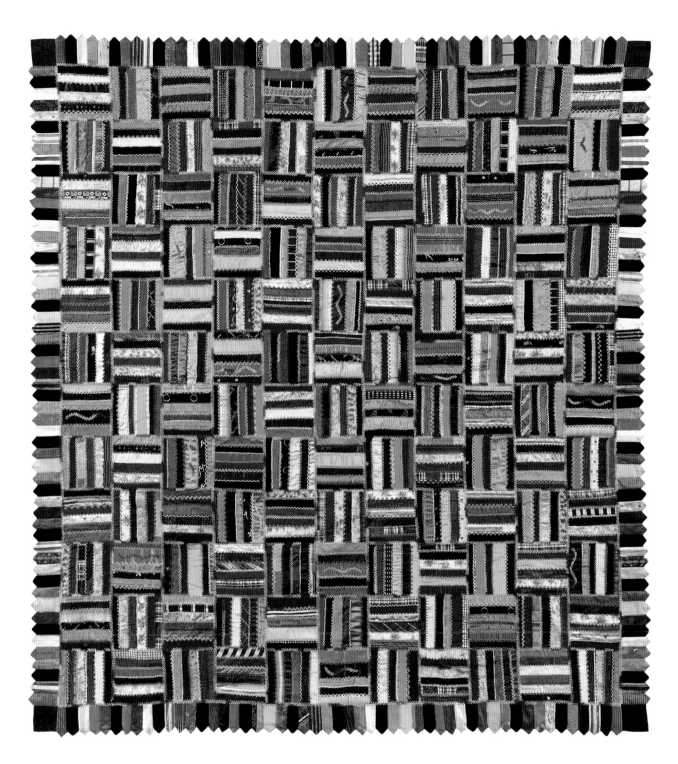

FIGURE 115. Pieced quilt, "Rail Fence," made by Ida Mae (Davis) Wood (b. 1855) of Pittsfield, c. 1890. Silk (59″ × 54 ½″). Collection of the Berkshire Museum, Pittsfield, Mass. (1993.5). *Photograph by David Stansbury.* MQ 2079.

field with his family as a child. One of his first positions as an adult was managing a sewing machine company, but after a few years, in 1882, he and his brother Joseph opened a music store, which is still in business over 125 years later as the Wood Brothers Music Company. They sold musical scores and instruments as well as made repairs.[15]

Every respectable Victorian parlor demanded a piano or organ. Before the turn of the twentieth century, most pianos were either horizontally strung, massive, square instruments, or the vertically strung new uprights. "Parlor" organs were pumped by the player's feet, with the sound being produced by air through reeds. William Wood also became a partner in the Wilcox & White Organ Company in Connecticut, makers of mechanical ("player") pianos and organs. All these keyboard instruments provided good surfaces for draping crazy quilts and other "dressing" for a tasteful room. Perhaps the "Rail Fence" quilt served this role in the Wood home.

Ida stitched her strips of silk to a foundation fabric, constructing a total of 132 blocks, each measuring about four and three-quarter inches square. She used a variety of embroidery stitches in varying colors to embellish the seam lines; a few of the strips also have a line of embroidery down their centers, and the seams where blocks were joined are similarly ornamented. The colors chosen for this top include the familiar black found in most crazy quilts, but also many strips that are bright peach and yellow-green. This contrast contributes to the woven effect of the quilt, achieved through the placement of the strips. Around the edge of the quilt, Ida set a border of the same strips perpendicular to the pieced blocks. This kind of border is now often called "piano keys," another nod to the musical connections of the Wood family. Ida finished the border strips with a point, stitched down to a foundation to achieve a smooth edge. The backing, which is attached to the top only at the edges, is brown sateen with a pink border on all sides about three inches wide. Ida did not use a filling.

The colors and combination of a simple block pattern with decorative stitching make this a visually striking example of late nineteenth-century

quiltmaking. Ida's quilt also provides a document of the social history of Massachusetts, symbolizing the rise of an urban upper middle class and the increasing leisure of women in that economic group, who could make quilts purely for decoration, not utility.

—MC

NORTH ADAMS LADIES AID SOCIETY QUILT
(FIG. 116)

Between 1890 and the end of the First World War, hand-embroidered outline motifs worked on plain white cotton (or occasionally linen) blocks became popular with quiltmakers. Red was the preferred color for the cotton embroidery floss, leading to the common descriptor "redwork" for this style of quilt. Sometimes incorporating a few fancier stitches for details along with the primary outline stitches, motifs included florals, animals, and human figures, complemented with names, dates, and phrases. These designs were readily available from commercial sources, sometimes pre-printed on fabric (see fig. 61/MQ 2312).

Redwork was also very popular in the late-Victorian and Edwardian era for signature quilts. In contrast to the mid-nineteenth-century signature or friendship quilts, these later quilts are more accurately considered as "names" pieces, because the embroidered writing generally does not follow the individual's unique signature; rather, it appears in a standardized cursive style. Redwork signature quilts often were undertaken as fund-raising projects by church, social, and charitable organizations— the Red Cross, for example, dominated the World War I period (see fig. 191/MQ 3239). For a contribution, a person's name was embroidered on the piece, often in a size or location that reflected the amount of the contribution. These "names" quilts promised a lasting memorial to the signers or those whom they wished to honor.

Records of the First Methodist Church Ladies Aid Society of North Adams note the decision to "have an autographed quilt to make a little money"

FIGURE 116. Signature quilt, blocks made by the Ladies Aid Society of the First Methodist Episcopal Church, North Adams, 1904, assembled 1982. Cotton (27" × 56½"). Collection of the First Methodist Episcopal Church, North Adams, Mass. *Photograph by Kevin Kennefick.* MQ 2417.

on May 4, 1904. In mid-September, the Society announced the "great success of the autographed quilt, quite a sum being realized and put in the bank where the men could not get hold of it."[16] The final amount earned was $260, but how the money was spent is unknown. Collecting money and names seems to have expended the energy of the organization, because they did not finish the quilt. These fifteen blocks were discovered in a box at the Historical Society in Jefferson, Maine, in 1981, their fate between the autumn of 1904 and 1981 unknown. (The North Adams First Methodist Church burned in 1927 and was rebuilt in 1929, probably contributing to the temporary misplacing of the blocks.) The Jefferson Historical Society returned the blocks to North Adams, and in 1982, women of the church assembled them with red lattice strips to match the embroidery and then quilted it. The finished piece was framed for display in the church.

The quilt is constructed of fourteen blocks that

North Adams was a center for the manufacture and especially the printing of textiles. Wool carding began in the early 1800s. The first cotton mill, which did carding and spinning, opened in 1810, and the first printworks began operations in 1829. In 1904 when these blocks were made, North Adams had been independent of the town of Adams for about thirty years and had a population of over twenty thousand. About two thousand hands were employed in at least four textile operations. The Arnold Printworks made calicoes and novelty panels for stuffed toys; the Windsor Printworks made cotton flannels as well as calico; Johnson's wove gingham; and the Blackinton mill, on the northeast side of town, wove woolens. The Hoosic River, with a narrow valley poorly suited to large-scale agriculture, provided the power for these mills. North Adams industry also included leather tanning and shoe manufacturing companies, along with an iron casting foundry that employed almost as many people as the textile works.

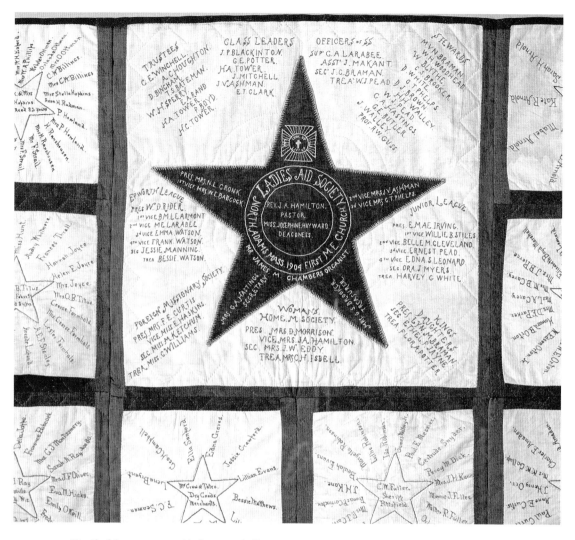

FIGURE 117. Detail of the center star with signatures in First Methodist Episcopal Church quilt. *Photograph by Kevin Kennefick.*

are each just under ten inches square, surrounding one larger block that measures nineteen by nineteen inches. This large block has a five-pointed red star appliquéd in the center. Embroidery on the red background is in gray floss; embroidery on off-white cotton is in red floss. On the red star is the crest of the Ladies Aid Society, the names and positions of all the officers of the group, the name of the church and town, the minister, and the organist. On the white background fabric of this block are the names of other organizations within the church and their officers. Each of the smaller fourteen blocks has a star with a name (an individual, a business, and in one case a date and location—perhaps a memorable outing connected with this project—"Block Island, July 1904"); radiating from the star are additional names arranged like the spokes of a wheel.

There are 366 names in total embroidered on these blocks. The names of families connected with the local textile mills are prominent. Half of the names on one block belong to various Arnolds, and Blackintons are also present. Albert C. Houghton, a trustee of the church, had been the first mayor of North Adams. Other local businessmen include the pharmacist Mr. Hastings, the grocer Mr. Bateman, as well as Mr. Brayton, the banker. Although the church ladies left their blocks to be finished by a later generation, their project tells a story of women's economic, social, and domestic history, as well as of the church and town.   —MC

Chapter 8

The Textile Industry

New England, and especially Massachusetts, became the epicenter of the Industrial Revolution in America in the early nineteenth century. The transformation of the Bay State's agrarian villages into industrial towns and cities owed much to the transatlantic movement of technology and skilled workers from Britain, which furnished Massachusetts with the means to start its own textile industry. None of it could have been achieved, however, without water power. Massachusetts' fast-running rivers and falls provided the vital source of power to turn water wheels, making it the ideal location for new factories.

COTTON INNOVATIONS

A bit of early industrial espionage combined with Yankee ingenuity set the revolution in motion. When well-to-do Boston merchant Francis Cabot Lowell (1774–1817) visited England in 1811, he toured a number of cotton mills in Manchester, the hub of the English textile industry. When viewing the impressive machinery, he was not allowed to take notes, but he recreated from memory what he had seen in the Manchester mills when he returned home to Massachusetts.

In 1813, Lowell formed the Waltham Company (later renamed the Boston Manufacturing Company) with his brother-in-law Patrick Tracy Jackson. A gifted mathematician, Lowell began to work out the figures needed to create his own power loom. With the help of local mechanic Paul Moody (1779–1831), the two men patented six new machines in two and a half years, including a power loom, warp-ing/dressing machines, a water wheel regulator, a double speeder, a dead spindle, and a throstle fitting frame, all necessary for fabricating cotton thread and fabric.[1]

Unlike the British mills (which parsed out the varied tasks of cotton production to separate establishments), Lowell envisioned his factory performing all functions, from making cotton thread to weaving cotton cloth, in one building. His first mill, built along the Charles River in Waltham, was the first mill in the world to combine all processes of cotton manufacture under one roof, and in 1816 he produced 1,242 yards of cotton cloth.[2]

Buoyed by the success of the Waltham factory, Lowell and Jackson expanded their operations to the Pawtucket Falls in Chelmsford. Under the guidance of Kirk Boott (1790–1817), who supervised all the mill enterprises, land and water rights were quickly purchased, followed by the construction of canals and mill buildings. In 1821, the Merrimack Manufacturing Company was established and the town of Lowell, named after Francis Cabot Lowell, was incorporated.

As the home of the Hamilton Manufacturing Company (1825), Appleton Company (1828), Lowell Company (1828), Suffolk Tremont and Lawrence Company (1829), the Boott Mill (1835), and the Massachusetts Company (1839), along with a multitude of related textile interests, Lowell was the most important textile center in early nineteenth-century America.[3] Unlike the English mill system, which employed whole families including small children, the workforce in Lowell was made up almost entirely of young, unmarried women. The Lowell

FIGURE 118. *Wamsutta Mill*, by William Allen Wall, oil on canvas, c. 1850. The textile industry offered employment opportunities for thousands of New Englanders and immigrants in the nineteenth and early twentieth centuries. *Photograph courtesy of the New Bedford Whaling Museum, New Bedford, Mass.*

"mill girls" were the educated daughters of Yankee farmers recruited from the local countryside. As such, they needed to be protected and were housed in special purpose-built boardinghouses, under the watchful eyes of matron supervisors, paid by the mill owners. Women remained the key work force between 1830 and 1850, at which point the social experiment began to break down.

Between 1814 and 1850, cotton mills inspired by the Waltham-Lowell system sprang up all over Massachusetts. The mills in Fall River became one of the largest cotton manufacturing centers in America, only threatened in scale by the mills of neighboring New Bedford, specializing in fancy cotton stuffs. Other enterprises included the cotton works in Clinton and North Adams. By 1850, eighty-five thousand textile workers were producing cloth goods in excess of $68 million.[4] New immigrants, eager for work, began to pour into cotton manufacturing towns such as Lowell, irrevocably changing the makeup of the work force from the original native Yankee farm girls, to Irish, Portuguese, and French-Canadians.[5]

The large-scale manufacture of woolen cloth developed slightly later than that of cotton due to several key factors. The first hurdle to surmount was the quality of native wool. American sheep produced a poor grade of wool fleece suited only for coarse clothing and blankets. This dilemma was resolved by the cross-breeding of native sheep with strains from Europe, and in the early nineteenth century, farmers began importing Spanish merino, French Rambouillets, and English Southdown breeds. By the 1830s, the quality of wool had vastly improved.[6]

Industrialization also was hampered by the lack of suitable machinery. The first power looms had been devised for cotton, and were too severe on the more delicate wool yarns. Early manufacturers accommodated this problem by combining wool yarns with sturdy cotton (or linen) to form a stronger warp, woven with the wool weft. This middling grade product was known as "satinet."

Some of the early experiments in wool manufacture took place in Pittsfield, Massachusetts. Lemuel Pomeroy's weaving establishment was followed by the work of Arthur Schofield, who invented a new wool-carding machine. The Housatonic Mills in Pittsfield, incorporated in 1812, was another early establishment for early broadloom weaving, but was eclipsed by the Pontoosuc Woolen Mill, organized in 1826, which became one of the nation's largest woolen mills in the 1830s.

All wool power weaving required the invention of new machinery, and in 1840, British émigré William Crompton devised a new power loom with multiple harnesses that could weave wool in complex patterns.[7] By 1860, the manufacture of woolens had greatly expanded with over twelve hundred establishments, including carpet and worsted specialties. The Civil War, however, gave the greatest boost to the woolen industry, as civilian and military demand for woolen garments skyrocketed, and many cotton mills converted to wool mills.

One of the significant developments in the expanding wool industry was the increased importance of the worsted woolen industry. Worsted wools were the longer, straighter, more lustrous fi-

bers (as opposed to the short, crimped wools) that were used for fine suiting fabrics. Taste in fashions and the growth of the ready-to-wear clothing industry all contributed to the increased importance of this worsted wool production.

By the late nineteenth century, Lawrence had emerged as the worsted wool capital of the world. Like its neighbor, Lowell, it was the brainchild of Boston entrepreneurs, many who had stock interests in the Lowell cotton mills. The city, incorporated in 1847, bears the name of one of those entrepreneurs, Abbott Lawrence. Immigrants flocked to Lawrence to work in the mills, arriving from as far away as Russia, Italy, Syria, Quebec, Poland, Germany, and Britain. By this time, whole families were employed in the mills, and manned the fulling, carding, and power looms of the Bay State, Washington, Atlantic, Pacific, Everett, Pemberton, Lawrence, and Arlington mills. The American Woolen Company, alone, was comprised of thirty-six mills including the Ayer, Prospect, and Wood mills, and manufactured more than half of all the menswear worsted woolens produced in Lawrence by 1914.[8] Later, the Pacific Mills became the largest mill in the world. Its complex of buildings stretched over a mile long and included a worsted wool division, a cotton division, and the Pacific Print Works, selling products to more than fifty-nine countries worldwide.[9]

SILK INDUSTRY

By comparison, the silk industry was a more modest endeavor in Massachusetts. Early attempts focused on the raising of silk worms, *Bombyx mori*, and were undertaken by groups steeped in progressive, utopian ideology. After several unsuccessful efforts, sericulture was abandoned, and silk manufacturers shifted to importing raw silk from Asia, which later formed the basis of several highly successful industries specializing in the production of machine twist and sewing thread.

Samuel Whitmarsh (1800–1875) is credited as having made some of the earliest attempts at producing silk on a large scale in Massachusetts. In the early 1830s, he purchased Fort Hill in Northampton, planting mulberry trees and building mill buildings and coccooneries for silk worms. The mulberry tree mania of the 1830s collapsed under the weight of its investors' expectations for financial gain; by 1839, Whitmarsh was bankrupt. Nevertheless, other attempts at sericulture soon followed. In 1840, the Northampton Association for Education and Industry was established on the very land that Whitmarsh had developed. Founded on abolitionist principles (Lydia Maria Child was a member—see fig. 133/MQ 4961), this utopian community expanded its production of silk threads with modest success. Despite winning awards for its silk threads at several local fairs, the Northampton Association succumbed to internal struggles and disbanded in 1846.[10]

Out of their ruins, however, emerged former member, Samuel Hill, who started a new company called the Nonotuck Silk Company in 1855. Using new technology, Hill produced a new type of smooth, strong, three-ply silk thread, called "machine twist," from imported raw silk. This new thread could sustain the tension of Isaac Singer's newly improved sewing machine, and he soon became one of Nonotuck Silk Company's most devoted customers.

Nonotuck marketed its silk thread under the "Corticelli" brand name, capitalizing on the allure of European silk. It produced silk for sewing machines, buttonhole thread, knitting, crocheting, darning, embroidery, even dental floss and surgical thread. Nonotuck continued to thrive in the 1860s and 1870s. At the 1876 Centennial Exhibition in Philadelphia, Nonotuck hosted a large display, featuring not only its signature Corticelli threads, but also machines for throwing and finishing silk. By 1878, it had become the largest manufacturer of quality silk thread in the United States. So important was the Nonotuck Silk Company to the community of Northampton, the mill area was renamed Florence after the Italian city famous for its elegant silks.[11]

In 1900, the Nonotuck Silk Company was one of 483 silk manufacturers in America. In Massachusetts, other silk establishments focused on finishing, weaving, and dyeing silk threads. In the 1920s, Nonotuck's fortunes declined, and it eventually merged with Belding Brothers, the Connecticut

firm formed by three brothers who, ironically, had gotten their start in the silk industry by selling Nonotuck silk threads door to door.   —LW

LILLIAN HIMMELREICH DICK QUILT
(FIG. 119)

Lillian Himmelreich was born in Lawrence on December 7, 1886, to German immigrants Paul and Louise (Schuster) Himmelreich. When she was fourteen, Lillian and her family moved to Lowell; she resided there the remaining forty-three years of her life. In 1906, Lillian married Hugo P. Dick (1884–1963), also from Germany, and together they raised two sons. A woman of small stature (under five feet), Lillian was known for her energetic work as a homemaker—she was a wonderful cook, gardener, and quiltmaker. Hugo worked at the Merrimack Mills of Lowell, eventually becoming the head dyer.[12]

By 1821, the Boston Manufacturing Company (also known as the Boston Associates) began to purchase land in East Chelmsford where the Merrimack River and Pawtucket Falls offered the necessary power for their planned textile mill. Construction of the Merrimack Manufacturing Company began in 1822, the same year as its incorporation. On September 4, 1823, it began operation, bringing to fruition the hopes and dreams of its investors and visionaries.[13] They intended to transform the community into a textile industry giant. Kirk Boott, who learned his drafting skills while in military school, designed the town's layout. "As first agent of the Merrimack Company, he laid out streets, designed mills, oversaw their construction and established rules for workers."[14] In 1826, East Chelmsford was renamed in honor of Francis Cabot Lowell, the founder of the Boston Manufacturing Company.[15]

Located in the northwest corner of Lowell, the Merrimack Manufacturing Company incorporated the integrated process of cloth manufacturing begun earlier in Waltham. It enjoyed great success, and for approximately twenty-five years was the largest and

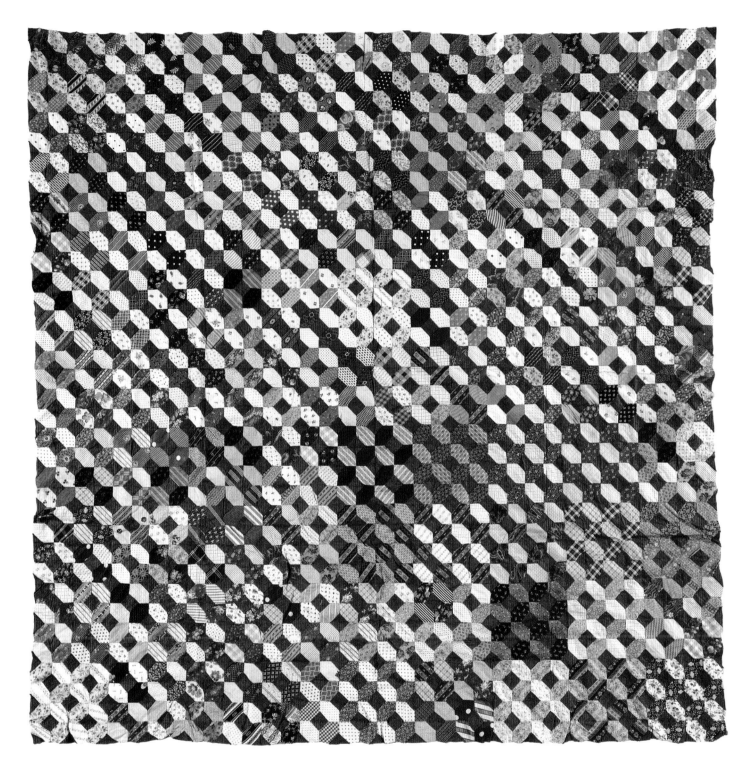

FIGURE 119. Pieced quilt top, "Old Fashioned Quilt" or "Ozark Tile
Pattern," made by Lillian (Himmelreich) Dick (1886–1957), Lowell, c.
1875–1900. Cotton (79" × 79"). Private collection. *Photograph by David
Stansbury.* MQ 4809.

FIGURE 120. Detail of calicoes in Lillian Dick quilt. *Photograph by David Stansbury.*

most profitable textile company in the country. In the 1890s, Merrimack Mills' production quotas were challenged by textile mills in Fall River, inspiring the Merrimack to change its product to "cut velvet cloth in rich midnight blues, deep maroons and lush dark greens."[16] The Merrimack, as well as other Lowell mills, found themselves plagued by stiff competition and employee strikes over wage issues. The Depression of the 1930s further contributed to the woes of the mills and the city; Merrimack Mills was sold, but the premature death of the new owner caused further problems for the troubled company.

Demand for goods remained low until the late 1930s, when the winds of war began to blow. The remaining mills in Lowell began to increase production to meet war needs, resulting in corporate profits, increased employment, and an improved standard of living for its workers. This proved to be a temporary situation, however, for as soon as World War II ended, so did the demand for goods produced in Lowell. The Merrimack Mills survived until the 1950s; a decade later, its buildings and accompanying boarding houses were razed to accommodate the construction of housing projects in misguided attempts at "urban renewal." As a result of the loss of these and other historic structures, a group of Lowell citizens developed a plan to revitalize Lowell by preserving its past and saving a number of the remaining mill buildings and boarding houses. Today, Lowell is a dynamic city, vigorous with museums, galleries, historic sites, festivals, and a variety of cultural activities.

This quilt top, in the "Old Fashioned Quilt" or "Ozark Tile" pattern, is one of several passed down through the maker's family.[17] It is striking in its geometric pattern and color selections. The fabrics came from a number of Lowell mills, including the Merrimack Mills and Hamilton Manufacturing Company.[18] Also included are fabrics printed at another New England mill, the Cocheco Manufacturing Company of Dover, New Hampshire.[19] The quilt top features several centennial prints, including white stars on royal or indigo blue grounds, and red and white striped fabric paired with an indigo and white print. Each of the 324 individual octagonal blocks measures four and a half inches. Lillian's design of the top is strongly graphic; the centers of solid red cotton are framed with dark fabrics on the diagonal from left to right, and light fabrics—mainly shirtings—from right to left. The work was completely hand stitched.

The Dicks both lived to see the closure of the Merrimack Mills, and Hugo may have lived to see the buildings removed. They were just two of the many thousands of people who lived and worked in Lowell, helping the city to play a key role in the Industrial Revolution.   —VLS

JESSIE GILLIES KENT QUILT
(FIG. 121)

Mention of the glamorous Art Deco style conjures images of architecture such as the Chrysler Building, or the elegant fashions of Erté.[20] The Art Deco movement of the 1920s and 1930s combined various contemporary artistic influences and updated old traditions with new colors or emphasis to celebrate the modernity of the early twentieth century. Textile designer Paul Poiret and artist Tamara de Lempicka epitomized the use of motif repetition, intense colors, and sharp black design emphasis.[21] Women who appliquéd brightly colored Sunbonnet Sues, parasols, or butterflies, and outlined them in black cotton thread, as Jessie Gillies Kent did with her butterfly quilt, also integrated Art Deco influences into their needlework, whether they realized it or not.

Jessie arranged her quilt design within a grid framework of bright "bubblegum" pink cotton; nine rows of seven blocks with printed cotton butterflies are stitched to a plain white cotton ground. Using the same template to cut her sixty-two butterflies,

Jessie incorporated forty-three different printed cottons into their wings, which she then outlined with black hem stitching. The butterflies on each half of the quilt and the middle row are turned toward the center block, which contains a flower motif.[22]

Born in Scotland in 1874, Jessie Gillies Kent likely immigrated to Lawrence to work in the booming textile industry. She produced not one, but two butterfly quilts during her life; a smaller crib quilt (using the same butterfly templates) features a yellow cotton grid and border. Both quilts descended through one of Jessie's daughters to its current owner, her granddaughter.[23]

One of the striking aspects of this quilt is the variety of printed cottons that appear in the butterflies. Only eighteen of the forty-three printed patterns are repeated in the quilt, and usually only twice. According to family tradition, the fabrics all came from the Pacific Print Works of Lawrence, where Jessie's husband, John L. Kent, worked for twenty years. As foreman of the engraving department at the Pacific Print Works from 1916 until his death in 1933, Kent had easy access to all the printed cotton fabrics, and likely brought them home for his wife. Most of the textile designs in the quilt are florals in small-repeat patterns and larger-scaled chintz furnishing fabrics; however, the quilt also contains examples of striped, paisley, and modernist designs in bold palettes.

The tremendous variety in fabric patterns, which were the responsibility of the engraving department, reflects the enormous scale of the Pacific Print Works operations. Built in 1911 on the site of a former print establishment, the Pacific Print Works (which also housed the bleaching department) was the third leg of the massive Pacific Mills complex that included separate cotton weaving and worsted-wool weaving divisions. In the early twentieth century, the Pacific Mills was physically the largest textile complex in the world, and one of the leading manufacturers and distributors of textiles, furnishing cloth to fifty-nine different countries worldwide.[24] In 1928, the Pacific Print Works could produce six and a half million yards of cloth per week with its fifty-one printing machines and eighty bleaching kiers. In the cotton division alone, the cloth was

FIGURE 121. Pieced and appliquéd quilt, "Butterflies," made by Jessie Gillies Kent (1874–1937) of Lawrence, c. 1930. Cotton (80" × 64"). Private collection. *Photograph by David Stansbury.* MQ 2006.

FIGURE 122. Engraving Department, Pacific Print Works, Lawrence, Mass. c. 1929–1930. *Photograph courtesy of Helen Glinos.*

used to make "women's dress fabrics, men's shirts, underwear, nightclothes, beachwear, aprons and smocks, negligees, children's dresses, household linens, uniforms, bags, caskets, men's habits, and ecclesiastical robes," among other products.[25]

This quilt is a charming product of the Art Deco style during the Depression era; it is also a symbol of the textile preeminence of the Pacific Mills of Lawrence, Massachusetts, in the early twentieth century. Pacific Mills' position would disappear within twenty years, as textile manufacturers—ever in search of workers who would labor for lower wages—moved out of New England and into the southeastern United States. —LW and DCA

SUSAN FLORENCE KINNEAR AND ESTHER EDNA KINNEAR QUILT

(FIG. 123)

Thousands of French- and English-speaking Canadians came to the Northeast during the nineteenth and early twentieth centuries to find work and begin a new life, many of them settling in Massachusetts textile mill communities, including Lowell, New Bedford, Lawrence, and Clinton.[26] Quiltmaker Susan Florence Kinnear and her husband, Samuel Kinnear (born c. 1838), migrated to Massachusetts from New Brunswick in 1887 with at least two of their children. Susan (recorded as Susannah in the 1900 census, Susanne in the 1910 census, and Susan in both the 1920 and 1930 census) was approximately twenty years younger than her husband, and widowed by the time of the 1930 census. According to these records, the couple had thirteen children, six of whom survived.

The Kinnear family initially settled in Clinton, on Woodlawn Street, where Samuel obtained employment as a dyer in one of the area mills. Two daughters were also mill workers—Bessie H., a winder, and Ida M., a carpet weaver. By 1910, additional children were recorded in the household, including Lillian (born 1891), Esther (born 1893), and William S. (born 1889). Between 1910 and 1920, Samuel and Susan moved to Ash Street in Clinton, and were joined by their daughter Esther and her husband Harold Card, another émigré from New Brunswick. Harold, employed as a cotton mill engineer, became the "head of household" by 1920, as recorded by the U.S. census.

Lancaster, Massachusetts, was a rural farming community until the Industrial Revolution secured itself on the banks of the Nashua River. In 1850, the factory village section of Lancaster, which produced combs, woven cottons, wool tweeds, and carpets, split off and became the town of Clinton. The Lancaster Mills had been incorporated six years earlier.[27] Its founders, inventor Erastus B. Bigelow and his industrialist brother Horatio N. Bigelow, were the major forces behind Clinton's transformation. Erastus Bigelow invented a loom to produce cotton check fabrics, which became a mainstay of the

FIGURE 123. Pieced quilt top, "Crown of Thorns" made by Susan
Florence Kinnear (1856–1939) and Esther Edna (Kinnear) Card (1893–
1970) of Clinton, c. 1915. Cotton (67" × 58½"). Private collection.
Photograph by David Stansbury. MQ 1882.

FIGURE 124. Detail of ginghams in the Susan and Esther Kinnear quilt. *Photograph by David Stansbury.*

Lancaster Mills.[28] Long known for his abilities as a "genius for mechanics," he previously had used his skills developing machinery in the Lowell mills.[29] In 1849, Erastus Bigelow's development of an improved carpet loom initiated the town's most famous product: Bigelow Carpets, which graced the White House, the House and Senate chambers, the SS *Titanic*, and famous hotels around the country.[30] By the time of Clinton's incorporation as a town, the Bigelow brothers' mills employed over seven hundred people and annually turned out approximately seven million yards of fabric and coachlace (a decorative woven tape used in upholstery).[31] The Lancaster Mill operations continued until approximately 1931.

Exactly which mill or mills employed members of the Kinnear and Card families is uncertain, although Esther's family reports that she worked at the Lancaster Mill for a short period of time after her marriage. Family tradition indicates that some

of the fabric in the quilt top came from that mill. Susan and Esther worked together to hand piece the top, using light and medium indigo blue, plus light and medium pink cotton solids in the forty-two blocks. Various shirtings contrast with the blue-and-white check fabrics believed to have been manufactured at the Lancaster Mill. Susan and Esther gave some attention to fabric pattern direction and placement, but in a number of places they incorporated non-matching pieces of fabric to complete the blocks, providing visual interest (whether intended or not) to an otherwise very regular design. The quilt remained unfinished until 2000, when Esther's daughter, Ruth Browchuk, completed it.

The mill town that the Kinnear and Card families knew was transformed again with the construction of the Wachusett Dam and Reservoir, beginning in 1901. This project dammed the south branch of the Nashua River in Clinton in order to supply Boston with water. As with the Quabbin Reservoir which would follow in thirty years (fig. 152/MQ 3041, fig. 153/MQ 3029, fig. 155/MQ 4244, and fig. 157/MQ 4233), the section of the town to be inundated had to be cleared and scraped clean. The Wachusett Dam is the largest hand-dug dam in the world, and its construction drew yet more immigrants to the area.

Although simple in appearance, this quilt illuminates the history of the Kinnear family, the industrial vision of two brothers, and the history of a town. For the quiltmakers' descendants, it is a tangible link to the past. —VLS

ZELIA LABADIE CHABOTTE QUILT
(FIG. 125)

Zelia LaBadie was born of French-Canadian parents, Clovis and Alphonsine H. LaBadie, who immigrated to Massachusetts in 1902 and settled in New Bedford. There, Zelia's father found employment as a picker in a textile mill. When Zelia and her brothers were old enough, they also went to work in a textile mill—Zelia as a spinner, Roland as a carpenter, and Dieudonner (Daniel) as a back boy.[32] At the age of twenty-five, Zelia married Alfred Chabotte of New Bedford, a native of Rhode Island with an American mother and Canadian father. Alfred was employed at a textile mill as a loom fixer, and Zelia by that time had become a web drawer.[33] According to family reports, at some point in her life, Zelia went to work for the Berkshire Hathaway Textile Mills.

The Berkshire Hathaway Textile Mills began as the Hathaway Manufacturing Company in 1888, a producer of cotton goods. The company prospered until just after World War I, at which time it experienced a decline in profits resulting from the drop in demand for goods no longer needed for the war effort. The company rallied after the Depression, continuing production for a short period of time until profits began to fall again. This resulted in a merger with the Berkshire Fine Spinning Associates

Inc. in the early 1950s. Under the corporate name of the Berkshire Hathaway Textile Mills, the organization ran for several more years, headquartered in New Bedford, until the late 1950s, when the return of declining profits resulted in the closure of plants throughout the area. In 1962, Warren Buffett purchased shares in the Berkshire Hathaway Company and turned it into an investment conglomerate. Today, the company exists as one of the most successful investment companies in the world.

Zelia's quilt is geometric in its design and has an unusual setting for log cabin blocks, creating a large X design in the center. Although one can argue the block setting is a variation of the "Barn Raising" pattern, the overall effect is unusual. Constructed from a variety of indigo blue prints and classic off-white print and striped shirtings, the contrast of colors adds to the graphic nature of this work. Each of the forty-eight blocks measures nine and one-half inches square, and the heavy hand quilting is executed in a "Baptist Fan" pattern with lines three-quarters of an inch apart. The quilt is backed with an off-white muslin, and bound with a straight-applied blue/black cotton print.

Zelia LaBadie Chabotte's story is one that has been repeated many times by French-Canadian émigré families. Seeking a better life and a new start, they came to the United States (and in particular to New England) to work in the mills. Life was very difficult for this ethnic group; the Irish and old-stock Yankees, in particular, discriminated against French-Canadians both socially and economically.[34] In spite of these difficulties, Zelia and other French-Canadians like her continued to work and live in this country. Zelia remained in the New Bedford area for the balance of her life. As a senior citizen, she lived in one of the renovated mill buildings, taking great pleasure in telling her relatives and friends that she was once employed in the same building. —VLS

FIGURE 125. Pieced quilt, "Log Cabin," "Barn Raising" variation, made by Zelia LaBadie Chabotte (1900–1988) of New Bedford, c. 1925. Cotton (92" × 82"). Private collection. *Photograph by David Stansbury.* MQ 2813.

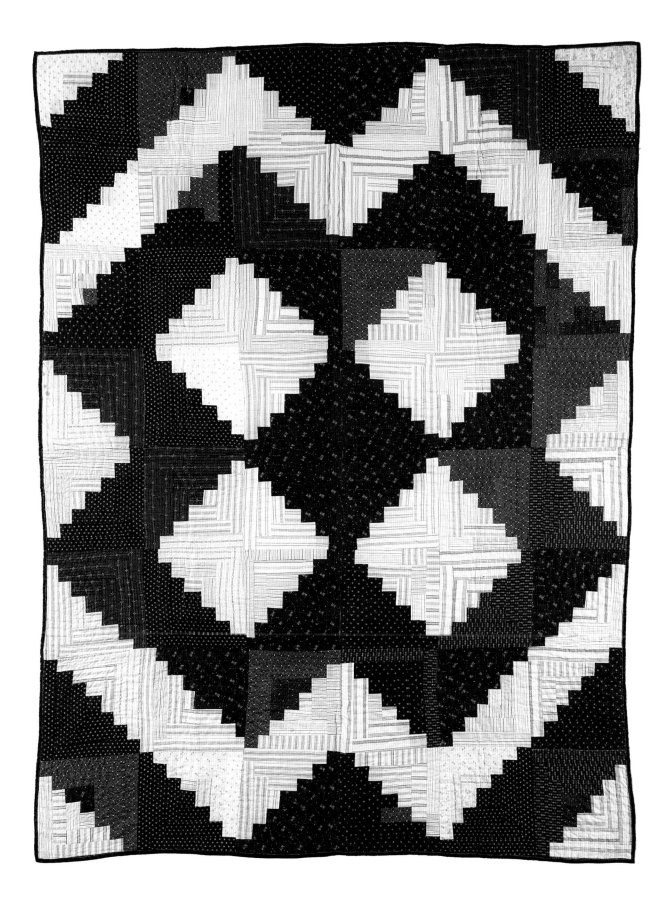

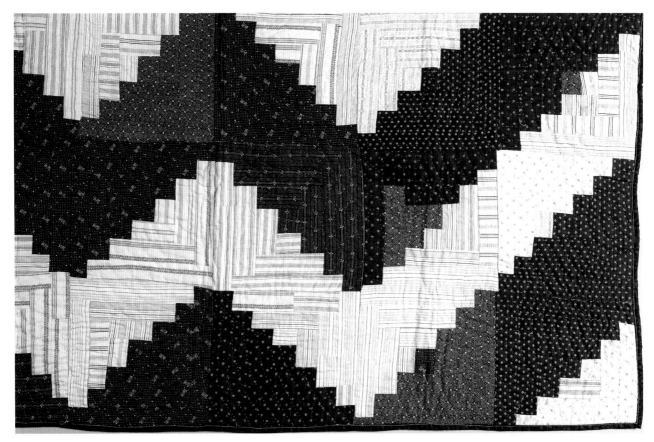

FIGURE 126. Detail of shirting fabrics in Zelia Chabotte quilt.
Photograph by David Stansbury.

MARY SPENCER RAMSDELL QUILT
(FIG. 127)

Mary Spencer was born and raised in Williams-ville, a village of West Stockbridge in Berk-shire County. Her father, Thomas Spencer, was a machinist. A teacher by training, Mary taught in Williamsville as well as Matanzas, Cuba. In 1873, she married Theodore G. Ramsdell (1833–1903), the superintendent, manager, majority stockholder, and vice president of Monument Mills in Housatonic.

Located along the Housatonic River, on the western slopes of the Berkshire Mountains, the vil-lage of Housatonic in Great Barrington was first oc-cupied by Mohican Indians migrating from upstate New York. They named the area "usi-a-di-en-uk" meaning "beyond the mountain place." The river's potential for industrial power was recognized early

in the nineteenth century. The village's first textile mill, Housatonic Mills, was replaced by the Monu-ment Mills after being destroyed by fire. Monument Mills specialized in cotton manufacturing and, by 1870, jacquard Marseilles bedspreads.[35] Theodore G. Ramsdell assumed ownership of the mill in 1886. The mill ran successfully until about 1950, attracting Polish and Italian immigrants for its labor force.

Theodore began work at the age of fourteen in a cotton mill in New Hampshire, advancing to over-seer in a spinning room by the age of sixteen. In 1864, at the age of thirty-one, Theodore moved to Housatonic to work in Monument Mills. Fam-ily history claims that Theodore and Mary met at the Housatonic Congregational Church; Theodore would walk Mary home from church services carry-ing her bible, a distance of several miles. The couple married on June 12, 1873, and had five children, all but the first surviving to adulthood. Male members

FIGURE 127. Pieced quilt, "Centennial Touching Stars," or "Stonewall Jackson," made by Mary (Spencer) Ramsdell (1841–1920) of Housatonic, c. 1876. (Cotton 99" × 88"). Private collection. *Photograph by David Stansbury.* MQ 86.

of the Ramsdell family went on to hold prominent places in the Monument Mills and the extended family chose professions in law, ministry, and medicine. The women "bore children, did good work, and made quilts."[36]

Family members believe that this visually striking quilt was inspired by the 1876 Centennial celebration of the United States. Ten star blocks, made from brown, red, off-white, and double pink solid and print cottons form the overall pattern. Diamonds of white cotton are formed between the stars, which connect at their points; the appearance of a hexagonal block is thus created. The center star, with differing fabrics from the other stars, is constructed with a center of white stars on a field of blue, surrounded by red and white alternating strips forming the larger star pattern. The approximately four-inch-wide border is also made of red, white, and blue solid cottons in diagonal strips. Adding to the beauty of the work, Mary finely quilted it with ten stitches per inch. The quilt is finished with a quarter-inch straight-applied binding, accented by a narrow red piping. The excellent workmanship indicates an experienced hand.

Mary Spencer Ramsdell, in additional to raising a family, was known for her charitable works through the Congregational Church in Housatonic. Theodore Ramsdell contributed further to the lives of Housatonic residents by requesting that his family donate $25,000 from his estate to establish a library. Opened in 1908, the library still bears the family name.[37] Today, the structures of the Monument Mills house a flourishing community of artists.

—VLS

ANNA CUSSON KANE QUILT
(FIG. 128)

Anna Cusson was born in North Adams on July 10, 1898. Her parents, Edmond and Emma Jane (Johnson) Cusson, came originally from Bouctouche, in Canada's New Brunswick province, and were of French-Canadian and American Indian heritage. Anna married Norman Kane (1898–1979) of New Bedford; there Norman worked as an electrician and Anna became a cloth inspector for the Wamsutta Textile Mills.

Wamsutta Mills, established in 1848 on the banks of the Acushnet River, was the first textile mill to succeed in New Bedford.[38] It took its name from Wamsutta, the leader of the Wampanoag Indian tribe, who participated in the first Thanksgiving and established early alliances with the English settlers of Plymouth Colony. For the mill's first twenty-five years, its economic importance was overshadowed by New Bedford's well-established whaling industry. Other towns and cities in Massachusetts, including Lowell and Fall River, already had established thriving textile industries, but it was an additional thirty years before New Bedford began to define itself as a manufacturing center for textiles, after the decline of the whaling industry, when local investors needed to find other business ventures.

Wamsutta Mills' growth continued into the next century in spite of the rise of competition from new textile mills that sprang up around it during the last quarter of the nineteenth century. With the development of the steam engine and its ability to increase horsepower, the Mills increased its size and output of goods. By 1900, forty-two textile mills had established themselves in New Bedford, drawn by the area's damp climate, which was conducive to fine spinning and weaving.[39] The Wamsutta Mills took advantage of these climatic conditions and produced fine percale sheeting, earning a reputation for quality goods.

Anna Kane's employment with the Wamsutta Mills gave her access to advertising literature, which she used as template papers for her "Grandmother's Flower Garden" quilt top. During the second quarter of the twentieth century, the hexagon shape found renewed popularity in a number of variations.[40] Its history as a popular early American and British piecing pattern made it a favorite of the twentieth century's Colonial Revival.

In mathematics, the hexagon is a geometrical figure where all six sides and interior angles are equal; inspiration for the artistic use of the hexagon design can be traced to nature, including the honeycomb and patterns on a turtle's shell. This tessellating pat-

FIGURE 128. Template-pieced quilt top, "Grandmother's Flower Garden," made by Anna (Cusson) Kane (1898–1985) of New Bedford, c. 1930. Cotton (92" × 82"). Private collection. *Photograph by David Stansbury.* MQ 2294.

tern is conducive to piecing and lent itself to the small and medium pastel floral and figured prints popular during the second quarter of the twentieth century. A variety of piecing methods were used, including the English paper-piecing or whip-stitch method.[41] This is the case with Anna's quilt top, assembled from over two thousand hexagons, each measuring one and one-quarter inches. Anna took great care in stitching her blocks together, beginning with a feedsack print center, surrounded by a Nile green solid, and finishing with a variety of prints and colors. She incorporated a soft pink cotton solid to connect the "flowers," extending to each edge. Many of the template papers are still in the top, especially around the edge.

Although little is known about Anna Kane's personal life, her workmanship speaks for itself. She had a skilled hand and fine color sense. The Wamsutta Mill, which left New Bedford in the mid-twentieth century and moved to Fort Mill, South Carolina, continues to enjoy a reputation for fine bed linens.

—VLS

CELESTINE BACHELLER QUILT
(FIG. 129)

Wyoma, a ward of Lynn, Massachusetts, sits surrounded by several large connected ponds that were the site of leisure activity, as well as the power source needed to run local manufactories. Wyoma's earliest settlers included members of the Bacheller family, who became so well established in the area by the eighteenth century that it was known as Bacheller Plains or Parrish. By the nineteenth century, new industries, including textile dyeing and printing, were established by the local residents, and the ward earned the title Dyehouse Village.[42] The Bacheller family became involved with the silk-dyeing trade in the early nineteenth century, when Jerry and Alfred Bacheller opened a dye works near one of the ponds.[43]

Alfred built his home across the street from the dye works at 395 Broadway in 1835, and his children probably spent many happy hours sailing in

the ponds and collecting the lilies that flourished in the waters.[44] Alfred and his wife Hannah Rowles had eight children. Two sons, Hartshorn and Lindley, followed their father into the silk trade and became finishers.[45] Their oldest daughter Celestine became a seamstress and used her talents to create a unique crazy quilt that depicted scenes from around Wyoma and Lynn.

The crazy-quilt format emerged during the third quarter of the nineteenth century. It was often referred to as "kaleidoscope" or "Japanese patchwork" because of the haphazard arrangement of the brightly colored silks, often embellished with elaborate embroidery.[46] This style of quilt design was fostered by the greater availability of a wide range of lushly dyed silk fabrics often used in dress goods and upholstery. It is tempting to think that a number of the silk swatches used by Celestine came from her father's dye works, but the colors and types of cloth used are very similar to those of other crazy quilts and probably date from the 1870s or 1880s, when crazy quilts were at the height of their popularity. By that time, Celestine, her mother, and her two younger sisters were living on Washington Street in Boston.[47] Alfred Bacheller lost his life in 1861. Caught up in the fervor that surrounded the conflict between North and South, he enlisted in the 38th Regiment of the Massachusetts Volunteers, and, sadly, was killed during the Battle of Baton Rouge. [48]After Alfred's death, it appears that his family fell on hard times. According to the 1880 census, Celestine worked as a seamstress while her younger sisters entered into domestic service to support themselves and their mother. In her spare time, Celestine must have made the crazy quilt, capturing happier times and her former life in Lynn.

While most crazy quilts are characterized by a seemingly haphazard arrangement of textile scraps, Celestine used the scraps to depict twelve scenes from Lynn and Wyoma, each contained in a sepa-

FIGURE 129. Foundation-pieced pictorial crazy quilt, made by Celestine Bacheller (1839–c. 1922) of Lynn, 1875–1900. Silk (74¼" × 57"). Collection of the Museum of Fine Arts, Boston; gift of Mr. and Mrs. Edward Healy in memory of Mrs. Charles O'Malley, 1963 (63.655). *Photograph © 2007 Museum of Fine Arts, Boston.* MQ 2491.

rate square. She included an image of her home on the corner of Broadway and Springvale (top row, middle scene), local residents boating in one of the ponds (top row, left scene), a girl collecting pond lilies and the willow trees planted at the foot of Flax Pond by her ancestor James Bacheller (third row, right scene).[49] Celestine used her sewing skills to create a masterwork of the quilter's art and a remembrance of life in Wyoma and Lynn during the middle of the nineteenth century.   —PP

Massachusetts and the Sewing Machine

The need for a workable sewing machine was rooted in both home and commercial venues.[50] The production of clothing and linens for the home was historically women's work, a skill passed from mothers to daughters. Sewing skills were essential in a successful household; as well as producing items for their own family members, many women produced clothing and linens for others in order to earn money.[51] Even very skilled needleworkers needed an immense amount of time to produce articles of clothing by hand: for example, about fourteen hours for a man's fine shirt and about six and one-half hours for a simple dress.[52] By the mid-1830s, due to advances in mechanized weaving and printing techniques, textiles for clothing became far more readily available and much less expensive.[53] Clearly a ready market existed for a practical sewing machine.

Although many versions of the sewing machine appeared as inventions before 1850, not all were manufactured for actual use. By 1831, Barthelemy Thimmonier, a French tailor, invented a chainstitch machine first intended for embroidery work, but later used it in a commercial operation for stitching army clothing. Several other developments in the 1830s and 1840s preceded the practical sewing machine: Walter Hunt's lockstitch machine; Edward Newton and Thomas Archbold's chainstitch machine for decorating gloves; John J. Greenough's straight-stitch machine for seaming leather work;

Benjamin W. Bean and James Rodgers' running-stitch machines; and George Corliss' two-needle machine for leather work. All either were not commercially produced or proved to be of very limited use.[54]

Elias Howe, Jr. (1819–1867), from a family of inventors, was born in Spencer, Massachusetts. At age sixteen, he apprenticed in a textile mill in Lowell, then in a precision machine shop in Cambridge, where he became interested in the problem of the sewing machine.[55] Howe patented the first sewing machine in 1846, incorporating several elements essential to a practical machine. His machine used an eye-pointed needle with thread supplied from a spool to make a lockstitch with the thread from a shuttle and a toothed wheel to move the cloth that was hung vertically on pins projecting from a baster plate. The machine had to be stopped and the cloth repositioned at the end of the pins in order to produce a long, continuous, straight seam. Howe, unable to get financial support for his invention in the United States, traveled to England and sold his English patent rights to William Thomas in 1849. Howe returned to the United States to discover that other inventors had worked on improving his ideas and were manufacturing their own machines, among them Isaac Merritt Singer.[56]

Singer, an itinerant actor and inventor of machines for drilling rock and carving wooden type, turned to the sewing machine after seeing the 1849 J. H. Blodgett and S. C. Lerow machine manufactured by Orson C. Phelps in Boston. With the financial backing of Phelps and George B. Zieber, Singer incorporated previous inventors' ideas, including the eye-pointed needle, the lockstitch shuttle, the yielding presser-foot and vertically reciprocating needle-bar to produce the "Perpendicular Action Sewing Machine" in late 1850. Singer added needle-thread control, an overhanging arm housing the needle-bar and needle-bar drive, facility to sew straight and curved seams, and an underneath feed wheel for continuous feed of the cloth.[57]

Massachusetts became the home of several major and some lesser sewing machine companies in the middle of the nineteenth century. Among them were, in Boston, the Grover & Baker Sewing Machine Company (champion of the chainstitch), the Finkle & Lyon Sewing Machine Company, and I.M. Singer & Company (which eventually moved to New York, and then to Elizabethport, New Jersey); in Orange, the Clark & Barker Company that first became A.F. Johnson & Company, and then the Gold Medal Sewing Machine Company, which later became the New Home Sewing Machine Company (which merged with the Free Sewing Machine Company in 1930 and was acquired by Janome in 1960); in Florence, the Florence Sewing Machine Company; and, in Chicopee Falls, the Shaw & Clark Company (running and chainstitch machines).[58]

Patent-infringement suits (primarily those initiated by Elias Howe) consumed the sewing machine industry in the 1850s. In 1856, the Sewing Machine Combination, a new model for the business world, combined the patents held by Elias Howe; Wheeler, Wilson, & Company; I. M. Singer Company; and Grover & Baker Company that covered the essential features of the sewing machine. The industry became stabilized and extremely profitable, especially for Elias Howe and the Singer Company.[59]

The sewing machine entered the homes of the United States very quickly in the 1850s. A major impetus for sales of machines to the home market was the hire-purchase plan for monthly installment buying, the idea of Singer's partner, Edward Clark, in 1856. Clark later also initiated the idea of the trade-in, allowing an old machine to be turned in for a fifty dollar credit toward the purchase of a new model, which resulted in a forty percent increase in machine sales for the Singer Company.[60] By 1860, a half-million sewing machines were in use in the United States, including those for domestic and commercial use. In New England, clothing factories had up to three thousand machines in use at a time. A pleated shirt that previously took ten to fourteen hours to complete by hand could be done in fifteen minutes with a machine.[61] It is not surprising that in July 1860, the editor of *Godey's Lady's Book* called the sewing machine, "The Queen of Inventions."[62]

—ABL

FIGURE 130. Chromolithograph trade card of the New Home Sewing Machine Company, Orange, Mass., c. 1880. *Courtesy of Lynne Z. Bassett.*

PART II

COMMUNITY

Chapter 9

Cooperative Quilting, 1770–1850

In 1802, Elizabeth Huntington admitted to her mother, Elizabeth Porter Phelps of Hadley, "I have a quilt or two to piece and I want your help extremely, it is a dull business for me alone."[1] For Elizabeth Huntington and many other Massachusetts women, helping hands and pleasant company greatly alleviated the tedium of a large quilting project.

Assistance with time-consuming and repetitive tasks was part of rural New England's tradition of cooperatively exchanged labor (or, as they called it, "changing works"), which often was combined with social activities such as conversation, eating, and dancing. Entries from the diaries of Massachusetts quilters record assistance from outside the quilter's household for the completion of all types of quilting projects, including bed quilts, petticoats, and quilted cloaks. The diaries make it clear that the entire process—beginning with spinning thread and carding bats, then weaving, dyeing, cutting and piecing fabric, putting the quilt into the frame, stitching, and finally finishing the edges—was most often the combined effort of two or more people in the eighteenth and early nineteenth centuries.

Bed quilts were finished with remarkable rapidity. Speed was desirable, for keeping the quilt laid out in its frame for an extended period of time in the already-cramped quarters of most New England homes was very inconvenient. Typically, a quilt was finished and out of the frame within two or three days. Perhaps a particularly complicated quilting design or too many interruptions caused Ruth Henshaw of Leicester to take an especially long time to finish a quilt in 1803. With some relief, she noted

on August 18 that "Aunt Wheeler B Honeywood quilted with us & we finished the bedquilt at dusk having been [in] the frame 18 days."[2]

In a partially fictionalized reminiscence of life in 1830s central Massachusetts, published in 1893, Francis Underwood described how the quilt itself was prepared before the guests arrived:

> When the patchwork was completed, it was laid upon the desired lining, with sheets of wadding between, and the combined edges were basted. Long bars of wood—the "quiltin' frame"—were placed at the four sides; the quilt was attached to the bars by stout thread, and the bars were fastened at the corners with listing [strips of cloth]; then the whole was raised upon the backs of chairs, one at each corner, to serve as trestles.[3]

Surviving quilting frames from the eighteenth and early nineteenth centuries hint at the congeniality of these parties. Frames with four equal sides such as Underwood depicted could accommodate the most quilters. With each side measuring nine or ten feet long, a dozen quilters could work together easily. However, accommodating so large a quilt frame, along with so many quilters, was another matter. "The quilting frame so nearly filled the sitting-room that there was little space behind the chairs," Underwood declared.[4] For women with smaller homes, a free-standing quilting frame with only two long sides, as seen in Lucy Cleveland's fabric sculpture, *The Quilting Bee*, was more suitable (see figure 131/MQ 5075). Six quilters might comfortably work with such an arrangement.

It was not unusual to plan a week of quilting in

order to complete several bed quilts or petticoats. The Westborough home of the Reverend Ebenezer Parkman was thrown into a flurry of activity with the marriage of each daughter, as he, his wife, friends, neighbors, and relations all assisted in gathering bed linens, furniture, and pots and pans to set up the new bride for housekeeping. At these times, Parkman (who preferred to have his "tabernacle at peace") had his studies interrupted for five or six days in a row by loquacious young women come to help with the quilting.[5]

"It rains so hard that the Young Women, Quilters, tarry all night," the Reverend Parkman noted in his diary in 1771.[6] In fact, friends invited to a quilting (or in some cases, the women hired to help quilt) often "tarried" overnight in order to finish the project. Generally, though, the quilters went home in the late afternoon or early evening, in time to have supper at home. Ruth Henshaw Bascom noted on an October day in 1809 that the weather was "very warm, till the shower at 5 oclock which made [a] wet walk for my quilters."[7] If necessary to complete the quilt, the ladies worked around the frame until 10 or 11 o'clock at night: "Old Mrs Scott & myself quilted all day P.M. had 6 assistants. . . . Finished the quilt at 10 evening," Ruth wrote in her diary on another autumn day in 1803.[8]

Informal afternoons spent stitching with two or three neighbors provided the most common type of quilting assistance. Cooperative quilting also sometimes came in the form of a large work party, called a "quilting" or "quilting party." (The term "quilting bee" was not used until late in the nineteenth century.) Ruth Henshaw noted in 1800 two quilting parties given by her family, the first of which was attended by "19 young ladies," while the second was enjoyed by thirteen neighborhood friends.[9] Invitations were given by word-of-mouth or, less often, by written invitation, a day or sometimes just a few hours in advance. "[B]rother Jos here & invited us to a quilting," Ruth noted the day before she attended her sister-in-law's quilting in 1803.[10]

Ruth tended to list in her diary the people who attended quiltings, both those she hosted and those at which she appeared as a guest. In the years before her first marriage in 1804 (which ended with the

death of her husband the following year), the same family names appear regularly—Wheeler, Lynde, Sergeant, Flint, Henshaw, and so forth. After Ruth married her second husband, the Reverend Ezekiel Bascom in 1806, she gave and received considerably more visits than she really preferred. No longer was every face around her quilting frame familiar. Many names listed in her diary after this period appear only once, and sometimes she didn't even know the guest well enough to know her name for certain: a "Polly or Molly" with an indecipherable last name attended one of Ruth's quiltings in 1809.[11] Despite her fatigue with the constant round of entertaining, Ruth understood the importance of these quilting parties in helping her husband to build relationships and maintain ties in the community.

An afternoon of quilting with the ladies sometimes was followed by an evening of games or music and dancing with men, but less frequently than is now generally thought.[12] In Shirley, Massachusetts, James Parker and his wife were very fond of frolics, as James notes attending more huskings, raisings, and quiltings than other diarists. In 1774, Mrs. Parker hosted a quilting with "about 20 Girls & about as many young men at Evening." Another quilt was stitched for the Parker family in 1780 and they celebrated with "a fine Dance at night [with] a Fiddle."[13] Ruth Henshaw also enjoyed the occasional frolic, dancing "till 12" to the fiddle music of "D. Ball" after a neighbor's quilting in 1802.[14]

Women who gathered together to quilt enjoyed the satisfaction of completing a project, as well as the opportunity to chat and exchange news. Indeed, the importance of even informal afternoon gatherings, like that of other types of cooperative work, went far beyond the need to complete a bed quilt or petticoat. Cooperative quilting strengthened the bonds among neighbors and relatives. The forlorn notation of spinster Rebecca Dickinson of Hatfield underscores the significance of these social interactions in the lives of women: ". . . yersterday was at brother bilings quilted of a Pink Silk Quilt [petticoat] for Polly church there was Lindy murry there Eunis White in the afternoon come the wife of joseph Dickinson the wife of Rufus Smith tha both quilted in the Silk quilt how lonesome to Come to this old hous after So much Company."[15] For lonely widows and spinsters, busy mothers, excited young women about to be married, frazzled ministers' wives, and exhausted farmwives, the hours spent at the quilting frame with female relatives, friends, and neighbors offered a welcome variation in their routine.

As nineteenth-century industrialization forced massive economic and social change and transformed New England communities, the practice of cooperative quilting declined.[16] Diaries indicate that beginning early in the century, fewer women gathered with their neighbors to quilt, and with increasing frequency through the century, they quilted alone. Nostalgia for a time supposedly free of social tension began to infuse the memory of quiltings by the 1840s. Conveniently forgetful of the sometimes raucous character of cooperative work parties, local historian George Davis used a rose-colored description of an old-fashioned quilting party to point out the superiority of our ancestors in his 1856 history of Sturbridge and Southbridge, Massachusetts:

> It must be borne in mind, that our ancestors always connected something profitable with their recreations. This was especially the case in reference to the old-fashioned Quiltings. . . . if the reader could travel back nearly a century, and desire to witness a group of healthy, blooming, rotund, and cheerful countenances, he might be gratified with such a scene as [a quilting] . . . presented. . . . Would you witness beauty unadorned there it might be seen. Would you see an exhibition of plain hospitality, unaffected civility, and cheerfulness, without extravagance in any of its modern forms, go back to those days of primitive simplicity.[17]

Eighteenth-century quilters, who understood the role of cooperative work parties in developing important social networks and establishing family and business alliances, would not have recognized such "primitive simplicity" in themselves.[18] Such romantic notions as promoted by George Davis gained popularity with the Centennial celebration of 1876, and continued to infuse the interpretation of American quilts and quilting for another hundred years.

—LZB

LUCY CLEVELAND FABRIC SCULPTURE

(FIG. 131)

In the mid-nineteenth century, an image of women quilting suggested more than the production of a domestic textile. At a time when Americans were increasingly affected by industrialization and urbanization, this image projected an idealized sense of community, cooperative labor, and a romanticized view of the past.

Lucy Cleveland's *The Quilting Bee* is a rare three-dimensional depiction of nineteenth-century quilting, especially because it is made primarily of textiles. Born in Salem, Lucy Hiller (Lambert) Cleveland was the daughter of a silversmith and the wife of a merchant and sea captain involved in the international maritime trade with China and the East Indies.[19] She was also a children's book author and a textile artist. Cleveland's family and friends preserved a sizeable body of work and primary source documentation that provides deeper insight into her life and work than is available for many women of that time.

Cleveland fabricated "figures of rags" or textile and mixed-media vignettes that portray domestic, social, and political themes. She exhibited them at charitable fairs to raise money for causes that she supported. These included the relief of impoverished female garment workers and the abolition of slavery. Although doll vignettes and other figural constructions were popular with women in the nineteenth century, Cleveland's work is significant in that approximately a dozen works attributed to her survive in the Peabody Essex Museum's collection.

The Quilting Bee is unusual among Cleveland's works in that it is smaller in scale and less intricately fashioned than other vignettes. In the other known examples, Cleveland meticulously created individual identities for her figures through the selection of textiles, the types of clothing, and by sculpting poses and gestures that signified the role of each person within a story. Cleveland appears to have drawn inspiration for her subject matter from prints and book and magazine illustrations of the day. An illustration entitled "New England Kitchen: A Quilting

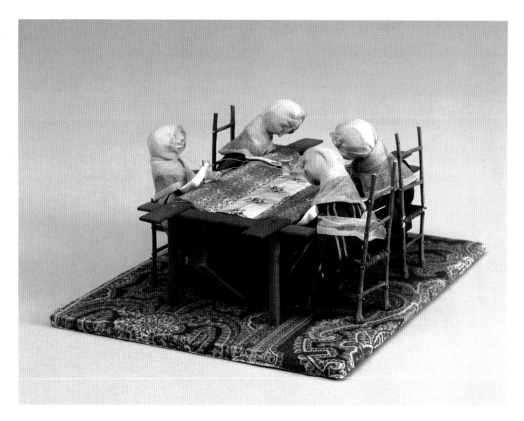

FIGURE 131. *The Quilting Bee*, sculpture made by Lucy Cleveland (1780–1866) of Salem, circa 1850–1865. Cotton, silk, linen, wool, paper, metal, wood, and hickory nuts (4½" × 9¼" × 7¼"). Collection of the Peabody Essex Museum, Salem, Mass., gift of Amey Willson, 1937 (122891). *Photograph courtesy of the Peabody Essex Museum.* MQ 5075.

Party" from Frank B. Goodrich's *The Tribute Book: A Record of the Munificence, Self-Sacrifice and Patriotism of the American People During the War for Union* (New York: Derby & Miller, 1865) depicts a scene of older women in white caps and collars that resembles this sculpture's composition.

Seated at a free-standing quilting frame with two long sides, four women bend over a quilt of printed

FIGURE 132. Lucy Cleveland, c. 1860. *Photograph courtesy of the Peabody Essex Museum.*

striped cotton fabric with an appliquéd center panel of floral sprigs on a white ground. A unique feature of *The Quilting Bee* is the use of hickory nut heads on the figures instead of the carefully modeled faces of kid leather or tinted silk crepe that Cleveland used in most vignettes. Each quilter wears a similar white fichu and cap over a dark silk dress, which creates a sense of uniformity and anonymity. Perhaps unintentionally, Cleveland's vignette draws attention to how collaborative creativity and cooperative labor obscured women's individual identities and contributions to communal activities such as quiltmaking in the nineteenth century. By practicing the virtues of modesty and self-effacement, women placed more value on the quilt itself and the good purposes for which they made it than in the recognition of individual achievement. While Cleveland's *The Quilting Bee* is an interesting depiction of quiltmaking in New England during the nineteenth century, it also can be viewed as commentary on the efforts and accomplishments of generations of anonymous women to the history of quilt-making in America.   —PBR

Chapter 10

Anti-Slavery Quilts

Women's participation in social reform movements during the first half of the nineteenth century was manifested in large part in the North as opposition to slavery. Antebellum society idealized the domestic role of women while denying them formal participation in political activities; however, women were accustomed to playing active roles as church members, having been encouraged to be "spiritual guardians of the household" and to carry the message of salvation to their families since at least the Great Awakening in the eighteenth century.[1] This religious energy extended to altruistic targets outside the home, particularly missions (both foreign and local), and included concern for the well-being of women in their communities. This "benevolence empire" is traced to the end of the eighteenth century when societies for the relief of women and children began to appear.[2] It flowered in the 1820s with temperance, anti-prostitution, and Sunday School movements, and then developed into the anti-slavery movement around 1830.[3] At the same time, education for women expanded through schools run by the Quakers (see fig. 135/MQ 2028) and seminaries founded by Emma Willard and Mary Lyon (see fig. 196/MQ 3518).

While sentiments against slavery were strong among such northern groups as the Quakers and free Blacks, there was not agreement on how to end it—total abolition by law, expatriation to Africa, voluntary freeing by owners—or who should be involved in the movement and how. The place of women in the discussion was a sore issue, in part because it raised questions of propriety, but also be-

cause significant women involved in the anti-slavery movement associated it with other issues such as property rights, suffrage, and temperance, which they saw as philosophically related to ending slavery.[4] This inclusive message was given by Lucy Stone of West Brookfield, Massachusetts, in 1847 when she pledged: "I expect to plead not for the slave only, but for suffering humanity everywhere. *Especially do I mean to labor for the elevation of my sex*."[5] The internal controversies of the anti-slavery advocates were often as challenging to the movement as the external opposition.[6]

When Massachusetts native William Lloyd Garrison published an anti-slavery poem by "a female" in his paper *The Liberator* in 1831, women's visibility in the movement became unmistakable. The next year he established a "Ladies Department" in the paper, which included discussion of how women could contribute to the movement. The suggestions still sound familiar to grassroots organizers: boycotts of slave-produced goods, intentional patronizing of businesses run by African Americans, and using "free produce" certified as not involving slave labor. Historian Julie Roy Jeffrey points out the appropriateness of such actions as in keeping with the nineteenth-century view of women as "unselfish, practiced in self-denial, and morally insightful."[7]

More direct actions suggested to women were public speaking and the circulation of petitions, especially as methods to be used in gender-segregated meetings and organizations sympathetic with the anti-slavery movement. Many churches lent their support to the anti-slavery movement, providing both space for meetings and general sanction to the cause, again in keeping with the view of women's "spiritual nature" (see fig. 202/MQ 3092). Pledging oneself to this movement sometimes resembled testifying to a religious conversion.[8]

Recruiting adherents was certainly an achievement, but women's ability to raise money was perhaps even more valued. Money was needed to pay for travel expenses as speakers fanned out across New England and west into the free states to spread the message. Before mass communications and speedy mail delivery, oratory was a major source of inspiration, and lectures drew large crowds, even in small towns. The fundraising fair was a major intersection of quilts, the anti-slavery movement, and women's traditional support for missionary endeavors. Women themselves frequently lacked independent incomes, inheritances, or other access to cash, but they had learned how to get others to contribute.[9]

The first anti-slavery fairs were the successors to other benevolent societies' efforts to raise funds for missions and domestic charities. By the time the anti-slavery societies became major fair sponsors in the mid-1830s, fairs already had a mixed reputation—acknowledged sources of money for causes, but somewhat arch rituals of young women exploiting the pocketbooks of potential suitors. The split between the radical (legal abolition) and evangelical (individual moral suasion) wings of the movement in the 1840s also detracted from the fairs' earning potential, but their popularity and success was undeniable.

Antebellum fairs typically were held in crowded, lavishly decorated halls, and offered food and objects for sale, in addition to fortune telling and auctions to benefit the cause. Even the more modest versions of these events, held in small towns or by less affluent groups than the urban societies, aimed at the appearance of plenty and generosity.[10] Quilts as well as such handmade items as potholders, penwipers, and needlebooks were among the goods offered. Many of these carried anti-slavery sentiments, such as the quilt Lydia Maria Child made and donated to a fair in the mid-1830s (fig. 133/MQ 4961). The amount raised by one of these fairs could be as much as $5,000.[11] Fairs continued up to and during the Civil

War to benefit the anti-slavery societies and later the United States Sanitary Commission (a forerunner to the Red Cross), which supplied Union soldiers and their families with needed goods and funds.

The connection of quilts with opposition to slavery has been suggested by a number of people as a force in the Underground Railroad.[12] Quilt historian Barbara Brackman, among others, has pointed out the lack of documentation of the use of quilts as signs to runaway slaves, but people whose houses sheltered the escapees on their way to safety certainly made and used quilts on their beds.[13]

Other quilts directly associated with the anti-slavery movement that were listed by the Massachusetts Quilt Documentation Project include a signature quilt made in Hingham (MQ 5012, not included in this book) and the quilt associated with Abby Kelley Foster, a veritable collection of tracts denouncing slavery (fig. 135/MQ 2028). In addition, the quilts attributed to Abigail May Alcott are pieces constructed during the antebellum period by a family dedicated to abolition (fig. 33/MQ 4692, fig. 35/MQ 4697).

While these quilts serve as examples of women's contributions to the anti-slavery movement, it is the movement itself that offered a stepping stone for women to enter political life and have a larger role in deciding their own fates. The quilts helped to support this revolution, which eventually transformed into the woman suffrage movement and the campaign for civil rights.   —MC

LYDIA MARIA CHILD QUILT
(FIG. 133)

Lydia Maria Child is credited as the maker of this small quilt. It was among the items sold at the fundraising Anti-Slavery Fair held in Boston on December 22, 1836. Hand sewn and hand quilted, the quilt incorporates a mix of white background fabrics and scraps of several calico prints. There are sixty-three pieced star blocks set side by side in nine horizontal and seven vertical rows. The central block has a poem, usually attributed to the Quaker poet Eliza-

FIGURE 133. Pieced cradle quilt, "Sawtooth Star," attributed to Lydia Maria Child (1802–1880) of Boston, 1836. Cotton (45½" × 36"). Collection of Historic New England, gift of Mrs. Edward M. Harris (1923.597). *Photograph by Peter Harholdt, courtesy of Historic New England (digital ID 000224).* MQ 4961.

Mother! when around your child
You clasp your arms in love,
And when with grateful joy you raise
Your eyes to God above,—
Think of the negro mother, when
Her child is torn away,
Sold for a little slave—oh then
For that poor mother pray!

FIGURE 134. Detail, inscription on the Lydia Maria Child cradle quilt. *Photograph by Peter Harholdt, courtesy of Historic New England (Digital ID 0000984).*

beth Margaret Chandler (1807–1834), handwritten in ink:

> Mother, when around your child
> You clasp your arms in love,
> And when with grateful joy you raise
> Your eyes to God above—
> Think of the negro-mother, When
> Her child is torn away,
> Sold for a little slave—oh then
> For that poor mother pray!

Anti-slavery fairs began in the 1830s and continued until the Civil War, their place taken then by the Sanitary Commission Fairs. The Anti-Slavery Fairs sold handicrafts and other objects often decorated with abolitionist mottoes and images to support the cause. In a letter dated January 1837, now in the collection of Brown University, Child reported "My cradle-quilt sold for $5.00." It was purchased by Francis Jackson for his recently married daughter, who was an active member of the Boston Female Anti-Slavery Society.[14]

Lydia Maria Child was the youngest of seven children born to Convers Francis and Susannah (Rand) Francis of Medford. Encouraged by an older brother, Lydia read extensively and educated herself in world religions. Throughout her life, she explored the doctrines of various religions, but was never quite satisfied with any of them, feeling she was left with too many questions. Her inquiring, open mind also gave her sympathy for Native Americans, reflected in her first novel, *Hobomok: A Tale of Early Times*, published in 1824. The popularity of *Hobomok*, the first American historical novel, led Child to write more books and articles; in 1827 she took the position of editor of *The Juvenile Miscellany*, one of the first children's magazines ever published.

In 1828, Lydia married David Lee Child, who shared Lydia's idealism but, unfortunately, not her competence. Throughout their marriage, it was Lydia's writing that supported them financially and covered the debts incurred by David's impractical projects. After William Lloyd Garrison began publication of *The Liberator* in 1831, David and Lydia Child became active in the abolitionist movement.

Along with other followers of Garrison, they joined the Northampton Association for Education and Industry, a utopian community active from 1842 to 1846 (see chap. 8). The Association's primary goal was to undercut the slave economy of the South by cultivating silk to replace cotton. Despite the good intentions of its participants, including ex-slave and abolitionist Sojourner Truth, the utopian experiment was a failure.

Her own straitened circumstances led Lydia to write her most popular book, *The Frugal Housewife* (1829, later retitled *The American Frugal Housewife*), which gave recipes and suggestions for running a home efficiently. Though childless herself, she also had great success with *The Mother's Book* (1831) and her writings for children. All of her publications project a "democratic humanitarianism" that goes well beyond a guide for taking care of babies and children, and serve as a precursor to her political writings on issues of slavery and the treatment of Native Americans.[15] Lydia became a regular contributor to William Lloyd Garrison's paper *The Liberator* and similar abolitionist publications. While her novels, poems, and articles were very well known in her own day, 150 years later, only one of Lydia Maria Child's poems remains in the American consciousness: "Over the river and through the wood to grandfather's house we go. . . ."[16] Her militant stand on abolition lost her some fans of her domestic writing and her position as editor of *The Juvenile Miscellany*, but that did not unnerve her. Lydia Maria Child's political ideals were present in all her books—and in this quilt.   —MC

QUILT ASSOCIATED WITH ABBY KELLEY FOSTER
(FIG. 135)

No records can be located regarding this quilt's maker or its acquisition by the Worcester Historical Museum, but tradition connects it with Abby Kelley Foster, a prominent figure and popular speaker in the abolition movement. It may have been made for a fundraising anti-slavery fair.

FIGURE 135. Pieced signature quilt, "LeMoyne Star and Diamond in the Square," associated with Abby Kelley Foster (1811–1887), unknown maker, c. 1845. Cotton (84" × 79"). Collection of the Worcester Historical Museum, Worcester, Mass. *Photograph by David Stansbury.* MQ 2028

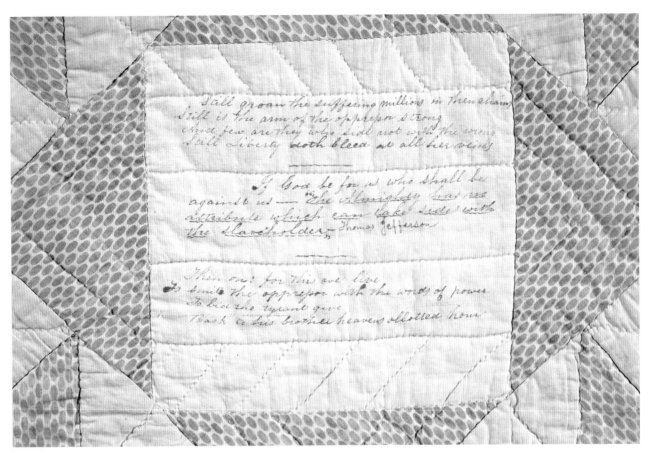

FIGURE 136. Detail, inscription on the Abby Kelly Foster signature quilt. *Photograph by David Stansbury.*

Over its life, the quilt has faded and yellowed, but its original colors were probably off-white and rose. The rose-colored calico is a closely spaced lozenge print on a light background. The quilt alternates blocks of the eight-pointed "LeMoyne Star" with "Diamond in the Square" blocks. Set on point, the latter provide eighteen blank spaces, each almost eight inches square, for inked messages such as: "Though distant be the hour, yet come it must. Oh hasten it in mercy gracious Heaven! When freedom—precious freedom shall be given to every race, complexion, caste and clime." In contrast with the almost prim design of the top, the sentiments written on the top are radical denunciations of slavery, including biblical references, and quotations from reformer Dr. Charles Follen and Thomas Jefferson. There is also a message that hints at the connection to fundraising fairs, possibly the source of this quilt:

Dedicated to the cause by a few friends in Everettville, Princeton, Mass. While ye are sleeping on your beds of down covered with quilts and costly tapestry, many a slave lies on the cold damp ground, covered with naught but Heaven's broad canopy. Remember the Massachusetts Anti Slavery Fair.

Made in a four-poster shape, the quilt was intended for use on a bed, but it seems that only the clearest of consciences could slumber under it without feeling that sleep was a luxury when more must be done to rid the world of slavery.

Abby Kelley was born in Pelham, in western Massachusetts, but her family moved while she was a baby to the Worcester area, where she spent most of her life. Her education was accomplished largely in a Quaker boarding school in Providence, Rhode Island, where girls were taught the same subjects as the boys but in separate classrooms. In 1836, she went to teach at a Quaker school in Lynn, where she was introduced to the organized abolition movement.

Although she had heard William Lloyd Garrison speak while she was still in Worcester, it was in Lynn that Abby Kelley joined the local, largely Quaker, Female Anti-Slavery Society. This group was already busy in the mid-1830s sewing articles for sale at the local and Boston fairs and circulating petitions condemning slavery. After her father's death, when she was twenty-six, Abby seems to have emerged from her grief even more committed to abolition, and she spent less time at teaching in order to raise funds for the cause, including contributing much of her inheritance.[17]

Abby reluctantly left the Society of Friends in 1841 in frustration over their position of "moral suasion" or individual choice in freeing slaves, as well as practices within some meetings that kept Blacks segregated.[18] Her commitment to abolition was by this time making her a very popular speaker on the abolition circuit, and she often spoke on programs with Frederick Douglass, William Lloyd Garrison, and Wendell Phillips, as well as speaking and traveling alone. Speaking tours took her through most of the Northeast and to Ohio. It was at this time that she became friendly with Stephen S. Foster (1809–

1881), another abolitionist speaker, whom she married in 1845.

Their daughter, Paulina Wright Foster (called "Alla"), was born in 1847, a few months after they settled on a farm in the Worcester area that would be their home for the rest of their lives.[19] Abby and Stephen both continued to speak in favor of abolition, but during the 1850s the movement became quarrelsome. Different factions were stubborn about their pet issues, ranging from women's rights to the Republican Party and its candidates, to John Brown's attack at Harper's Ferry. It was increasingly difficult to raise the sums of money needed to maintain the speaking tours. As the outbreak of the Civil War approached, many personal as well as political battles raged within the movement; by the end of the war, abolitionist newspapers—such as Garrison's *Liberator*, the *Anti-Slavery Bugle*, *North Star*, and *Freedom*—which had stirred so many to support the cause, had ceased to publish.

After the war, the Fosters continued to be political activists, including refusing to pay taxes on their farm as a protest against women's lack of the vote. By the 1870s, however, many of the people who had led the fight for abolition were dying. Other reform causes, especially women's rights, inherited both the fervor and controversy that had fueled this movement.   —MC

Chapter 11

Agricultural Fairs and Quilts

The quilts in this section all appeared at Bay State agricultural fairs during the nineteenth and twentieth centuries. The first agricultural fair in the United States convened in Pittsfield, Massachusetts, in 1810. The brainchild of Elkanah Watson, the Berkshire Agricultural Society and similar organizations offered a practical means of education for local farmers.[1]

Watson's inspiration partially came from reading reports of Boston's Massachusetts Society for Promoting Agriculture (MSPA), which was chartered in 1792 and catered to the city's elite gentleman farmers. Watson wanted to find a more practical means to assist the smaller local farmers in his part of the state. In turn, the MSPA soon followed Watson's lead and held their first fair in 1816. They were the first to add a plowing match to a fair's schedule, which increased interest and drew larger crowds.[2]

While Watson's aims were educational and practical, he also realized that he needed to have a social element to maintain interest. To increase participation, the 1811 fair was bigger and grander with a parade and awards for the best entries. By 1813, the Berkshire Agricultural Fair included an "Agricultural Ball" and invited women to compete for prizes with their textiles. At first, according to Watson, the local women were hesitant to enter because he required the winners to claim their prizes in person and none wanted to be the first recognized in this way. However, with the encouragement of Watson's wife, female Pittsfield neighbors started to turn out for the fair, to enter their work, and to claim their prizes.[3]

By 1860, there were over seven hundred county and local agricultural societies in the north and the west of the United States, most modeled on Watson's "Berkshire Plan."[4] Although initially shy to participate, women quickly took a more visible role by assisting with decorating the display areas and entering fancy work and various types of foodstuffs in the competitions. Agricultural fairs offered women a socially acceptable means of achieving recognition for their work, allowing them to build self-esteem and make a contribution to their community. As historian Linda Borish observed, "While many farmers criticized and underappreciated farm women's labors at home, when women showed these labors for all to see in public, suddenly, her skills became acclaimed and she held some cultural power."[5] As mechanized industrialization spread across the state during the mid- and late-1800s, the displays of "domestic manufactures" at the annual agricultural fair offered a touchstone for residents who were anxious about the changes. The exhibition of quilts and other handmade needlework was reassuring to men and women alike, allowing them to preserve connections with their mothers and grandmothers—and with what was quickly becoming a romanticized view of pre-industrial American life.[6]

While women overcame their reticence to compete for prizes, they still rarely participated on the judging committees for the fancywork categories. The male judges, without personal experience of the skills involved, were drawn to examples completed by the very old and the very young, or those quilts comprised of thousands of tiny pieces. Local newspaper accounts are full of descriptions like the one for a quilt made by seventy-year-old Mrs. Elizabeth

Sargeant of Lancaster, considered "meritorious for its example of industry in age."[7]

Undoubtedly partially inspired by the growing number of agricultural societies and fairs dotting the state, Massachusetts established its own agricultural college in 1867, through the Morrill Land-Grant Act, which had been signed into law by Abraham Lincoln in 1862. Under the act, the state received federal land to be used toward establishing and funding an educational institution to teach agriculture, engineering, and military tactics. In Massachusetts, the land grant college was built on 310 acres of land in Amherst. When it opened in 1867, the institution, which would come to be known affectionately as "Mass Aggie," had four faculty members, four buildings, fifty-six students and a curriculum with offerings in modern farming, science, and the liberal arts. In 1947, "Mass Aggie" became the University of Massachusetts at Amherst. A desire for agricultural education and assistance also supported the founding of a Grange chapter in Massachusetts in 1873 and a 4-H chapter in 1908.

In addition to being the home of the first American agricultural fair in 1810, Massachusetts also claims the first national quilt contest, held in 1932 in West Springfield at Storrowton Village on the grounds of the Eastern States Exposition. More than six hundred quilts were submitted, all seeking the first prize of $50. Judges for this first contest included the editor of *Good Housekeeping*, Anne Orr, and Mary Reynolds of *Farm Journal*.[8] While many of the local and county agricultural fairs that used to be annual attractions for Massachusetts farmers and their families have slowly died out, the Eastern States Exposition remains an anticipated event each fall.

The quilts in this section tell more than just the personal stories about their makers. Taken together, they also provide new ways of understanding Massachusetts history and culture: The quilt from the Nantucket Agricultural Society shows how an entire community came together with hope for the future; Mollie Rice's quilt shows how the tradition of piecing passed from generation to generation; Edna Towne's quilt demonstrates how the agricultural society movement inspired the organization of the

National Grange; and Mrs. Baker's elegant white-work quilt exemplifies the pride that Massachusetts quilters took in their work as they hung their quilts at fairs held from Cape Cod's beaches to the hills of the Berkshires. —AEN

CHARLES FREDERICK COFFIN QUILT

(FIG. 137)

By the mid-1800s, Nantucket's whaling industry was in decline and residents were forced to consider new ways to make a living. This quilt helps trace the island's post-whaling history of the mid- and late 1800s.

Nantucket's population in 1840 was about ten thousand, but as the whaling industry waned, thousands of islanders left their homes to pursue alternate ways of making a living. By 1870, the population had declined to four thousand people.[9] In an attempt to turn the island's economy around, a group of island residents gathered in April 1856 to establish the Nantucket Agricultural Society. Chartered by the state, the Society was formed "for the encouragement of Agriculture and Mechanic Arts, in the County of Nantucket, by premiums and other means." The Society quickly set to work encouraging residents to farm the land in order to offset the loss of the whaling industry. On October 28–30, 1856, the Society held its first fair.[10] According to newspaper accounts, attendance at the fair was overwhelming. Its popularity spilled into a second day when twelve hundred people attended, prompting fair organizers to hold it open for a third consecutive day.[11]

While the Society's goals and activities were similar to many other New England agricultural societies, it seems to have been more progressive in allowing women to hold leadership roles. While most societies had committees of men to judge the fair entries—even those items considered "women's work" such as textiles and cheese—the Nantucket Society's "Committee on Fancy Articles" had ten female members out of the group of twelve. In

FIGURE 137. Pieced Friendship quilt, "Broken Sash," made for the Nantucket Agricultural Society, 1856. Cotton (95" × 78"). Nantucket Historical Association, Nantucket, Mass. (1970.2.1). *Photograph by Jeffrey Allen, courtesy of the Nantucket Historical Association.* MQ 981.

FIGURE 138. Detail, inked eagle from center block of Nantucket Agricultural Society quilt. *Photograph by Jeffrey Allen, courtesy of the Nantucket Historical Association.*

addition, four of the Society's Finance Committee members, charged with raising the funds necessary to be recognized by the state, as well as to put on the initial fair, were women.[12]

Island women had a long tradition of playing more public roles than their counterparts on the mainland. Nantucket's Quaker population encouraged education for women and maintained separate "meetings" for women and men. In addition, with many of their husbands, fathers, sons, and brothers working in the whaling industry—often on voyages that lasted four or five years—Nantucket women were used to overseeing family affairs and business at home. With this history, it comes as no surprise that women worked alongside men to form the Nantucket Agricultural Society and to strengthen

the island's economy. Newspaper accounts recount that the women of the Society decorated and arranged the exhibits of fruits, vegetables, and fancy goods. Women were also active in the evening programs writing songs, conducting choirs, and receiving complimentary toasts. They also created this quilt, presumably as a fundraiser for the Society.

The quilt contains about 218 signatures, with others that are now too faint to decipher and some that may have faded completely. Many of the signers can be traced through island genealogical records; sometimes mother, father, and child each signed their own block. In addition to the names, the quilt also includes many verses, some relating directly to agriculture, such as that on the square signed by Eliza W. Mitchell ("Long life and success to the farmer"), or the one on the square signed by Nathaniel Barney ("He that ploweth should plow in hope"). Other verses reflect more standard sentiments including, "God is love" and "As the twig is bent the tree is inclined." The center square of the quilt is larger than the pieced blocks and has an inked drawing of an eagle with a faint verse written underneath reading, "Nantucket Agricultural Society, incorporated / in the year one thousand, eight hundred, and / fifty six. / Lucy S. Mitchell."

Details on why the quilt was made are frustratingly vague in the newspaper accounts and Society records, but one of the island newspapers included the following in its account of the first fair: "An Album Quilt was exhibited by the Society, composed of squares marked with the autograph of the maker, each square made by a different person."[13] Despite this description, it seems more likely that the quilt was made by a small group of women and then signed by people who attended the agricultural fair, perhaps paying a small fee for the privilege. The Society's records suggest that the quilt may have been auctioned off. On the last evening of the fair, a song by the Glee Club was "followed by the 'auction bell,' calling all to the sale of the remaining articles donated to the fair."[14]

The quilt is pieced in a simple square block, known alternatively as "Friendship Album Quilt," "Broken Sash," and "Dutch Tile."[15] The blocks have muslin centers and scraps of printed cottons at the corners in pink, brown, blue, and other colors. It is hand-quilted in a grid pattern combined with an "X" through each block. The quilt is backed with a printed pink cotton fabric and bound with brown striped twill tape.

Newspaper accounts of the fair reprint several of the songs performed during the evening activities, including one called "The Agricultural Fair," written by Miss Margaret Getchell (1841–1880), who also signed one of the quilt's blocks. One stanza of the song reads, "Here's GARDNER with his plenteous horn, In Album Quilt displayed, With colored squares and stitches fine, That ladies fair have made; With MRS. MITCHELL's eagle proud, In centre-piece outspread, And MRS. FOSDICK's model plough, With not a line mislaid." The song verse seems to be de-

scribing the signature quilt with its central square showing an inked eagle. No Mrs. Mitchell or Mrs. Fosdick is listed as premium winners in the quilt category at the fair, but "Mrs. H. Fosdick" did receive special mention for "handsome specimens of marking with indelible ink" shown at the fair.[16] "Lucy S. Mitchell" is the name in the central square with the inked eagle, suggesting that she is the Mrs. Mitchell named in the song. Hannah M. Fosdick (1809–1864) and Lucy S. Mitchell (1794–1865) also signed multiple blocks in the quilt, lending further credence to the idea that they were instrumental in creating it.

On the back of the quilt is a handwritten inscription: "C. F. Coffin." Charles Frederick Coffin was born in 1835, son of Henry Coffin, one of the island's wealthiest whaling merchants and ship-owners. When he died in 1919, Coffin's obituary included the information that "he was identified with the agricultural fairs."[17] If the quilt was auctioned as a fundraiser at the fair, perhaps Coffin was the winning bidder. Or, he may have been given the quilt in recognition of his service to the Society. Regardless of how Coffin came to own the quilt, it was passed down in his family until it was given to the Nantucket Historical Association in 1970.

Today the quilt serves as a symbol of the struggle of mid-nineteenth-century Nantucket residents as they tried to save their beloved island from a devastating economic depression. Although the Nantucket Agricultural Society experienced success, continuing to sponsor annual fairs until 1934, tilling the soil ultimately did not save the economy. Instead, tourism offered promise for Nantucket, as off-islanders discovered the healthful air and peaceful landscapes. But the Society did achieve its secondary purpose—fostering a sense of pride among Nantucketers and celebrating "the spirit that makes our Island so free."[18]

—AEN

FIGURE 139. Pieced-quilt top, "Uneven Nine Patch" or "Puss in the Corner," made by Mary (Mollie) Rosina Rice (1889–1970) of Barre, 1899. Cotton (68" × 56¼"). Private collection. *Photograph by David Stansbury.* MQ 3459.

MARY (MOLLIE) ROSINA RICE QUILT

(FIG. 139)

In 1899, the Worcester County West Agricultural Society held its forty-ninth annual fair in Barre. The local newspaper reported a "conservative estimate" of thirty-five hundred attendees on the first day, September 28, and a record-breaking attendance the next day, as "crowds of people in holiday attire poured through the several entrances into the enclosure, and viewed with pleasure and admiration the various fine exhibits of the society. It was a lively and animated scene."[19]

The entries on view included this pieced quilt top, made by ten-year-old Mollie Rosina Rice of Barre. As the local paper reported, "Miss Mollie Rice, ten years old, was awarded a premium of seventy-five cents for a patchwork quilt, which she made." The fair had a special category for entries by children, awarding premiums for those under the age of fifteen in embroidery, crochet, and knitting. Mollie's quilt top won for "plain sewing and patchwork done by a girl under twelve years of age." It was the only premium awarded in that category and matched the amount awarded in several of the women's categories for needlework. Like many newspaper accounts of local agricultural fairs, the reporter called attention to entries by the very young and the very old, in this case, Mollie Rice's quilt and a patchwork quilt made by an octogenarian "containing 1480 pieces."[20]

Forty-two six-and-a-half-inch square blocks placed on point constitute Mollie's hand-pieced quilt top. She seems to have used scrap fabrics, perhaps left over from her family's clothing. Many of the fabrics are dark blues and browns, with additional pieces cut from light-colored shirtings and small prints. The tags from the agricultural fair still hang from one corner.

Originally established as the town of Hutchinson in 1774, Barre (pronounced "Barry") was reborn with Revolutionary fervor in 1776, trading the name of Massachusetts royal governor, Thomas Hutchinson, for that of an Englishman who opposed the taxation of America, Colonel Isaac Barre. Lo-

cated on the Ware River, Barre has been home to countless mills over the centuries, including fulling mills, powder mills, saw mills, and mills to make potash, linseed oil, and saltpeter.[21] According to one 1830s visitor, the town was "a large, flourishing, and well-built village." At that time, it had a cotton mill with twenty-five hundred spindles employing seventy-five people, as well as two woolen mills producing thirty-five thousand yards of cloth and employing sixty-six people.[22]

As late as 1905, Barre also had 286 farms within its borders.[23] When the Worcester County West Agricultural Society formed in 1851, Barre's central location and space for fairgrounds made it the logical home for the Society's annual cattle show and fair.[24] By the time Mollie entered her quilt, the fair was considered "one of the best, if not the best, in the state."[25] Despite the rise of industry through-

FIGURE 140. Detail, agricultural fair exhibit tags attached to Mollie Rice quilt top. *Photograph by David Stansbury.*

out Massachusetts by 1899, small communities like Barre still invested land and resources in farming to supply growing urban areas with fresh produce, milk, and meat. Honorable John L. Bates, the featured speaker at the cattle show dinner (attended by over four hundred), painted a rosy picture of the state's agricultural future. The newspaper reported, "he thought the outlook for the future of farming very bright . . . agricultural products had shown an increase of more than half a billion dollars in value. All kinds of stock had increased in value [over last year]."[26] However, less than thirty-five years later, in 1933, the Society dissolved as the Great Depression hit its lowest point and radically changed farming in the state and the nation.[27]

The Rice family was numerous in Barre when Mollie displayed her quilt. In an area of town known as "Rice Village," several family members manufactured carriages and wagons, as well as produced granite curbing, hitching posts, and house foundations.[28] The quiltmaker's branch of the fam-

FIGURE 141. The Rice children; Mollie is seated at the bottom, c. 1900. *Photograph courtesy of Bertyne Smith.*

ily apparently lived briefly in Charlton, for she was born there on May 22, 1889, the daughter of Daniel Herbert Rice (1863–1930) and his first wife, Helen Rosina White (1863–1889). They soon moved back to Barre. Helen Rice died shortly after Mollie's birth and Daniel Rice married again in 1891. With his second wife, Jennie Adelaide Adams (1864–1938), Daniel had four children. On the 1900 U.S. census, Daniel is listed as a grain dealer. By 1910, he seems to have given up agricultural pursuits and is listed as Deputy Sheriff, as he would be listed in 1920 and 1930.

In 1891, Mollie's widowed grandmother, Elizabeth Fitch (Rawson) Rice sold her farm and moved to a smaller house in town, just down the street from Mollie's father's house. According to family history, two-year-old Mollie moved in with her sixty-three-year-old grandmother. When Elizabeth Rice died in 1905, Mollie moved back into her father's house. In 1910, the census lists Mollie as a "shorthand teacher" living with her father. Mollie continued to teach, working at both public and private schools. In 1933, when she was forty-four, Mollie Rice married Guy Edward Rice (1894–1958) in Worcester. In 1945, the couple moved to Ashfield, where Mollie died in 1970.[29] The quilt's current owner is the maker's niece, and both she and the quilt continue to reside in Barre. —AEN

NELLIE EDNA GROTTO TOWNE QUILT
(FIG. 142)

During the 1930s and 1940s, many quilters took inspiration from the designs and color arrangements that they saw at public quilt shows and exhibitions, such as those at local agricultural fairs. This quilt, which still has its blue ribbon from the 1945 Essex Grange Fair pinned to one corner, undoubtedly impressed fair visitors with its 1,599 one-and-a-half-inch squares, and also may have inspired some viewers to adapt its arrangement of color and pattern.

The quilt is machine-pieced with scraps of count-

FIGURE 142. Pieced quilt, "Trip Around the World," made by Nellie Edna (Grotto) Towne (1881–1961) of Essex, circa 1935–1945. Cotton (80" × 65"). Private collection. *Photograph by David Stansbury.* MQ 2673.

FIGURE 143. Essex Grange Fair exhibit tag and first-prize ribbon attached to Nellie Towne quilt. *Photograph by David Stansbury.*

FIGURE 144. Nellie and Albert Towne, c. 1930s. *Photograph courtesy of Jean Towne.*

less colorful cotton prints. Hand-quilted with seven stitches to the inch, the quilting pattern consists of squares radiating from the center with a diamond grid between each "block." The single outer border matches the sashing, and the quilt has a knife-edge finish. A thin cotton batting and a plain pink cotton backing complete the quilt.

Nellie Edna Grotto was born in Gloucester on March 3, 1881, to English-Canadian parents. At the age of seventeen, she married Albert Lucius Towne (born c. 1874) and together they had two sons, Earle McKinley Towne and George Edward Towne. According to the 1910 and 1920 U.S. censuses, Albert Towne worked as a carpenter at a shipyard and, later, as a contractor. On the 1930 census, Albert and Nellie were empty-nesters, living alone in their home. Albert continued to work as a carpenter.

The family lived in Essex, where Nellie sold fruit and vegetables from her garden. She made at least

a dozen quilts. According to family history, Nellie learned to quilt at church quilting bees; she also may have learned to use paper templates from her English-Canadian mother. Unfortunately, she left the newspaper templates in some of her quilts, causing the fabrics to disintegrate.

Nellie Towne's quilt won first place at the Essex Grange Fair in 1945. The National Grange, also known as the Order of the Patrons of Husbandry, formed in December 1867 "to unite private citizens in improving the economic and social position of the nation's farm population."[30] One of the oldest fraternal organizations in Massachusetts, the first state Grange began in Greenfield in June 1873. Following the Civil War, the country was mired in an economic depression. Many Massachusetts farmers struggled to make a living and were attracted to Grange membership as a forum for sharing ideas and as a source of assistance. One hundred Grange chapters were formed in Massachusetts by 1875, though growing pains caused a drop in membership within a few years. Today, over eighty local and Junior Grange chapters still function in Massachusetts.[31] In addition to holding regular agricultural fairs, the local, state, and national Grange pursues lobbying activities in Washington, D.C., educates schoolchildren through classroom programs, and works to support many environmental and health causes.

Based on the ribbon pinned to her quilt, Nellie Towne and her family were involved with the Massachusetts Grange at its peak. In 1949, the state had over fifty-one thousand members.[32] Although the Grange was progressive in admitting women as members on equal footing with men, existing records do not list Nellie Towne as a Grange member. (Entrants in the Grange fairs were not required to be members.) While no membership records exist for Nellie Towne or her husband, Albert, there are membership records for their two sons: Earle Towne joined on April 4, 1928, at the age of twenty-six, and George Towne, along with his wife Ethel, joined on October 25, 1933, at the age of thirty-three. Continuing the family tradition, George and Ethel's son, Arthur, became a Grange member at the organization's youngest acceptable age (fourteen) in February 1955.[33]

Nellie Edna (Grotto) Towne died in Danvers, Massachusetts, on July 1, 1961. The quilt was passed down in the family and is now owned by her grandson.   —AEN

NANCY CHEEVER BAKER QUILT
(FIG. 145)

During the second quarter of the 1800s, whitework quilts held a high level of cachet for their makers and users. As urban style-setters like Eliza Leslie started to look down on patchwork, writing, "Patch-work quilts of old calico are only seen in inferior chambers," elegant whitework quilts became the pinnacle of fashion.[34] This quilt, magnificently quilted with nine stitches to the inch, almost certainly was its maker's prized possession. Indeed,

the quilt was prize-winning as well. When donated to Old Sturbridge Village in 1979, a silver medal from the 1841 fair organized by the Massachusetts Charitable Mechanic Association in Boston accompanied it.[35]

The Massachusetts Charitable Mechanic Association (MCMA) was founded in Boston in 1795 with Paul Revere as president. The group intended to pursue state legislation on the problem of runaway apprentices, but instead quickly turned its attention to promoting the mechanical arts and providing funds for members' widows and children. Incorporated in 1806, the MCMA pursued opportunities for training and educating its members, including founding a library and an evening school.[36] The Association first organized an exhibit in 1818, with prizes totaling $35 to be awarded to "coopers' apprentices for the best casks, to be made by their own hands."[37]

In 1837, the MCMA organized a much bigger fair, held at Quincy Market and Fanueil Hall, opening on September 18. The displays included textiles as well as paintings, machines, tools, and many other items from hundreds of exhibitors. Gold medals were awarded to the most outstanding items, with silver medals for "not as perfect a specimen but one worth considerable praise."[38] In later years, bronze medals and diplomas were added to the prize structure. At the 1839 fair, over seventy thousand people attended to view the work of almost twelve hundred exhibitors. Entrants claimed 25 gold medals, 153 silver medals, and 254 diplomas.[39]

This quilt was entered in the MCMA's September 1841 fair, where it was awarded a silver medal. The fair program describes the quilt as "a Quilted Counterpane in imitation of Marseilles. More beautiful than *any* other in the Exhibition."[40] This description of the quilt helps illustrate the contemporary distinctions between whitework quilts and "Marseilles quilting." Starting in the seventeenth century, Provence textile workers made a variety of quilted whitework items including quilts, petticoats, and men's waistcoats. These goods were exported through the port of Marseilles and sold in England and America, becoming known as "Marseilles" goods. In the mid-eighteenth century in England,

FIGURE 145. Drawing of whitework quilt, attributed to Nancy
Cheever Baker (dates unknown) of New Bedford, 1841. Cotton (104"
× 95"). Old Sturbridge Village, Sturbridge, Mass. (26.23.138). *Drawing
by Lynne Z. Bassett, courtesy of Old Sturbridge Village.* MQ 4619.

a loom-quilting process was developed and used to weave yardage resembling the French product (see fig. 24/MQ 5073). The loom-quilted and hand-quilted versions of whitework were widely available in America during the eighteenth and nineteenth centuries. The description of Mrs. Baker's quilt suggests that the loom-quilted version was known as "Marseilles," while a hand-stitched whitework quilt was often referred to as a "white quilt" or a "white quilted counterpane."[41]

The elegance of whitework quilts and the skill required to make them were widely recognized. The writer for one of the Boston newspapers covering the fair identified this quilt as something special among the hundreds of entries: "Proceeding a little way we noticed an elegant quilted counterpane by Mrs. D. Baker of New Bedford . . . the neatness and perfection of the work plainly showed that [this lady was not] accustomed to 'eat the bread of idleness.'"[42]

The quilt has a straight-applied binding and a thin batting. The backing is composed of plain white cotton like the front. The elaborate quilting design has an oval center with floral and foliate designs. Both the inner border of undulating feathers and the outer border of grapevines were designed carefully to avoid overlapping at the corners. Diagonal lines placed three-eighths of an inch apart fill the design's background.

Unfortunately, few details are known about the maker's life. The MCMA fair pamphlet and the medal list the maker as "Mrs. D. Baker" of New Bedford. This is probably Nancy Cheever Baker, who married David Baker of New Bedford on December 27, 1836. She was the widow of Thomas K. Cheever of Boston. David Baker is listed in New Bedford city directories from 1836 to 1852 as a dealer of mathematical instruments and sealer of weights and measures.[43]   —AEN

Chapter 12

Politics and Patriotism in Quilts

Among the many reasons for quiltmaking is the opportunity for political or patriotic expression. The names of numerous patterns evoke political sentiments, and names such as "Whig Rose," "Democratic Rose," the "Rocky Road to Kansas," or "Bourgoyne Surrounded" come to mind for many of us. But cloth itself also could be a political statement.

Printed fabrics venerating American politicians date from the late eighteenth century, when French and British manufacturers created toiles featuring George Washington or Benjamin Franklin.[1] Early nineteenth-century politics, however, created a new abundance of campaign paraphernalia that could be incorporated into quilts. The 1828 campaign of Andrew Jackson is often cited as the beginning of the modern American political campaign. Jackson's Democratic followers so successfully garnered support by distributing ribbons, vestings, and buttons, that the opposing Whig party imitated them in 1840, producing slogan-bearing buttons, snuff boxes, ribbons, torches, and sheet music of their own. Soon everyone knew of "Tippecanoe, and Tyler, too," or the benefits of "Log Cabins and Hard Cider." Just as modern political activists pass out tee-shirts, bumper stickers, and yard signs, nineteenth-century politicos distributed such campaign tokens at political meetings and rallies.[2] Quiltmakers incorporated campaign ribbons or message-bearing bandanas, sashes, or kerchiefs into their work, literally stitching their support together.

During the early years of the Republic, when women were not permitted to vote, few publicly expressed their political or social beliefs. There were

notable exceptions, particularly among the Quakers who believed women as well as men should promote justice. By the 1840s, Lucretia Coffin Mott (originally from Nantucket), Lucy Stone of West Brookfield, Abby Kelly Foster of Worcester (fig. 135/MQ 2028), and others were successfully challenging the notion that ladies should be seen but not heard. Many women spoke before groups of other women, a practice that had been acceptable since the earliest European settlers, but Stone, Foster, and Mott broke convention by speaking before mixed, or "promiscuous" audiences. They were shouted down, doused with ice water, and mobbed, yet they continued to speak out against slavery and for women's rights. Only after the Civil War did it became acceptable for women of all classes to speak publicly before a mixed audience.[3] For many women then, a more comfortable way to express their political opinions was with needle and thread. Certainly the woman who produced the Benjamin Harrison quilt (fig. 146/MQ 5617) decades before she would have been eligible to vote, made her support of the Republican President evident.

Patriotic themes appeared early in American quilting, for the United States and individualized quiltmaking came of age together. It is easy to forget the newness of the nation during the early nineteenth century, yet the number of patriotic motifs incorporated into quilts testifies to quiltmakers' awareness. Particularly during times of war, the American flag or eagle were embroidered, appliquéd, or pieced into quilts as Massachusetts quiltmakers sewed hopes for peace and support for their country into their work. Even midway through the twentieth century, as the European war approached America, a German immigrant raised in the United States patriotically celebrated the 150th anniversary of Washington's inauguration (fig. 148/MQ 4420).

The power of women's political voice became louder and more public as the nineteenth century progressed. It became easier for women to speak from platforms, to carry placards, and ultimately to vote. Yet for many, even in an era when a woman is a leading presidential candidate, quilts continue to provide an important outlet of political and patriotic expression.
—DCA

FIGURE 146. Pieced quilt of Benjamin Harrison political handkerchiefs, made by Christiana King Shelley (1832–1919) of Holyoke, c. 1888. Cotton (95⅛" × 93⅜"). Private collection. *Photograph by David Stansbury.* MQ 5617.

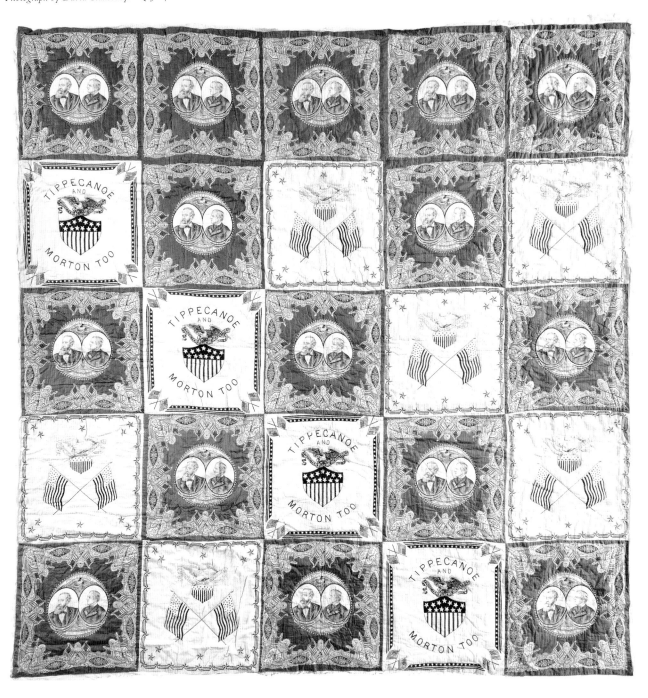

CHRISTIANA KING SHELLEY QUILT

(FIG. 146)

Christiana King Shelley, who is profiled earlier in this book (see fig. 110/MQ 92), was a prolific quiltmaker. At least one of her quilts reveals her political sympathies. Decades before women could vote, they successfully used quilts to support social reforms and express political opinions. In the quilt featured here, Christiana combined varieties of "Tippecanoe and Morton, too" handkerchiefs to create her evocative quilt. Benjamin Harrison, the twenty-third president of the United States, served from 1889 to 1893. His grandfather, military hero and ninth president of the United States William Henry Harrison, was nicknamed "Tippecanoe" for his role in the defeat of the Chief Tecumseh. William H. Harrison's 1840 presidential campaign produced the alliterative and memorable slogan "Tippecanoe and Tyler, too." Forty-eight years later, in 1888, the slogan reappeared to promote Benjamin Harrison and his running partner Levi P. Morton.

Republican Benjamin Harrison campaigned in support of protective tariffs through legislation intended to stabilize American factories by making it more difficult for foreign goods to compete in the American market. Such a policy would have been favored by those working in an industrial center such as Holyoke.[4] Although the twenty-five handkerchiefs used in the quilt are made up of three different types of pro-Harrison motifs, each features the slogan "Protection of Home Industries." Christiana's quilt preserves evidence of her family's involvement in the Harrison campaign and her own political awareness.   —DCA

HANNAH DUSTIN BURKE QUILT

(FIG. 147)

Flags, eagles, and other patriotic symbols have been popular motifs in American quiltmaking for more than two centuries, particularly at times of celebration and commemoration, or during national crisis and war. Although examples can be found throughout the history of quilting in America, a proliferation of flag quilts occurred at several notable periods. These included the American Civil War, the Centennial celebration in 1876, during United States military engagements in the nineteenth and twentieth centuries, at the American Bicentennial in 1976, and most recently following the terrorist attack on the New York World Trade Center on September 11, 2001. The popularity of quilts featuring this bold symbol of national identity spans the country, reflecting many regional styles from the album quilts of Baltimore to the distinctive quilt-making traditions of Hawaii. Quilters incorporated flags into their design vocabulary using a variety of techniques, including pieced, appliquéd, embroidered, printed, stenciled, or stamped fabrics. Flag and patriotic quilts provided women with an opportunity to express themselves about political movements and events that shaped their lives and the history of their country.

When the Peabody Essex Museum acquired this quilt in 1982, the donor recorded that it was made by Hannah Dustin Burke of Seekonk, Massachusetts, in 1912, on the occasion of Arizona's admission to the Union as the forty-eighth state and the last of the continental states to join the Union.[5] It is not known whether Hannah Dustin Burke had a personal or family association with Arizona. However, the quilt demonstrates her awareness of national events and pride in the territorial expansion of the United States. Her selection of the flag motif also may have been influenced by an Executive Order issued by President William Howard Taft in 1912 that defined the size, arrangement, and proportion of the stars and stripes of the American flag, which previously had minimal regulation. The forty-eight-star flag served as the official flag of the United States for forty-seven years (1912–1959), longer than any previous flag and only recently eclipsed in longevity by the fifty-star flag first issued in 1959.[6]

Hannah Dustin Burke pieced the quilt by machine, centering the flag on a ground of alternating red and blue stripes. The surface of the quilt is dot-

FIGURE 147. Pieced comforter, American flag design, made by Hannah Dustin Burke (dates unknown) of Seekonk, 1912. Cotton (76" × 81"). Collection of the Peabody Essex Museum, Salem, Mass., gift of Lillian J. Noekles, 1982 (135664). *Photograph courtesy of the Peabody Essex Museum.* MQ 2791.

ted by hand-stitched white cotton ties that connect the quilt top to its blue cotton backing.

In 1912, Seekonk, a small town in Bristol County near the Rhode Island border, was largely agricultural in character. In the twentieth century, Seekonk has become increasingly a residential suburb of Providence, Rhode Island, located only four miles to its west.　　　　　　　　　　—PBR

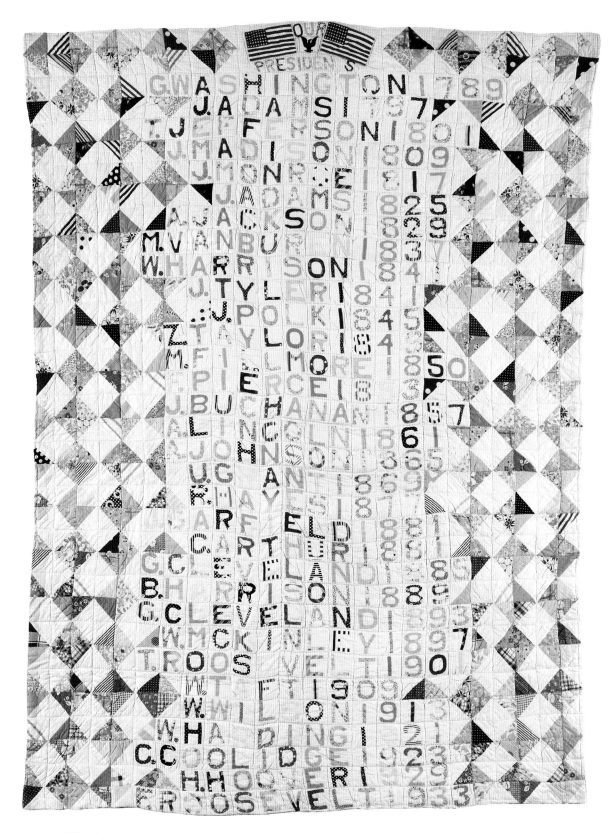

FIGURE 148. Pieced and appliquéd quilt, "Presidents Quilt," original design made by
Martha (Katzschmann) Mielke (1887–1973) of Easthampton, c. 1935. Cotton (89½" ×
63½"). Collection of Pocumtuck Valley Memorial Association, Memorial Hall Museum,
Deerfield, Mass. (2008.7). *Photograph by David Stansbury.* MQ 4420.

MARTHA KATZMANN MIELKE QUILT

(FIG. 148)

Martha Katzschmann was born in Germany in 1887 and came with her family to the United States when she was about two years old. Her family lived first in Holyoke, where at least one sister worked at the silk mill as a "quiller" (someone who fills bobbins).[7] After her marriage to Otto Mielke, the family lived in an immigrant neighborhood in nearby Easthampton, where they raised their children. Otto worked as a weaver in the suspender mill, where their daughter Gertrude later was employed as a silk winder and where Martha's two sisters also worked.[8]

Despite her immigrant background, the quilts Martha made show her strong allegiance to the United States. Her impulse to make these patriotic quilts is unknown; she became a naturalized citizen as a child, so it cannot be connected to that event. Clearly, she was just proud to be an American. In addition to the "Presidents Quilt," she made a quilt consisting of replicas of four historic American

FIGURE 149. Framed photograph of Martha Mielke, c. 1910. *Photograph by David Stansbury, courtesy of Brenda Rice.*

FIGURE 150. Detail, "Presidents Quilt." *Photograph by David Stansbury.*

flags and other patriotic symbols, such as the Liberty Bell. A snapshot of this quilt exists in the family collection, but the whereabouts of the quilt itself is unknown.

The "Presidents Quilt" is a list of all the presidents of the United States up to the time of its making, including the year of each man's first inauguration. It is somewhat unusual that Martha chose to list the year of inauguration rather than election, the year more commonly associated with presidential terms. One possible explanation coincides with family memories that unfortunately have not been documented: that this quilt was made for a contest sponsored by Macy's Department Store connected with the New York World's Fair of 1939 to 1940. The year 1939 marked the 150th anniversary of Washington's first inauguration (held in New York City). No records have been found of this quilt being entered in this contest and Martha is not among the recorded winners, though her family recalls going to the fair and they possess souvenirs from their trip.

The quilt primarily utilizes everyday fabrics: a mix of cotton print scraps, typical of women's housedresses and aprons, with white, somewhat heavier cotton used as the background fabric. The title "Our Presidents," centered with two American (forty-eight-star) flags, appears at the head of the quilt, along with a blue eagle similar to the symbol used by the National Recovery Act (1933–1935). Martha probably purchased these ready-made motifs and then appliquéd them by hand. Below the title, the list of the first initials (with a period after each) and last names of the presidents and their inauguration dates appear centered down the middle of the quilt, each president occupying his own line. Hourglass blocks set on point flank this list. The letters and numbers are mixed scraps, hand-appliquéd on white squares that measure two and three-quarters inches square. Machine stitching joins the squares, accomplishes the quilting in a simple grid pattern following the block centers, and top-stitches the knife edge.

This example of political folk art combines humble materials with a carefully conceived design recording the presidents' names and inaugurations. Even though the Great Depression was a difficult time for people working in the mills, this quilt sends a message to later generations from its immigrant maker, indicating her devotion to the United States and its leaders, as well as displaying her knowledge of American history and government. —MC

Chapter 13

Lost Towns of the Quabbin

In the late nineteenth century, Boston started looking for a new water supply. Officials identified the Swift River Valley in the middle of the state as the most appropriate place to create a reservoir, as its hills and bedrock would provide a strong foundation for the necessary dams. The region was known as "Quabbin," a Native American word meaning "many waters," for here the Swift River, Beaver Brook, and several smaller streams, along with Quabbin and Greenwich lakes, provided an ample supply of clear, clean water. A generation passed, temporarily easing the valley's residents' fears, but in 1927, the Swift River Act finalized the decision that the Commonwealth of Massachusetts would take the valley to create a reservoir for Boston.

Four towns—Greenwich (pronounced "Green-witch"), Enfield, Dana, and Prescott—and several villages would have to be abandoned; their twenty-five hundred residents relocated, their houses, churches, banks, mills, hotels, and stores demolished, the coffins from their cemeteries moved, their trees cut and burned. Amazingly, the citizens accepted the Commonwealth's demand with little protest, perhaps due to a sense of political helplessness. The largest protest actually came from Connecticut, which fought Massachusetts all the way to the Supreme Court over the effect that damming the Swift River would have on its own water supply. Connecticut's complaint was dismissed in 1931.[1] In contrast to Connecticut's suspicion, the valley's residents trusted "the generosity, justice, and honor of the Commonwealth," in the words of John H. Johnson at the ceremony noting the demise of the town

of Dana. But many citizens of the Swift River Valley were sadly disappointed.[2] The state paid residents for their real estate, but often at reduced prices because values had fallen due to the state's inaction in determining the fate of the valley.[3] The cost of lost business inventory or of reestablishing a business in another town was not reimbursed at all.

Most valley residents moved to surrounding towns, including Belchertown, Pelham, New Salem, Orange, New Braintree, Hardwick, and Ware; a few even moved their houses with them.[4] Savvy real estate investors snapped up vacated buildings for a song and moved them to towns around central Massachusetts and up to Vermont. Most buildings, however, were demolished. For several years, smoke hung over the valley like a pall, as acres and acres of trees were burned to smooth the valley floor for the reservoir.

The Quabbin Reservoir project came at a good time for Massachusetts, as the Great Depression smothered the national economy following the stock market crash of 1929. Clearing the valley and building the dams and other necessary structures created thousands of jobs (three thousand Boston Irish were hired just to cut trees)—and the men who labored on the project fueled the local economy, mostly in the town of Ware, for they and their families needed to be housed, fed, clothed, and entertained.[5]

Clearing began in 1928. Eleven years and $65 million later, the valley began to fill with water; by 1946, it was full. With 412 billion gallons of water, Quabbin Reservoir is "the largest body of untreated drinking water in the country."[6] Winsor Dam (named for the project's engineer) and Good-

FIGURE 151. View of the Quabbin Reservoir from Enfield Lookout. *Photograph courtesy of Lynne Z. Bassett.*

nough Dike, about three miles apart at the southern end of the reservoir, are each about half a mile long. The water backs up behind them for eighteen miles at an average of ninety feet deep.[7] It is then funneled through the Quabbin Aqueduct, a tunnel large enough to paddle a canoe through, to the Wachusett Reservoir in Worcester County and from there sent to Boston, a total of sixty-five miles.

Today, the thousands of acres of protected watershed area provide protected space for recreational walking, hiking, limited biking and fishing, and picnicking. Moose, beaver, bobcats, fishers, wild turkeys, and bald eagles have returned to the area, and possibly even mountain lions in the more remote northern regions of the watershed. It is a resource of beauty and tranquility for regional residents, but always with the knowledge that so many people gave up their homes and livelihoods for the benefit of the Commonwealth.   —LZB

MARTINDALE SISTERS DOLL QUILT

(FIG. 152)

Farmed by English and Scottish settlers since the second quarter of the eighteenth century, Enfield was incorporated as a town in 1816. In *Quabbin*, Francis Underwood described the town as lying between three hills, Great Quabbin, Little Quabbin, and Ram Mountain, "while the river, which is the life of the valley, glides in swift curves" at their bases.[8] From Little Quabbin, the view "embraced the cove, the river winding through meadows, the village, tufted with maples and elms, the white spire standing out from the northern hill."[9] It was a farming community, with a few other businesses (including a textile mill that produced satinets, flannels, and cassimeres) adding some diversity to the economy.[10]

In his fictionalized reminiscence, Underwood described the people and events of Enfield in the 1830s. A quilting party offered the author an opportunity to describe the common process, and to poke a little fun at the ladies attending.

> Co-operation among the women of Quabbin took the form of an afternoon quilting followed by tea.
> . . .
> Around the quilt, so stretched out at a convenient height, a dozen (more or less) might be at work, seated at the four sides, all following in their stitching the pattern laid down. The pattern was fanciful,—in zigzags, parallels, octagons, or concentric circles. . . .
> A more favorable arrangement for a social afternoon could hardly be imagined. The work demanded no thought on the part of those who were familiar with it; and the women, all facing inward as at a square table, and all in best gowns, cambric collars, and lace caps, could gossip to their hearts' content."[11]

Surely, many a "good, old-fashioned time," was enjoyed over quilting frames in Enfield—until the conversation turned in the late nineteenth century to worried rumors that the valley would be flooded for Boston's water supply.[12]

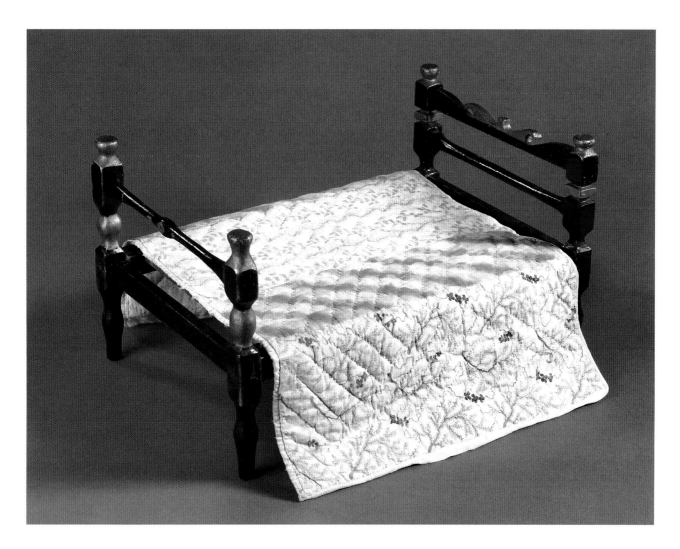

FIGURE 152. Pieced doll quilt with doll bed, belonged to Martha Elizabeth Martindale
(1874–?) and Mary Diana Martindale (1875–1952) of Enfield, c. 1875. Cotton (13¾" × 21¾").
Collection of the Swift River Valley Memorial Historical Society, New Salem, Mass.
Photograph by David Stansbury. MQ 3041.

In the period that Underwood remembered, Enfield was at its most populous, with over one thousand inhabitants. The population held fairly steady from 1830 to 1900, then began to fall as the inevitability of its being taken for the creation of the reservoir was realized. By 1930, it was down to 495 people.[13] The last day for the town came on April 27, 1938. A farewell ball was held that evening at the Town Hall. The next day's *Springfield Union* described the town's end:

> Under circumstances as dramatic as any fiction or in a movie epic, the town of Enfield passed out of existence at the final stroke of the midnight hour.

> A hush fell over the Town Hall, jammed far beyond its ordinary capacity, as the first note of the clock sounded; a nervous tension growing throughout the evening had been felt by both present and former residents and casual onlookers.

> The orchestra, which had been playing for the firemen's ball throughout the evening, faintly sounded the strain of Auld Lang Syne . . . muffled sounds of sobbing were heard, hardened men were not ashamed to take out their handkerchiefs."[14]

Not all of Enfield's residents were forced to leave their homes; two elderly sisters, Martha ("Mattie") Elizabeth Martindale Vining and Mary Diana Martindale were allowed to stay because their farm lay far enough beyond the Winsor Dam that it did not impinge on the work area. The Martindale family had owned the farm ("one of the most prosperous farms in the district") since the 1870s.[15] There Mattie and Mary played with the little doll bed and quilt featured here. As Underwood would have described, the simple, strip-pieced doll quilt was made of fabrics from "the skirts of the calico gowns worn by the female members of the family."[16] In this case, possibly from the skirts of their grandmother, as the calicoes are typical of the 1830s or 1840s.

Mattie married Orrin William Vining, a toolmaker at the Springfield Armory, in 1897. They had no children. After Orrin's death in 1929, Mattie returned to her family home in Enfield to live with Mary, who had never married. Donald Howe, chronicler of the Quabbin towns, described their home as "one of the most sumptuous farm homes in the area."[17] After Mary retired to a rest home in Springfield, Mattie continued to live in the home alone, "her simple wants . . . attended to by her nephew, Emory H. Bartlett of Belchertown."[18] Upon her death, the house was taken by the Commonwealth.

The site of the old Martindale farm lies along Webster Road, named for Mattie and Mary's mother's family. In this area within the Quabbin Reservoir watershed, Webster Road is unpaved, tree-lined, and quiet—a popular area for local residents to walk and watch birds and deer. Along its length can be seen old stone walls that once outlined fields, the foundations and a lone stone porch of old houses and outbuildings, and even fragments of abandoned equipment now enveloped by a tree trunk. No evidence of the Martindale house remains except for a flattened spot on the hillside.

—LZB

MRS. CHARLES LINDSEY QUILT
(FIG. 153)

Too many men by the name of Charles Lindsey are listed in Dana census records to be able to document which one married this quilt top's

maker. Local historian Donald W. Howe notes several of the numerous Lindsey family members as being prominent for their profession or their activism; those found in the census records are laborers and tradesmen.[19]

The town was incorporated in 1801 after seventy years of gradual settlement by families from surrounding towns. Never a large town, Dana's population peaked in 1860, with 876 inhabitants.[20] More than a hundred small farms on the rocky hillsides provided a living to the hard-working residents, but the local economy grew and diversified with the coming of the railroad to the northern part of Dana (afterwards called "North Dana") in 1873.[21] Around that time, an anonymous resident penned a description of the town:

> Few villages of its size enjoy two stores and a post office so complete and neat in arrangements and appearance. The residences and premises are universally neat, and well-kept; the citizens are thrifty and enterprising. The proprietors of the cloth mill, hat factories, box company, and lumber mill are all spirited, energetic, and courteous to strangers. No railroad station can boast of a more courteous and gentlemanly occupant than this.[22]

The cloth mill mentioned by the writer was a shoddy mill, which chopped up old fabrics and spun and then wove the short fibers into rough, cheap cloth (thus the term "shoddy" for poor quality). An old photograph of North Dana shows rows of outdoor wooden racks for laying out the lengths of fabric to dry after fulling.[23] Undoubtedly, the anonymous writer romanticized Dana to some degree, but the description reveals the residents' affection for their town.

Dana now lies under the Quabbin or within the reservoir's protected watershed. An old road on the east side of the reservoir leads to the abandoned Dana town common. Granite fence posts mark the front yard of what was once a comfortable home, now an empty lot, and the old stone foundations of houses and barns now provide shelter only for chipmunks and garter snakes.

A variety of late nineteenth-century silks from dresses and probably men's vests and ties consti-

FIGURE 153. Template-pieced and painted quilt top, made by Mrs.
Charles Lindsey (dates unknown) of North Dana, c. 1890–1910. Silk
(66" × 59"). Collection of the Swift River Valley Memorial Historical
Society, New Salem, Mass. *Photograph by David Stansbury.* MQ 3029.

FIGURE 154. Detail, Mrs. Charles Lindsey quilt. *Photograph by David Stansbury.*

tute the quilt top. Many of the pieces are seamed to make them large enough for the one-and-a-half-inch hexagons. The quiltmaker added beauty to this piece by painting the plain black silk hexagons with flowers, including tulips, lilies, carnations, roses, goldenrod, and a multitude of unidentifiable posies. While the painting of the flowers is more charming than skilled, the overall effect of the quilt is lovely, with a carefully considered distribution of light and dark colors. It was clearly intended as a showpiece modeled after the quilts made of more elegant silk brocades and velvets fashionable with the economic elite. The quilt top was backed, tied, and bound in 1998 by a member of the historical society that now owns it. —LZB

MARION SKINNER BROWN QUILT

(FIG. 155)

A faded photograph of Marion Skinner Brown shows her standing in a vegetable garden with a chicken-wire perimeter. She wears her white hair in a bun on top of her head and a white apron is tied around her ample waist; she gazes with a shy smile at the photographer. Marion was remembered in an unpublished Brown family genealogy as "a handsome woman of kindly disposition and auburn hair. She was generous and kindly in all her ways and never afraid to help her sick or needy neighbors in their day of trouble."[24]

Marion was the daughter of carpenter Darius Skinner and Candace (Jenokes or Jenks) Skinner of Dana, who sent her to North Brookfield Academy for her education. Her mother also provided an

FIGURE 155. Template-pieced comforter, "Hit and Miss" variation, made by Marion Candace
Skinner Brown (1848–1927) of New Salem, c. 1890–1900. Cotton (84" × 72"). Private
collection. *Photograph by David Stansbury.* MQ 4244.

FIGURE 156. Detail, calicoes of Marion Skinner Brown comforter.
Photograph by David Stansbury.

important part of Marion's education, teaching her housekeeping skills, including how to quilt.In 1870, Marion married Damon Kilgore Brown (b. 1847) of New Salem. Damon was a railroad station master at the New Salem depot, and later a conductor on the Athol-Springfield run of the Boston and Albany Railroad. (Called the "Rabbit Line" for its frequent stops, this rail line had to be abandoned when the Quabbin Reservoir was created.) Ill health—probably tuberculosis—forced Damon to give up his railroad job, so he and Marion bought a farm in New Salem and Damon started a meat peddlar's route. Unfortunately, while driving his meat cart one bitter winter's day in 1899, he contracted pneumonia; he died the following April.

Marion and Damon had four children, two of whom, Miner Damon (b. 1871), and Clarence Mager (b. 1876), survived beyond young adulthood. The 1900 U.S. census finds Marion living with her son-in-law, Charles S. Wheeler, and five-month-old grandson in Worcester; her daughter Barbara probably died due to complications of childbirth. Marion's losses continued. After the death of her daughter-in-law, Hannah C. (Day) Brown, Marion raised her two grandsons, Murry (1905–1999) and Ralph (b. about 1909). The Brown family genealogy states that Murry and Ralph would "always remember her for the love and care she gave in the absence of a mother." Murry grew up to be an engineer. In his retirement, this renaissance man built an observatory in the yard of his home in Orange to pursue his interest in astronomy, and made violins, including a reproduction of a seventeenth-century Stradivarius. Murry inherited Marion's quilts and passed them along to his good friends and neighbors, James and Anna Cullen.

The comforter featured here is pieced in a "Hit and Miss" variation, with light and dark colors alternating, giving the pattern a braided effect. The calicos are typical late nineteenth-century shirtings and work dress fabrics, undoubtedly recycled from family garments. The design is accented with scattered solid orange and red patches, and red triangles along the top and bottom edges. Tying rather than quilting this utilitarian but attractive top indicates the haste with which Marion had to produce the covers to keep her family warm.   —LZB

EVA RAND STEVENS GOODFIELD QUILT
(FIG. 157)

Eva Rand Stevens was raised in Dana, the youngest of four children born to Frank D. and Susan E. Stevens. Frank was the grocer and postmaster in town. With an education from the New Salem Academy and undoubtedly some experience in her father's store under her belt, she went to work as a bookkeeper in the general store in Gilbertville, a town located to the southeast of Dana. In 1909, Eva married Arthur Granger Goodfield (1875–c. 1952), the son of William C. Goodfield, a native of Canada, and Susan E. (Granger) Goodfield. Eva and Arthur became farmers in Gilbertville, like Arthur's parents. The couple soon began having children: Alvin, William, Chester, and Alice were all born between 1910 and 1918. Eva and Arthur established themselves on a farm in the next town, New Braintree, where they specialized in dairy cows. (Undoubtedly, they knew the pointlessness of taking a farm in Eva's hometown of Dana, as it was doomed by the 1920s to be inundated as a water supply for Boston.) Eva's mother-in-law, Susan Goodfield, came to live with the family after she was widowed, and helped Eva to raise the children and keep house. Grandmother Susan celebrated with the family when another daughter, named Susan like both of her grandmothers, arrived in 1923.[25]

In 1937, Eva and Arthur moved their family to the Mixter farm in Hardwick, which is said by their granddaughter to have kept the largest herd of Guernsey cows in the world. For the next fifteen years, the Goodfields produced huge quantities of dairy products, even shipping cream to Europe. By the twentieth century, dairy farming had been an important part of Massachusetts agriculture for over a hundred years. The growth of cities with the Industrial Revolution created large markets for farm-

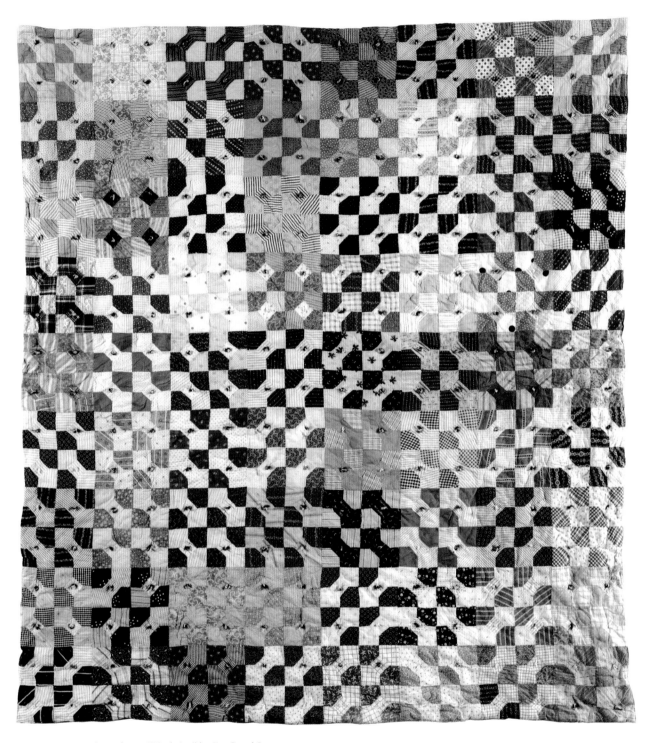

FIGURE 157. Pieced comforter, "Neckties," by Eva Rand Stevens Goodfield (1884–1953) of New Braintree, c. 1900–1920. Cotton (82" × 74"). Private collection. *Photograph by David Stansbury.* MQ 4233.

ers' products. Regions in Worcester, Hampshire, Middlesex, and Essex counties especially were devoted to dairy farming.[26] Eventually, refrigerated containers on trains and trucks made it possible for dairy products to be shipped from the Midwest, and family dairy farms in Massachusetts, which could not sustain such large herds as farmers farther west, began to go out of business. Eva and Arthur sold their dairy farm in Hardwick in the early 1950s; the next owner was not able to keep it in business.

Eva's comforter was made of old dress and shirting scraps in the early twentieth century. Her lack of concern for arranging the "neckties" in a consistent direction, or of making them in a consistent light-dark pattern, gives the quilt top movement and visual interest, though perhaps unintentionally. She was more careful to balance the light and dark blocks in the overall arrangement, however. Large blue and white yarn ties punctuate the center of each necktie.   —LZB

FIGURE 158. Eva Rand Stevens Goodfield (seated) with her husband, son Chester and daughter-in-law Lois Goodfield, c. 1940. *Photograph courtesy of Alice Lowell.*

Chapter 14

Family Quilts

Almost all of the quilts described and pictured in this book have a family story or were passed down for generations, or both. Quilts are particularly powerful family touchstones, conveying warmth and comfort while conjuring memories of a beloved grandmother or cherished mother. The quilts in this section have rich family stories and, in two cases, offer the especially fruitful resource of multiple quilts made by members of the same family—in one case, over one hundred years apart.

The quilt collections from the Wilber family of Swansea and from the Healy and Robbins family of Blandford visually document the family connections made with quilts. Each collection spans at least two generations and demonstrates how women used the quilts of their ancestors to inspire their own work. Similar block patterns and arrangements of color and design are immediately evident from one look at these quilts. For Massachusetts women of the eighteenth and nineteenth centuries, who had no formal political voice and who left few written documents behind, making a quilt offered a way to be heard and remembered.

The other two quilts in this section were made by boys while they recuperated from illness or injury. The scholarship on how girls were taught patchwork, plain sewing, and embroidery is voluminous. We have many examples of how a girl served her "apprenticeship" at the knees of her mother in their own home. However, these quilts made by boys expand our understanding of the past; we can see that gender boundaries were not as strict as we might think. In addition, we learn something of how quilts were understood and used by both the male and female members of Massachusetts families.

Finally, by studying these quilts and others with family histories, we start to see a new pattern of female property use and value. Official records and countless history books document that women often were legally prohibited from owning property once they were married.[1] While the property most often referenced by these sources consists of land, buildings, stocks and bonds, little is specifically mentioned about "movable goods," like quilts and other furnishings. The quilts in this section and throughout this book, along with the stories told about them, suggest that they were understood by their makers and their families to hold value. Moreover, they were often understood—in reality, if not in actual, legal fact—to be the maker's to use as she saw fit. One quilt historian recently has suggested that "quilts functioned as a kind of currency in an informal, female-centered economy based on kinship, mutual support, and the transformation of ordinary materials into objects of significance and value."[2] Indeed, these quilts did that and more—they taught new skills, they reminded children and grandchildren of those who came before, and they were gifts at joyful times, and consolations during difficulty.

—AEN

The Wilber Family Quilts

Like many old Massachusetts families, the descendants of the Wilber family of Swansea accumulated a large collection of textiles made and used by their ancestors, including clothing, household textiles, and needlework. Fortunately, Wilber Doe (with his wife, Mary), a member of the family's tenth generation, recognized the value of his family's collection and gave over one hundred items to Old Sturbridge Village in the mid-1980s. This generous gift offers the opportunity to explore what was saved, what was reused and remade into other items, and how these items compare to textiles owned and used by earlier generations.

The Wilber family collection includes seven quilts spanning three centuries. The four quilts shown here document the evolution of quiltmaking in Massachusetts from the late 1700s to the early 1900s. Old design practices and fabrics are recycled and reused in the quilts to create new textile traditions. The quilts also reveal the family's memories and cherished connections to earlier generations.

The first Wilber family member to live in Swansea was Daniel Wilber (1666–1741), who was born in Portsmouth, Rhode Island. He settled in Swansea in 1680, on land purchased by his father, William Wilber (1630–1710). Daniel married Ann Barney (d. 1741). They were farmers and made their living with the assistance of slaves.[3] Daniel Wilber's son, also named Daniel (1697–1759), married Ann Mason (d. 1751); together they had one daughter and one son. When he died in 1759, Daniel Wilber left an estate valued at over 1,000 pounds "lawful money" (including two slaves), indicating that he prospered as a farmer. His probate inventory also suggests that the family produced textiles. The appraisers listed forty-eight sheep and twenty-seven lambs, 160 weight of wool, four pairs of wool cards and two wool wheels, along with 118 pounds of flax, 20 pounds of hetcheled flax, 24 pounds of hetcheled tow, two flax wheels, 18 yards of linen cloth, and one hundred skeins of linen yarn.[4]

Daniel and Ann's son, once again named Daniel (1749–1821), was born in Swansea in 1749. This Daniel served in the Revolutionary War and continued to farm the land. He married Mary Barnaby (1744–1826) in 1772; they had nine children; seven of whom survived to adulthood. This generation also produced textiles. In Daniel's will, he left one-half of all his weaving utensils to his wife; he gave the other half to his daughter, Mary, along with

"a privilege in the garret to set looms and other things."[5] Two of the quilts featured here are associated with his children.

Continuing the family tradition, Daniel Wilber's grandson was also named Daniel (1817–1896). He was from the family's seventh generation, lived in Swansea, and married Nancy Lee (1828–1915) in 1846. The couple had a son, William Irving Wilber (b. 1863). William, in turn, married Caroline (Carrie) Eliza Eddy (b. 1863) in 1886, and had two daughters. Mary Eddy Wilber (b. 1886) married Arnold Richardson Doe and had a son, Wilber Stanley Doe (b. 1916). Her sister, Elizabeth Sherman Wilber (b. 1890) married Charles William Frost and had a daughter, Virginia Frost (b. 1915). In the mid-1980s, Wilber Stanley Doe gave the family textile collection to Old Sturbridge Village in memory of his cousin, Virginia Frost.[6]

Swansea is located in southeastern Massachusetts, bordered by Rhode Island on the west. First settled in 1663, the town was founded on the premise of religious tolerance for all. Early settlement was disrupted in 1675, when the town witnessed the first bloodshed of King Philip's War. Indian attacks decimated the houses and garrison, but the townspeople rebuilt after the war. Most families pursued farming, with forges, ironworks, and fishing also offering employment. As the surrounding towns of Fall River and Taunton industrialized in the late 1800s, Swansea took on a suburban character, and served as a summer destination for residents of those communities.   —AEN

ELIZABETH (SHERMAN) WILBER QUILT
(FIG. 159)

Probably created around the time that Elizabeth Sherman married James Wilber (1774–1848) in October 1797, this early quilt is made of elegant imported French and English fabrics. James was the son of Daniel and Mary (Barnaby) Wilber. Elizabeth's sister, Sarah, married James's brother, Daniel, a few months earlier that same year. The circa 1781

FIGURE 159. Pieced quilt, "One Patch," attributed to Elizabeth (Sherman) Wilber (1776–1823) of Swansea, c. 1800. Cotton and linen (96" × 102"). Collection of Old Sturbridge Village, Sturbridge, Mass. (26.23.153). *Photograph by David Stansbury.* MQ 4613.

inventory of Elizabeth and Sarah's father, Zephaniah Sherman, suggests that the sisters performed some textile production. The inventory includes eighteen sheep, four bushels of flax seed, two linen wheels, and one wool wheel. In 1802, about five years after his marriage, James Wilber purchased a 150-acre farm in Swansea, with a house, a barn, and other outbuildings for $6,000. James and Elizabeth had nine children, eight of whom survived to adulthood.[7]

A popular style in the 1790s and into the early nineteenth century, the quilt has a pieced center

FIGURE 160. Detail of calicoes, Elizabeth Wilber quilt. *Photograph by David Stansbury.*

with ruffled drops forming the characteristic New England "T-shape." The one-patch squares, cut from English block-printed dress fabrics, may have been recycled from garments worn by Elizabeth and her sisters. A red and white copperplate-printed French or English fabric with a chinoiserie pattern of figures, foliage, and other motifs comprises the drops.

The quilt is pieced by hand with sixty-three eight-and-one-quarter-inch squares making up the center section. This section is hand-quilted with seven stitches to the inch in cross-hatched parallel lines set about one and a half inches apart. The quilting is done with dark and light threads to match the fabrics. Like most early quilts, it has a knife-edge finish. The quilt is filled with a medium-weight batting and backed with white linen.

The fabrics suggest a late 1790s or early 1800s date for the quilt, making it possible that it was made in preparation for Elizabeth Sherman's wedding. Historical myths about wedding quilts abound in twentieth-century literature. Romanticized ideas about quilts were perpetuated by many writers during the Colonial Revival, including Alice Morse Earle, Ruth Finley, and others. When quilts were "re-discovered" by feminist historians and quilt-makers in the 1970s, they appropriated many of these same myths.[8]

Recent scholarship provides a more realistic understanding of quiltmaking in the 1700s and 1800s, including a refutation of the wedding-quilt myths.[9] There is no evidence that young women made thirteen quilts in preparation for their marriage, or that the last quilt was stitched with a heart-influenced quilt design. Instead, probate inventories and diary evidence suggest that most families owned far fewer than thirteen quilts at a time. One survey of thirty-four diaries kept between 1754 and 1850 found that women under thirty spent an average of slightly over three days each year quilting, while women over thirty spent an average of about two and a half days quilting each year, hardly enough to make more than one or two quilts.[10] There does seem to have been a New England tradition for a young woman's mother to give her a quilt as a wedding gift.[11] And, in many eighteenth- and early nineteenth-century families, daughters were given a share of their father's estate in moveable goods at the time of their marriage. This usually included beds and related bedding, including quilts.[12] This quilt was probably made by Elizabeth Sherman in preparation for her marriage, with the assistance of her mother and sisters—but it was not one of thirteen. Nor does it have any kind of heart-shaped quilting design or other indication of a bride. Instead, it offers an early interpretation of the evolving American—and Massachusetts—passion for pieced quilts and vibrant arrangements of color and pattern.

—AEN

MARY WILBER QUILT
(FIG. 161)

This hand-pieced and tied quilt, known during the early 1800s as a "comforter" or "comfortable," is made frugally from several pieces of two blue-and-white printed cottons. The center fabric may have been recycled from eighteenth-century bed hangings used by an earlier generation of the family. The back is similarly pieced together, using seven pieces of a plain-woven white cotton, probably recycled from scraps of other household textiles. The thick wool batting is secured with knotted cotton ties throughout.

The center fabric is blue and white resist-printed cotton with a large-scale flowering vine pattern. Such fabrics were made by applying wax, starch, or (later) a chemical paste in the desired pattern to white fabric; when the fabric was dipped into the indigo bath, the paste "resisted" the dye, leaving the fabric white. The process was repeated to make multiple shades of blue. Starting in the

1660s, English textile producers sent design suggestions to India for these fabrics, and then imported them for sale in England and America. Large-scale arborescent designs, like the one seen here, were popular.[13] The quiltmaker added borders of an early-nineteenth-century cylinder-printed chintz with birds, urns, and foliage to the sides, top and bottom.

The quilt is attributed to Mary Wilber, based on the inked initials visible on the back in one corner. The initials "W.W." are presumed to stand for her brother, William Wilber (1783–1868), who inherited the "rest and residue" of his sister Mary's estate when she died in 1846. Mary Wilber was the daughter of Daniel and Mary (Barnaby) Wilber. She never married and evidence from the wills of her parents suggests that she was a weaver. Her father, also a weaver, bequeathed half of his weaving tools and the right to live in the northwest front chamber of the family home to Mary.[14] It is possible that Mary wove some or all of the fabrics used in the backing of this quilt.

Mary's will lists bequests to her siblings, nieces, and nephews totaling $3,500, a considerable sum for a single woman in the 1840s. Likewise, her probate inventory included property worth over $8,600, ranging from debts owed to her, land in Swansea and Fall River, a share of a pew in the Swansea Village Meetinghouse, and a long list of household goods. Her inventory not only listed spinning and weaving equipment (wool wheel, linen wheel, loom, warping bars, and weaving harnesses), but also seven quilts worth $14 together, and one other quilt with no value listed.[15]

—AEN

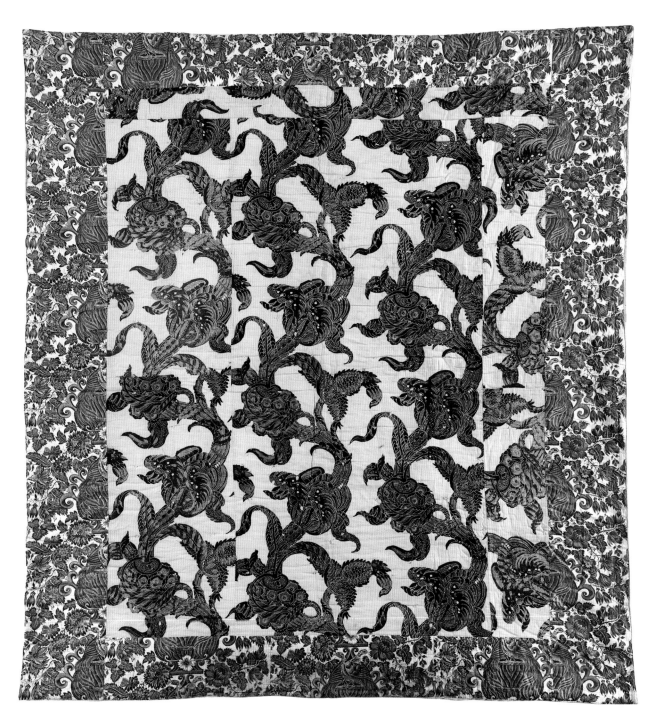

FIGURE 161. Pieced and tied comforter, possibly made by Mary
Wilber (1781–1846) of Swansea, c. 1835–1840. Cotton with wool
batting (95½" × 91"). Collection of Old Sturbridge Village,
Sturbridge, Mass. (26.112.13). *Photograph by David Stansbury.* MQ 4601.

WILBER FAMILY "FOUR PATCH" QUILT

(FIG. 162)

This vibrant quilt has a top composed of 168 pieced blocks of plain and glazed cottons that are slightly over five inches square. It is hand-quilted in a simple cross-hatched design with eight to nine stitches per inch. Using such a simple pattern of parallel lines allowed a woman to finish quilting in a day or so. A recent survey of New England diaries from the late 1700s and early 1800s found a number of references to putting a quilt on a frame and "quilting it off" in a single day. Whether quilting alone or with friends and family, a woman had practical reasons for finishing the quilting as quickly as possible. Chief among these reasons was the inconvenient crowding that undoubtedly occurred with the quilting frame set up in the parlor or sitting room.[16]

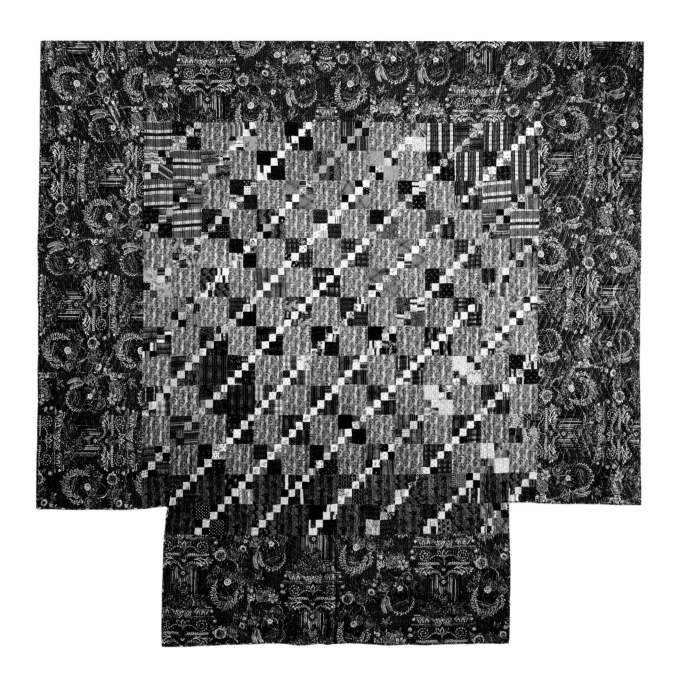

An elegant chintz pillar print comprises the border. The binding is straight-applied in some places and front-to-back in others. A thin cotton batting and a white cotton backing complete this bed covering, which has cut-out corners to help it drape smoothly around the bed posts.

Cross-stitched initials, "SS," mark the top center of the back. Learning to make such marks was the practical purpose behind stitching a sampler as a schoolgirl. The marks allowed a woman to keep track of how many linens she owned and also assisted in identifying them quickly, ensuring their prompt return when they were sent out for laundering or just spread out to dry on the bushes in the yard. A woman could prevent uneven wear by rotating her linens regularly according to their marks.

These are probably the initials of Sarah Slade (1816–1841). Sarah was the daughter of William Slade (1759–1850) and Mary Sherman (1775–1858), the older sister of Elizabeth and Sarah Sherman, who married brothers James and Daniel Wilber in 1797. (The one-patch quilt described previously is attributed to Mary's sister, Elizabeth Sherman Wilber.) Mary and William Slade married in 1795 and had two sons and three daughters, including Sarah, their youngest child.[17]

This quilt represents a step forward in the evolution of Massachusetts quilt style, from the circa 1800 one-patch quilt discussed above. Quilts from the early 1800s often employed relatively simple patterns such as the "Four Patch," "Nine Patch," or "Eight-Pointed Star," but manipulated them into visually stunning arrangements overall by adding or subtracting sashing, setting them straight or on point, or by placing them in vertical, horizontal, or diagonal stripes. Making this quilt particularly vibrant is the array of cylinder-printed fabrics used in the top. Starting in the 1810s, cylinder-printing technology made colorful printed cottons far more economical for middling New England women to purchase. In

addition to the decreased prices, women were drawn to the precise patterns, crisp appearance, and bright colors of these fabrics.　　　　　　　—AEN

WILBER FAMILY "MONKEY WRENCH" QUILT
(FIG. 163)

The fourth quilt from the Wilber family brings the family story into the twentieth century. Just as the previous three quilts are objects of their respective eras, so this quilt employs fabrics popular during the late 1800s and early 1900s, including shirtings, plaids, checks, rich dark prints, and pretty pastels. It is tied rather than quilted, helping to illustrate how the women of the family may have had less time or interest to devote to quiltmaking by the end of the 1800s.

Like Mary Wilber's blue and white resist-print quilt described above, this bedcover was also known as a "comforter" or "comfortable," because the three layers are tied rather than quilted. Nineteenth-century women always seem to have distinguished between quilts and comforters, often noting in their diaries that they "tied comforters." Probate inventories also note the difference, generally valuing comforters lower than quilts.[18]

The top is pieced by hand in the "Monkey Wrench" pattern with eighty-one blocks that are nine-and-a-quarter inches square. It is bound with bias-cut twill-woven cotton. And, like the blue and white resist comforter, this bedcover reuses older materials to make something new and fresh. A second quilt was incorporated into the piece; a close examination of the comforter reveals that the newer top was attached over a "Log Cabin" pieced bedcover and that the backing was not altered—it is the backing used for the "Log Cabin" quilt.

The red and white fabric on the back is copper-plate-printed in a floral pattern with scenes of children playing games. It dates to about 1790—one hundred years earlier than the current top. Despite the proliferation of reasonably priced printed cottons available to Wilber family members at the end of

FIGURE 162. Pieced quilt, "Four Patch," from the Wilber family of Swansea, c. 1835. Cotton (112" × 109¾"). Collection of Old Sturbridge Village, Sturbridge, Mass. (26.23.154). *Photograph by Thomas Neill, courtesy of Old Sturbridge Village.* MQ 4614.

FIGURE 163. Pieced and tied comforter, "Monkey Wrench," from
the Wilber family of Swansea, c. 1890–1920. Cotton (84¼" × 83½").
Collection of Old Sturbridge Village, Sturbridge, Mass. (26.112.10).
Photograph by David Stansbury. MQ 4602.

FIGURE 164. Copperplate-printed fabric on back of "Monkey Wrench" quilt. *Photograph by David Stansbury.* MQ 4602.

In addition to the four quilts shown here, the Wilber family textile collection includes numerous examples of everyday household items ranging from handkerchiefs to towels, as well as clothing. The collection includes three more quilts that further illustrate the family's history, as well as their penchant for recycling old materials into something new. One of the three quilts is a quilt made of red and brown wools and backed with a gold wool and cotton fabric, probably home-dyed and home-woven (osv 26.107.7). The quilt dates to the early 1800s; sadly the maker's name has been lost. Another quilt, made of three block-printed, late-1700s printed cotton dress fabrics, may have been made around the time of the 1797 weddings of Elizabeth and Sarah Sherman (osv 26.23.152/MQ 4611). In this quilt, a central square made by stitching strips of one fabric together is surrounded by a border of the second fabric; the third dress print is used across the top of the quilt. The third quilt dates from the 1810s and is pieced in a "Nine Patch" variation with an effect similar to the circa 1835 quilt described above (osv 26.23.157/MQ 4612). It is marked with the initials "SS." This quilt uses printed cottons in red, pink, white, and blue, and has an English roller-printed blue-and-white border.

the 1800s, someone frugally chose to reuse an older quilt for their bed covering. While this certainly did save the maker some money, it also provided an emotional reward, whether conscious or unconscious. Each night, the quilt's owner wrapped herself in one hundred years of family history and ancestry.

—AEN

The Healy Family Quilts

The three quilts shown here (FIG. 165), all made by members of the same family, visually demon-strate the tradition of quiltmaking in Massachusetts, where quiltmaking skills in some families have been passed down from generation to generation since at least the eighteenth century. These family quilts symbolize the connections between a woman and her daughters and granddaughters; they also embody a skill and craft that often served as a voice for women. All three quilts employ a similar pieced pattern, color palette, and fabric arrangement.

The oldest quilt of the three is shown at the top right. The block pattern had special meaning for the quiltmaker: The pattern is composed of four "H"s signifying the quiltmaker's last name, Healy, along with her middle name, Harmony. Sarah Harmony Healy probably made this quilt between 1900 and 1925, during her teens or twenties, prior to her marriage. Sarah was born in Blandford on March 5, 1889, the daughter of Winfield Dennison Healy (b. 1854) and Sarah Caroline Snow (b. c. 1858). According to the 1900 U.S. census, Winfield Healy was a farmer. Sarah Snow Healy stayed at home to care for the couple's five children, including Sarah, known as "Sadie."

Incorporated in 1741, Blandford is located in Hampden County, on an early travel route between Springfield and Albany, New York. While there were two mills in town by the 1830s, most residents pursued dairy farming.[19] Winfield Healy supported his family by farming throughout the 1910s and 1920s. The 1910 census also lists a boarder living with the Healy family. Seventy-seven-year-old Joseph Phillips, a shoemaker, helped the Healy family by providing extra cash and, in return, received shelter without needing to perform a lot of heavy labor to care for his own home or farm.

Sarah Harmony Healy, who made the quilt at top right as well as the quilt in the center of the photograph, learned to quilt from her grandmother. A favorite family story explains that if her grandmother wasn't satisfied with the stitches, she would rip them out and make Sarah do it again. Sarah's quilt at top right consists of thirty eleven-inch-square blocks pieced from a variety of fabrics including conversation prints, sheeting, indigo prints, and large-scale patterns. She quilted it by hand in a grid with seven to eight stitches to the inch. The quilt has cotton

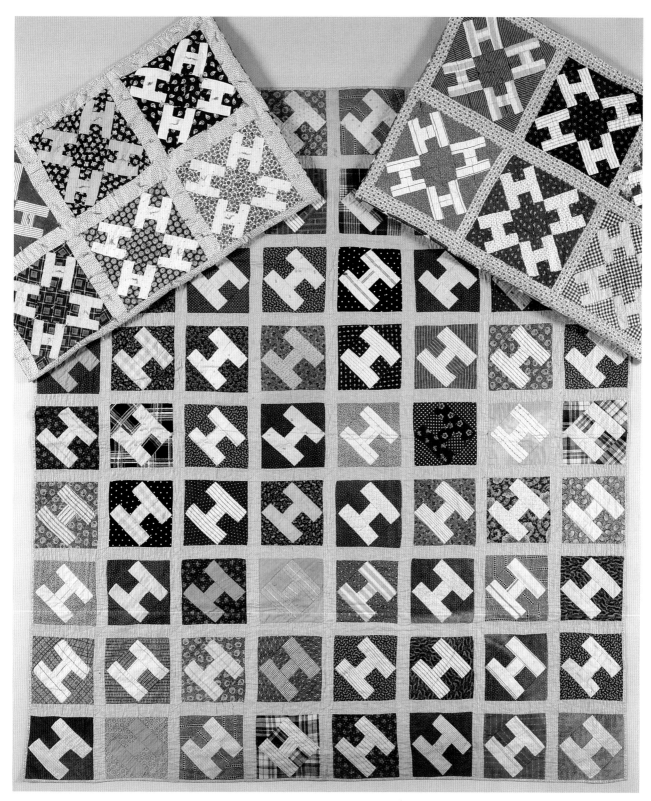

FIGURE 165. Three pieced quilts: *(Top right)*, "H Square," made by Sarah Harmony Healy (1889–1981) of Blandford, c. 1900–1925. Cotton (76½" × 64"). Private collection. MQ 3511. *(Center)*, "Letter H," made by Sarah Harmony Healy (1889–1981) of Blandford, c. 1930. Cotton (80" × 71"). Private collection. MQ 3573. *(Top left)*, "4-H Club Block," made by Alta Robbins Rhodes (b. 1921) and Sarah L. Robbins (b. 1922) of Blandford, c. 1935. Cotton (80" × 66"). Private collection. MQ 3574. *Photograph by David Stansbury.*

batting and a back-to-front binding that is partially machine sewn.

Sarah Harmony Healy also hand-pieced the quilt in the center, probably around 1930. The blocks are smaller, approximately seven and a half inches square, with seventy-two blocks making up the quilt top. Like her earlier quilt, Sarah used a variety of light and dark fabrics, including shirtings, indigos, and other patterned and plain textiles. The quilt is hand-quilted "in the ditch" with six to seven stitches per inch. The back-to-front binding is machine sewn. The quilt has a thin cotton batting.

In 1920, Sarah married Philip L. Robbins (1889–1984) in Blandford. According to the 1930 U.S. census, Philip worked as a chauffeur for a private family. Sarah kept house for her family, consisting of two sons and two daughters. Just as she learned to quilt from her grandmother, Sarah taught her daughters to stitch. The third quilt, pictured at top left, was made by Sarah's daughters, Alta (b. 1921) and Sarah (b. 1922), around 1935.

Sarah Harmony Healy's quilt from the early 1900s probably served as a model to inspire her daughters. Their quilt is tied rather than quilted and is pieced by machine. This evidence from the quilt itself suggests how quiltmaking and needlework changed during the early twentieth century, in Massachusetts and throughout the country. Many quilts from the 1920s and 1930s were expected to receive less use than those made in earlier eras. Women could buy inexpensive machine-made blankets for warmth as well as store-bought bed coverings for decoration.[20] While their mother and grandmothers learned to make quilts to acquire important sewing skills and to provide for their future families, Alta and Sarah Robbins undoubtedly had different reasons for making their quilt. Stitching the blocks together provided a sense of connection between the sisters and their mother. The quilt served emotional and psychological needs, more than the practical functions of education and physical comfort.

Just like their mother's quilt, this one has a top comprised of thirty blocks that are eleven inches square. It also has light-colored lattice strips between the blocks. Most importantly, the quilt is made with light-colored "H"s on darker background fabrics, including a colorful variety of patterned calicoes. The single border is made from the same pink, red, and white fabric as the lattice strips. Like their mother's quilts, this one has back-to-front binding and a cotton batting.

Fittingly, the block used for Alta and Sarah's quilt is known as the "4-H Club Block"; the girls made the quilt as a 4-H project. With Blandford's history as a dairy town, 4-H had a ready audience among the community's youth. Many 4-H programs were established throughout the country during the late 1890s and early 1900s in order to improve agricultural education for young people. In 1914, the Smith-Lever Act established the Cooperative Extension Service, providing public financial support for related programs, including 4-H. In Massachusetts, 4-H started in 1908. During the 1930s, when Sarah's daughters were active in the club, 4-H expanded projects for girls to include clothing, home management, food and nutrition, and other home economics projects. By 1942, 4-H had one and a half million members nationally and 4-H'ers were responsible for over 77,000 head of dairy cattle, 246,000 swine, and 210,000 other livestock; in addition, they contributed over 40,000 tons of forage crops and 109,000 bushels of root crops.[21]

Sarah Harmony (Healy) Robbins's quilts are still owned by her daughters. Alta Robbins became a nurse and Sarah Robbins pursued a career in banking. Both women continue to live in the Blandford area where they grew up.   —AEN

Boys' Quilts

QUARTUS MOORE QUILT
(FIG. 166)

Quilts made by young girls abound in museums and private collections—see the examples made by Mollie Rice (figure 139/MQ 3459) and Ella Hapgood Ward (figure 80/MQ 5076) in this volume. While their brothers served apprenticeships outside the house to learn a craft or trade that would allow them to support their future family, most girls served their own version of an apprenticeship

FIGURE 166. Pieced quilt, "Album Block," made by Quartus Eugene Moore (1849–1864) of Leverett,
1855. Cotton (79½" × 81"). Private collection. *Photograph by David Stansbury.* MQ 3166.

at home with their mother learning to sew, quilt, cook, and clean. However, boys and men of the 1800s occasionally did make quilts, including the two bed coverings in this section. For boys, needlework was usually a lesson in patience assigned by their mother, often as a way to pass the time while bedridden due to illness or injury.

Six-year-old Quartus Eugene Moore of Leverett made the earlier of these two quilts around 1855. A handwritten card attached to the quilt explains, "Quilt pieced by Quartus E. Moore when he was 6 years old (about 1855) while recovering from a broken leg." In a time without television, video games, or action figures, the activity of piecing quilt blocks offered Quartus's mother the opportunity to keep him occupied, while also teaching him a practical skill. Quartus was born on September 3, 1849, the second son of George W. Moore (1818–1894) and Rhoda M. (Babcock) Moore (1818–1893).

Incorporated in 1774, the small, rural town of Leverett borders Amherst, Shutesbury, Sunderland, and Montague. In the late 1830s one observer noted, "This is principally an agricultural town."[22] While many other Massachusetts towns and villages were starting to industrialize by the 1830s, Leverett boasted only two scythe manufactories, producing 2,400 scythes in 1837; it also produced as a cottage industry an astounding 30,400 palm-leaf hats.[23] The wives and daughters of farmers during this period often exchanged the braided palm leaf for credit at the local store in order to purchase machine-made goods and other items that could not be produced on the farm.

The quilt's forty-two blocks (with sixteen half-blocks and four quarter-blocks) each measure nine inches square and are hand-pieced, set on point, and sashed with a light-blue striped fabric. While young Quartus pieced the blocks, family tradition holds that his mother put the top together and quilted it. The quilt is hand-quilted with six stitches to the inch. The blocks are quilted "in the ditch" and the lattice strips have a diamond pattern. A nine-inch-wide fine linen strip was attached across one end, probably sometime in the early twentieth century. It features three cross-stitched motifs of flowers and a floral basket in the center. Often called a "beard protector," this strip reinforced the top of the quilt, protecting it from the natural oils on one's neck and chin (and beard), helping to preserve the quilt's fabrics along that edge. The quilt has a single border, front to back binding, and cotton batting. The backing is composed of seven pieces of pattern-woven brown cotton, probably recycled from previously used household textiles. The center block has an inked inscription by an older hand, probably Quartus's mother, reading, "Quartus E. Moore Aged 6 years Leverett, Masstts."

Quartus died on December 20, 1864, at the young age of fifteen, a victim of diphtheria. His younger sister, Jerusha Elizabeth (b. 1851), died less

than a month later, in January 1865, of the same disease. The quilt undoubtedly was treasured by Quartus's mother and has been passed down in the family. In effect, the quilt became a "sentimental collaboration" of the maker's actions in creating it and his mother's emotions after his death, allowing her to feel his presence after he was gone.[24] The sentimental value of the quilt could only increase after the death of his sister Jerusha.   —AEN

DWIGHT BRADLEY QUILT
(FIG. 167)

Almost thirty years later, seventeen-year-old Dwight Bradley made his quilt top while recovering from an accident with an ax. The top is composed of twenty-five hundred one-and-a-half-inch-square blocks, hand- and machine-pieced together. The range of fabrics used in the top date from the 1860s up to the 1880s. Dwight's mother, Mary Celina (Reed) Bradley (1843–1909), was a dressmaker; family history suggests that the fabrics in Dwight's quilt came from fabrics left over from the garments she created. Dwight hand-stitched the individual squares together and then his mother used her sewing machine to sew the long strips to each other.

Dwight Bradley was born on July 27, 1867, in West Stockbridge. Located in the Berkshires, West Stockbridge was a farming community with significant quarries for marble and iron ore as well. His father, Luther Bradley (1841–1907), was a carpenter who later switched to farming to support his family. Dwight recovered from his injury and eventually married. With his wife Maud, Dwight moved to Lee, where he worked as a teamster for the coal company, according to the 1920 Census. Maud kept house for Dwight and their two sons. The quilt was passed down in the family and is now owned by the maker's great-niece.

Although most nineteenth-century sewing handbooks directed their instructions to girls and women, boys were not unaware of fabric, sewing, and quilts. They saw quilts made by their moth-

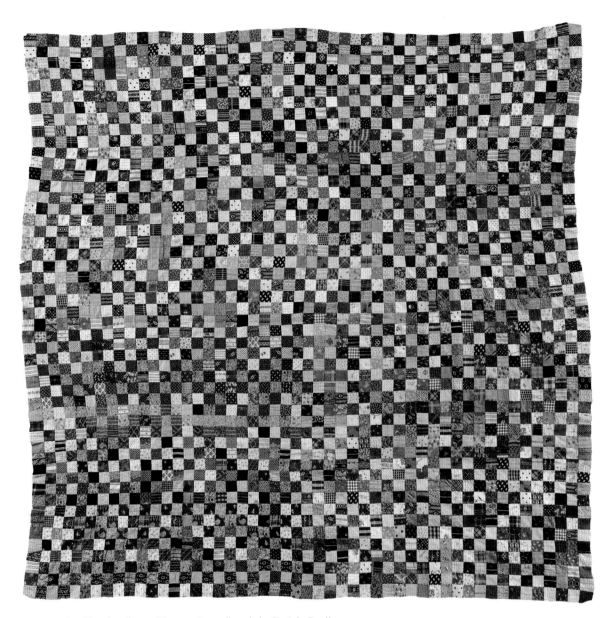

FIGURE 167. Pieced quilt top, "Postage Stamp," made by Dwight Bradley (1867–1936) of West Stockbridge, 1884. Cotton (64" × 62"). Private collection. *Photograph by David Stansbury.* MQ 4414.

ers and sisters take shape, eventually sleeping under them each night. In addition, many nineteenth-century primers and children's books used problems about fabric yardage to teach basic arithmetic skills.[25] And husbands and fathers often were charged with purchasing fabric and other sewing supplies for their female relatives at local and regional stores.

While stitching their quilts together, Quartus Moore and Dwight Bradley learned the same les-

sons of self-discipline and precision that sewing was intended to teach their sisters. In addition, these young men might relate the skills they learned for precise piecing to woodworking and carpentry once they were well.[26] By helping their sons to make a quilt, Dwight's and Quartus's mothers fulfilled their mothering role by teaching the boys new skills and nurturing important virtues, while also keeping them occupied as they recuperated in bed.   —AEN

Chapter 15

Immigrant and Ethnic Communities

For its first two hundred years of European settlement, Massachusetts' population was very homogeneous. Although native communities persisted through this period and the slave trade introduced a small African population, at the time of the first U.S. census in 1790, ninety-five percent of this state's inhabitants were of English heritage.[1] Beginning in the 1820s, events both here and abroad altered this demographic. Most important of these occurrences, as pointed out by historians Richard D. Brown and Jack Tager, is that "Massachusetts became industrial and urban before the rest of the nation."[2] The multitude of mills and factories built along the state's rivers offered employment to thousands of workers, as did the canals and railroads that connected the mills to their markets. Immigrants escaping famine, economic depression, and religious persecution in their home countries came by the tens of thousands to find work in Massachusetts, hoping to make a better life for themselves.

The first to come in large numbers were the Irish, escaping English oppression and then the potato famine, which began in 1845. In 1847 alone, over 37,000 Irish came to Boston; by 1855, 181,000 Irish immigrants inhabited the commonwealth.[3] Irish laborers took the dangerous jobs of building the infrastructure—the canals, dams, railroads, and huge stone factory buildings—that supported the new industrial economy. So many Irish women went into domestic service that the name "Bridget" became synonymous with "maid."[4] And the Irish went to work in the textile mills, working for lower wages than the native New Englanders would take. Exacerbated by the trauma of sudden and dramatic societal change, friction between the Catholic Irish and the Protestant Yankees over religious differences and jobs escalated into violence and riots in Boston and the industrial towns.

In general, the Irish suffered from terrible discrimination ("No Irish Need Apply") and often atrocious living conditions. In the textile mill town of Lawrence, the dirt-floor, one-room shacks that typically housed a large Irish family and often a boarder or two inspired the term "Shanty Irish."[5] Lowell mill girl Lucy Larcom recalled the poverty of some early Irish immigrants in her reminiscence, *A New England Girlhood*:

> Now, too, my childish desire to see a real beggar was gratified. Straggling petitioners for "cold victuals" hung around our back yard, always of Hibernian extraction; and a slice of bread was rewarded with a shower of benedictions that lost itself upon us in the flood of its own incomprehensible brogue."[6]

Hard work and perseverance paid off eventually. Within two or three generations, the Irish became an economic, social, and political force in the commonwealth. Of course, today Massachusetts is famed as the home of the Kennedys, a powerful political family of Irish heritage.

In the period after the Civil War, French Canadians escaping an agrarian depression in Quebec began coming to work in the Massachusetts mills. By 1880, twenty-five thousand French Canadians had arrived in the Bay State.[7] Like the Irish before them, they often met with discrimination and maltreatment—including from the Irish, who felt their

FIGURE 168. Photograph, *Portuguese Navy Yard*, c. 1910. Many Portuguese
immigrants settled along the southern shore of Massachusetts, working as fishermen.
Here, Portuguese children play among the shanties near the harbor in New Bedford.
Photograph courtesy of the New Bedford Whaling Museum, New Bedford, Mass.

hard-won jobs and communities were threatened by the interlopers. The owner of two quilts documented by MassQuilts wrote of her ancestor's coming to Lowell in 1874:

> Georgiana [Jondreau] and her family entered the U.S. hidden under hay in a wagon, escaping a smallpox epidemic, and joined relatives living in Little Canada in Lowell. She immediately went to work in a twine mill on Merrimac St. near the Concord River. She walked to work accompanied by her father armed with a bat to protect her from the Irish boys.[8]

This short passage illustrates much about the immigrant experience in Massachusetts: most foreigners, like Georgiana, came after a few intrepid family members or friends had established themselves here and written home, enticing others to join them; they tended to settle among their own kind in neighborhoods—such as "Little Canada" or "Little Italy"; and turf protection was rampant among gangs of immigrant and Yankee boys and young men.

At the turn of the twentieth century, the greatest wave of immigrants hit the shores of the Bay State. Over a million eastern and southern Europeans came to New England between 1890 and 1910, fleeing religious persecution and poverty.[9] They came from Poland, Russia, Lithuania, Austria-Hungary, Italy, Greece, Portugal, and many other countries.

They worked in the mills and they established themselves in business. The Portuguese were fishermen who settled mainly along the South Shore and Cape Cod; many of the Polish were farmers who found particularly rich soil to till in the Connecticut River Valley; many Russian Jews became tailors and grocers in eastern Massachusetts. Like their predecessors, they had a difficult time in the beginning. The famous case of Sacco and Vanzetti in 1921 — two Italian immigrants accused of and eventually executed for the crimes of robbery and murder — rocked the nation because the judgment seemed to many to be biased. (Today, in the Italian North End of Boston, you can find an historical marker noting the spot where the bodies of Sacco and Vanzetti lay on view in their coffins.)

Barely a hundred years after the emergence of Massachusetts as an industrial state, the composition of its population had switched from largely Yankee to a true melting pot of cultures. The 1920 federal census documented that almost seventy percent of Massachusetts residents were immigrants or the children of immigrants.[10] It was still, however, largely white: African Americans made up only a small percentage of the population of Massachusetts until the mid-twentieth century, when Blacks from southern states came north to find work in Massachusetts industries. Asian and Hispanic immigrants also did not come in substantial numbers until later in the twentieth century.

Not all of the immigrant groups that came to live in Massachusetts quilted. Of the hundreds of quilters identified by MassQuilts, only three were of Eastern European (Polish) heritage. No Jewish quilters were found at all. Inquiries to organizations representing these cultures uncovered no pre-1950 quilts, but did generate some interesting comments. Louise Silk declares in her book, *The Quilting Path: A Guide to Spiritual Discovery through Fabric, Thread, and Kabbalah*, "In my experience, quilters were not Jewish, and Jews did not quilt."[11] The research of Ronda McAllen on Jewish quilters in mid-nineteenth-century Baltimore shows that, in fact, Jews sometimes did quilt.[12] What appears to matter is region, rather than religion or ethnicity. The Jews of Baltimore were from Germany; the Jews of Massachu-

setts were mostly from Russia. Eastern European immigrants in general appear to have followed their tradition of sleeping under blankets and thick down-filled duvets. MassQuilts member Martha Supnik recalls also the social isolation of her own Jewish family who emigrated around 1905,

> Striving to preserve their cultural identity, they had little social contact with Christian women who were making quilts in church groups at that time. My mother said that my great-grandfather, who died in 1931, once made a patchwork quilt out of fabric samples from his son's custom tailoring shop. That quilt disappeared long before I was born in 1947.[13]

In contrast, scores of French-Canadian and Irish quilts turned up at MassQuilts documentation days. Quilts with British-Canadian, Italian, Portuguese, German, Scottish, and Armenian makers also appeared. This chapter explores the stories of these quilts and their immigrant families.　—LZB

MARY CLANCY QUILT
(FIG. 169)

Near the end of Brookfield's Tercentenary Program is a page of black and white, postage stamp–sized photographs. Even through the shades of gray, the bright, pretty eyes of Mary Clancy sparkle.[14] Never married, she was an "unclaimed treasure."[15] The "Log Cabin" comforter pictured here is also a treasure, though not unclaimed. It is one of many works created by the talented and always busy hands of Mary Clancy.

Mary was the oldest child of John (b. 1861) and Catherine Harrington Clancy (b. 1866) who immigrated to the United States as young children, John from Ireland and Catherine from Wales.[16] The Clancys arrived in Brookfield shortly after Mary's birth in 1884. Attracted by its rich soils, Europeans settled in the area by 1673 — early for a town that was neither on the coast nor on the Connecticut River. By the nineteenth century, manufacturing supplemented the local agricultural economy.

FIGURE 169. Pieced comforter, "Log Cabin," made by Mary Clancy (1884–1976) of Brookfield, c. 1890. Cotton (85" × 78"). Private collection. *Photograph by David Stansbury.* MQ 3271.

Shoe manufacturers, cotton and paper mills, and carriage makers all prospered. Merchants stocked goods from around the world, and lawyers, surgeons, and doctors offered their services.[17] Today, Brookfield's town common, where residents' sheep and cows once grazed, typifies the appearance of a serene New England village: Its white gazebo hosts concerts and speeches, benches beneath shady trees provide places to visit with friends, and large clapboarded houses line the streets.

Number 8 Kimball Street, the Clancy family home, stands less than half a mile from Brookfield Common. Kimball is a quiet, narrow road, visually little different from when the Clancys purchased their two-story Queen Anne–style house over a hundred years ago. Most of Mary's neighbors were Yankees, but French-Canadian, Polish, Italian, and of course Irish families also lived in the vicinity. The street, new and incomplete in 1870, soon connected to Mill Street and the flourishing paper mill.

Mary first appears on official records as a twenty-five-year-old finisher at the paper mill, which also employed her father and sister. She remained at the mill throughout her wage-earning years, changing duties as her experience and age progressed.[18] Mary's mother's expectations, however, freed her sons from becoming mill laborers. Catherine wanted all of her children to be well educated, but believed her boys in particular should attend college "at all cost." Two of her four sons complied: William became a chemist at the paper mill, and John became a dentist. The Clancy girls did not go to college, but their intelligence is evident. Sister Nellie became an accountant at the mill and youngest sister Annie became a dental assistant. Mary's formal education ended at eighth grade. Her wages helped support her younger siblings.

Although the Clancy daughters never married, Mary had been engaged to a railroad engineer. Like many oldest daughters, Mary felt a strong sense of responsibility to her parents and siblings, and was instrumental in raising her younger brothers and sisters. She spent years nursing her mother, ill with pancreatic cancer, and upon Catherine's death, Mary ended her engagement in order to continue managing her widowed father's home. By 1930, her broth-

ers had moved out, so the sisters added a boarder to their household.[19] When Mary's father died in 1944, her dentist brother, John, returned to the Kimball Street house.

Mary, Nellie, and John resided on Kimball Street until they were in their nineties, and theirs was a house filled with children and laughter. After Mary's retirement, her great-nieces and nephews were regular visitors, where they played school, always found molasses cookies in the jar, and gathered to say the rosary at one o'clock every afternoon.

St. Mary's Church received much of Mary's time. Every evening, Mary walked the short distance from Kimball Street to make sure the flowers were fresh and the priests' vestments were clean and ready—a dedication that Mary learned from her parents, who had funded a stained glass window during the 1891 church renovation. "She *was* the Alter Guild" declares her niece-in-law.

Mary, who also tatted and crocheted, made numerous quilts, often working with her sister Nellie to "keep their hands busy." Many of Mary's quilts survive, and her preference for the "Log Cabin" pattern is evident in the number of quilts and tops pieced in this pattern. Some tops contain bright silks and velvets. Others are more somber. The featured comforter is comprised of printed cottons from the late nineteenth century, arranged with a clear appreciation of color and tonal balance. However, Mary was a consummate saver who even at her death in 1976 at the age of ninety-two had an impressive fabric stash, so this comforter may well have been constructed in the twentieth century using the earlier fabrics.

Mary Clancy was a petite woman, with a gentle manner, and a sweet sense of humor. A proper woman who never appeared outdoors without her white gloves and hat, she was modest of her contributions. She was one of many whose quiet sacrifices put others through school, kept households functioning, and made churches serene.   —DCA

MARY MARGARET DE VEAU QUILT

(FIG. 170)

Mary Margaret De Veau, born April 17, 1870, in the Canadian province of Nova Scotia, immigrated to Massachusetts at the age of eighteen. Margaret (as she was called by her family) lived most of her adult life in Haverhill, and returned to Canada the year before her death in 1935. She never married. Although Margaret lived and worked in the Haverhill area, family members believe that she remained a citizen of Canada, and never applied for United States citizenship. This was a common experience of French-Canadian workers in Massachusetts; because of the relatively short distance between their Canadian home and Massachusetts, they came and went as work opportunities, family obligations, and homesickness drove them.[20] Members of Margaret's family can be traced to Washington Avenue in Haverhill, a primarily French-Canadian neighborhood and one of the poorer sections of town. Whether she resided with them is unknown, for no further record can be found of her. Although little is known about Margaret, her sewing artistry is preserved in the crazy-quilt top she left in the care of her family.

Crazy quilts abound in the United States, and Massachusetts has its healthy share. Silks in satin and velvet weaves, along with many other fancy fabrics, were readily available from mail-order companies, local shops, and stashes of remnants at home. Department stores, including Boston's Jordan Marsh, profited from the fashion by selling bags of scraps for one dollar each.[21] The crazy-quilt fad swept the nation primarily during the last quarter of the nineteenth century, although occasional examples of the style can be found earlier and later. It was particularly strong in the mid-1880s. The decline of the crazy-quilt fashion at the turn of the twentieth century probably caused many examples to be left unfinished, as with Margaret's crazy quilt.

Constructed from thirty-five blocks, each twelve and a quarter inches square, this work is constructed of late nineteenth-century silk velvet, taffeta, and satin fabrics, plus grosgrain, commemorative, and ombré ribbons. One pink commemorative ribbon, printed in gold letters with "Nantucket," perhaps was a souvenir of a pleasant vacation. Other pieces of fabric are embroidered with the initials "AR" and "ARD" and the name "Helen," probably friends and relatives of Margaret who assisted with her quilt top. Margaret used many of the embroidery patterns popular during that period, including three interlocking rings (representing the Odd Fellows' symbol of Friendship, Love, and Trust, or the Holy Trinity), butterflies, fans, and flowers, floral bouquets tied with ribbons, and figures of animals and children.[22] Margaret attached the individual crazy pieces with embroidery to foundation fabrics made primarily of cottons.[23] Margaret's quilt is unusual for its light color palette; traditionally, crazy quilts are made in maroon, brown, blue, and other dark colors. This design choice is consistent with what textile historians Linda Welters and Margaret Ordonez found in their study of French-Canadian quiltmakers in Rhode Island. They note in the exhibit catalogue, *Home from the Mill*, that this cultural group showed "a marked preference for light colors."[24]

Like so many women throughout history, little is known of Margaret. The main evidence of her life lies in her quilt. The quilt reveals that she had access to elegant fabrics, perhaps through her employer or through her own well-considered purchases, and that she paid careful attention to detail. Excellence marks her color sense and embroidery skills.   —VLS

FIGURE 170. Foundation-pieced crazy quilt top, made by Mary Margaret DeVeau (1870–
1935), of Haverhill, c. 1890. Silk (86" × 61½"). Private collection. *Photograph by David
Stansbury.* MQ 5003.

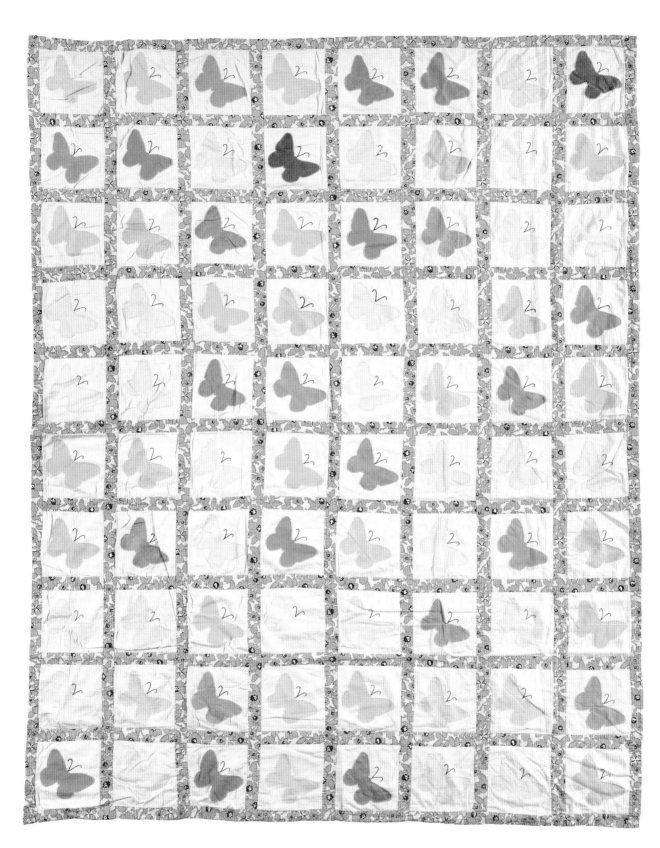

FIGURE 171. Appliquéd quilt, "Butterflies," made by Harmeline "Minnie" Giroux Louison (1892–1979) of North Adams, c. 1935–1945. Cotton (82¼" × 65¼"). Private collection. *Photograph by David Stansbury.* MQ 4838.

HARMELINE GIROUX LOUISON QUILT

(FIG. 171)

The crash of the stock market in 1929 and the Great Depression that followed stimulated a psychological need for thriftiness and frugality in America that found expression in the pieced and appliquéd quilt revival of the 1930s. Among the many quilt patterns that proliferated during this period, butterfly appliqué patterns were particularly popular (see also figure 121/MQ 2006).[25]

One such quilt was made by Harmeline Giroux, born in 1892 on a farm in Quebec. Upon the Giroux family's arrival in North Adams in 1906, Minnie (as her family called her) went from being a farm girl to a factory worker.[26] She began working at the Berkshire Fine Spinning Corporation in 1907 at the age of fifteen, and continued working there for the next fifty years.[27] For most of that time she was a weaver.

In 1910, eighteen-year-old Minnie married coworker Adolph Louison, another French-Canadian immigrant. The couple's only child, a son, was born within two years. The Louisons remained at the mill for most of their married lives. Adolph died in 1958, the year after Minnie retired.

Minnie's son, Adolph, Jr., whom the family called "Doug," was the undisputed "apple of his mother's eye." Minnie's inclusive heart, however, embraced also her daughter-in-law, Renée, and grandchildren; she also became acting grandmother to some of Renée's siblings' children, including the current quilt owner.

Although family and work took up much of Minnie's time, she was a member of Saint Thomas Aquinas Church in nearby Adams. After being widowed, Minnie joined the Golden Age Club, and hosted Friday night sewing bees at her home during the 1950s and 1960s.

Minnie moved frequently during her life in North Adams, eventually settling in a large house on Commercial Street that was subdivided into apartments and rented to various relatives. Her early farm years trained her to keep chickens for eggs, manage a thriving vegetable garden, and preserve large vats of *kapusta*, a type of sauerkraut, every year—a recipe learned perhaps from a Polish neighbor. Minnie's love of needlework is evidenced not only by her quilt, but by the numerous doilies, afghans, and cheerfully embroidered pillowcases and handkerchiefs that she created. During her later years, the short, bespectacled Minnie usually wore a full apron with an embroidered handkerchief tucked in the pocket, but her love of colorful brooches and cameos echoed a younger woman's fondness for dressing up. Her butterfly quilt reflects that early fashion sense, and was always displayed prominently on her own bed. Minnie Louison's expansive sense of family brought warmth and stability to her home and those she loved. Upon her death, the quilt became a cherished memento.   —DCA

JULIA KRUSZYNA STEUER QUILT

(FIG. 172)

At the time of this writing, quiltmaker Julia Kruszyna Steuer was ninety-three years old, still living in her home in North Adams, and still "relishing pierogies."[28] Sponsored by his brother Thomas, Julia's father, Joseph Kruszyna, came to the United States in 1889 from Kosworat, Galicia, which was then in Austria. Joseph arrived at Castle Garden on Manhattan, America's first official immigration center (established in 1855), and from there went to work in the textile mills of Ware, Massachusetts. The 1900 U.S. census finds Joseph working as a weaver in a cotton mill and living with his brother's family in Adams. There, he met and married Justyna Izyk, a native of Jaslo, Poland, who had come to Adams in the 1890s. The number of Polish residents in Adams boomed between 1895 and 1900, as recruiters sent by the Berkshire Fine Spinning Company successfully enticed Polish farmers to immigrate. As Julia's daughter states of her family, "They all hoped to have farms in the U.S.; Uncle Tom did in Cheshire, but most settled for mills."[29]

Unfortunately, Joseph died young in 1916, leaving Justyna with four small children, including two-year-old Julia. She married her second hus-

FIGURE 172. Pieced comforter, "Grandmother's Flower Garden," made by Julia Agnes (Kruszyna) Steuer (1914–) of North Adams, started c. 1934 and finished 1970s, Cotton (95" × 75"). Private collection. *Photograph by David Stansbury.* MQ 4345.

band, John Durda, who came to Massachusetts from Austria-Hungary around 1905, and whom she knew from the Polish National Catholic Church in Adams. Together, Justyna and John had two more children. Justyna and her family assimilated into the American culture more quickly than did some of their Polish neighbors. Julia's daughter relates that "Those who belonged to St. Stanislaus, the Roman Catholic Church, . . . [and who] attended Polish school . . . maintained their Polish traditions much more than the families who belonged to the Polish National Catholic Church and attended public school, as did my mother." Nevertheless, the Kruszyna-Durda family still "observed Christmas Eve customs, prepared and ate Polish foods . . . , danced the polka, listened to Polish programs on the radio, [and] played Polish pitch at every picnic."[30]

It fell to the second generation to experiment with quiltmaking. Although Justyna sewed, she did not make quilts. According to her granddaughter, "quilting was not big in the Polish community; crocheting afghans seems to have been much more common; every family has afghans handed down." Julia started her quilt top around the time of her wedding in 1934 to Edward G. Steuer, a high school teacher whom she had met at church. (Edward's father was an immigrant from Bavaria, who set up shop as a barber in Adams.) After her marriage, Julia was soon busy raising a daughter, keeping house, doing charity work, and sewing clothing and slipcovers for clients. After she was widowed in 1966, Julia went to work at a local dress shop, which was run by the Venezuelan nephew of the Italian immigrant founder and employed a German tailor, a Honduran seamstress, and (later) a Japanese tailor— creating a "virtual League of Nations."[31] While Julia hooked and braided rugs, and sewed "many mother-daughter outfits, Halloween costumes, and even bathing suits when her daughter was growing up," she did not get back to her quilt until the 1970s, when the event of her daughter's wedding spurred her to finish it.

Julia hand-stitched the hexagons of the "Grandmother's Flower Garden" pattern. She used a thin blanket for the batting, and tied the layers together with pink and white yarns. The knife-edge finish is stitched carefully around the contours of each outer hexagon. Julia expressed confidence in her sewing skills and her desire to participate in the latest American quiltmaking fashion by choosing the "Grandmother's Flower Garden" design for her first pieced quilt. Perhaps, though, its predictable pattern and picky precision did not satisfy her artistic side, as it also was her last quilt. While the Polish community did not add significantly to the tradition of quiltmaking in Massachusetts, their contribution to the Bay State's economy and culture is immeasurable.

—LZB

JOSEPHINE ROSSI ANZALONE QUILT
(FIG. 173)

Artistry motivated Josephine Anzalone to make her silk double-sided comforter. A creative woman who knitted, crocheted, tatted, and even painted, Josephine was willing to "try any handwork."[32] Born Josephine Rossi in Avellino, Naples, Italy, she was only eight years old when she immigrated in 1893. Josephine was the oldest daughter of Luigi and Filomena (Ventola) Rossi. Her family settled in Boston's North End near other Avellino families. Most immigrants congregated in neighborhoods with others from their country of origin. Italians, however, specifically sought out family or former neighbors from their own villages, a practice that helped preserve cultural traditions, but also made them more insular.[33] In December of 1903, Josephine became the eighteen-year-old bride of fellow immigrant and shoemaker Joseph Anzalone and settled in Cambridge; a brash move among the Avellino community. There they rented and eventually purchased a three-decker house and raised their two sons and four daughters.

Italian immigration to the Americas began in the mid-1700s, but the majority of Italian immigrants came in the late nineteenth and early twentieth centuries. Burdened by drought, epidemics, a destructive grapevine parasite, and eruptions of Mount Aetna, nearly seven million

FIGURE 173. Pieced comforter, obverse pattern "Attic Window,"
reverse pattern "One Patch," made by Josephine (Rossi) Anzalone
(1885–1966) of Cambridge, c. 1910–1920. Silk (73" × 60¾"). Private
collection. *Photograph by David Stansbury.* MQ 4472.

FIGURE 174. Pieced back, "One Patch," of the Josephine Anzalone quilt. *Photograph by David Stansbury.*

southern Italians and Sicilians emigrated to the United States between 1884 and 1924.[34] Among them were the Rossis and Anzalones.

Josephine's early life was not peaceful. All immigrants are subject to discrimination and stereotyping, but Italians suffered particularly harsh treatment; they were lynched at a rate second only to those of African Americans. In 1891, Italy temporarily ended diplomatic relations with the United States when the lynching of eleven Italian immigrants and Italian Americans in New Orleans met with minimal legal response.[35] Closer to Boston, the xenophobic trial and execution of Sacco and Vanzetti received international notoriety in the 1920s. Gang violence between Italians and Irish groups resentful of the newer immigrants filled Josephine's earliest years.[36] In January 1919, the Anzalone family listened in horror to the news that a great wall of molasses, fifteen feet high, coursed through Boston's Italian North End neighborhoods, leveling buildings, sweeping train trestles and houses from their foundations, and killing twenty-one people.[37] Surprisingly, this tumult created, as Josephine's granddaughter recalls, a woman "generous in spirit," who graciously accepted and cherished her children's spouses, regardless of nationality.

Josephine mixed her love of food and family with her artistry. Sporting slacks when few women publicly did so, she regularly visited the Boston Museum of Fine Arts, and painted her own works. Josephine and her friend, "Mrs. Bly," created extraordinary fashion shows at the local theater; Josephine also lent Portuguese immigrant, Mrs. Bragga, a designing hand at her millinery shop. Yet she regularly served three-course meals complete with generous servings of traditional Napoli tomato sauce or "gravy," and babysat for her grandchildren. Never competitive of her talents, Josephine delighted whenever anyone tried something new; praising her daughters-in-law, and supporting them.

Embodying Josephine's own complexity, her quilt is double-sided. Her granddaughter remembers Josephine's ability to reproduce clothing seen in magazines, and it is likely she drafted her quilt patterns in a similar fashion. On the front of the quilt, three-inch squares and triangles were pieced in the "Attic Window" pattern.[38] The reverse is a simple "One Patch," but the alternating dark and light blocks are arranged to create concentric bands of color. White, black, and claret are the predominant colors on the front, while deeper blues and olive greens appear on the back. The relatively airy feel of the front suggests that Josephine embraced the lighter-hued colorways of the early twentieth century. Family tradition theorizes that Josephine's sister, who became a dressmaker, provided the fabric. The quilt probably dates from 1910 or 1920, when Josephine had three sisters in the dressmaking business who might have provided materials.

Josephine taught her daughters and granddaughters many skills, but not quilting. Nevertheless, two of her son Salvatore's daughters became quilters, including the current quilt owner, Janice Bakey. Janice became a quilter while helping her dying sister finish quilts for her grandchildren. Now, quilting has become the link to her past and future. "I've made things out of my sister's material for her children and granddaughters. I taught my sister's granddaughter how to quilt. Quilting keeps that [family] connection." As a woman who admired creativity, Josephine Anzalone would have approved.   —DCA

ADDIE EFFINGTON BAILEY QUILT

(FIG. 175)

Addie (Effington) Bailey's "Court House Steps" quilt radiates with the syncopated style and vibrant colors attributed to southern African-American quilters.[39] This is no surprise, since she grew up quilting in the small village of Bogue Chitto, Mississippi. Born on her family's 200-acre "farm and a half," Addie learned to quilt from her mother, who gathered friends and relatives around a large quilt frame erected outdoors to finish her works. Many of Addie's quilts were created during what has been dubbed Mississippi's "Golden Age of Quilting."[40]

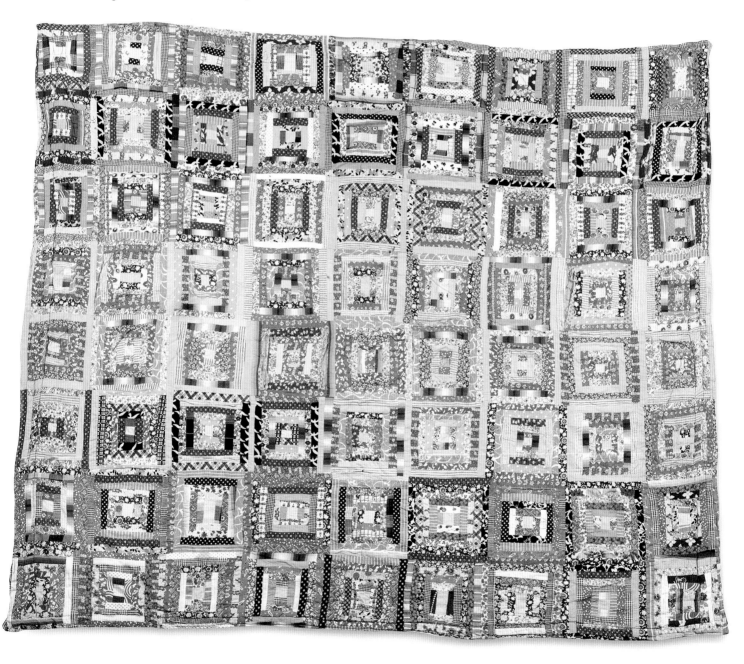

FIGURE 175. Pieced quilt, "Court House Steps," made by Addie (Effington) Bailey (1912–1993) of Springfield, c. 1940s. Cotton (72½" × 64"). Collection of Peabody Essex Museum, Salem, Mass., 2006 museum purchase, (PEM 138635). *Photograph by David Stansbury.* MQ 3458.

"Court House Steps" is one of many variations of the "Log Cabin" pattern made of narrow strips of fabric arranged into blocks. The maker intermingled pastel prints of the Depression era with the brightly colored printed cotton fabrics of the 1940s. Her use of yellow center blocks and the thoughtful alignment of bands of yellow, red, blue, and striped fabrics reveal an intuitive and playful use of color. Addie reused a blanket as quilt batting between the quilt top and the lining.

Mississippi life was difficult even for formerly prosperous farmers like Addie's family. The 1920s boll-weevil infestation pushed even lucrative farmers into economic jeopardy, and the Depression further contributed to the demise of small Mississippi towns. Moreover, persistent Jim Crow laws codifying racial segregation and discrimination encouraged many African Americans to migrate north. Although not free from prejudice, northern urban centers often offered greater educational and economic stability.

In 1953, Addie's husband, Nathaniel Bailey,

FIGURE 176. Addie Bailey, c. 1960. *Photograph courtesy of Irma Foster.*

decided to join their four oldest children in Massachusetts. Addie reluctantly agreed, and at age forty-one she "stuffed" four adults, four "big" children, and trunk-loads of goods into a single car; the family then spent a week making their way north. Despite the need for strategic packing, Addie brought several of her quilts.

Upon arriving in Massachusetts, Addie and Nathaniel acquired a small house in Springfield. Nathaniel worked in a nearby foundry where his two older sons were already employed; he later became a Baptist minister. Addie managed the house, finished raising the youngest of their eight children, kept chickens for eggs, a milk cow, and supplemented the household income by working at a nearby restaurant. She was an accomplished seamstress and dressmaker and made many garments for her family. She was active in the Baptist Church, serving as a Springfield missionary for more than twenty-five years.

Erecting a frame in Addie's small house was difficult, and the New England weather made outdoor quilting less attractive, yet she continued to make quilt tops in Springfield. She was a generous quiltmaker who gave many of her pieces away. This one was presented as a wedding gift to her youngest daughter many years after it was completed.

Addie died at age eighty-one, and her quilts might have been lost to anonymity like so many others. Instead, recognition of her contributions to American quilt history recently became assured when the Peabody Essex Museum acquired her striking quilt, the first example by an African-American quilter in the museum's collection.

—DCA and PBR

THERESA OLIVER MELLO QUILT
(FIG. 177)

Founded on high principles and benevolence, the textile manufacturing center of Lowell employed young women from rural New England eager to leave the drudgery of farm work for the promise of wages that would enable them to have better lives. As the search for profit supplanted the ideals of

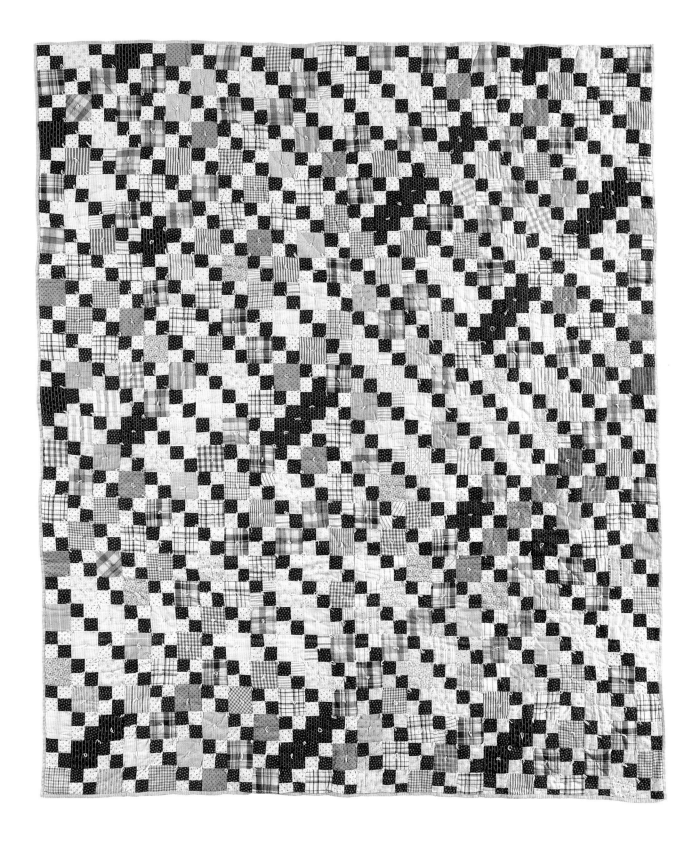

FIGURE 177. Pieced comforter, "Four-Patch," made by Theresa
(Oliver) Mello (1875–1921) of Lowell, c. 1910. Cotton (82" × 70").
Collection of the New England Quilt Museum, (2000.07). *Photograph
by David Stansbury*. MQ 2049.

FIGURE 178. Workers at the Boott Cotton Mills, c. 1915. Theresa Mello is seated in the second row, third from right. *Photograph courtesy of Anne and Jean Keating.*

their founders, mills became less attractive to these women and labor unrest among them arose. In the 1840s and 1850s, Irish immigrants and then, in the 1860s and 1870s, French Canadians began to fill the ranks of mill workers in Lowell. By the 1880s, they were joined by Greeks, Poles, Russian Jews, Armenians, Lithuanians, and Portuguese. All were seeking a better life in America.[41]

Among the Portuguese mill workers was Theresa Oliver, the third child of John and Mary (Bettencourt) Oliver.[42] Theresa was born on the island of St. George in the Azores and immigrated with her family to Provincetown, Massachusetts, in 1892. Theresa later moved to Lowell, where she lived with a married sister, and began working in the Boott Cotton Mills as a weaver, tending twelve looms that produced canvas. In Lowell, Theresa met and married Frank F. Mello (1867–1943), originally from

Terceira in the Azores. At one time, Frank was a foreman at a factory that made boxes to encase upright pianos, and later, during World War I, worked in a factory that made boxes for rifles. They had two children, Amelia Frances (1904–1968) and Americo John (1907–1999). The Mello family resided in a top-floor apartment in the three-story Saunders Block, which housed the Saunders Market on the ground floor. The block, long since demolished, was located in the heart of the Portuguese community at the corner of Gorham and Summer Streets. In April of 1921, while lifting a heavy bundle (probably a roll or rolls of canvas), Theresa injured herself, resulting in hospitalization and surgery. She died shortly thereafter and was buried in St. Patrick's Cemetery in Lowell. Her family has speculated that she suffered a hernia, and then developed peritonitis after the surgery, causing her death.[43]

FIGURE 179. Theresa Mello with daughter Amelia and son Americo, c. 1915. *Photograph courtesy of Anne and Jean Keating.*

According to her granddaughters, Theresa was known for her good works in the Portuguese community, tending to the sick and giving assistance to those in need. As a group, Portuguese women were known for their fine handwork, though mostly lace-making and embroidery, rather than quiltmaking. Theresa's mother and sister also made quilts, as did many of their neighbors, but, unfortunately, none survived their use as warm bedding. Theresa left many examples of fine handwork herself, but most of her work was for utilitarian purposes, such as lace-edged table runners, embroidered towels from material produced at Boott Mills, and twelve wool "Log Cabin" quilts, and eight cotton "Four Patch" quilts, all incorporating fabrics from the Lowell mills. The quilt illustrated here is composed of 672 blocks, each approximately three inches square, set in "Four Patch" blocks in twenty-eight vertical rows by twenty-four horizontal rows. Filled with cotton batting of medium thickness and tied rather than quilted, the quilt was meant to be used during the cold Lowell winters, not as a show piece. Yet the deliberate setting of the reds in a diagonal pattern punctuated by the random blue and orange patches

belie a wonderful color sense, as is also evidenced by her "Log Cabin" ("Barn Raising" variation) quilt still in the possession of a family member, and two other quilts in the collection of the New England Quilt Museum.[44]   —ABL

ANTARAM MANOOGIAN BARSAMIAN QUILT

(FIG. 180)

World War I caused tectonic shifts in world culture. It spelled the end of the Ottoman Empire, which once covered the Middle East, northern Africa, and southeastern Europe. The last vestiges of this once-powerful Muslim empire were centered in Turkey in the early twentieth century. Like many countries at that time, the Turkish government encouraged a strongly nationalistic culture, but the consequences of that nationalism were particularly heinous. The Armenians, a Christian minority who for centuries had lived alongside their Muslim neighbors (although they were subject to prejudice and periodic violence), became the target of the Young Turk government, which desired their eradication. The Armenian genocide began in 1915, with the murder of three hundred Armenian leaders who had been called together for a purported meeting in Istanbul. By the end of World War I (which largely distracted the world from the actions of the Young Turks), one and a half million Armenians— well over half of all Armenians in the Ottoman Empire—were killed by starvation, overwork in labor camps, or outright murder.[45]

Recognizing the impending disaster, Movses Manoogian came to the United States in an attempt to find a way out of Turkey for his family. Tragically, he was not successful. His wife and children all were murdered—except Antaram, who at the age of about seven had the presence of mind to pretend she was dead in order to survive the massacre. She was rescued and taken to an orphanage near the Russian border, where she was well treated and learned to speak Russian. Antaram lived at the orphanage for three years.

At the orphanage, she made the center of this

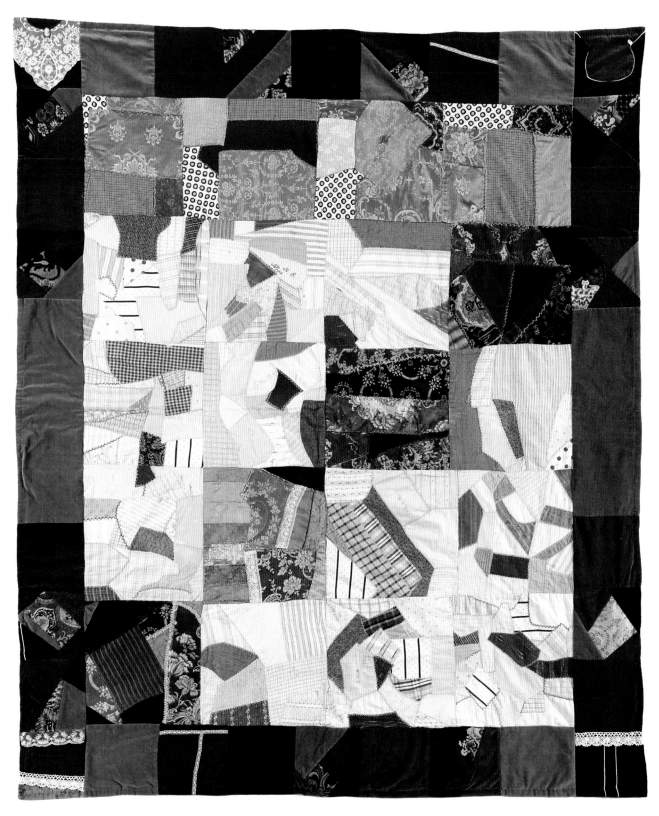

FIGURE 180. Foundation-pieced, embroidered crazy quilt, made by Antaram
(Manoogian) Barsamian (1907–1999) of West Roxbury, started c. 1915, finished 1999.
Cotton, silk, and synthetic fabrics (74" × 45"). Private collection. *Photograph by David
Stansbury.* MQ 2003.

FIGURE 181. Anataram Barsamian with her granddaughters, 1999. *Photograph courtesy of Kaye Barsamian.*

crazy quilt. Its childish stitches and haphazard use of fabrics tell of a little girl desiring to please her caretakers, but perhaps not actually enjoying the task set out for her. Antaram included cotton flannel and calico from orphanage clothing, as well as the more expected silk brocades, in her crazy quilt. Crazy patchwork was not familiar to her—Armenians traditionally favored lacemaking, embroidery, and appliqué as needlework techniques.[46] Although Antaram never made another quilt, the deeply felt significance of this piece is evident in the fact that she kept it throughout her life, despite her many relocations. Unfortunately, the family no longer knows to whom the initials and names that appear on the quilt belong—perhaps they were embroidered by fellow orphans.

After the war, Movses Manoogian returned to Turkey to try to find his family. He learned that only Antaram had survived, but no one knew where she was. After years of searching, he found that she had gone to Argentina. To reunite with her father and his new wife, Antaram sailed for America from Buenos Aires in 1924 at the age of seventeen. Land-

ing on Ellis Island, she proceeded to Hopedale, in southeastern Worcester County, where she finally joined the remains of her family.

Massachusetts offered a new life for many Armenians who escaped the Turkish massacres of the 1890s and the campaign of genocide of 1915 to 1916. Like so many other Eastern Europeans who came to the Commonwealth at that time, Armenians were attracted by employment opportunities in the factories, settling particularly in Worcester County. A major product of the Hopedale factories were Northrop looms, which were used widely by American and international textile manufacturers.[47]

A traditional man, Movses preferred that Antaram marry rather than attend school. In 1925, Antaram became the wife of Mihran Barsamian (1907–1950), who had come to America before the massacres. Jordan Marsh, Boston's elite department store, employed Mihran as their Oriental rug repair and design man. Antaram and Mihran lived in South Boston, where they raised six children; in 1948, they moved to West Roxbury, another Boston suburb.

Supporting her adopted country during World War II, Antaram went to work in a local factory, building submarines for the war effort.[48] Adolph Hitler was strongly influenced by the Armenian genocide of World War I, commenting chillingly in 1939, "Who, after all, speaks today of the annihilation of the Armenians?"[49] Antaram undoubtedly understood the tragedy unfolding again in Europe —the Jewish Holocaust and the annihilation of Poles and anyone else who stood in Germany's way.

After Mihran's death in 1950, Anataram stayed at home in West Roxbury to raise her children, the youngest of whom was only two. She never learned to drive, but stayed in touch with the world in part through an Armenian-language newspaper, which she received every day. Following Antaram's death in 1999, her crazy quilt was finished by a family friend, who created a border for it with pieces of the dresses of Antaram's beloved granddaughters. —LZB

FIGURE 182. Appliquéd quilt, "Dahlia," made by Ann (Hollos) Davison (1879–1970) of North Adams, c. 1930s. Cotton (88" × 74"). Private collection. *Photograph by David Stansbury.* MQ 4833.

ANN HOLLOS DAVISON QUILT

(FIG. 182)

Ann Hollos Davison loved quiltmaking. As a child, she made quilts with her grandmother, and as a mother and grandmother, she made them for her adult children and grandchildren. According to one of her granddaughters, the "Dahlia" pattern shown here was her favorite.[50]

Born in 1879 in Soothill, Yorkshire, England, Ann was the daughter of William and Sarah Hollos and worked in the woolen mills there as a young girl. In 1897, she married Alfred Davison (born 1874), a glass blower at the local glassworks. About twelve years later, the couple and their first four children immigrated to North Adams, Massachusetts.

Located in the northwest corner of the Berkshires, North Adams is home today to the Massachusetts Museum of Contemporary Art, one of the largest modern art museums in the country. Historically, however, it was industry, not art, that defined the city. Originally inhabited by the Pocumtuc Indians, North Adams's location on the Hoosic River made it an attractive mill site.[51] By the mid-1800s, the city housed machinery shops, sleigh and wagon makers, and numerous shoe and textile fac-

tories. Arnold and Company, established in 1860 and boasting the most innovative textile printing equipment of its time, became a leading producer of printed fabric and the largest employer in North Adams until the 1930s.

As elsewhere in Massachusetts, the North Adams factories attracted numerous immigrants. Most were Irish, Italian, or French Canadian, but the English arrived, too, including Ann's father, William Hollos, who worked in the printing mill. Missing family, he requested that one of his children join him in North Adams. Alfred came first; then in 1909, Ann and their children followed, sailing from Glasgow, Scotland, to Boston, then traveling across the state. They rented a house behind the factory, where Alfred and the older children joined William at the print works. This section of town was called "Blackinton," after the owners of the local wool mill (see fig. 116/MQ 2417). Ann didn't like it at first, saying "it's a God forsaken land he's brought me to," but the family stayed.[52] In 1917, Ann, Alfred, and their four oldest children became naturalized citizens; the six additional children they had after 1913 were born American citizens.

U.S. census records show that in 1920 Alfred worked as a salesman for the local department store, but by 1930, around the time this quilt was

FIGURE 183. Ann Davison (*seated*) and her family, c. 1920. *Photograph courtesy of Kathy A. West.*

FIGURE 184. Ann Davison (*standing*) with her quilting friends, c. 1950. *Photograph courtesy of Kathy A. West.*

made, he had returned to the print works, working in the bleaching department. In that year, three of Alfred and Ann's children who lived with them worked in the textile mills: Robert, age twenty-six, was a packer at the print works; Gladys, age sixteen, worked as a design painter; and fifteen-year-old William worked with his father in the bleaching department. Although money was tight and life was difficult at times, Ann focused on her family, volunteering, and quiltmaking.

A large part of Ann's volunteer work centered on St. John's Episcopal Church. Ann joined the Afternoon Guild, which did charitable sewing, and she was president of the Rector's Aid Society for twenty years until she turned ninety. The Rector's Aid Society raised funds for the pastor through a variety of means, including quilting. Ann was a skilled quilter in her own right, yet occasionally paid to have her tops quilted by the women in the Rector's Aid Society. The "Dahlia" quilt featured here was one of two matching tops completed by them in the 1930s.

Ann's relief work during World War II included fundraising dances and card parties, collecting food and clothing, and knitting and sewing. The British Government awarded her the medal of "Service for the Cause of Freedom" from King George V.

As an English-trained quilter, it is not surprising that Ann used paper-piecing, and taught her children and granddaughters to quilt in the same fashion. She kept a frame in her house, and her son and daughter-in-law quilted with her until the end of her life at age ninety-one.

Ann Hollos Davison is remembered as a dedicated volunteer, the maker of marvelous Yorkshire pudding, and a kind, loving grandmother. But, her granddaughter notes, it is her quilts that keep her memory alive. "Quilts tie you in. I don't know if she knows I make quilts, but I like to think so. Quilts keep the quiltmaker alive. Now I have grandchildren and I show them things, and they can keep the story alive." —DCA

Chapter 16

Quilts in War Time

War is a time of fear, hope, courage, loss, and commitment—not a time generally connected to the domesticity or artistry of quiltmaking. But countries at war, particularly if the battlefields are within their boundaries, are called upon to sacrifice not only their sons and sometimes daughters, but material goods such as food, clothing, and bedding as well. Bed quilts may even be a byproduct of war: textile and costume historians have long noted that jackets were used as padding under chain-mail, and that compactly quilted garments themselves sometimes served as a form of armor.

The first acknowledged American connection between war and quilts occurred during the Revolutionary War. In Massachusetts, as elsewhere in the colonies and would-be United States, provision officers during the Revolutionary War collected food, clothing, blankets, and quilts to feed and warm the Continental Army.[1] Men received the credit for gathering and transporting the supplies, but it was often women's labor that produced the collected cheese, stockings, meat, blankets, yarn, and quilts.

Provisioning the Army became significantly more organized during the Civil War, thanks in part to the United States Sanitary Commission. Initially organized as a means to improve facilities where wounded soldiers were treated, the Sanitary Commission quickly became a resource for nurses, healthy foods, clean clothes, and bedding. Boston-born New York clergyman the Reverend Henry W. Bellows and Massachusetts' social reformer Dorothea Dix were instrumental in the commission's creation. The first state Sanitary Commission was established in New York in 1861 and within months a reluctant President Lincoln authorized the creation of a national commission. Under the auspices of Frederick Law Olmsted, the United States Sanitary Commission designed guidelines for the manufacture and shipping of necessary supplies. Goods were gathered or created in cities and towns and then shipped to a state office, and in turn to a specific part of the army. Many supplies were forwarded first to the Army of Virginia and later the Army of the Potomac from the central Massachusetts office at 22 Summer Street in Boston, which received supplies also from Vermont, New Hampshire, and Maine. In addition to food and clothing, light quilts, heavy quilts, and comfortables all were requested.[2]

In total, the United States Sanitary Commission collected and distributed over 250,000 quilts and comforters.[3] It is not clear how many quilts Massachusetts towns supplied to the Boston office. Town records varied from noting that "The Ladies of Wayland, . . . held frequent meetings . . . [and] among those articles forwarded were 14 blankets, 53 quilts, 88 bed sacks . . . ," to the much more vague notation that "The ladies of Reading met two or three times a week during the war to prepare lint bandages, and clothing for the soldiers and forwarded them to the Army and to the Sanitary Commission. They kept no record of their good works; one of them Miss Emily Ruggles, furnished a representative recruit 'for three years service.'"[4]

By the start of the Great War (World War I), quilts were less likely to be found among the official supplies shipped to soldiers. Factory-made bedding was readily available, and women's efforts focused on providing bandages, mittens, or stockings. Yet quilting was still a war effort. Just as Americans gave up silk stockings to make parachutes, and adopted white, greasy margarine to send butter to the front lines, they also were encouraged to make scrap quilts to save factory-made blankets for the armed forces.[5]

War-time quilt production continued as women made individual gifts for sweethearts and sons, as fundraisers for the war effort—most notably the Red Cross quilt described in this section (fig. 191/ MQ 3239), and as means of filling lonely hours anticipating the return of distant soldiers (fig. 194/MQ 4955). Quiltmakers always have found solace in their work, and worried wives and mothers continued to stitch their concerns into their quilts (see also fig. 40/MQ 1538).

Quilts served as gifts of gratitude for war-time service, such as the signature quilt presented to Clara Barton by the G.A.R. encampment named in her honor (fig. 189/MQ 3487), or to give comfort to those injured or imprisoned, such as the quilt presented to James George (fig. 185/MQ 4026). And most poignantly, quilts serve as memorials for those who gave their lives or as a comforting reminder that others acknowledge and share the grief of the deceased's family. Such Massachusetts war-time quilts continue to be made today through the state's participation in the "Home of the Brave Quilt Project," which seeks to present quilts to the families of those killed in Iraq and Afghanistan.   —DCA

ANDERSONVILLE PRISONER OF WAR QUILT

(FIG. 185)

On approaching Gettysburg on the morning of that day I soon saw what was before us and what we had to expect;—at such time one can think of many things in a few seconds. I thought on you and the dear children—and offering a mental prayer—for you and for courage and resignation to bear whatever might befall myself. I felt strengthened and the words of our 'Saviour' came to my mind "that not

a sparrow falls to the ground without the knowledge of your heavenly father" and the next minute we were under the terrible fire which—brought down so many of our men, but I remained untouched. For these mercies My Dear Wife—we should be humbly thankful and may God hasten the time when the efforts of the Country shall be crowned with final victory and peace. I conclude with love to you all.

From Your Affectionate Husband James George[6]

Five months after South Carolina secessionists fired on Fort Sumter, propelling the nation into civil war, James George (1828–1871) of Cherry Valley, New York, volunteered as a private for "H" Company, 76th Regiment, New York Infantry. After almost three years of action in some of the bloodiest battles of the war, including Gettysburg and Fredericksburg, James was captured during the vicious Battle of the Wilderness on May 5, 1864, and imprisoned in the infamous Andersonville Prison. James was fortunate—his incarceration at Andersonville was only about six months, but that was long enough for the cruel starvation and unsanitary conditions suffered by all prisoners there to permanently affect his health.

James George probably received this signature quilt as a gift from well-wishers while he recuperated in a Washington, D.C., hospital sometime between February 1865 and his discharge from the Union Army in June 1865.[7] This quilt, now owned by the New England Quilt Museum, is notable for its provenance, display of anti-slavery sentiment, and the fact that very few quilts used by soldiers during the Civil War have survived. The central block notes that the quilt was begun February 22, 1864, and finished February 9, 1865. Its narrow width suggests that it was made for a hospital or camp bed.

During our nation's Civil War, many small, industrious groups were established to make much-

FIGURE 185. Pieced and appliquéd "Album Quilt," made by R. A. Sibley, Rosa Aldrich, Mary Slone, A. Ludworth, E. G. Fitsgerald, Alice Coburn, and Annie M. Watsen of Boston, 1865. Cotton (87½" × 58¼"). New England Quilt Museum (2004.17). *Photograph by David Stansbury.* MQ 4026.

needed items for soldiers. Women in both the North and the South organized knitting, sewing, and quilting groups as part of larger socially conscious organizations or as separate entities. One such group was formed in the Boston area, possibly as part of the U.S. Sanitary Commission. In 1865, Mrs. R. A. Sibley, Rosa Aldrich, Mary Slone, A. Ludworth, E. G. Fitsgerald, Alice Coburn, and Annie M. Watsen came together to donate their time and talents to make this heartfelt album quilt. The towns of residence noted by four of the women are all in Boston or the surrounding area.[8] One of the many blocks made by Mrs. Sibley included her full address: 12 Bowdoin Street, Boston.[9]

The 1860 U.S. census suggests that "Mrs. R. A. Sibley" was Rebecca A. Sibley, age forty-eight, the wife of Boston physician Rodney Sibley. Rebecca and Rodney had two sons and a daughter. Their eldest son, David J., born around 1835, was of an age to be a soldier in the war—reason enough for Rebecca to engage in activities for soldiers' relief. Mary Slone was born in Massachusetts in 1831. She and her husband, John (an office worker and native of England), had three children. They lived in Cambridge, immediately north of Boston across the Charles River. Rosa Aldrich, the daughter of Jerome B. and Sabrina Aldrich of Boston, was the youngest of three girls and would have been fifteen years old at the time this quilt was made. Alice Coburn, born about 1828, lived in various places in Massachusetts during her life. She remained single and held occupations as a mill hand in Lowell, housekeeper in Dracut, and teacher in Boston. Little is known about Annie M. Watsen other than that she lived in the Boston area. A. Ludworth and E. G. Fitsgerald could not be found in any census records of the period.[10]

The quilt is constructed with thirty-five pieced blocks, each measuring twelve inches square and assembled from a variety of cotton solids and prints, along with chintz prints. Each maker hand-pieced and quilted her block, with the exception of the machine-quilted center block. All blocks were

FIGURE 186. Back of the "Album Quilt," showing the individually bound blocks. *Photograph by David Stansbury.*

FIGURE 187. Detail of Album Quilt, with inked drawing of soldier and tent, and inscription: "Lo speed thy way to southern burghs / to sheet the soldier's bed, / and shield him from the chilly damps / That fall around his head." *Photograph by David Stansbury.*

FIGURE 188. Detail of the "Album Quilt," with inked drawing of plantation overseer with whip, and inscription: "O! Massa do some pity take / And spare my back for Dinah's sake, / She'll miss my care, & greatly need / My help to pick the cotton seed. / The South as it was. / R. A. Sibley / 12 Bowdoin St. / Boston." *Photograph by David Stansbury.*

completed, including quilting and binding, before insertion into the quilt. The center of the quilt forms a nine-patch medallion made primarily with red, white, and blue fabrics.

Most blocks contain biblical and inspirational verses. In addition, three are embellished with ink drawings and anti-slavery dialogue. Only one block is signed by Mrs. Sibley, but the style of drawing and lettering matches other blocks in the quilt. One of the verses that Mrs. Sibley wrote on a red-and-white striped block echoed the sentiments of many young women:

> A number of young girls with pretty good cheer
> Have determined to work for the Soldier's this year
> Therefore a quilt with these names all right
> Written in each square, Will gladden your sight
>
> Some of the girls are young and fair,
> Some have blue eyes with long curly hair
> Some are quite old but not out of date.
> Hoping some day (time) for the marriageable state.
>
> And as the young lass who can sew and knit
> Always industrious and can work very quick
> Alert for each duty and ever says can,
> Is surely entitled to a very good man.
>
> And if I should ask them I know they would say
> "Give me a man [crossed out], soldier who is on his
>   way
> Home from the field of danger and strife
> For he only is worth[y] of a New England wife."
>   R.A.S. 12 Bowdoin St. Boston

The Confederates paroled James on or about December 5, 1864, from Florence, South Carolina, and he finally was discharged from a military hospital early in the summer of 1865.[11] At the time of his discharge, James held the rank of sergeant.[12] Returning to Cherry Valley, James rejoined his wife, Thomasine (1833–1894), daughters Elizabeth, Julia, and Alice, and son, Hubert. Mr. George was employed as the Proprietor of the Rail Road Hotel, Cherry Valley, Otsego County, New York, and was also a member of the Cherry Valley N.Y. Independent Order of Odd Fellows, Lodge No. 102.[13] Two more children, a son and daughter, were born to

James and Thomasine after the war. After James's death on March 4, 1871, William Stephens, an inmate with James George, testified in a pension affidavit for Thomasine that James George's health had been "ruined and his early death caused by his imprisonment at Andersonville."[14] The quilt descended in the George family, along with his military documents, battlefield letters, newspaper articles, and a chess set made in Andersonville Prison from rat bones. The family presented the quilt to the New England Quilt Museum in 2004.

From its inception as a means to help and serve, to today's reminder of who we are and where we have come from, the lovingly sewn pieces of this quilt deeply touch all people who see it. It has accumulated a remarkable provenance, from its early beginnings in Boston, to a soldier wounded as the result of battle in the South, to Upstate New York, to its subsequent passage to various family members in the northeast, until finally resting in Massachusetts, where it began.   —VLS and ABL

CLARA BARTON POST QUILT
(FIG. 189)

Clara Barton (1821–1912), Civil War nurse and founder of the American Red Cross, was born and raised in North Oxford, Massachusetts. Led by her four much older brothers and sisters, Barton's early education placed her far beyond her peers by the time she officially started school at the age of four. She began to teach school herself at the age of seventeen, in Worcester County. After more than ten years in the profession, she chose to become a student again and attended the Liberal Institute in Clinton, New Jersey. After studying languages and writing there, she opened a free school in Bordentown in southern New Jersey. Quitting in disgust when a man was hired as the principal in spite of her successful leadership of the institution, Barton found employment as a clerk in the United States Patent Office in Washington, D.C. She was the first woman ever to work for the Patent Office, and she did so at the rate of pay given to her male colleagues, a remarkable achievement in itself.

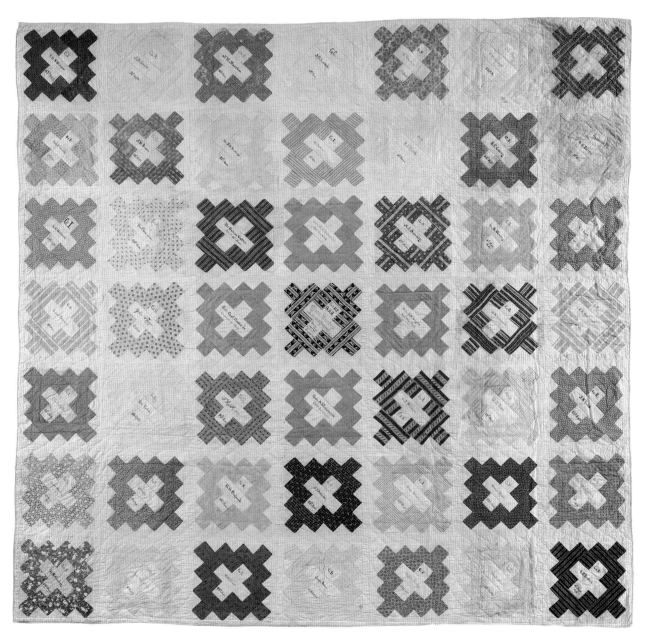

FIGURE 189. Pieced Friendship Quilt, created by the G.A.R. Post 65 Clara Barton Encampment, Warren, c. 1876. Cotton (90" × 83"). Collection of the Clara Barton Birthplace Museum, North Oxford. *Photograph by David Stansbury.* MQ 3487.

Thus, Barton resided in the nation's capital when the Civil War broke out. She was inspired to organize a relief program for soldiers upon the arrival in the city of the 6th Massachusetts Regiment, which had been bloodied and harassed by rioting secessionists in Baltimore. The experience marked the beginning of Barton's lifetime of philanthropy and caring for others. Clara Barton never had any particular medical training beyond nursing an invalid older brother, yet she came to be known as the "angel of the battlefield."

The fact that many of the wounded soldiers from the First Battle of Bull Run suffered from a lack of medical supplies led Barton to advertise for donations back in her home state, in the Worcester newspaper, the *Spy*. Her success (assisted by Massachusetts Senator Henry Wilson) in creating an organization to distribute medical supplies, stockings, blankets, and other necessities brought her to the attention of Surgeon General William A. Hammond, who granted her a general pass to travel with army

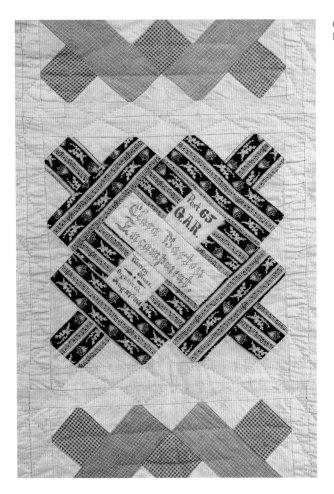

ambulances "for the purpose of distributing comforts for the sick and wounded, and nursing them."[15] For the rest of the war, Barton followed the army in Virginia and South Carolina, tending to the ill and injured. Her kindness and nursing skills—and her bravery on the front lines of battle—attracted national attention. In 1864, she became the superintendent of nurses under the command of Major General Benjamin F. Butler.

After the war, Barton organized a system for locating soldiers missing in action. By interviewing Federal soldiers released from southern prisons, writing thousands of letters of inquiry, and posting lists of names in newspapers, she and her assistants discovered the fate of twenty thousand missing men and notified their families.

In addition to heading the effort to locate missing soldiers, Barton lectured around the country about her experiences on the battlefield and worked with

the nascent suffragist movement. She worked herself into a collapse and, on doctor's orders, went to Europe for a vacation. Even in Europe, though, Barton was compelled to help those who suffered, assisting the relief effort during the Franco Prussian War (1870–1871). Her experience in Europe informed her of the Red Cross, established there by the Treaty of Geneva in 1864. Inspired to establish the American Red Cross in 1881, Barton served as its president until her retirement in 1904. She died at her home in Glen Echo, Maryland, in 1912, and is buried in the Barton family plot in Oxford, Massachusetts.

An important item in the Clara Barton Birthplace Museum is a signature quilt believed to have been presented to Clara Barton around the time of this country's Centennial celebration.[16] The quilt was created by the G.A.R. Post 65 of Warren, Massachusetts—called the "Clara Barton Post." The quilt is composed of forty-nine "Chimney Sweep" or

"Album Patch" blocks, set on point and measuring approximately thirteen inches square. The Post 65 block, made of cotton printed in a Centennial design of madder stripes with shields bearing the word "Peace" and the musical notation for "Hail Columbia," is placed prominently in the center.

Established in 1866, the G.A.R., or Grand Army of the Republic, supported Union veterans of the Civil War, and their widows and orphans. By the 1890s, its members (all of whom were honorably discharged Union veterans) numbered over four hundred thousand.[17] The nationwide organization was broken down locally into "posts," headed by a commander. (Warren's Post 65 was established in 1868.) There were national and regional "encampments," multi-day events at which members generally camped out together to hold formal dinners and memorial activities. The G.A.R. established veterans' homes and worked to gain pension legislation. An important political force into the early twentieth century, it is the G.A.R. to whom we owe thanks for this country's annual observation of Memorial Day every May.

Written on the G.A.R. Post 65 block in the center of the quilt is "Clara Barton Encampment," suggesting that this quilt was made while men who signed it had gathered together for an encampment in Warren. Their wives, many of whom were undoubtedly members of a G.A.R. auxiliary (either the Ladies of the Grand Army of the Republic or the Women's Relief Corps), probably took charge of making the quilt. Twelve of the forty-eight men whose names appear on the quilt were from Warren. Dr. Calvin Cutter (1807–1872) was a skilled surgeon and author of the 1850 textbook, *Cutter's Anatomy, Physiology and Hygiene*, the first of its type.[18] He was also an abolitionist, and volunteered for duty in the Civil War at age fifty-three. His nineteen-year-old daughter, Carrie, served as a Union nurse and is believed to be the first female casualty of the war.[19] John G. Leach (1840–1930), a future commander of Post 65, is represented in a block in the top row. In the Civil War, Leach served in Company C, 25th Massachusetts Volunteers of Southbridge. He was a founder and later president of the Warren Steam Pump Works, and led the Memorial Day parades in

Warren "well into his 80s." He was the last surviving member of the Clara Barton Post 65.[20]   —LZB

RED CROSS SIGNATURE QUILT
(FIG. 191)

The American Red Cross was founded by Clara Barton in 1881 (see the preceding essay). While its early projects aided victims of natural disasters and epidemics, its war-related activities began in the years prior to the United States' entrance into World War I. Although Americans held mixed opinions about entering the war in Europe, young men who supported England and France volunteered to be ambulance drivers for the Red Cross and other volunteer organizations, or joined British and Canadian military units. Textile scholar Beverly Gordon reports that making Red Cross quilts hit a peak before this country entered the war in 1917.[21] Enthusiasm continued during World War I and experienced a resurgence just before and during World War II. The American Red Cross provided medical supplies and personal items for military use, and also became a catalyst for women to organize, raise funds, and create quilts.

Unlike the Sanitary Commission's use of quilts as bedding for soldiers during the Civil War, Red Cross signature quilts provided a way to collect money for the organization's relief and medical projects. A large number of these quilts have found their way into local historical societies and museums because their real usefulness was to raise funds rather than to be bedcovers. The typical Red Cross quilt of the World War I era was generally a modest collection of signatures. In its December 1917 issue, ladies' magazine *The Modern Priscilla* published a pattern and detailed directions for making a Red Cross quilt, including specifying the charge per signature in order to earn just over $1,000.[22]

The Montague Red Cross quilt does not follow that published pattern, although both feature a large central red cross. It has approximately 230 signatures and initials that have been hand-embroidered, red on white and white on red, in the checkerboard sur-

FIGURE 191. Red Cross signature quilt, made by members of the Montague
Unitarian Alliance, 1915. Cotton (73½" × 61½"). Collection of the Pocumtuck
Valley Memorial Association, Memorial Hall Museum, Deerfield, Mass.
(1957.6). *Photograph by David Stansbury.* MQ 3239.

rounding the cross. Likely, one or two people did the embroidery, as the similarity of the writing suggests that the names are not actual autographs. The central cross contains the identification of the group and the date. It is not known how much money the quilt raised, but the museum does have a letter from one contributor making a pledge of $1.00.

The quilt was presented to the pastor of the Montague Unitarian Church, the Reverend Richard Birks, upon his retirement. (Mrs. Birks' signature is near the center.) Reverend Birks was born in England, while his wife hailed from Massachusetts. Their daughters, Ellen and Florence, also were born in England. By 1910, the United States census listed the family as living in Deerfield; Reverend Birks was then sixty-five years old. Perhaps their pastor's British roots inspired the Alliance members to give him this symbol of support for those serving in the Great War. Florence Birks donated the quilt to Memorial Hall Museum in 1957.   —MC

CELINA RHODIER BALISE QUILT
(FIG. 193)

As Massachusetts' factories flourished and its population grew, more and more people left the farms of their childhoods to settle in urban areas— but not Celina Rhodier Balise. Born in Hadley in 1872 to French-Canadian farmers, Celina moved to nearby Hatfield to become a farmer's wife.

Throughout the state, enterprising farmers developed farms specializing in dairy, produce, or fresh meat, and carried their goods into thriving city markets. In the Connecticut River Valley, the rich soils permitted farmers to also raise shade tobacco for wrapping cigars. Tobacco was so profitable that Canadian immigrants recruited as labor often stayed and purchased their own farms. Thus it was tobacco, not textiles, that brought Celina's parents and in-laws from Canada to Massachusetts.

A young bride of seventeen, Celina and her husband Paul Napoleon Balise (b. 1869) initially shared Paul's parents' home on Chestnut Street in Hatfield. Motherhood came early and often to Celina; she

FIGURE 192. Celina Rhodier Balise, c. 1940. *Photograph courtesy of Dorothy and Carol Balise.*

bore ten children, five girls and five boys. Sorrow came too, as two daughters died in infancy. The family's main source of income remained tobacco, but Paul Balise also repaired carriages. Celina's second son, Peter, expanded his father's carriage shop to include automobiles, and today Balise Motors is one of the largest auto dealers in southern New England.

During Celina's life, though, it was the Balise women who were celebrated locally. Celina and daughters Beatrice and Edna shared a March 29 birthday and local newspapers regularly covered the human interest story.[23] Celina managed a boisterous household, filled with good food, laughter, and miscellaneous cats and dogs. She was also a prolific quilter whose works frequently received prize ribbons at the Three County Fair in Northampton. Celina's afternoon quilting parties combined her love of sewing with company, coffee, and food.

Like most quilters, Celina recognized that her handwork was a tangible reminder of her love for

FIGURE 193. Pieced quilt, "Double Wedding Ring," made by Celina
(Rhodier) Balise (1872–1942) of Hatfield, 1941. Cotton (79" × 63½"). Private
collection. *Photograph by David Stansbury.* MQ 4151.

her family. Each of her children received a quilt, usually when they married. Patriotic pride, though, motivated Celina to make her son Robert's quilt— this double wedding ring quilt was among her last.

Nineteen-year-old Bob joined the Army in 1940 and completed his term of service later that year, but when the United States entered the war in 1941, he re-enlisted. That was when sixty-nine-year-old Celina began piecing her concern and pride into her work, tucking the completed quilt away until Bob's homecoming. Celina never got to give Bob his quilt, though. She died in 1942 before his return. Prompted by Bob's marriage plans in 1947, Celina's youngest daughter, Beatrice, presented the vibrant quilt to his bride-to-be, Dorothy, as a token of Celina's love for her son, and the Balise family's welcome to its newest member.

The cotton scrap quilt contains bits of the popular pastels of the 1930s, but its predominant colors, red, white, and blue, reflect the war-time patriotism of its maker and intended recipient. Well loved and well used, its worn binding was replaced in the 1960s. Bob died in January of 2007, not quite sixty years after Celina's final quilt was bestowed on him. Dorothy, the daughter-in-law Celina never met, will pass the quilt on to her own daughter as a treasured reminder of the woman who loved her family so much. —DCA

PAM COLLETTE QUILT

(FIG. 195)

With the onset of World War II, many young couples rushed to marry prior to the serviceman's departure overseas. This left young brides at home, many still living with their families, attending to daily chores or employed outside the home in order to build a nest egg for their lives together once the war was over. Women put their handwork skills to use by knitting and crocheting articles of clothing such as socks, sweaters, hats, and scarves. These items were made for loved ones overseas or shipped to orphanages in need of supplies, as had been the practice in World War I. Some women made quilts

FIGURE 194. Pam and Normand Collette on their wedding day, October 31, 1942. *Photograph courtesy of Pam Collette.*

for their future homes, answering the call to "make scrap quilts for their own use and leave the blanket supply 'for the boys over there.'"[24]

Quilting, which had seen a revival in the 1920s and 1930s, continued during this period, although it declined somewhat in popularity. Various national contests sponsored by well-known organizations and companies, including *Woman's Day* magazine, helped maintain interest in quilting during the 1940s.[25] Many periodicals published quilting patterns; in addition, women shared patterns with one another, or drafted them from existing quilts.

Pam Collette was one of these young women. This young bride from Spencer married her serviceman sweetheart, Normand, in 1942. As a member of the all-volunteer Flying Tigers, Normand was due to ship out to China within days of their wedding. Pam stayed behind and put her skills to work, sew-

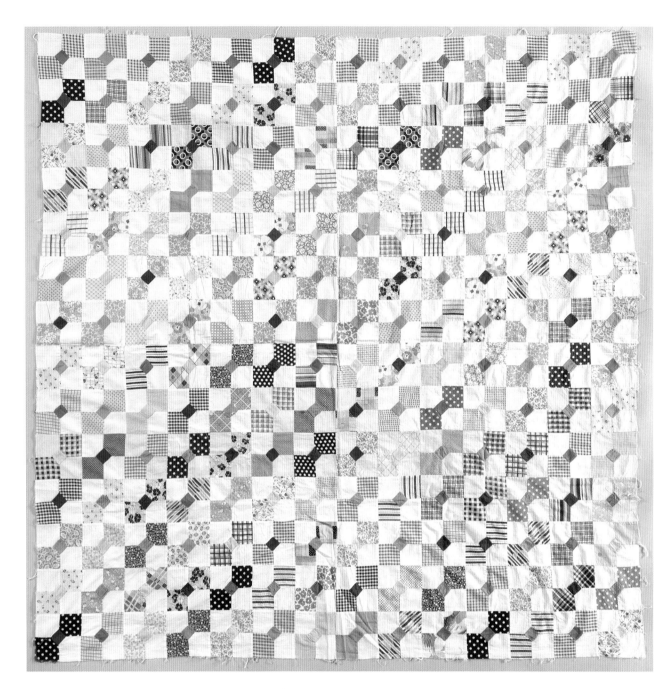

FIGURE 195. Pieced quilt top, "Necktie," made by Pam Collette,
Spencer, 1942. Cotton (68" × 70"). Private collection. *Photograph by
David Stansbury.* MQ 4955.

ing Army boots in the local shoe factory. She had learned to sew at her mother's knee and embraced this skill with enthusiasm for the rest of her life; she continued to improve her skills after marriage by taking eight years of adult education courses in sewing and dressmaking.[26]

Pam recalled climbing into the attic of her family's home as a young woman to retrieve boxes of scraps left over from clothing made by members of the family. These scraps were assembled into quilts. The "Necktie" quilt top seen here had particular significance for her. While her husband was fighting in China, Pam constructed it of brightly colored and patterned cotton fabrics from the mid- to late 1930s and early 1940s. It incorporates two hundred pieced blocks, each approximately five inches square. The center of each necktie is made from a solid pastel or primary colored square, while the outer portions of the ties are constructed from floral, striped, checked, or polka dot prints. The remaining portion of each block is pieced from an off-white cotton.

Normand returned from World War II in 1945 and lived happily with his wife until his death on July 4, 2005. Pam made clothing and quilts for her family throughout her sixty-year marriage. The World War II quilt top, although never completed, remains part of Pam's memory of a time when piecing bits of fabric helped to pass the long hours waiting for her sweetheart to come home.   —VLS

PART III

MEMORY

Chapter 17

Quilts as Memory

Friendship Quilts

Friendship quilts became a fad of the 1840s and 1850s, beginning in the mid-Atlantic region and spreading from there.[1] The argument has been made and frequently repeated that signed friendship quilts became possible in this period because of improvements in commercially available ink and the invention of the steel nib pen, but in fact, the reasons were far more complex—and interesting.[2] Friendship quilts were the result of a confluence of social, economic, religious, and political events that created a period now known as the Romantic Era. Massachusetts played a key role in American thought during the Romantic Era, so exploring the issues to explain more fully the appearance of friendship quilts is particularly appropriate to this book.

The Romantic Movement had its roots in Europe in the eighteenth century; it began in philosophical discussions reconsidering the significance of the individual person. The English religious leader John Wesley (1703–1791) repudiated the predestination doctrine of Calvinism and the hierarchy of the Church; instead, he preached the value of the individual soul and the salvation that comes through faith. French social commentator Jean-Jacques Rousseau (1712–1778) also emphasized the goodness of the individual person and rejected the concept of original sin. The influence of these two philosophers, among others, laid the groundwork for a democratization of religion and the Second Great Awakening, a religious revival that began in the 1790s in Europe and spread to the United States in the first decades of the nineteenth century. Beginning in the southern and mid-Atlantic regions, the Second Great Awakening was a Protestant movement that offered a doctrine of salvation through personal faith and good works. Rather than man being at the mercy of a wrathful God, man had control of his destiny.[3] This religious philosophy held particular appeal for the American people, who recently had won their independence from England and did, indeed, feel that they controlled their own destiny. The Second Great Awakening peaked in the late 1820s and 1830s.

The democratization of religion fertilized the roots of Romantic Era fashions in architecture, dress, and the decorative arts. Looking back to earlier centuries (particularly the highly religious medieval period) provided comfort and an escape from the stresses of the early nineteenth century's rapidly changing society. Gothic ideals of chivalry and faith prevailed, while the economic and cultural triumph of the Renaissance was represented by the adaptation of sixteenth- and seventeenth-century styles for Romantic Era clothing fashion.

The Romantic Movement in America began around the 1810s, and reached its height in the second quarter of the nineteenth century. In this country, the Romantic Movement particularly emphasized the landscape, giving rise to a literary and philosophical movement known as Transcendentalism. Ralph Waldo Emerson and Henry David Thoreau of Concord, Massachusetts, argued the perfectibility of man through the contemplation of nature. Nature and religion—which were practically the same thing—offered an antidote to an increasing social anxiety over the rapid loss of what was recalled nostalgically as a "quiet" and "simple" rural life to the tumult and dangers of urban industry. More and more immigrants came into the country in this period, bringing strange customs, languages, and appearances, threatening the familiar homogeneity. Young families, moving west to seek fertile land and new opportunities, left behind worn-out and over-crowded farmlands—but also their family, friends, and homes.

In response to these traumas and worry over increasing materialism, Americans embraced the Romantic Movement and cultivated a fashionable sentimentality for the home, family, friends, nature, and death—impulses that came together to create a new form of textile, the friendship quilt. The embodiment of this movement was the wife and mother, who was expected to be a stabilizing force, creating a loving, beautiful, and serene home for her husband's comfort after a hard day working in the brutish business world—a social movement termed "the cult of domesticity" by historians. Advances in printing technology, including lithography, stereotype plating, and the cylinder steam press, allowed books and magazines to be produced faster and more inexpensively than ever before, making gothic romances and their ideals of perfect womanhood widely available. The highly sentimental art and literature of the Romantic Era thus reinforced this vision of women as angelic protectors of family, home, and religious virtue.

The evangelical quality of the Second Great Awakening was the catalyst for the reform movements of the early nineteenth century. Armed with moral authority and religious fervor, women in particular (as sanctified protectors of the home) set out to eradicate social ills, including slavery and the consumption of alcohol. Women gathered together to sew quilts for the poor or to raise money for the anti-slavery cause. The Boston Female Anti-Slavery Society was particularly active in this arena, producing fairs with offerings of handmade articles—including quilts—often inscribed with anti-slavery verses (fig. 133/MQ 4961 and fig. 135/MQ 2028).

Women were beginning to think of quilts as vehicles for political and cultural expression, as well as personal expression. And they were writing on their quilts, undoubtedly inspired by the bound friendship albums that appeared early in the Romantic Era. In these albums, women gathered expressions of love and concern, quotations, verses, and the signatures of friends and relatives. The verses were often quite morose, pondering the inevitability of death but the hope for eternal life. Similar verses sometimes were penned on friendship quilts, but the difficulty of writing on fabric restricted most signers to short phrases of remembrance or perhaps a verse from the Bible if they ventured beyond their signature at all. Indeed, the responsibility of writing on the blocks of a friendship quilt sometimes was delegated to the individual who had the greatest skill with the pen (whether it was a quill or tipped with a steel nib) and ink.

Departed loved ones were often memorialized on friendship quilts along with living friends and relatives. The possibility—indeed, likelihood—of suffering the death of a loved one, or being concerned with the possibility of dying oneself, was a part of everyday life in the early nineteenth century, as it had been throughout history. Attitudes towards death altered significantly, however, during the Romantic Era. Of course, the period's religious ferment had something to do with this, but the overarching sentimentality of the period also played a role. No longer were the dead buried in "coffins," but in "caskets," the term for a jewel box. And no longer were the weedy and neglected plots where the dead lay at rest called "burying grounds," to be avoided until the next grave was dug; they became "cemeteries" meaning "sleeping place," and they began to be landscaped and decorated with architectural elements and sculpture other than gravestones. (The Mount Auburn Cemetery, established in 1831 in Cambridge and Watertown, Massachusetts, was the first cemetery in the United States designed with a park-like setting. It was, in fact, America's first public park.) Cemeteries became places for picnics and bucolic strolls.

In the same way that cemetery art and landscapes reflected this heightened interest in sentiment, so too did quilts. The Romantic Era invested cloth remnants of dresses and shirts with powerful emotions. An essay written in 1842 for the Lowell, Massachusetts, mill girls' periodical, *The Lowell Offering*, portrayed "The Patchwork Quilt" as an object both commonplace and precious. The writer, using the pen name "Annette" (probably Harriet Farley) recalled the family members associated with each scrap of fabric:

> Yes, there is the PATCHWORK QUILT! Looking to the uninterested observer like a miscellaneous collection of odd bits and ends of calico, but to me it is a precious reliquary of past treasures; a storehouse of valuables, almost destitute of worth; . . . a bound volume of hieroglyphics, each of which is a key to some painful or pleasant remembrance . . . Gentle friends! It contains a piece of each of my childhood's calico gowns, and of my mother's and sisters. . . .[4]

Another element in the rise of the friendship quilt that is important to consider is the romanticization of cooperative quilting (as discussed previously in this book). By the time that friendship quilts came into fashion, the cooperative quilting party was in decline due to industrialization and population shifts.[5] In popular literature, such as the well-known *Godey's Lady's Book* short story, "The Quilting Party" from 1849 and novels by Harriet Beecher Stowe and Catherine Maria Sedgwick, quilting parties and quilts are romanticized as part of a vanishing world.[6]

Friendship quilts were the product of a highly religious and sentimental society that romanticized friendship, death, nature, and the home. Scraps of calico, along with the process of quilting itself, evoked cherished (if not always accurate) thoughts of loved ones and revered ancestors. Inked signatures and sentimental phrases of remembrance gave comfort to those who were separated from their friends and relatives, or memorialized deceased loved ones. The horrors of the Civil War effectively ended the Romantic Era in the United States, but it was on the decline anyway. As the Romantic Era waned in the 1860s, so too did the friendship quilt fashion—though it never completely disappeared.   —LZB

EMILINE CROSS QUILT
(FIG. 196)

On November 8, 1837, when Mount Holyoke Female Seminary in South Hadley opened, students arrived to find many chambers yet unfurnished. Supporters of the school nailed down carpet, begged and borrowed spoons and bedsteads, stuffed pillows, and stitched quilts in the last rush of the long, hard-fought battle to establish this institution of higher learning for women—the first permanent, college-level school for women in the nation. Inspired or cajoled by founder Mary Lyon (1797–1849), rich and poor alike across New England gave what they could toward her cause, despite a terrible economic depression and the diatribes of those who believed that educating women was a waste of time and even dangerous to society.

A more determined woman than Mary Lyon perhaps never lived. Growing up in a poor and fatherless family in the Massachusetts hilltown of Buckland, Mary struggled to gain an education. Recognized early on for her exceptional intelligence, she taught at a number of schools and eventually became associated with other women who were committed to educating girls and women, including Zilpah Grant, Emma Willard, and Catherine Beecher. But it was Mary Lyon's vision to establish a college for women that was financially endowed and not dependent on a single, dynamic personality for its success, a revolutionary idea in the early nineteenth century.[7]

In 1854, Emiline Cross graduated from Mount Holyoke, and friends from school and from her home in Blandford made this friendship quilt to honor her accomplishment. Penned on the block of Elizabeth "Lizzie" Hanmer, the phrase "Sharer in all the joys and sorrows of Holyoke life" hints at the fond friendships, academic challenge, religious devotion, homesickness, and hard physical labor experienced by the early students at Mount Holyoke Female Seminary. The school consisted of a one-hundred-room building housing both classroom and dormitory space for approximately three hundred students and teachers. To convince nonbelievers that

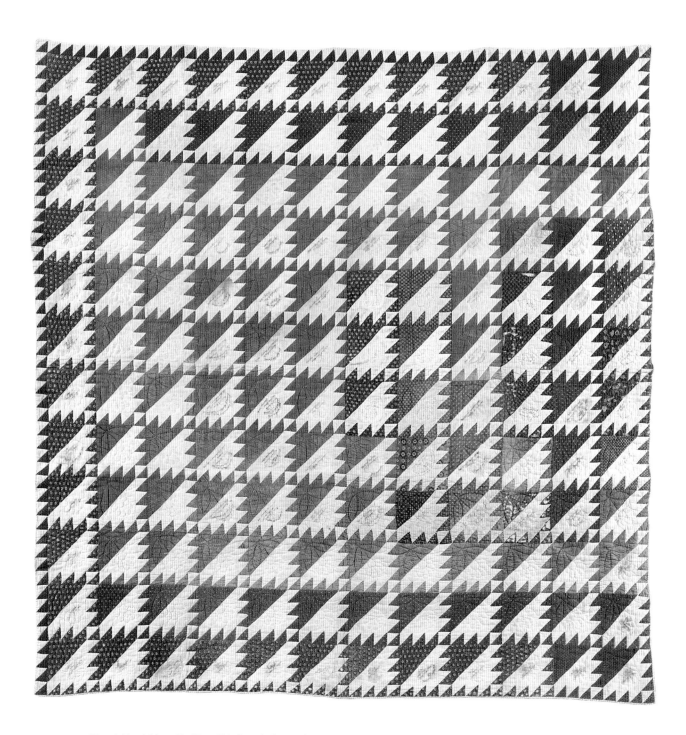

FIGURE 196. Pieced friendship quilt, "Lost Ship," made for Emiline
Cross of Blandford, 1854. Cotton (80" × 80"). Collection of the
Blandford Historical Society, Blandford, Mass. *Photograph by David
Stansbury.* MQ 3518.

FIGURE 197. Detail, inscribed block, "Sharer in all the joys and sorrows of Holyoke life, Lizzie Hanmer, Wethersfield, Conn." *Photograph by David Stansbury.*

women could handle both scholarly pursuits and traditional housekeeping duties—as well as to save money and keep tuition costs down—the students did all the cleaning and cooking at the school.

Letters in the Mount Holyoke College archives written by students in this period reveal their appreciation for the opportunity to receive an excellent education, which included courses in astronomy, botany, chemistry, philosophy, rhetoric, history, algebra, geometry, and Latin. As has been true for students throughout history, the academic demands caused great anxiety, but comfort was found in food: "Tell Mother she does not make her Peach pies right, she must come here if she wants to eat a peach pie; the crust is put into a deep plate and the peaches wiped and put in whole so that it makes a delightful pie," Anna Walker (Class of 1852) wrote to her brother.[8] One hopes he had enough tact not to pass along the message.

The girls who lived in proximity to each other called themselves a "family." Frances Tower wrote on Emiline's quilt that she was "A much loved member of 'our family circle' / Consisting of the N. H. [New Hampshire] girls & the Blandford girls." Another member of the family circle, Mary Ellen Wilder, penned her block with a reminder of "The fine times in the No. 94 / When 'the whole family' was together." Lizzie Hanmer, "sharer in all the joys and sorrows of Holyoke life," may well have been Emiline's roommate. Roommates particularly developed a close bond. As was common practice in earlier centuries, they shared a bed as well as a room. Anna Walker noted in a letter home that roommates walked "with their arms around each other (that is the way you always see them walk no matter where)."[9]

Student letters also reveal the sorrows of seminary life, often with a wry sense of humor. Not

every student appreciated the requirement to attend church on Sunday and to spend an hour every day in private devotions. Charlotte B. Mead of the Class of 1853 noted that with such spiritual attentiveness, ". . . truly one ought to be holy here."[10] In addition to their rigorous academic course and daily worship, students were expected to attend to their house-keeping duties for about seventy minutes every day. Some students did the baking and cooking, while others scoured knives, wiped crockery, swept the classrooms, or even scrubbed the toilet seats. Every student hauled firewood daily from the basement up to the little Franklin stoves in their rooms, which may have been as far up as the third floor. Anna Benton (Class of 1850) noted that it was "90 stairs" from her room to one area of her work duties.[11] Required daily calisthenics and frequent outdoor walks proved that women's bodies were capable of enduring protracted physical exertion, just as their minds could withstand protracted study. Hikes up to the top of Mount Holyoke, for which the school was named, were more pleasant—the beautiful view of the Connecticut River Valley was popular with tourists and artists, as well as students.

So regimented and full were the hours of each day that Anna Benton wrote to her aunt: "I never

lived in such a hurry in my life. . . . it seems some days as if I should go crazy." Many students wrote of the lack of time to get all their chores and studying done. Mary Elizabeth Dewell (Class of 1850) went so far as to write a lament, "I have no time," to fulfill her weekly composition requirement. Her wish for more hours in the day belies the notion of a slower-moving lifestyle in the past: "Where is time! Oh could I but meet with some one, that would tell me where it might be found, how quick would I avail myself of the opportunity."[12]

Bells signaled the shift from one activity to another. Josephine Kingsley wrote on her block for Emiline's quilt, "These Holyoke bells! These Holyoke bells! / How many a tale their music tells!" However, the ringing of the bells was decidedly *not* music to most students' ears. The bells signaling "retiring" (9:45) and especially the time to get out of bed in the morning caused particular anguish. Frances Harback of the class of 1854 moaned in her letter to a friend, ". . . it is but half past five in the morning—now don't you think that it is too bad to rouse a poor body out of bed so early?" She also felt terribly constrained by the innumerable rules: ". . . and oh the rules that we have it is enough to kill any one. . . ."[13]

While letter-writer Anna Benton eventually became accustomed to the rigors of Holyoke life, Anna Walker, Charlotte Mead, Mary Elizabeth Dewell, and Frances Harback did not stay long enough to graduate. Emiline's friend Lizzie Hanmer also did not graduate from Mount Holyoke. Indeed, whether due to exhaustion or lack of money, most students attended the school only a year or two and did not graduate, making Emiline Cross's accomplishment all the more notable.

Lizzie Hanmer went on to be a teacher in Wethersfield, Connecticut. At least two other friends who signed Emiline's quilt had careers as teachers: Frances E. Tower, who earned a master's degree and taught at Rutgers, and Mary Ellen Wilder, who moved to the Midwest and married a fellow teacher.[14] Emiline, "As good as she is pretty," according to the block penned by Sarah Fowler, married Edward L. Tinker in 1856 and bore two sons. She died young in 1863, and is buried in Plainville, Connecticut.

Mount Holyoke Female Seminary became a college in 1888. Today, twenty-one hundred students from seventy countries attend this internationally renowned school for "Uncommon Women," and while they no longer have to cook or sweep the classrooms, they do still enjoy the view from the mountain that shares the college's name.　　—LZB
(MOUNT HOLYOKE COLLEGE CLASS OF 1983)

NORTH FALMOUTH
CONGREGATIONAL CHURCH
QUILT
(FIG. 199)

> When we this little present make
> though tis uttered not
> we're striving friend to keep awake
> In those whose words of kindness spake
> and fear to be forgot.

With phrases of esteem and friendship inked on its white patches, members of the North Falmouth Congregational Church presented this quilt to the Reverend Asahel Cobb (1793–1876)

and his wife Helen Maria (Hamblen) Cobb (1803–1869) in 1850. This "free will offering for Mr. & Mrs. Cobb, Jan. 8, 1850" was intended as a good-bye gift, as several of the blocks are inked with phrases of remembrance, such as "Absent but not forgotten," "I think of thee," and "Though lost to sight to memory dear / Absent friends are still remembered." Asahel Cobb served the North Falmouth Congregational Church from 1844 through 1848. The Reverend Cobb kept his home in nearby Sandwich—home also to some of the quilters—although he moved on to preach in New Bedford. His 1876 obituary states that he was "beloved and respected by all who knew him, without regard to sect or creed."[15]

Each of the twenty-four squares is pieced in a pattern known as "Odd Fellows" or "Flying Geese" and set on point. The blocks of vibrant blue, pink, and brown cotton prints are sashed with an unusual squiggly pink-and-white pattern originally printed as a striped fabric. This stripe also is used around the cut outs of the lower corners. The white cotton center of each square contains a name, a phrase, or a date (the earliest being 1849). One square states "Quilted at Mrs. Tobey's Jan. 3, 1850"; Mrs. Tobey's house still stands today on Main Street in North Falmouth.

The North Falmouth Congregational Church was built and dedicated in 1832 by members of the First and Second Congregational Churches in Falmouth. The twenty-three original members are noted in the church records as ". . . inhabitants of North Falmouth, desirous of enjoying religious privileges in this place . . . [who] do hereby withdraw from the first Congregational society in Falmouth and form ourselves into a religious Society, and take the name of North Falmouth Congregational Society." Of these original members, eleven were husbands or fathers of the quilters.

The occupations of the men related to the quilt's thirty-six signers (who were all women) represent a cross-section of the economy of Falmouth, a town on the western edge of Cape Cod. Eleven husbands of quilters were master mariners according to the 1850 federal census, underscoring Falmouth's reliance on the sea. The husbands of another thirteen

FIGURE 199. Friendship quilt, made by members of the North
Falmouth Congregational Church, 1850. Cotton (86" × 78").
Collection of the Falmouth Historical Society, Falmouth, Mass.
(1999.116.01). *Photograph by David Stansbury.* MQ 2956.

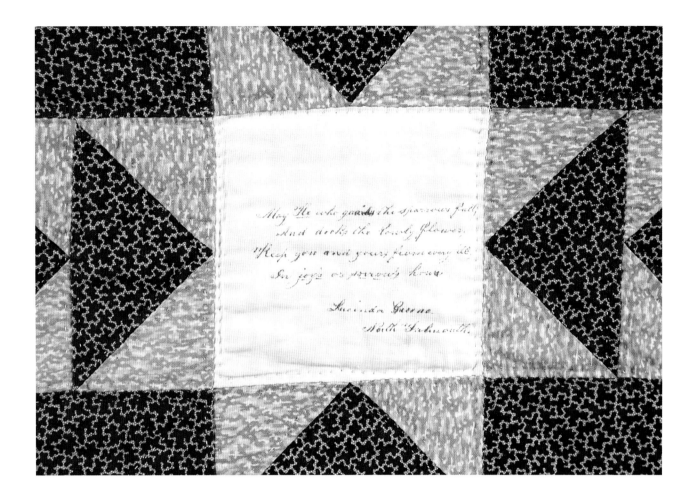

quilters were farmers, representing the other critical aspect of Falmouth's economy. A doctor, a merchant, a drover, painters, and carpenters also played necessary roles in the Falmouth community.

In 1850, there were about fifty families living in separate households in town. Many of the quilt's signers were descended from North Falmouth's original seventeenth-century settlers, and they were related to each other. Twenty-nine quilt signers are buried in the North Falmouth Cemetery. In life also, many of them were located in close proximity, in houses along Old Main Road. Undoubtedly, they shared much in their lives, including the loneliness of long separations from their husbands gone to sea, anxiety over a son gone to the California in search of gold (a child of Harriet Goodspeed Nye), happiness over the return of loved ones, and sadness over the deaths of family members and friends.

Crowell and Nye family members are especially well represented on this quilt. Both are old local

FIGURE 200. Detail, close-up of inscribed block, "May he who guides the sparrows fall, / And decks the lovely flowers / Keep you and yours from every ill / In joy's or sorrow's hour. / Lucinda Greene / North Falmouth." *Photograph by David Stansbury.*

FIGURE 201. Detail, calicoes, North Falmouth Congregational Church quilt. *Photograph by David Stansbury.*

families, with streets or sections of town named for them. One signer of the quilt, Almira Davis Nye, along with her husband James, assured future ministers of the North Falmouth Congregational Society of housing near the church. Because all of the Nye's four children died before them, James Nye left his house in his 1871 will to the church "to be used as a parsonage" after the death of his wife, which came in 1890; the house was sold by the congregation in the 1950s. While none of the other signers were able to leave such a large gift to show their devotion to the community, this beautiful quilt survives as their legacy.   —LZB and HE

REVEREND THOMAS TREADWELL STONE QUILT

(FIG. 202)

In the varied patchwork of our individual character let us put only strong fabricks and lasting colors, lest, thro' the "wear & tear" of life, we prove but a shabby coverlet to wrap an immortal soul in.

Inscribed in ink on this autograph quilt, this verse presents quiltmaking as a metaphor for human life and character. Signed by eighty-two women, the quilt was given to the Reverend Thomas Treadwell Stone, who was installed as a minister of the First Church in Salem in July 1847. Several of the blocks are inscribed with dates that range from June 1847 to January 1848. In addition to the inscription above, three other squares feature short verses:

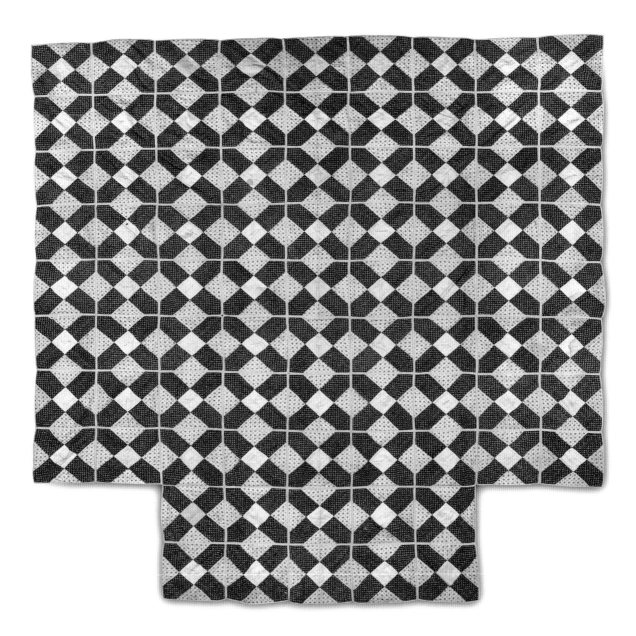

FIGURE 202. Friendship quilt, made for the Reverend Thomas Treadwell Stone (1801–1895) of Salem, 1847–1848. Cotton (85½" × 96"). Collection of the Peabody Essex Museum, Salem, Mass., gift of Martha E. Waite, 1924 (PEM 11/691). *Photograph courtesy of the Peabody Essex Museum.* MQ 3092.

Love not sleep lest / Thou come to poverty / Robin M. Deland [Proverbs 20:13].

Our hearts unite / In the parting prayer / And the kind good night / L. E. M.

Sleep sit dove-like on thy breast. / E. Merritt.

A comparison of the names on the quilt with a membership list of First Church, Salem revealed that almost thirty or approximately one-third of the names on the quilt belonged to members of the Reverend Stone's congregation. This suggests that the quilt may have been a presentation piece or a gift to the new minister of the church and his family.[16]

Another possibility also exists. Several of the women who signed the quilt were also members of

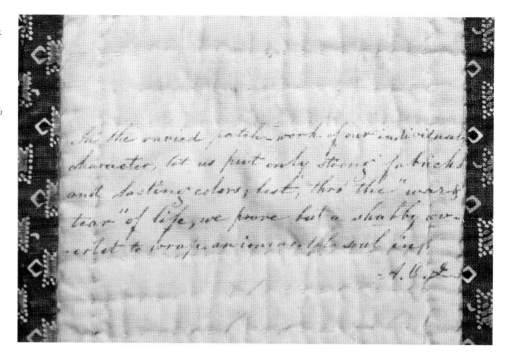

the Salem Female Anti-Slavery Society, to which the minister's wife, Laura Poor Stone, belonged. These included Lucy Ives, the wife of William Ives, publisher of the newspaper, *The Salem Observer*, who served for several years as the society's president. In 1847, while the quilt was under construction, Laura Stone served as the vice president for the society and in September of that year, the Reverend Stone accepted the society's invitation to deliver an anti-slavery lecture in Salem. During the fall of 1847, members of the Salem Female Anti-Slavery Society prepared goods to be sold at the Fourteenth National Anti-Slavery Bazaar held at Faneuil Hall in Boston on December 21 to 31. During the eleven days that the fair was open, several "persons of distinguished eloquence" presented evening lectures in support of the anti-slavery movement. The speakers included noted abolitionists Frederick Douglass and Wendell Phillips, along with the Reverend Thomas T. Stone.[17] Antebellum charitable fairs typically sold a wide array of textiles and other goods made by women to raise money for causes they supported. Because of the close connection between the Reverend Thomas and Laura Stone and these abolitionist organizations and events, this quilt could have been associated with this occasion.

In the years following, the Reverend Stone's abolitionist stance became the source of increasing tension with some members of his congregation. Public debate about slavery grew more heated in Salem during the spring of 1851 when a runaway slave was captured in Boston and returned to the South under the provisions of the Fugitive Slave Act adopted by Congress in 1850. In sermons that were published later, Stone voiced outrage at the institution of slavery and political compromises that attempted to sustain the union through concessions to slave holders.[18] In August of 1851, the First Church voted to give six months' notice to the Reverend Stone; he concluded his ministry in Salem in February of 1852. As he departed for Bolton, Massachusetts, where he lived for the remainder of his life, individual members of the congregation gave the Reverend Stone one thousand dollars, "cordially presented to him upon the close of his ministerial connection with them."[19] Ironically, when the Reverend Stone died in 1895 at the age of ninety-two, his funeral service took place at Salem's First Church with the abolitionist minister Edward Everett Hale delivering the eulogy. While reasons for Stone's departure remain vague, in 1903, an article in the *Salem Evening News* recounted that the Reverend Stone was "driven from this pulpit because he preached abolition sermons . . ."[20]

Each of the eighty-two blocks of this quilt features a pieced cross-like pattern made of turkey red printed cotton on a ground constructed from white printed cotton with a small floral sprig pattern. The center block of each square made of white cotton muslin bears the signature or initials of an individual woman. Each block is bound in white cotton twill tape and the overall effect of the quilt is of a simple but bold lattice-like pattern.

In 1924, Martha E. Waite of Bolton, Massachusetts, offered to the Essex Institute (now Peabody Essex Museum) this "album quilt given my father (Rev. Thomas T. Stone) when he was minister of the First Church in Salem." She commented that "It is in very good condition."[21] Made of "strong fabrics" and "lasting colors," Reverend Stone's quilt is still vibrant 160 years later. Not only a fine example of an autograph or friendship quilt, it also serves as a poignant reminder of the life and character of an individual whose convictions embroiled him in the tumultuous times and events that led to the American Civil War. 　　　　　　　　　—PBR

Signature Quilt

SARAH F. GALLUP QUILT

(FIG. 204)

Although women could not vote in the nineteenth century, they nevertheless demonstrated a passion for politics and other social issues. Their political and patriotic expressions often took the form of quilts. Around 1880, Sarah F. (Colburn) Gallup, the wife of James B. Gallup, a comb maker in Leominster, gave herself the project to create a signature quilt as a fundraiser for Union veterans of the Civil War.[22] In fact, she decided that she would make two quilts: one to give away in a contest and the other to keep for herself. She sent two squares of white linen to one hundred famous people of the day; eighty-eight responded. Those who responded included four presidents, four vice presidents, five

cabinet members, three first ladies, six Massachusetts governors, and six United States senators. With the exception only of 1880 democratic presidential candidate and Civil War Union hero Winfield Scott Hancock (1824–1886), all of the politicians who signed the linen squares were Republican, the party of Abraham Lincoln.[23]

Mrs. Gallup also solicited signatures from famous cultural figures of the day, including the Reverend Henry Ward Beecher (brother of *Uncle Tom's Cabin* author Harriet Beecher Stowe), and Massachusetts literary figures John Greenleaf Whittier, Oliver Wendell Holmes, Sr., Louisa May Alcott, Henry Wadsworth Longfellow, Edward Everett Hale, and Thomas Wentworth Higginson. People prominent in various reform movements added their signatures to the quilt, including Frederick Douglass and Mary A. Livermore, nationally known reporter, editor, lecturer, and president of the Massachusetts Women's Suffrage Association, as well as president of the Massachusetts Women's Christian Temperance Union. In short, this quilt is a compendium of America's political, military, and cultural leaders of the Gilded Age. It is a remarkable testament, in particular, to the prominence of Massachusetts literary figures.

Mrs. Gallup finished only one of her two quilts. One set of the white autographed squares was pieced together with red cotton to form "Ohio Star" blocks, which were then sashed with blue (now faded to gray). The quilt was tied rather than quilted. A local newspaper noted when and where the quilt would be displayed, and how one might win it as a prize: "The quilt will be at the G.A.R. Fair December 17, 18, and 19. Send her fifteen cents and the right answer to the following problem and the quilt is yours." The problem followed:

> Three men went to town. One had ten eggs. One had twenty eggs. One had thirty eggs. They agreed to sell them at the same rate. On their return home they each had the same amount of money for the sale of their eggs. Now, how did they sell their eggs? Who gets the quilt?

The answer was that each man sold his eggs for 10 cents each; the second man brought ten eggs home,

FIGURE 204. Signature quilt, made by Sarah F. Gallup (1833–after
1910) of Leominster, c. 1880–1881. Cotton and linen (79" × 79").
Private collection. *Photograph by David Stansbury.* MQ 4903.

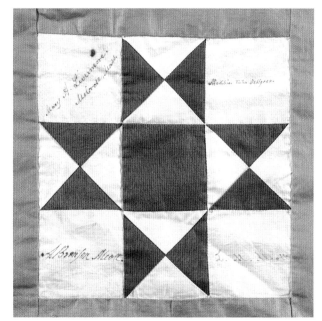

FIGURE 205. Detail of block with signature of President James A. Garfield, who was shot while in office in 1881; the block bears a single black bead in the center as a symbol of mourning. Other signatures on this block include Garfield's wife, Lucretia Rudolph Garfield, and his mother, Eliza Ballou Garfield, and his Secretary of State James G. Blaine. *Photograph by David Stansbury.*

FIGURE 206. Detail of block with signatures of Mary A. Livermore, Madeline Vinton Dahlgren (born into an important Ohio political family, she became an author and arbiter on etiquette), A. Bronson Alcott, and Louisa May Alcott. *Photograph by David Stansbury.*

while the third brought twenty eggs home. It is not known who came up with this answer and won the quilt, nor how the quilt came to be in the antiques shop in Waltham, Massachusetts, where the current owner purchased it in the 1970s.[24]

Signatures on the quilt include:

PRESIDENTS

Ulysses S. Grant (1822–1885), served 1869–1877
Rutherford B. Hayes (1822–1893), served 1877–1881
James A. Garfield (1831–1881), served 1881;
    assassinated in office (Garfield's block on this quilt
    bears a single black bead, probably in recognition
    of his death.)
Chester A. Arthur (1829–1886), served 1881–1885

VICE PRESIDENTS

Chester A. Arthur (became president after the
    assassination of Garfield)
Schuyler Colfax (1823–1885), Grant's vice president
Hannibal Hamlin (1809–1891), Lincoln's first vice
    president
William A. Wheeler (1819–1887), Hayes's vice
    president

CABINET MEMBERS AND DIPLOMATS

George S. Boutwell (1818–1905), Secretary of the
    Treasury under Grant
Elihu Washburne (1816–1887), Secretary of State
    under Grant
Thomas L. James (1831–1916), Postmaster General
    under Garfield
James G. Blaine (1830–1893), Secretary of State
    under Garfield
George Bancroft (1800–1891), Secretary of the Army
    and Navy under Polk
Charles Francis Adams (1807–1886), Minister to
    Great Britain 1861–1868 (grandson of John and
    Abigail Adams)

FIRST LADIES

Julia Dent Grant (1826–1902)
Lucy Ware Webb Hayes (1831–1889)
Lucretia Rudolph Garfield (1832–1918)

MASSACHUSETTS GOVERNORS

Alexander Hamilton Rice (1818–1895), served 1876–
    1879
Alexander H. Bullock (1816–1882), served 1866–1869

John D. Long (1838–1913), served 1880–1883

Nathaniel Prentiss Banks (1816–1894), served 1858–1861

Thomas Talbot (1818–1886), served 1874–1875 and 1879–1880

William Claflin (1820–1887), served 1869–1872

SENATORS

George F. Edmunds (1828–1919) of Vermont

John A. Logan (1826–1886) of Illinois

William Windom (1827–1891) of Minnesota (candidate for president in 1880, and served as Secretary of the Treasury under both Garfield and Benjamin Harrison)

George F. Hoar (1826–1904) of Massachusetts

Eugene Hale (1836–1918) of Maine

MILITARY HEROES

General Philip Sheridan (1831–1888)

General William Tecumseh Sherman (1820–1891)

Major General John M. Schofield (1831–1906)

Thomas Wentworth Higginson (1832–1911, most famous for his correspondence and friendship with Emily Dickinson of Amherst; he was the first editor of her poetry, along with Mabel Loomis Todd)

Winfield Scott Hancock (1824–1886)

LITERARY FIGURES

John Greenleaf Whittier (1807–1892)

Oliver Wendell Holmes, Sr. (1809–1894)

Louisa May Alcott (1832–1888)

Henry Wadsworth Longfellow (1807–1882)

Edward Everett Hale (1822–1909)

Madeline Vinton Dahlgren (1825–1889)

REFORM FIGURES

Frederick Douglass (1818–1895)

Mary A. Livermore (1820–1905)

Bronson Alcott (1799–1888)

—LZB

Mourning Quilt

HENRIETTA BRYAN LAMBIE QUILT

(FIG. 207)

Viewed without an awareness of its history, the grief that this crazy quilt symbolizes is not immediately apparent. Made of typical late nineteenth-century silks and velvets, it is embellished with the Japanese-inspired motifs of handscreens, lotus flowers, and Oriental vases that one usually finds on such quilts. Careful study, however, reveals a story: painted and embroidered pansies, representing "thoughts" or sympathy in the Victorian language of flowers; daisies, representing childhood's innocence, embroidered along with the name "Ethel"; forget-me-nots painted on cream satin; multiple embroidered motifs of children; and a hen with her chicks all suggest a mother's loss of a child. In fact, two children are commemorated in this quilt.

In 1875, Henrietta Bryan of New York City married Jasper Eadie Lambie (1845–1898) of Easthampton, Massachusetts. Jasper and his brother John were the prosperous owners of a dry goods shop on Main Street in Northampton. J. E. Lambie & Co. advertisements in the Northampton City Directories of the 1880s and 1890s reveal that they offered "Rich Dress Goods, Silk and Fancy Goods, Dress Trimmings, Buttons, Hosiery, Corsets, Gloves, Ladies' and Gents' Underwear, &c." Henrietta and Jasper spent the first ten years of their marriage in nearby Easthampton. In 1879, Ethel Henrietta was born. Another daughter, Emily Mary, came along in 1882. Grief came to the family in 1884 when five-year-old Ethel died in February. Because one block in the quilt is dated April 30, 1884, it seems that the quilt began as a memorial to Ethel, but when two-year-old Emily died in August that same year, the quilt became her memorial as well.

In copperplate script, Henrietta wrote a note to keep with the quilt, describing the fabrics she used. Her husband's ties are the black and white and purple silks—all colors of mourning. Ethel's pink sash and red and blue ribbons are used, along with the white silk lining to Emily's cloak, which Henrietta

FIGURE 207. Foundation pieced, embroidered, and painted crazy quilt, made by
Henrietta Bryan Lambie (1852–1932) of Northampton, 1884. Silk (66" × 57"). Collection
of Historic Northampton (68.49). *Photograph by David Stansbury.* MQ 4061.

painted with forget-me-nots. Much of the rest of
the quilt was made from pieces of Henrietta's own
clothing, to which she added "the red satin . . . to
brighten." Henrietta and Jasper's daughter Margaret, born in 1885, noted when she donated the quilt
to Historic Northampton that "sympathetic friends"
also contributed blocks for the quilt, which explains
the various initials and names such as "Davis" and
"Newman" that appear on the quilt.[25]

Henrietta Lambie's declaration in the 1900 Federal Census that she was the mother of six children,

along with the span of four years from her wedding date to the birth of Ethel, suggests that she lost
two babies in the first years of her marriage. Perhaps in part to escape the sad memories of their
losses in Easthampton, in 1885 the couple moved to
Northampton. Two more children were born: Margaret, who became a prominent lawyer in Washington, D.C., and Morris (b. 1888), who also survived
to adulthood and became a professor at the University of Minnesota. Henrietta suffered one more
grievous loss when Jasper died in 1898. The dry

FIGURE 208. Detail of Henrietta Lambie quilt, showing painted pansies and embroidered daisies. *Photograph by David Stansbury.*

PHOTOGRAPHER.

FIGURE 209. Henrietta Bryan Lambie, dressed in 1830s garb for a pageant, c. 1890s. *Photograph courtesy of Historic Northampton.*

goods business continued under the supervision of her brother-in-law into the 1920s, probably providing some income to Henrietta, as she appears to have continued to live comfortably in Northampton. She was active in the community, participating in Colonial Revival pageants (as seen in figure 208, where she is dressed in 1830s garb), and lending her beautiful contralto voice to church choirs throughout the vicinity.[26] In 1914, Henrietta and her two surviving children moved to New York City to join Henrietta's family. In her old age, Henrietta lived with Margaret in Washington, D.C., where she died at age eighty. —LZB

Family Register Quilt

ELIZA SUMNER QUILT

(FIG. 210)

This bed cover was made not only to warm the Sumners of Spencer, but to document the birth and death of each family member. It is the unique vision of its maker, Eliza Sumner, the daughter of William and Lucena (Fletcher) Sumner, who married in 1799.

The first thing that strikes the viewer is the unusual color scheme of this 1848 quilt. The yellow, blue, and white combination at first appears unlikely for a mid-nineteenth-century quilt, but closer examination reveals that the glazed blue and white cottons used are the typical "cambric" lining fabrics found in women's dresses in this period. The yellow silk is likewise a common lining fabric of the period, called "sarsnet," while the yellow gingham was a popular fabric used for children's clothes and women's work aprons.[27] Eliza chose these fabrics carefully to execute her celestial design, with large medallions of "A Representation of the Starry Heavens," "The Dipper," "The Seven Sisters," "The Sun and its Rays in their irregular order," and the moon at night. The knowledge of astronomy, along with the carefully planned geometry and calculated measurements of the various blocks, indicate that Eliza had advanced schooling, probably at a young ladies' academy.

Another unusual aspect of this bed cover is that it is constructed like a duvet cover, an envelope to accept a quilt or blanket inside. The back is detachable along each side, being stitched only at the corners, and is fastened to a lip of the white cambric with small, white porcelain buttons and tape loops. The back is decorated with narrow white cotton tape laid out in a diamond grid pattern, with the tape twisted into small circles along each line. Small porcelain buttons, typically used on children's clothes and everyday clothes in this period, along with brass studs, create starburst patterns. Round patches of the white cambric edged with narrow strips of purple and yellow cotton are laid out in a symmetrical pattern of interlocking diamonds. The bed cover is edged along three sides with a scalloped ruffle trimmed with the narrow white tape and tiny thread buttons.

The unique and curious features of Eliza's bed cover do not end there. Perhaps most unusual are the linen patches that have been custom printed with religious verses and a family register in the center of the front. "The Title Diamond" at the top center of the front explains Eliza's motivation for making this bed cover:

TO
REMAIN
IN THE FAMILY
OF MRS. WILLIAM SUMNER,
AND HANDED DOWN TO
FUTURE GENERATIONS,
By line of descent, in Remembrance of
Their Ancestors.
Names of the descendants to be added. Those
in nearest connection to be placed upon the
REGISTER.
Wrought by Eliza Sumner.
Daughter of Dea. Wm. Sumner.
Spencer, Ms.
1848.

Above the Title Diamond is Eliza's "Dedicatory to 'Album Quilt,'" in which she offers herself and her quilt to the Lord's work: ". . . it is my reasonable duty to devote my time, talent, and all for Thy service from time and eternity. Great God, help me thus to do, and prepare me for all Thy will while on earth I live."

Scattered throughout the bed cover, front and back, are short verses of religious devotion, at least some of which were drawn from well-known hymns at the time: "Blessed by [*sic*] the tie, that binds / Our hearts in Christian love / The fellowship of kindred minds / Is like that above."[28] "Waiting to receive thy spirit / Lo the Saviour stands above / Shows the glory of His merit / Reaches out the crown of love."[29] These and other verses reflect the doctrine of salvation through faith that characterized the Second Great Awakening, a religious movement that was at its height in New England in the second quarter of the nineteenth century.

FIGURE 210. Pieced, appliquéd, and reverse-appliquéd bed cover, original pattern by Eliza Sumner (1802–1856) of Spencer, 1848. Glazed and plain cotton, linen, silk, and porcelain and brass buttons (92" × 104"). Private collection. *Photograph by David Stansbury.* MQ 4100.

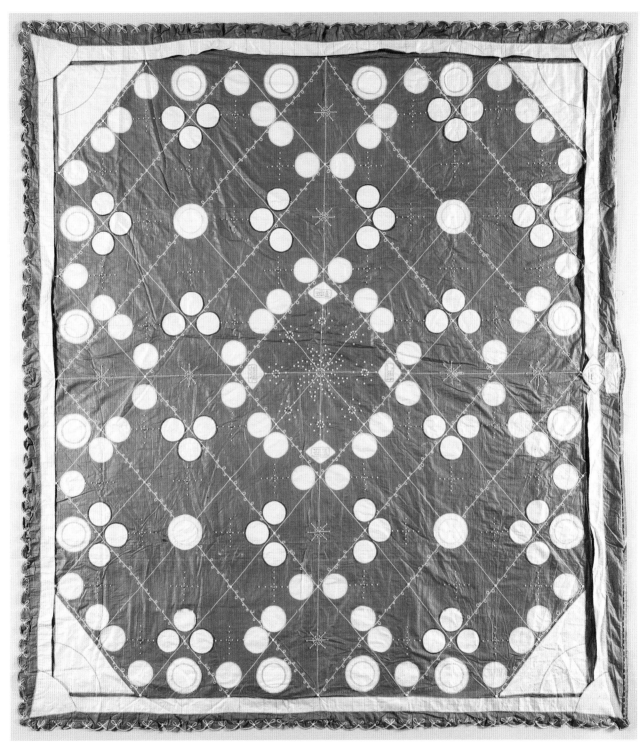

FIGURE 211. The back of Eliza Sumner's bed cover is decorated with small white porcelain buttons, brass studs, narrow white braid, and medallions printed with religious verses. *Photograph by David Stansbury.*

FIGURE 212. Detail of the "Selected Dedicatory to 'Album Quilt,' and 'The Title Diamond.'" *Photograph by David Stansbury.*

(See the essay on friendship quilts at the beginning of this chapter.) Eliza was primed to receive the preaching of this religious revival, as she was raised in a religious family and her father was a deacon in the church.

In the center of the front is a large panel, printed at the top with "FAMILY RECORD" under which appears "NAMES," "MARRIAGES," and "DEATHS." Such family registers were extremely common in the period, though printed on paper, not cloth. Where did Eliza acquire this register and the unique linen patches printed with pious verses? A kit for letter-press printing by amateurs at home, called a "novelty press," did not become available until 1867—too late for Eliza to have produced the patches for her "Album Quilt" herself.[30] She must have had them custom-made at a professional print shop. The closest print shop to Spencer belonged to one of rural New England's most successful printers, Ebenezer Merriam (1777–1858), in business from 1798 to 1848. He was located in the western section of Brookfield, the town located just to the west of Spencer.[31] As the Sumner family lived at the western edge of Spencer, it was a ride or walk of about eight miles to place an order at the E. & L. Merriam print shop.[32]

The "Album Quilt" appears to have been a gift to Eliza's mother, Lucena, as the dedication states that it was to remain in the family of "Mrs. Wm Sumner." Eliza intended for the vital information about each family member to be written in the respective columns of the register. However, the register was never filled in—it is blank. Perhaps it was the sorrowful fact that Lucena outlived most of her family that kept her from filling out the register. Six of her eleven children were deceased by the time Eliza presented her with the quilt; her husband William,

also, was gone, having died of consumption in 1839. Eliza, too, would die five years before her mother, in 1856. The "Album Quilt" was kept safely folded up in a trunk for three more generations, passing to Eliza's only surviving brother, William, Jr., a piano teacher in Worcester, and then down to his daughter and granddaughter. The contents of the Sumner house in Worcester were sold in the 1990s, and thus the present owner came into possession of this special textile, a unique item of American folk art.

—LZB

Chapter 18

The Colonial Revival

In the early twentieth century, quiltmaking experienced renewed vigor brought about by events and cultural movements that were shaping American life. One important influence was the Colonial Revival, an aesthetic and cultural movement that appropriated and reinterpreted the American past in response to forces of modernity in contemporary life and as a means to express American identity. The Colonial Revival was an aesthetic style expressed in architecture and in the fine and decorative arts, but it was also a social agenda conveyed in many forms of popular culture. Although its roots can be traced to the time of the American Civil War, expressions of the Colonial Revival became increasingly widespread following the American Centennial in 1876 and continued to evolve through the Depression era of the 1930s.

The Colonial Revival presented an idealized, romanticized, and modernized version of the American past that blended elements of style drawn from the colonial period and the first decades of the new republic. These included iconic symbols that mythologized historical events and individuals such as the Pilgrims and the landing of the Mayflower, heroes of the American Revolution such as George Washington, Paul Revere, or Betsy Ross, and figures such as Priscilla Mullins, who was brought to fame by Henry Wadsworth Longfellow's poem, "The Courtship of Myles Standish" (1858). The values and character embodied by these individuals were upheld as examples of American patriotism and morality. Prized heirlooms of colonial life, antique objects such as grandfather clocks, spinning wheels, candlesticks, hearths, and sailing ships took on symbolic meaning as emblems of integrity, longevity, handcraftsmanship, and industry. Social activities of colonial life—dancing the minuet, tea-drinking, or quiltmaking—were celebrated as emblems of hospitality and cordial and productive social interactions. These images served as an antidote to aspects of societal change and unrest affecting the lives of Americans such as urbanization, industrialization, immigration, labor disputes, faster-paced life styles, increasing mobility, and national and international events, including the First World War and the Great Depression.[1]

Massachusetts played an important role in the Colonial Revival. Several leading figures of this movement resided in Massachusetts and promoted the style to a national audience. Historic quilts and the activity of quiltmaking featured prominently in their works. Born in Worcester, author Alice Morse Earle (1853–1911) wrote over a dozen books that are important expressions of Colonial Revival ideology and material culture. Although often ignored or criticized by academic historians, Earle's books and articles were influential in recording the life-ways and material world of the colonial period and promoting the past as an exemplar for the present. Her book, *Home Life in Colonial Days*, published in 1898, contains the following description of quilt-making:

> The feminine love of color, the longing for decoration, as well as pride in skill of needle-craft, found riotous expansion in quilt-piecing. A thrifty economy, too, a desire to use up all the fragments and bits of stuffs which were necessarily cut out in the shaping, chiefly of women's and children's gar-

ments, helped to make the patchwork a satisfaction. The amount of labor, of careful fitting, neat piecing, and elaborate quilting, the thousands of stitches that went into one of the patchwork quilts, are to-day almost painful to regard. Women reveled in intricate and difficult patchwork; they eagerly exchanged patterns with one another; they talked over the designs, and admired the pretty bits of calico, and pondered what combinations to make, with far more zest than women ever discuss art or examine high art specimens together to-day.[2]

The author also commented on the superiority of fabrics available in the past, the fanciful names given to quilt patterns, and the sociability and productivity of quiltmaking as a collaborative activity, all reinforcing an impression of quiltmaking as a quaint and genteel endeavor.

Massachusetts resident Wallace Nutting (1861–1941), the clergyman, photographer, author, furniture manufacturer, and entrepreneur, also used quiltmaking as a potent symbol of an idealized American past. In his artfully contrived photographs, women in colonial garb stitch peacefully on quilts in softly lit colonial interiors creating impressions of domesticity and genteel industry. His book, *Massachusetts Beautiful*, published in 1923, featured several quilting scenes including "The Goose Chase Quilt—Quincy Homestead," "Patchwork Quilting—Newburyport," and "A Tree of Life Bedspread." Nutting used these benign images not only to encourage historic preservation but also to express an anti-modern world view in twentieth-century America.[3]

Textiles were a very important medium of expression for the Colonial Revival. Historic textiles such as samplers, quilts, clothing, and accessories were acquired by collectors and institutions as important relics and touchstones from the colonial past. In addition to collecting historic examples, artists and craftspeople created new textiles that reinterpreted historic designs and techniques for contemporary consumers. Probably the best-known expressions of colonial revival textiles are the embroideries and weavings by the Deerfield Blue and White Society of Deerfield, Massachusetts. Founded

in 1896, this textile cooperative promoted handcraftsmanship and production of domestic textiles based on historic designs as an alternative to industrialized consumer goods. Their designs often combined historic motifs of the colonial period or early nineteenth century with influences of Art Nouveau and the Aesthetic Movement.[4]

Publishing firms in the early twentieth century that catered to a national readership of female needlework enthusiasts produced magazines and patterns for embroidery, crochet, and quiltmaking. These included mass-market publications such as *Ladies Home Journal*, *Good Housekeeping*, and specialized textile publications including *Modern Priscilla* and *Needlecraft* magazines. Publishers often hired women artists to produce new designs featured in these periodicals. Massachusetts quiltmakers drew inspiration from published patterns by designers such as Anne Champe Orr of Tennessee, needlework editor of *Good Housekeeping*, and Marie Webster of Indiana, whose quilt designs appeared in *Ladies Home Journal* and were later published in her book, *Quilts, Their Story and How to Make Them* (1915). In 1915, Carrie A. Hall and Rose Kretsinger of Kansas published *The Romance of the Patchwork Quilt in America*, both a history of quiltmaking and a guide to hundreds of quilt patterns that were used by women around America.[5]

Colonial Revival quilts often featured adaptations of eighteenth- and nineteenth-century pieced and appliquéd quilt patterns. In these quilts, an impression of historicism was often more important than an exact reproduction of an actual textile from the colonial period. The fabrics used to create these quilts are an important feature in distinguishing those of the Colonial Revival era from historic examples (compare, for example, figure 128/MQ 2294 with figure 18/MQ 2798 or 76/MQ 1372). While emulating historic designs, Colonial Revival quilts often feature mill prints and shirting fabrics commonly associated with American textile production in the early twentieth century. During the Great Depression in the 1920s and 1930s, pastel and brightly colored printed dress fabrics created a distinctive aesthetic in quiltmaking that is now considered a characteristic of that era (fig. 64/MQ 3678, fig.

121/MQ 2006, fig. 128/MQ 2294, fig. 172/MQ 4345, fig. 175/MQ 3458, fig. 182/MQ 4833, fig. 192/MQ 4151, fig. 194/MQ 4955, fig. 213/MQ 3680). A new development in quiltmaking during the early twentieth century was the introduction of kit quilts. Manufacturers hired textile designers to create patterns and assembled materials and components into packaged kits that were sold in local dry goods or department stores, or through national mail-order companies (fig. 216/MQ 4022). Although individual quilters continued to produce fine examples, interest in quilting waned somewhat in the 1940s as women entered the workforce during World War II, which also caused shortages of materials.[6]

A distinctive form of American quiltmaking, Colonial Revival quilts are attracting attention in scholarly and collecting circles. Massachusetts quiltmakers and collectors promoted and contributed to the development of this aesthetic style and have left a rich heritage of quilts for future enjoyment and study; for example, Annie Strock Offen's collection (see fig. 218/MQ 5618). A highly creative and expressive artistic medium, quilting has enjoyed a resurgence of interest in the late twentieth century that builds on and honors the contributions and heritage of generations of quiltmakers such as those from Massachusetts featured in this publication.   —PBR

CORA BRUCE APPLING QUILT
(FIG. 213)

Living in Plymouth County, home of the Pilgrims, Cora Bruce Appling must have felt a strong connection to the Colonial Revival. Not only was her town named Carver after John Carver (1576–1621), the first leader of Plymouth Colony, but her own husband was the great-great-great-great-great-grandson of none other than William Bradford (1590–1657).[7] Bradford was the primary author of the Mayflower Compact (1620), the agreement signed by the Separatists—better known as the Pilgrims—establishing the basis for governance in the New World. He took over leadership of Plymouth Colony following the death of John Carver, acting

as governor for thirty years. It was Bradford who declared the First Thanksgiving in the autumn of 1621. Certainly, the Appling family could take pride in their distinguished heritage.

Like her "Sweetheart" comforter (fig. 64/MQ 3678), Cora made this comforter with the help of her quilting friends from the North Carver Grange and Congregational Church. Cora used feedsack prints, as well as finer calicoes in piecing this pattern, called "Martha Washington's Flower Garden"—a Colonial Revival name for an old hexagonal template-pieced design that had been practiced in America since at least the 1830s.[8] It is a variation on one of the most common quilt designs of the Colonial Revival, "Grandmother's Flower Garden," in which the small hexagonal pieces are arranged in concentric rings to create an abstract floral design. (See examples by Julia Steuer, fig. 172/MQ 4345, and Anna Kane, fig. 128/MQ 2294, in this book.)

Quilt historian Merikay Waldvogel notes that the soft pastel colors so popular in this period belie the difficult time of the Great Depression.[9] In the 1930s, Cora and her husband, Henry, were much better off than many Americans. The 1930 census notes that Henry was working as a "moulder" at the Plymouth foundry, probably to supplement their income as cranberry growers. The value of their home, at $2,500, was above average for their area—and they owned a radio. Nevertheless, in one way or another, the Depression affected everyone. Cora no doubt found some relief from the worries of the period in stitching her lovely quilts and comforters, and in the pleasant chatter of friends gathering to quilt in the church basement and Grange Hall.   —LZB

FIGURE 213. Template-pieced comforter, "Martha Washington's
Flower Garden," made by Cora Bruce Appling (1879–1969) of Carver,
c. 1930s. Cotton (78" × 76"). Private collection. *Photograph by David
Stansbury.* MQ 3680.

LUCETTIA MAY SHARP YOUNG QUILT

(FIG. 214)

Stitched on the reverse of this quilt is a cloth tape with a typed inscription, "L.M.Y. 33,148 pieces," which records the maker's initials and the magnitude of her accomplishment. Quilt designs made of small square blocks of approximately one inch in size are typically referred to as "post-age stamp" patterns. With cotton blocks measuring just three-quarters of an inch in size, this unfinished quilt top can be considered the micro-mosaic of postage stamp quilts. Composed of fifty-six blocks, the tiny squares are arranged and machine-stitched to form hearts that join at the base, forming an overall design of floral medallions with eight petals, in a pattern known as "postage stamp, hearts and gizzards."[10] Because the quilt top is unfinished, the back of the quilt reveals the astonishing regularity that the maker was able to achieve.

FIGURE 214. Pieced quilt top, made by Lucettia May Sharp Young (b. 1870) of Lynn, 1930. Cotton (90½" × 79½"). Collection of the Peabody Essex Museum, Salem, Mass., gift of Eben G. Young, 1940 (124251). *Photograph courtesy of the Peabody Essex Museum.* MQ 2761.

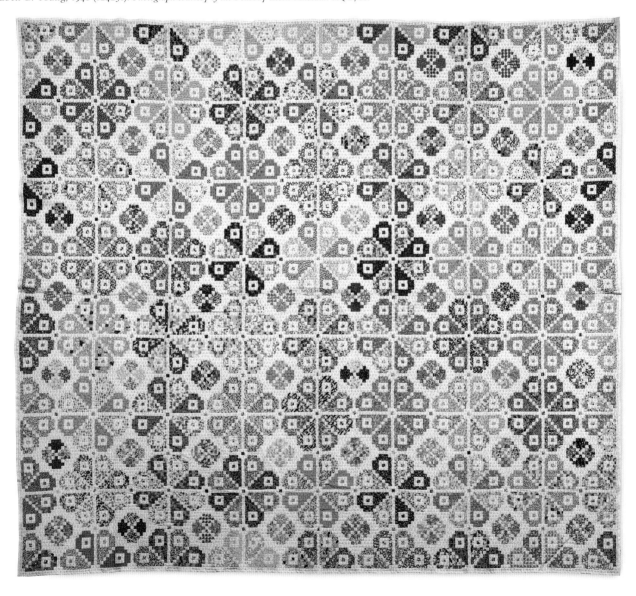

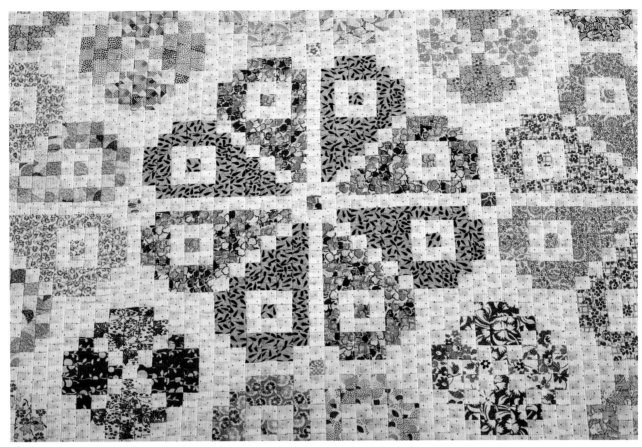

FIGURE 215. The pieces in Lucettia Young's postage-stamp quilt top are three-quarters of an inch square. *Photograph courtesy of the Peabody Essex Museum.*

The quilt is constructed from printed cotton dress fabrics in the bright pastel shades favored in the 1920s and 1930s. While embodying the aesthetics of the Depression era in the color of the fabrics, the pattern of floral medallions draws inspiration from the symmetry and regularity of early nineteenth-century woven coverlets. This reference to historic American textiles places the design of this quilt top into the context of the Colonial Revival with its appropriation and reinterpretation of earlier textile traditions for contemporary life.

When the Peabody Essex Museum acquired the quilt in 1940, it was approximately ten years old. The donor recorded the name of the maker as Lucettia May Sharp Young. Genealogical research suggests that Lucettia (Lusettia) H. Sharp, born in Lynn, was the daughter of Joshua F. Sharp and Jane Sharp, both immigrants to the United States from New Brunswick, Canada. In 1890, she married Eb-

enezer G. Young (b. 1862) who was born in Nova Scotia and later worked in the leather and shoe industry in Lynn.[11]　　　　　　　　　—PBR

MARY LOUISE DEWEY QUILT
(FIG. 216)

Mary Louise Dewey's crisp, bright summer spread marks an important change in design from quilts of the late 1800s. Made in the 1920s or 1930s, Dewey undoubtedly purchased a kit with pattern, instructions, and possibly even the fabric, to make her bed covering. In comparison to quilts made by women of her mother's and grandmother's generations, Mary Louise's quilt is less individualized and uses a lighter color palette and a more realistic depiction of flowers. Women all over the

FIGURE 216. Appliquéd summer spread in flower basket with bow
pattern, by Mary Louise (Walker) Dewey (1898–1951) of Great
Barrington and Longmeadow, c. 1923–1935. Cotton and polyester (96"
× 82"). Private collection. *Photograph by David Stansbury.* MQ 4022.

country made quilts and spreads like this one, influenced by the Colonial Revival.

The quilt, composed of solid-colored cotton fabrics, is appliquéd by hand using the whip stitch. Four blue baskets with lighter blue bows, joined by a floral garland of blue flowers and green leaves, comprise the center design. A scalloped swag accented with flowers borders the baskets. The blue cotton binding is bias-applied; white cotton sheeting is used for the backing. There is no batting or quilting.

Kit quilts became popular in the 1910s and 1920s as enthusiasm for the Colonial Revival increased in America. A 1917 issue of *Hearth and Home* magazine proclaimed, "the old-time 'laid work' or appliqué patchwork has come in again."[12] Women who learned to quilt as children returned to their needles as grown women to make fashionable bed coverings that reflected the popular Arts and Crafts and Art Nouveau styles. While family and friends usually exchanged new quilt patterns during the 1800s, the twentieth century offered a proliferation of quilt-themed magazine and newspaper columns that provided inspiration and ideas for contemporary bed coverings. By 1934, more than four hundred newspapers around the country included a quilt pattern column.[13]

Widely recognized as the tastemaker behind kit quilts, Marie Webster (1859–1956) published her first design in *Ladies' Home Journal* in 1911. Webster's innovations included the use of a pastel color scheme (by virtue of new fabric shades made possible with improved synthetic dyes), an overall design with strong borders recalling the medallion format of quilts from the late 1700s and early 1800s, and a more literal depiction of flowers, allowing specific plants to be identified.[14] Following in Webster's footsteps, a number of women designed equally distinctive and colorful quilts. Among the best known are Ruby McKim, Rose Kretsinger, and Anne Orr.

Quiltmaker Mary Louise Walker was born in Chicago, Illinois, in 1898, the daughter of Sydney and Harriet Walker. The Walkers had a large family; Mary Louise, known as "Marylou," was the second-youngest of nine siblings. Her physician father apparently specialized in ophthalmology, as he was called an "oculist" on the United States census.

Marylou enjoyed needlework and probably learned to quilt from her mother. Her interest in the domestic arts led her to be a home economics major at Simmons College in Boston. With degree in hand, Marylou taught home economics until 1923, when she married William F. Dewey in Evanston, Illinois. The couple relocated to Great Barrington, Massachusetts, shortly after their marriage. William Dewey was a consulting engineer and moved his family around according to his consulting jobs. In 1933, they moved to Ohio, followed by a stint in New York State. In 1941, the family returned to Massachusetts, taking up residence in Longmeadow.[15] Marylou and William had three children.

Marylou most likely made this quilt after her marriage in the 1920s or 1930s. She was diagnosed with multiple sclerosis while living in New York State during the late 1930s and was unable to sew as much as she had previously. Before her diagnosis, she completed several quilts in addition to this one, and started many more. Mary Louise Dewey's quilt was passed down in the family, where it remains today. Following in her mother's and grandmother's footsteps, the quilt's current owner is working on completing the quilts that Marylou started before her untimely death in 1951. —AEN

FIGURE 217. Mary Louise (Walker) Dewey, c. 1915. *Photograph courtesy of Betsy Giles.*

FIGURE 218. Appliquéd quilt, "Cape Cod Bridal Quilt," maker unknown, Osterville, c. 1840. Cotton (108½" × 107"). Collection of the Peabody Essex Museum, Salem, Mass., gift in memory of Annie Strock Offen, 2006 (138622.1). *Photograph courtesy of the Peabody Essex Museum.* MQ 5618.

Annie Strock Offen Collection

"CAPE COD BRIDAL QUILT"

(FIG. 218)

This quilt is a masterwork of the quilt and coverlet collection assembled by Annie Strock Offen (1899–2002), now owned by the Peabody Essex Museum. Comprised of sixteen blocks, the quilt features oak leaf, palm frond, and fleur-de-lis variations appliquéd in red cotton and interspersed with white blocks, stitched with a feather wreath motif in stuffed and corded quilting. Undulating feather vine and floral motifs in stuffed and corded quilting finish the quilt's edges. The information accompanying the quilt when it was acquired by the collector indicated that it was a wedding quilt made in Osterville, Massachusetts. Although it has been published as dating prior to 1810, the appliqué pattern suggests a date more likely in the 1840s.[16]

In early twentieth-century America, antique collecting became popular as a manifestation of the Colonial Revival movement that looked to the past for an idealized national identity. The Colonial Revival promoted a visual style associated with patriotic and traditional values in the present. Prominent American collectors, such as Electra Havemeyer Webb and Henry Francis du Pont, included quilts in the range of art, furniture, decorative art, and Americana acquired to furnish their homes, which later became the Shelburne Museum and the Winterthur Museum, respectively.[17] Other collectors have pursued a passion for collecting types of objects, such as American samplers or quilts. Each collector is drawn to certain works by complex intuitive responses that appeal to the intellect, senses, aesthetic tastes, and imagination.

Born in Boston, Annie Rose Strock Offen attended Boston's High School of Practical Arts, where she developed the skills and an appreciation for needlework. Widowed at the age of forty, Mrs. Offen enrolled in the Nursery Training School of Boston (now the Eliot Pearson School of Tufts University) to study early childhood education and later pursued a career in education. In 1944, she founded the Winchester Pre-School, a pioneering independent day care center in New England that enabled mothers to continue working outside the home while raising and educating their families.[18]

Mrs. Offen began collecting quilts and woven coverlets in the 1940s and initially was attracted to them as women's artistic expressions and as documents of women's history and industry. She acquired historic quilts and contemporary examples for her family's use. Much of her collecting took place in New England, although she also acquired examples on trips to Pennsylvania, Florida, and other destinations. She eventually amassed over two hundred examples from New England, the Mid-Atlantic, the South, and the Midwest, ranging in date from about 1800 to the 1970s. While she kept abbreviated records of her acquisitions, an overview of the collection reveals that she was drawn to certain types of quilts. The collection contains fine examples of appliquéd quilts, pieced geometric and abstract patterns, whitework quilts, Depression-era quilts, Bicentennial quilts, and overshot and jacquard woven coverlets. Intending to write a book on crazy quilts, Mrs. Offen collected a diverse array of this type. Although her goal of publishing was not realized, the collection offers many examples for those interested in this genre of quiltmaking.

Over the years, Annie Strock Offen shared her collection with the public through publication and exhibition. Her friend, author Lenice Ingraham Bacon, published a selection of quilts from the Offen collection in *American Patchwork Quilts* (1973), including the "Cape Cod Bridal Quilt." Mrs. Offen also lent quilts to museum exhibitions, including one held in honor of her ninetieth birthday at the New England Quilt Museum in Lowell in 1990; it featured over twenty of her quilts. In 2006, the collection was given in memory of Annie Strock Offen to the Peabody Essex Museum, where her collecting interests and dedication to promoting recognition of women's artistic and cultural achievements will continue to be shared with quilters, textile scholars, and museum visitors.   —PBR

NOTES

1. Early Quilts and Quilted Clothing (pages 3–33)

1. Early quilt historians, including Ruth E. Finley, author of *Old Patchwork Quilts and the Women Who Made Them* (1929), Carrie A. Hall and Rose G. Kretsinger, who collaborated on *The Romance of the Patchwork Quilt in America* (1935), and Patsy and Myron Orlofsky, authors of *Quilts in America* (1974), typically state that quilting was born of necessity and that patchwork was well known to the early colonists. Sally Garoutte was among the first to challenge this notion in her essay, "Early Colonial Quilts in a Bedding Context," published in *Uncoverings 1980*, (reprinted 1993): 18–27.

2. A purported seventeenth-century quilted petticoat fragment, said to have belonged to Elizabeth Alden Pabodie (1622/23–1707), is in the collection of the Pilgrim Society in Plymouth. The petticoat was cut to create a sleeve, following the line of the quilted feather along the petticoat's border to create the shoulderline. See *New England Begins: The Seventeenth Century* (Boston: Museum of Fine Arts, 1982), vol. 2, 348. Recent examination of this sleeve suggests that it is probably a fragment from an eighteenth-century petticoat, not from the seventeenth century. The face is fine pink silk, and the backing is woven with a linen warp and wool weft—it is not fustian (cotton and linen), as stated in *New England Begins*. The quilting pattern is typical of quilted petticoats from the latter half of the eighteenth century, and the sleeve shape is inconsistent with surviving seventeenth-century garments. The author wishes to thank Stephen C. O'Neill, curator of Pilgrim Hall Museum; Jill Hall, wardrobe and textiles manager at Plimoth Plantation; and Deirdre Windsor, textile conservator, for their assistance in analyzing this item.

3. Garoutte, "Early Colonial Quilts in a Bedding Context," 26.

4. George Francis Dow, "The Patchwork Quilt and Some Other Quilts," *Old Time New England* 17, no. 4 (April 1927); quoted in ibid.: 25.

5. Linda R. Baumgarten, "The Textile Trade in Boston, 1650–1700," in *Arts of the Anglo-American Community in the Seventeenth Century*, ed. Ian M. G. Quimby, 260–62 (Charlottesville: University Press of Virgina for the Henry Francis du Pont Winterthur Museum, 1975).

6. Ibid., 233.

7. Lynne Z. Bassett, *Telltale Textiles: Quilts from the Historic Deerfield Collection* (Deerfield, Mass.: Historic Deerfield, 2003), 5.

8. Baumgarten, "The Textile Trade in Boston," 220.

9. *The Weekly News-Letter*, Boston, June 22, 1727, no. 26.

10. Lynne Zacek Bassett, "Inspired Fantasy: Design Sources for New England's Whole-Cloth Wool Quilts," *The Magazine Antiques* (September 2005): 120–27.

11. Lynne Z. Bassett and Jack Larkin, *Northern Comfort: New England's Early Quilts, 1780–1850* (Nashville, Tenn.: Rutledge Hill Press, 1998), 15.

12. See advertisements in *New England Weekly Journal* 244 (November 22, 1731), 2; and "To be Sold by Phillip Audibert . . ." *The Boston Gazette*, July 23–30, 1733, 3.

13. "Lustring" or "lutestring" was a plain-woven silk "which had been stretched and, while under tension, smeared with a syrupy gum" to impart a crisp, lustrous quality. Florence Montgomery, *Textiles in America, 1650–1870* (New York: W. W. Norton & Co., 1984), 283.

14. A. Cecil Edwards, *The Persian Carpet* (London: G. Duckworth & Co., Ltd., 1953), 41.

15. Ibid.

16. *The New England Historical and Genealogical Register*, vol. 44, 1890, 55.

17. See the *Boston Gazette*, April 1–8, 1728, issue 437, 2; and the *Boston Evening Post*, July 2, 1739, issue 203, 2.

18. Jonathan Swift, *Directions to Servants* (1726), quoted in Deborah E. Kraak, "Early American Silk Patchwork

Quilts," *Textiles in Early New England: Design, Production, and Consumption, The Dublin Seminar for New England Folklife Annual Proceedings 1997* (Boston: Boston University, 1999), 14.

19. Oscar P. Fitzgerald, *Three Centuries of American Furniture* (Englewood Cliffs, N.J.: Prentice-Hall, 1982), 35–53. The term "Queen Anne" in reference to this decorative arts style is not related to the actual reign of Queen Anne, 1702–1714.

20. See Kraak, "Early American Silk Patchwork Quilts," 7–28.

21. Clark earned a bachelor's degree in 1712, and a Master of Arts in 1715. *Boston Gazette*, June 27, 1768, 2.

22. Quoted in Clifford K. Shipton, *Biographical Sketches of Those Who Attended Harvard College in the Classes 1701–1712* (Boston: Massachusetts Historical Society, 1937), 616.

23. See "Tituba's Story," *New England Quarterly* 71, no. 2 (1998); Elaine G. Breslaw, *Tituba, Reluctant Witch of Salem: Devilish Indians and Puritan Fantasies* (New York: New York University, 1996).

24. Paul Boyer and Stephen Nissenbaum, *Salem Possessed: The Social Origins of Witchcraft* (Cambridge, Mass.: Harvard University Press, 1974). See also John Putnam Demos, *Entertaining Satan: Witchcraft and the Culture of Early New England* (New York: Oxford University Press, 1982); Carol Karlsen, *The Devil in the Shape of a Woman: Witchcraft in Colonial New England* (New York: Vintage, 1987); and Mary Beth Norton, *In the Devil's Snare: The Salem Witchcraft Crisis of 1692* (New York: Random House, 2002). Bridget Marshall's website, http://ccbit.cs.umass.edu:80/parsons/hnmockup/witchcraft.html, provides an excellent overview of the literature on witchcraft in early New England.

25. Shipton, *Biographical Sketches*, 617.

26. *Boston Gazette*, June 27, 1768, 2.

27. Shipton, *Biographical Sketches*, 620.

28. *Boston Gazette*, June 27, 1768, 2.

29. J. W. Hanson, *History of the Town of Danvers, From its Early Settlement to the Year 1848* (Danvers: published by the author, 1848), 179; and *Boston Gazette*, June 27, 1768, 2.

30. *Boston Evening-Post*, March 11, 1765, 3; quoted in Shipton, *Biographical Sketches*, 620.

31. Shipton writes that Deborah was "the heiress of the well-off Deacon Peter Hobart of Braintree," *Biographical Sketches*, 617.

32. Kraak, "Early American Silk Patchwork Quilts," 7–28.

33. Paula Bradstreet Richter, *Painted with Thread: The Art of American Embroidery* (Salem, Mass.: Peabody Essex Museum, 2001), 6–7; Betty Ring, *Girlhood Embroidery: American Samplers and Pictorial Needlework, 1650–1850* (New York: Alfred A. Knopf, 1993), 31–35.

34. Saltonstall Quilt Linings Scraps of Paper (1702–1703). Saltonstall Family Papers, 1524–1969, MS N-2232, Box 39. Massachusetts Historical Society.

35. Lenice Ingram Bacon, *American Patchwork Quilts* (New York: Bonanza Books, 1973), 67, 69; *A Memoir Biographical and Genealogical of Sir John Leverett, Knt, Governor of Massachusetts, 1673–9 or Hon. John Leverett, F.R.S., Judge of the Supreme Court and President of Harvard College; and of the Family Generally* (Boston: Crosby, Nichols and Company, 1856).

36. Claude M. Fuess, *Andover: Symbol of New England, the Evolution of a Town* (Andover, Mass.: Andover Historical Society and North Andover Historical Society, 1959), 125.

37. Sarah Loring Bailey, *Historical Sketches of Andover (Comprising the Present Towns of North Andover and Andover), Massachusetts* (Boston: Houghton, Mifflin and Company, 1880), 110.

38. Ibid.

39. The author would like to thank Carol Majahad of the North Andover Historical Society for helping to clarify the garbled family genealogy that came with the quilt when it was donated to the McCord Museum.

40. Walter Eliot Thwing, *The Livermore Family of America* (Boston: W. B. Clarke Company, 1902), 35.

41. *Two Dedication Sermons, Delivered in Wilton, N.H., Before the First Congregational Church and Society in That Town* . . . (New York: John A. Gray, Printer, 1861), 16–17.

42. Ibid., 21.

43. Lynne Zacek Bassett, "Inspired Fantasy: Design Sources for New England's Whole-Cloth Wool Quilts," *The Magazine Antiques* 168, no. 3 (September 2005): 120–27.

44. For discussions of the Asian influences on English needlework, see Nicola J. Shilliam, "The Needle's Excellency: Tudor and Stuart Embroidery in the MFA," *The Magazine Antiques* (June 1996): 858–59; Liz Arthur, *Embroidery 1600–1700 at the Burrell Collection* (London: John Murray; Glasgow: Glasgow Museums, 1995), 39–40; and "Preserving the Past: An Indian Embroidered Coverlet," *Rotunda* 14, no. 2 (1981): 26.

45. Letter dated July 12, 1887, by Mrs. J. W. (Mary Irene) Fifield. Curatorial file (1972.910), Department of Textile and Fashion Arts, Museum of Fine Arts, Boston.

46. *The New England Weekly Journal* 403 (December 16, 1734): 2; and *Boston Gazette*, May 24–31, 1736, reprinted from Ann Pollard Rowe "Crewel Embroidered Bed Hangings in Old and New England," *Boston Museum Bulletin* 71, no. 365 (1973). 111.

47. Richard's first wife, Mary Thurston, was the mother of Mary Fifield Adams. Mary Thurston Fifield died in 1701.

48. Mary Allen's death date is unknown; Mary (and James) Allen appear in Boston real estate records until 1761, after which time they cease to appear.

49. Mary Avery bequeathed the quilt to her son, Joseph Avery White, who later gave it to his daughter, Charlotte (White) Kennard. Charlotte Kennard passed the quilt to her daughter, Mary (Kennard) Scott, mother of the donor, Mrs. E. (Mary Adams Scott) Emerson. Curatorial file (1972.910), Department of Textile and Fashion Arts, Museum of Fine Arts, Boston.

50. Curatorial file (31.694), Department of Textile and Fashion Arts, Museum of Fine Arts, Boston.

51. Susan S. Bean, *Yankee India: American Commercial and Cultural Encounters with India in the Age of Sail: 1784–1860*, (Salem, Mass., and Ahmedabad, India: Peabody Essex Museum, Mapin Publishing, and the Prashant H. Fadia Foundation, 2001), 31–34, 74–78; Richard J. Cleveland, *A Narrative of Voyages and Commercial Enterprises* (Cambridge: John Owen, 1842), 112.

52. Alice Baldwin Beer, *Trade Goods: A Study of Indian Chintz in the Collection of the Cooper-Hewitt Museum of Decorative Arts and Design* (Washington, D.C.: Smithsonian Institution Press, 1970), 32–33; John Irwin and Katharine B. Brett, *Origins of Chintz* (London: Her Majesty's Stationery Office, 1970), 3–23; Montgomery, *Textiles in America* (see n. 13), 314.

53. Edmund Janes Cleveland and Horace Gillette Cleveland, comps., *The Genealogy of the Cleveland and Cleaveland Families* (Hartford, Conn.: Case, Lockwood and Brainard, 1899), 498–502, 1076; Paula Bradstreet Richter, "Lucy Cleveland's 'Figures of Rags': Textile Arts and Social Commentary in Early Nineteenth-Century New England," in *Textiles in Early New England* (see n. 18), 557–58.

54. Josette Bredif and Natalie Rothstein, *Toiles de Jouy: Classic Printed Textiles from France 1760–1842* (London: Thames & Hudson, 1989), 50–51, 52–57, 141, 144.

55. See Jeremy Adamson, *Calico and Chintz Antique Quilts From the Collection of Patricia S. Smith* (Washington, D.C.: Museum of American Art Smithsonian Institution, 1997).

56. Mary Schoeser and Celia Rufey, *English and American Textiles from 1790 to the Present* (New York: Thames & Hudson, 1989), 52–53.

57. Celia Y. Oliver, *Enduring Grace: Quilts from the Shelburne Museum Collection* (Lafayette, Calif.: C & T Publishing, 1997), 47.

58. Florence M. Montgomery, *Printed Textiles: English and American Cottons and Linens, 1700–1850* (New York: Viking Press, 1970), 218, 235.

59. Ibid., 240.

60. Genealogical information was gathered from Charles Warren Spalding, *The Spalding Memorial: A Genealogical History of Edward Spalding of Virginia and Massachusetts Bay and His Descendants* (Chicago: American Publishers' Association, 1897).

61. Richard N. Smith, *Divinity and Dust: A History of Townsend, Massachusetts* (Lancaster, Mass.: Townsend Historical Society and Richard N. Smith, 1978), 96.

62. Ibid., 173, 96, 175, 241.

63. Bassett and Larkin, *Northern Comfort* (see n. 11), 61–62; "Fancy Needlework," in *The Lady's Book* (Philadelphia: Louis A. Godey, 1835), 10, 41.

64. Sumpter T. Priddy III, *American Fancy: Exuberance in the Arts 1790–1840* (Milwaukee: Milwaukee Art Museum, 2004), 83–96. See also Linda Eaton, *Quilts in a Material World: Selections from the Winterthur Collection* (New York: Abrams, 2007), 79.

65. "Fancy Needlework," 10, 41.

66. Rachel Cochran, et al., *New Jersey Quilts, 1777 to 1950: Contributions to an American Tradition* (Paducah, Ky.: American Quilter's Society, 1992), 61–62. The Heritage Project of New Jersey conjectured that this tape was distinctive to early quilts made in that state; however, this woven striped tape is seen frequently in New England's early nineteenth-century quilts. Despite the acknowledged geographical breadth of its use, it is commonly known as "Trenton tape," and will be referred to as such when discussed in this book.

67. Merchant sample book, 1828–1834, American, Peabody Essex Museum, American Decorative Arts department, 129931.

68. The author wishes to thank intern Jessica Zdeb, Harvard University, for genealogical research associated with this quilt.

69. *Boston News-Letter*, January 4, 1720. See Bassett, *Telltale Textiles* (see n. 7), 6–7.

70. Arthur Murray Kingsbury, *Kingsbury Genealogy* (Minneapolis: Burgess-Beckwith, 1962), 21.

71. Louis Coffin, ed., *The Coffin Family* (Nantucket: Nantucket Historical Association, 1962), 19, 43.

72. The author thanks Aimee Newell, former registrar of the Nantucket Historical Association artifact collection, for making available her research notes from the museum's curatorial files.

73. An exhibit label from 1979, written by Mrs. Henry Coffin Carlisle, Sr., reads: "Damaris Gayer stitched and was married in this skirt (petticoat) to Nathaniel Coffin Grandson of Tristram, in 1697 [*sic*—should read 1692] five generations of brides have worn this."

74. Mary Evelyn, *Mundis Muliebris: or, The Ladies Dressing-Room Unlock'd, and Her Toilette Spread . . .* (1690). Book online, available at the website of the Women Writers Resource Project of Emory University: http://chaucer.library.emory.edu/cgi-bin/sgml2html/wwrp.pl?act=contents&f=%2Fdata%2Fwomen_writers%2Fdata%2Fevelyn.sgm; accessed 19 April 2007. See also Iris Brooke and James Laver, *English Costume from the Seventeenth through the Nineteenth Centuries* (New York: Macmillan, 1937; reprint, New York: Dover Publications, 2000), 68.

75. Curatorial notes, acc. no. 2000.86.1, Aimee Newell, 28 February 2001, Nantucket Historical Society.

76. The interpretation offered by a museum label written by Mrs. Henry Coffin Carlisle, Sr., in 1977 that five generations wore the skirt is not possible, as there are only four generations from Damaris Coffin to Elizabeth Ramsdell.

77. Kevin Sweeny, "From Wilderness to Arcadian Vale: Material Life in the Connecticut River Valley, 1835–1760," in *The Great River: Art and Society of the Connecticut Valley, 1635–1820* (Hartford, Conn.: Wadsworth Atheneum, 1985), 21.

78. Marla R. Miller, "'And others of our own people': Needlework and Women of the Rural Gentry," in *What's New England about New England Quilts? Proceedings of a Symposium at Old Sturbridge Village* (Sturbridge, Mass.: Old Sturbridge Village, 1999), 19–33.

79. Professionally made imported petticoats tend to be more hastily quilted, with fewer stitches per inch. They also generally have a glazed, plain-woven worsted fabric called "tammy" used for the lining.

80. James Russell Trumbull, *History of Northampton, Massachusetts, From its Settlement in 1654* (Northampton: Gazette Printing Co., 1902), vol. II, 177.

81. Henry R. Stiles, *History of Ancient Wethersfield* (New York: Grafton Press, 1904), 815.

82. Ibid.

83. Trumbull, *History of Northampton*, 177.

84. Clare Rose, "The Manufacture and Sale of 'Marseilles' Quilting in Eighteenth-century London," *Bulletin du CIETA* (Lyon, France: Centre International D'Etude des Textiles Anciens), no. 76, 1999, 104–113.

85. The magnificent gambrel-roofed Dwight House, built in 1754 and the site of Betsy's marriage, was moved from Springfield and erected at Historic Deerfield in the mid-twentieth century to save it from demolition; its original Connecticut River Valley scrolled pediment doorway can be seen at the H. F. DuPont Winterthur Museum in Delaware.

86. Note in document file for F-495, Historic Deerfield registrar's office.

87. http://www.nps.gov/blac/planyourvisit/valley-sites-douglas-sutton-northbridge.htm

88. The author thanks Dr. Holly Izard, curator of the Worcester Historical Museum, for her assistance with family genealogy and comments on the relationship between Sarah and Mary.

89. Their real estate holdings jumped from $2,000 in 1860 to $6,860 in 1870, according to U.S. census records.

2. Northeastern Massachusetts (pages 34–65)

1. See http://www.massport.com/ports/about_histo.html; accessed 16 August 2007.

2. Ibid.

3. Richard D. Brown and Jack Tager, *Massachusetts: A Concise History* (Amherst: University of Massachusetts Press, 2000), 202.

4. Brown & Tager, *Massachusetts*, 202.

5. Ibid., 164–65.

6. Presidents John Adams and John Quincy Adams of Quincy, John F. Kennedy of Brookline, and George H. W. Bush of Milton; Psalms 107:23, King James Version.

7. *The Diary of William Bentley, D.D.*, (Gloucester, Mass.: Peter Smith, 1962), 4, 556–67.

8. Viola Hopkins Winner, "Abigail Adams and 'The Rage of Fashion,'" *Dress: Journal of the Costume Society of America* 28 (2001): 64–76; Abigail Adams to Hannah Quincy Lincoln Storer, Auteuil, 20 January 1785. *Adams Family Correspondence*, ed. Richard Alan Ryerson (Cambridge Mass.: Belknap Press of Harvard University Press, 1993), vol. 6, 66. Massachusetts Historical Society.

9. Lynne Z. Bassett, "A Classical Turn: Fashion in the Time of President John Adams," *White House History* 7 (Spring 2000): 46–55; Phyllis Lee Levin, *Abigail Adams: A Biography* (New York: St. Martin's Press, A Thomas

Dunn Book, 1987); Winner, "Abigail Adams and 'The Rage of Fashion.'"

10. John E. Morris, ed., *The Felt Genealogy: A Record of the Descendants of George Felt of Casco Bay* (Hartford, Conn.: Press of the Case, Lockwood & Brainard Company, 1893), 289–95; Eben Putnam, ed., *A Genealogy of the Descendants of John, Christopher, and William Osgood* (Salem, Mass.: 1984), 147–48. The author wishes to thank intern Jessica Zdeb, Harvard University, for research on Osgood family genealogy.

11. Will of Abigail Adams, 18 January 1815. Adams Family Papers. Massachusetts Historical Society.

12. Richard Newman, chief scientist at the Museum of Fine Arts, Boston, conducted both high-performance liquid chromatography (HPLC) and scanning electron microscopy/energy dispersive X-ray spectrometry (SEM/EDS) tests in February 2007. The major dye stuff was cochineal; however, the slightly more orange weft fibers of the satin-woven quilt top revealed the addition of brazilwood. The wool batting fibers were also dyed with cochineal and madder.

13. See Amy Butler Greenfield, *A Perfect Red: Empire, Espionage, and the Quest for the Color of Desire* (New York: Harper Collins Publishers, 2005).

14. The MFA collection contains a 1790s pink taffeta dress, two pairs of shoes, a hat, and a sash with bright pink tones. These objects, however, have not been analyzed for dye.

15. *The Massachusetts Centinel*, 17 January 1787, vol. 6, issue 35, 140. Other advertisements for silk quilts appear in *The American Herald*, 2 May 1785.

16. *Dictionary of American Biography* (New York: Scribner, 1980), 215.

17. File (49.886) in the Department of Textile and Fashion Arts, Museum of Fine Arts, Boston.

18. Letter from Daniel Davis to Col. Benjamin Welles, 15 March 1829, reprinted in William H. Sumner, *Memoirs of Governor Increase Sumner* (Boston: S.G. Drake, 1854), 27–28.

19. Rev. Wilson Waters, *History of Chelmsford, Massachusetts* (Lowell, Mass.: Printed for the Town of Lowell by the Courier-Citizen Co., 1917), 199, 209, 362, 681, 682.

20. Ibid., 366. The country was in tremendous debt following the Revolutionary War. In 1786, Captain Daniel Shays of Pelham led a revolt against the commonwealth government, protesting the ruinous taxes that were impoverishing farmers, particularly in western Massachusetts. He and his large band of followers

successfully closed the court in Northampton in August of 1786, keeping the judges from confiscating farms for debt. In January of 1787, Shays faced the militia during an attempt to take the arsenal at Springfield. Four Shaysites were killed and a number of others wounded. The rebels fled but continued to skirmish with the militia until they were defeated in the winter of 1787 in Petersham. Shays and his followers were tried for treason, but were pardoned. This revolt catalyzed the country into creating a more stable and unified federal government, leading to the adoption of the United States Constitution.

21. See Lynne Zacek Bassett, "Inspired Fantasy: Design Sources for New England's Whole-Cloth Wool Quilts," *The Magazine Antiques* 168, no. 3 (September 2005): 120–27.

22. Waters, *History of Chelmsford*, 447, 484–486. Producing gun powder was a very dangerous industry that frequently experienced fatal explosions; when the Chelmsford gun-powder factory blew up in 1820, "the report was distinctly heard for thirty miles"; it suffered explosions again twice in 1821, 1826, and 1830; ibid., 817–18.

23. Accession record for quilt 72.4.3, Chelmsford Historical Society. The author wishes to thank Judith Fichtenbaum for her generous sharing of this quilt and its history.

24. Barbara Brackman, *Encyclopedia of Pieced Quilt Patterns* (Paducah, Ky.: American Quilter's Society, 1993), 410–11, #3400.

25. Dean Lahikainen, *In the American Spirit: Folk Art from the Collections* (Salem, Mass.: Peabody Essex Museum, 1994), 36.

26. Joseph S. Robinson, *The Story of Marblehead* (Privately printed, 1936), 57; Samuel Roads, Jr., *The History and Traditions of Marblehead* (Marblehead, Mass.: N. Allen Lindsey & Co., 1897), 365–77.

27. Information for this essay came from Charles A. Howe and Peter Hughes, "Bronson and Abigail Alcott," http://www.uua.org/uuhs/duub/articles/bronsonalcott.html. See also Madelon Bedell, *The Alcotts: Biography of a Family* (New York: Clarkson N. Potter, Inc., 1980).

28. See http://www.alcott.net/alcott/home/fruitlands.html; Howe and Hughes, "Bronson and Abigail Alcott"; and Bedell, *The Alcotts*. Fruitlands is now a museum open to the public.

29. For more on Marion Cheever Whiteside Newton, see Naida Treadway Patterson, "Marion Cheever Whiteside Newton: Designer of Story Book Quilts, 1940–1965," *Uncoverings 1995*: 67–94).

30. See Bedell, *The Alcotts*, 236–51.

31. Thomas B. Wellman, *History of the Town of Lynnfield, Mass., 1635–1895* (Boston: The Blanchard & Watts Engraving Co., 1895), 142.

32. At that time, forty-one thousand men in Massachusetts (one out of eight) were employed in the shoemaking industry. W. H. Richardson, *The Boot and Shoe Manufacturers' Assistant and Guide* (Boston: Higgins, Bradley & Dayton, 1858), 16.

33. *Massachusetts Soldiers, Sailors, and Marines in the Civil War* (Norwood, Mass.: Norwood Press, 1931), vol. I, 347. Zachary T. Wiley was born in 1848.

34. Board of Trade, *Haverhill, Massachusetts: An Industrial and Commercial Center* (Haverhill, Mass.: Chase Brothers, 1889), 132.

35. Ibid., 132–33.

36. Ibid., 141.

37. George Wingate Chase, *The History of Haverhill, Massachusetts, From its Settlement, in 1640, to the Year 1860* (Haverhill, Mass.: Published by the author, 1860), 545.

38. Winifred Reddall, "Pieced Lettering on Seven Quilts Dating from 1833–1891," *Uncoverings 1980*: 56–63. Reddall describes a group of seven quilts with pieced lettering and lists sources where these quilts are illustrated or described.

39. Barbara Brackman, *Clues in the Calico: A Guide to Identifying and Dating Quilts* (McLean, Va.: EPM Publications, 1989), 120.

40. Stacy C. Hollander, "Talking Quilts," *Folk Art* 29 (Spring/Summer 2004): 38; Brackman, *Clues in the Calico*, 120.

41. Laurel Horton, *Mary Black's Family Quilts: Memory and Meaning in Everyday Life* (Columbia, S.C.: University of South Carolina Press, 2005), 8.

42. U.S. Bureau of the Census, 1900.

43. "People" Research File—ME–MN, Natick Historical Society, Natick, Massachusetts.

44. John Warner Barber, *Historical Collections . . . of Every Town in Massachusetts* (Worcester: Dorr, Howland and Company, 1840), 210.

45. Ibid., 212.

46. John J. Currier, *History of Newburyport, Massachusetts 1764–1905* (Newburyport: John J. Currier, 1906), 237.

47. Undated letter written by Alice G. (Brown) Brigham, private collection. Alice Gray Brown's diaries and letters are still owned by her descendants. I am indebted to Alice's granddaughter, Patricia Brigham Valiasek, for sharing the excerpts quoted here with me.

"Spoken," as used here, was a common nautical term referring to communication between ships.

48. Currier, *History of Newburyport*, 459.

49. Notes from Patricia Brigham Valiasek, sent to the author, December 2006.

50. August 1879 diary kept by Alice Gray Brown, private collection.

51. Mrs. M. L. Rayne. *What Can a Woman Do?* (Petersburgh, N.Y.: Eagle Publishing Co., 1893), 65.

52. Sylvain Cazalet, "New England Female Medical College and New England Hospital for Women and Children," accessed 23 February 2007; available at http://www.homeoint.org/cazalet/histo/newengland.htm.

53. Much of the specific information regarding Dr. Westergren was obtained from Jack Eckert, reference librarian at the Francis A. Countway Library of Medicine, Harvard Medical School, and Emily L. Beattie, head of Technical Services and Archives at the Alumni Medical Library, Boston Medical Center.

54. The authors thank Frances Collison for providing Westergren family information.

55. Barbara Brackman, *Clues in the Calico*, 154.

56. Ibid., 160.

57. Ibid., 155.

3. Southeastern Massachusetts (pages 66–76)

1. Richard D. Brown and Jack Tager, *Massachusetts, A Concise History* (Amherst: University of Massachusetts Press, 2000) 46–49.

2. See Victoria Lincoln, *A Private Disgrace: Lizzie Borden by Daylight* (New York: G.P. Putnam's Sons, 1967).

3. The author is indebted to Anita Loscalzo, curator at the New England Quilt Museum, for sharing the curatorial file on this quilt. For more on Lizzie Borden and her trial, see Walter L. Hixson, *Murder, Culture, and Injustice: Four Sensational Cases in American History* (Akron, Ohio: University of Akron Press, 2001); and David Kent, *The Lizzie Borden Sourcebook* (Boston: Branden Books, 1992).

4. *Representative Men and Old Families of Southeastern Massachusetts* (Chicago: J.H. Beers & Co., 1912), 418–19.

5. Account books for Cook, Borden and Company (covering the years 1863–1867, 1894–1896, and 1913–1914) are located at Special Collections and Archives, W. E. B. Du Bois Library, University of Massachusetts, Amherst, Massachusetts.

6. Brown and Tager, *Massachusetts*, 206.

7. The "Star of LeMoyne" or "LeMoyne Star" block is thought to be named after the family who founded the colony of Louisiana and the city of New Orleans. Barbara Brackman credits the block name to early quilt historian Ruth Finley, who collected quilt patterns and names in Ohio and the East. See Barbara Brackman, *Encyclopedia of Pieced Quilt Patterns* (Paducah, Ky.: American Quilter's Society, 1993), 452–53; Barbara Brackman, "What's In a Name? Quilt Patterns from 1830 to the Present," in *Pieced By Mother: Symposium Papers*, ed. Jeannette Lasansky, 112 (Lewisburg, Penn.: Oral Traditions Project, 1988); Ruth E. Finley, *Old Patchwork Quilts and the Women Who Made Them* (Philadelphia: J.B. Lippincott, 1929).

8. Barbara Brackman, *America's Printed Fabrics 1770–1890* (Lafayette, Calif.: C&T Publishing, 2004), 35.

9. Barbara Brackman, *Clues in the Calico: A Guide to Identifying and Dating Antique Quilts* (McLean, Va.: EPM Publications, 1989), 99.

10. Article on the history of Mansfield by Jennie F. Copeland, published in the Mansfield 150th Anniversary Program, 1925, now accessible online: http://www.mansfieldma.com/about/historical.htm.

11. *The Woman's Book, Dealing Practically with the Modern Conditions of Home-Life, Self-Support, Education, Opportunities, and Every-Day Problems* (New York: Charles Scribner's Sons, 1894), vol. I, 3.

12. See Deborah Harding, *Red and White American Redwork Quilts* (New York: Rizzoli International Publications, 2000).

13. Compare this quilt with a c. 1929 redwork quilt belonging to the Great Lakes Quilt Center/Michigan State University Museum, #2006:141.2; picture available at http://www.quiltindex.org/quarton.php; accessed 15 July 2007. The framed designs of children engaged in various activities are similar to this quilt's designs.

14. The authors thank the quilt's owner, the step-niece of Rose and Lumina, for sharing information about the quiltmakers.

15. The 1900 U.S. Census finds Cora and Henry living with their two-year-old son Harold next door to Henry's parents, George and Lucy Appling in Carver. Henry was employed as a laborer in a cranberry bog. Census records available at www.ancestry.com; accessed 19 July 2007.

16. The author thanks Dr. Claire Appling for her assistance in providing the family history of these quilts.

17. Barbara Brackman, *Encyclopedia of Appliqué: An Illustrated, Numerical Index to Traditional and Modern Patterns* (McLean, Va.: EPM Publications, 1993), 62, 179.

18. Brackman, *Encyclopedia of Pieced Quilt Patterns*, 521, 523.

19. Lydia Maria Child, *The American Frugal Housewife* (London: T. T. and J. Tegg, 1832; reprint, Bedford, Mass.: Applewood Books, n.d.), 117–118. Reprint of the twelfth edition of 1832.

20. See Joseph D. Thomas, ed., *Cranberry Harvest: A History of Cranberry Growing in Massachusetts* (New Bedford, Mass.: Spinner Publications, 1990).

4. Cape Cod, Nantucket, and Martha's Vineyard (pages 77–87)

1. Henry D. Thoreau, *Cape Cod* (New York: Thomas Y. Crowell and Company, 1908), 4.

2. *Three Centuries of the Cape Cod County Barnstable, Massachusetts 1685 to 1985* (Barnstable County, 1985), 3–4.

3. See http://www.priweb.org/ed/pgws/history/pennsylvania/pennsylvania.html; accessed 10 September 2007.

4. James Norton, "Saltworks in Holmes Hole," *The Dukes County Intelligencer* 25 (August 1983); Eleanor R. Mayhew, ed., *Martha's Vineyard: A Short History and Guide* (Edgartown, Mass.: Dukes County Historical Society, 1956), 53.

5. According to Linda M. Wilson, assistant librarian at the Martha's Vineyard Museum in Edgartown, Massachusetts, Parnall (or Parnell) was a common first name in the Mayhew family but does not appear in the Vineyard vital records as a last name. Carolyn (or Caroline) Newcomb was born in 1814 and married Frederick Lambert in 1833.

6. Charles Edward Banks, *The History of Martha's Vineyard*, volume 3 (Edgartown, Mass.: Dukes County Historical Society, 1966), 323, 403; additional family information in this essay comes from the United States Census and Martha's Vineyard vital records. I am indebted to Linda M. Wilson, assistant librarian at the Martha's Vineyard Museum, for assisting me with life dates for Ephraim Mayhew and Susanna Pease.

7. Louis Coffin, ed., *The Coffin Family* (Nantucket: Nantucket Historical Association, 1962), 230; James Carlton Starbuck, *Starbucks All 1635–1985: A Biographical-Genealogical Dictionary* (Roswell, Ga.: W.H. Wolfe Associates, 1984), 129; "75 Main Street," Nantucket Historical Association pamphlet, 1958, "Blue Files," Nantucket Historical Association Research Library, Nantucket, Massachusetts.

8. Collection Overview, Business Papers of Charles G. Coffin and Henry Coffin, Nantucket Historical Association Library.

9. John Warner Barber, *Historical Collections . . . of Every Town in Massachusetts* (Worcester, Mass.: Dorr, Howland and Company, 1840), 54–55.

10. Ibid.

11. I am indebted to the current owner of this quilt, who shared several pages of family history and genealogy compiled by one of her relatives. These notes included information from Shebnah Rich, *Truro Cape Cod or Land Marks and Sea Marks* (Boston: D. Lothrop and Company, 1884).

12. Kirk J. Nelson, *A Century of Sandwich Glass, From the Collections of the Sandwich Glass Museum* (Sandwich, Mass.: Sandwich Glass Museum, 1992), 4. The author would like to thank Kirk Nelson, former curator of the Sandwich Glass Museum; Dorothy G. Hogan-Schofield, curator of the Sandwich Glass Museum; and Barbara Knight, former owner of this comforter, for their generous assistance with the research for this essay.

13. Martha Hassell, "The Role of Women in the Sandwich Glass Industry," *The Acorn* 1 (1990), 17.

14. Ibid., 16.

15. Harriot Buxton Barbour, *Sandwich, The Town that Glass Built* (Boston: Houghton Mifflin Company, 1948), 276.

16. Conversation with Kirk J. Nelson, 5 August 2006.

5. *Worcester County (pages 88–107)*

1. Ellery Crane Bicknell, ed., *History of Worcester County, Massachusetts* (New York and Chicago: Lewis Historical Publishing Company, 1924), 2.

2. Zelotes W. Coombs, *Worcester and Worcester Common* (Worcester, Mass., 1945).

3. Richard D. Brown and Jack Tager, *Massachusetts: A Concise History* (Amherst: University of Massachusetts Press, 2000), 213.

4. Bicknell, *History of Worcester County*, 607.

5. Ibid., 608.

6. Brown and Tager, *Massachusetts*, 126.

7. Bicknell, *History of Worcester County*, 613.

8. Accession and donor records for the coat, #1976.787, Worcester Historical Museum, Worcester, Massachusetts. The author is indebted to Holly Izard, curator at the Worcester Historical Museum, for sharing these records.

9. Letter from Salem Towne, Jr., Boston, to Sally Towne, Charlton, 8 November 1821, Towne Family Papers, Old Sturbridge Village Research Library, Sturbridge, Massachusetts; *Columbian Centinel*, Boston, 26 November 1823; diary kept by Ruth Henshaw Bascom, 22 November 1805, American Antiquarian Society, Worcester, Massachusetts.

10. Michele Majer, "American Women and French Fashion," in *The Age of Napoleon: Costume from Revolution to Empire 1789–1815*, ed. Katell le Bourhis, 216–37 (New York: Harry N. Abrams, 1989); *Ackermann's Repository*, London, June 1827, 363–64. "En gigot" is the French term for a leg o' mutton sleeve.

11. Research notes, #1976.787, Worcester Historical Museum; Gilman Bigelow Howe, *Genealogy of the Bigelow Family of America* (Worcester, Mass.: C. Hamilton, 1890), 182; Patricia Bigelow, ed., *The Bigelow Family Genealogy* (Flint, Mich.: The Bigelow Society, 1986).

12. See the curatorial file, #26.23.181, Old Sturbridge Village, Sturbridge, MA.

13. John Warner Barber, *Historical Collections . . . of Every Town in Massachusetts* (Worcester, Mass.: Dorr, Howland and Company, 1840), 608; Joseph S. Clark, *An Historical Sketch of Sturbridge, Mass.* (Brookfield, Mass.: E. and L. Merriam, 1838), 25–26; George Davis, *A Historical Sketch of Sturbridge and Southbridge* (West Brookfield: O.S. Cooke and Company, 1856), 199–201; Francis DeWitt, *Statistical Information Relating to Certain Branches of Industry in Massachusetts* (Boston: William White, 1856), 539.

14. Nancy H. Goody, "Fiskdale: 1816–1850," privately published research paper, 1977, Research Library, Old Sturbridge Village, Sturbridge, Massachusetts, 8–16; DeWitt, *Statistical Information*, 539–40.

15. Frederick Clifton Pierce, *Fiske and Fisk Family* (Chicago, 1896), 256; Davis, *Historical Sketch of Sturbridge*, 12; *Vital Records of Sturbridge, Massachusetts to the Year 1850* (Boston: New England Historic Genealogical Society, 1906).

16. 1798 Federal Direct Tax, Research Files, Old Sturbridge Village, Sturbridge, Mass.

17. Town tax records, 1820 and 1830, Research Files, Old Sturbridge Village, Sturbridge, Mass.; U.S. Bureau of the Census, 1830 and 1850, transcription in Research Files, Old Sturbridge Village, Sturbridge, Mass.

18. Peace and Patience Kirby's collection of weaving drafts are in the collection of Old Sturbridge Village, Sturbridge, Mass.; Lynne Bassett and Jack Larkin, *North-*

ern Comfort: New England's Early Quilts 1780–1850 (Nashville: Rutledge Hill Press, 1998), 61.

19. The Charleston Museum, *Mosaic Quilts: Paper Template Piecing in the South Carolina Lowcountry* (Greenville, S.C.: Curious Works Press, 2002), 12.

20. The author is grateful to the quilt's owner for providing the family genealogy.

21. Ezra Hyde, *History of the Town of Winchendon* (Worcester, Mass.: Henry J. Howland, 1849), 62.

22. Alfred Free, *Winchendon: A Retrospect of One Hundred and Fifty Years* (Winchendon, Mass.: Town of Winchendon, 1914), 11.

23. Edgar Vinton Wilson, *Memorial: Frederic Almon Wilson (1822–1897), Cordelia Rebecca (Mack) Wilson (1827–1913)* (Athol, Mass.: privately printed, 1913), 17. The author wishes to thank the quilt owner for providing this reference, along with photographs of Rebecca's "best" quilt.

24. Hyde, *History of the Town of Winchester*, 60.

25. *Massachusetts Spy and New England Farmer*, passim for 1820s through 1850s; Virginia Gunn, "Quilts at 19th Century State and County Fairs: An Ohio Study," *Uncoverings 1988*: 117; Linda J. Borish, "'A Fair, Without *the Fair*, is No Fair At All': Women at the New England Agricultural Fair in the Mid-Nineteenth Century," *Journal of Sport History* 24 (1997): 171.

26. Lydia Maria Child, *The Mother's Book* (Boston: Carter, Hendee and Babcock, 1831), 61.

27. Charles Martyn, *The William Ward Genealogy* (New York: Artemas Ward, 1925), 364–65. The author is indebted to Paula Lupton, collection manager at the Artemas Ward House, for sharing the quilt and its Ward family history.

28. Linda Welters and Margaret T. Ordonez, eds., *Down By the Old Mill Stream: Quilts in Rhode Island* (Kent, Ohio: Kent State University Press, 2000), 230; Barbara Brackman, *Encyclopedia of Pieced Quilt Patterns* (Paducah, Ky.: American Quilter's Society, 1993), 26–27; Virginia Gunn, "Template Quilt Construction and Its Offshoots: From *Godey's Lady's Book* to Mountain Mist," in *Pieced By Mother*, ed. Jeannette Lasansky, 72–73 (Lewisburg, Penn.: Oral Traditions Project, 1988).

29. Sylvia G. Buck, *Warren: A Town in the Making 1741–1991* (Warren, Mass.: Sylvia G. Buck, 1994), 17, 78.

30. Ibid.

31. Richardson and Moore family information compiled by Sylvia G. Buck and given to the quilt's former owner; I am indebted to Carol Andrews for sharing this information.

32. Harriet Lombard Richardson was Arthur's great-aunt, so it is possible that he saw the "Tumbling Blocks" quilt being made or after it was completed.

33. Eliza Leslie, *The American Girl's Book* (Boston: Monroe and Francis, 1831); Lydia Maria Child, *The Little Girl's Own Book* (Boston: Carter, Hendee and Babcock, 1832), 225.

34. Family information provided to MassQuilts by Sylvia G. Buck, Librarian, Warren Public Library. The author is indebted for this information.

35. Quilt label by Sylvia G. Buck from Warren Public Library information file.

36. *Royalston, Massachusetts Directory 1885* (Fitchburg, Mass.: 1885), accessed via www.ancestry.com.

37. *Cemetery Inscriptions of Royalston and South Royalston, Massachusetts* (Westminster, Mass.: Central Massachusetts Genealogical Society, 2004), accessed via www.ancestry.com.

38. Both the darker fabric, which is printed with six-pointed stars and hexagons, and the crazy-patch fabric, which is used in one strip beginning in a corner, are pictured in Bobbie Aug, Sharon Newman, and Gerald Roy, *Vintage Quilts: Identifying, Collecting, Dating, Preserving and Valuing* (Paducah, Ky.: Collector Books, 2002), 133, 134.

6. The Connecticut River Valley (pages 108–134)

1. At the time, Enfield was part of Hampshire County in Massachusetts; it is now in Connecticut.

2. See Gerald Ward and William Hosley, ed., *The Great River: Art and Society of the Connecticut Valley, 1635–1820* (Hartford, Conn.: Wadsworth Atheneum, 1985).

3. Timothy Dwight, *Travels in New England and New York* (Cambridge, Mass.: The Belknap Press of Harvard University Press, 1969), vol. 2, 229. The four-volume travelogue was written while Dwight journeyed between school sessions beginning in the 1790s, and were first published posthumously in 1821 and 1822.

4. See Lynne Z. Bassett, "The Sober People of Hadley: Clothing in a Connecticut River Valley Town in the Seventeenth and Early Eighteenth Centuries," in *Essays on the History of Hadley, Massachusetts*, ed. Marla Miller (Amherst: University of Massachusetts Press, forthcoming 2009). See also Marla Miller, *The Needle's Eye: Women and Work in the Age of Revolution* (Amherst: University of Massachusetts Press, 2006).

5. Dwight, *Travels in New England*, vol. 2, 230.

6. James Russell Trumbull, *History of Northampton,*

Massachusetts, From its Settlement in 1654 (Northampton, Mass.: Press of Gazette Printing Co., 1898), vol. 2, 475–76.

7. Jane Nylander, "Textiles, Clothing, and Needlework," in *The Great River*, 371.

8. Sylvester Judd, *History of Hadley* (Somersworth, N.H.: New Hampshire Publishing Company, 1976), 380. First published in 1863; this reprint is taken from the 1905 edition.

9. Ibid.

10. Amelia F. Miller, *Connecticut River Valley Doorways: An Eighteenth-Century Flowering* (Boston: The Dublin Seminar for New England Folklife, 1983).

11. The author thanks Lynda Faye, former Conway town clerk, for her assistance in researching tax records.

12. Document records for 308057, National Museum of American History, Smithsonian Institution.

13. Deane Lee, ed., *Conway, 1767–1967* (Conway, Mass.: Town of Conway, 1967), 123.

14. For more on this quilt, see Doris M. Bowman, *The Smithsonian Treasury, American Quilts* (Washington, D.C.: Smithsonian Institution Press, 1991), 16.

15. Sarah Snell Bryant diary, Cummington, Massachusetts, 1796–1835, Houghton Library, Harvard University; 22 December 1822. Sarah Snell Bryant was the mother of poet William Cullen Bryant, one of America's leading writers and editors of the nineteenth century.

16. Document of the Overseers of the Poor, dated 3 September 1803. Dewolf family papers, Flynt Library, Deerfield, Massachusetts. Revealing the desperate circumstances of single mothers in that period, Esther apparently took back her wayward husband, Moses Rice, for she had two more children by him after 1807. See George Sheldon, *A History of Deerfield, Massachusetts . . .* (Deerfield, Mass.: Pocumtuck Valley Memorial Association, 1896), vol. 2, genealogy section, 267.

17. Copy of a court document dated 27 September 1805. Dewolf family papers.

18. Testimonial dated 15 February 1837. Dewolf family papers.

19. Account book of Walter and Orlando Ware, Deerfield, 1799–1819. Flynt Library, Deerfield.

20. Biographical information on Susannah Allen Anderson Howard comes from Probate Records of Hampshire County, Box 275, #8; Box 4, #59; Box 319, #15, Hall of Records, Northampton, Mass.; manuscript schedules of the Federal Censuses of Population for Massachusetts, 1820, 1830, 1840, and 1850, microfilm at the Old Sturbridge Village Research Library; Arthur Chase, *History of Ware, Massachusetts* (Cambridge, Mass.: The University Press, 1911); Jay Mack Holbrook, comp., *Vital Records for the Town of Ware, Massachusetts, 1735–1893* (Oxford, Mass.: Jay Mack Holbrook, 1983), microfiche. For additional information on Susannah A. A. Howard and her quilts, see also Lynne Z. Bassett and Jack Larkin, *Northern Comfort: New England's Early Quilts 1780–1850* (Nashville: Rutledge Hill Press, 1998), 5–10, 51–54.

21. John Warner Barber, *Historical Collections . . . of Every Town in Massachusetts* (Worcester, Mass.: Dorr, Howland and Company, 1840), 343–44.

22. Bassett and Larkin, *Northern Comfort*, 8–9. For a particularly disdainful description of patchwork quilts, see Eliza Leslie, *The House Book: or, A Manual of Domestic Economy* (Philadelphia: Carey and Hart, 1843), 311.

23. Curatorial files for 26.23.142 and 26.23.124, Old Sturbridge Village, Sturbridge, Mass.

24. For the history of the Rice family, see "The Edmund Rice (1638) Association, Inc."; available from www.edmund-rice.org; accessed 12 March 2007.

25. Barbara Tricarico, ed., *Quilts of Virginia 1607–1899: The Birth of America through the Eye of a Needle* (Atglen, Penn.: Schiffer Publishing, 2006), 34, 52, 59.

26. Barbara Brackman, *Clues in the Calico: A Guide to Identifying and Dating Quilts* (McLean, Va.: EPM Publications, 1989), 62–67.

27. Ibid., 58–62.

28. In fact, the designation "bachelor's" degree has been traced to the Latin name of the bay or laurel berry. See Mrs. M. Grieve, "Laurel (Bay)," from *A Modern Herbal*, first published in 1932, available from botanical.com/botanical/mgnh/l/larbay10.html, accessed 11 March 2007.

29. Shepherd family archives, box 5, folder 12, Historic Northampton.

30. Ibid.

31. Ibid.

32. King David was the second king of ancient Israel, slayer of Goliath, and a wise and powerful ruler who brought prosperity to his people.

33. Shepherd family archives, box 5, folder 14.

34. "The Shepherd Family of Northampton," archives introduction, p. 5.

35. See Elizabeth M. Sharpe, *In the Shadow of the Dam* (New York: Free Press, 2004) for a very complete account of the flood and its significance.

36. Quilters usually refer to this block pattern of six hexagons surrounding a center hexagon by the twentieth-century name, "Grandmother's Flower Garden," al-

though this design appears in the earliest of patchwork quilts.

37. Brackman, *Clues in the Calico*, 136, 138.

38. Virginia Gunn, "Quilts at 19th Century State and County Fairs: An Ohio Study," *Uncoverings 1988*, 117.

39. Barbara Brackman, "Fairs and Expositions: Their Influence on American Quilts," in *Bits and Pieces: Textile Traditions*, ed. Jeannette Lasansky, 95 (Lewisburg, Penn.: Oral Traditions Project, 1991).

40. The current owner dates the quilt as 1888 based on an understanding that it was given to her mother as a wedding gift. However, her mother's note, attached to the quilt, states that the quilt was received "when I was a young girl." Since the owner's mother was not born until about 1890, it seems more likely that the quilt was given to her in the 1890s rather than at the time of her marriage.

41. Aimee E. Newell, "A Stitch in Time: The Needlework of Aging Women in Antebellum America," Ph.D. diss., University of Massachusetts–Amherst, forthcoming.

42. Barbara Brackman, *Encyclopedia of Pieced Quilt Patterns* (Paducah, Ky.: American Quilter's Society, 1993), 262, #2098a.

43. Interview with Barbara Poppe, March 2007.

44. United States 1880 Census Records; the 1900 census states that Christiana's father was born in New York.

45. U.S. Bureau of the Census, 1850. Two Christiana Kings appear in Chicopee at this time. Both were born in New York in 1832. One resided in a boarding house with numerous other women her age. The second boarded with a family. No occupation is listed for either woman.

46. Reverend Elias Nason and George J. Varney, *A Gazetteer of the State of Massachusetts with Numerous Illustrations* (Boston: B.B. Russell, 1890), 380–83.

47. Hadley Falls Company was renamed the Holyoke-Water Power Company in 1859.

48. Nason and Varney, *Gazetteer of the State of Massachusetts*, 380–83.

49. Ibid.

50. The 1900 U.S. census records the number of births as well as number of living children a woman had. Christiana bore seven children; only five survived.

51. United States 1860 Census.

52. Holyoke City Directory, 1892; U.S. Bureau of the Census, 1900.

53. Suzanne L. Flynt, 1994, Memorial Hall Museum accession notes.

54. See http://www.mass.info/colrain.ma/description.htm; accessed 16 April 2007.

55. Flynt, accession notes.

7. Berkshire County (pages 135–144)

1. Research on the Belden and Mattoon families was provided to the owner of the quilt by Joseph L. Broom, a genealogist working in the 1990s, whose major sources were census reports. The author is grateful to the quilt owner for supplying these reports.

2. Ibid. Also consulted was the American Civil War Soldiers database at www.ancestry.com, accessed 7 May 2007.

3. Jane Stickle's quilt has been published widely, along with patterns for its many blocks. See Brenda M. Papadakis, *Dear Jane* (Warren, Mass.: E-Z Quilting by Wrights, 1996).

4. This national celebration of America's one-hundred-year anniversary was erected on 450 acres outside of Philadelphia, and included five major buildings (Main, Machinery, Agriculture, Art, and Horticulture) and assorted minor buildings. In the six months that it was open to the public, the exposition hosted eight million visitors.

5. http://libwww.library.phila.gov/CenCol/tours-womenspav.htm.

6. A search through *Godey's Ladies Magazine* from 1875 to 1880 has revealed no evidence of literary sources yet, but research is ongoing.

7. Katherine C. Westwood, Special Collections librarian, North Adams Public Library, via email correspondence with the author, 20 June 2007.

8. See Celia Y. Oliver, *Enduring Grace: Quilts from the Shelburne Museum Collection* (Shelburne, Vt.: The Shelburne Museum, 1997), 62.

9. Henry Joyce, *Art of the Needle: One Hundred Masterpiece Quilts from the Shelburne Museum* (Shelburne, Vt.: The Shelburne Museum, 2003), 48.

10. My thanks to Carolyn Ducey, curator, International Quilt Study Center, Department of Textile, Clothing, and Design, University of Nebraska, Lincoln, for pointing out the connection.

11. Curatorial files (#1997.007.0163), International Quilt Study Center, University of Nebraska, Lincoln.

12. Census and city directories for North Adams, Massachusetts, curatorial files (#1997.007.0163), Inter-

national Quilt Study Center, University of Nebraska, Lincoln.

13. See Thorstein Veblen, *The Theory of the Leisure Class* (New York: Macmillan, 1899; reprint, New York: Dover Books, 1994), especially chapter 4.

14. See Russell Lynes, *The Tastemakers* (New York: Harper & Bros., 1954), especially 30–31.

15. Information on the family's history was supplied by Mr. and Mrs. Ralph B. Wood to the Berkshire Museum at the time of the quilt's donation.

16. "The History of the Ladies Aid Society of the Methodist Episcopal Church of North Adams for 73 Years, 1856–1929," transcription by Mrs. Minnie Rosston. The author wishes to thank Jane B. Marino for providing this information.

8. The Textile Industry (pages 145–165)

1. Orra L. Stone, *A History of Massachusetts Industries* (Boston: S.J. Clarke Pub. Co, 1930), 91–92.

2. Perry Walton, *The Story of Textiles* (Boston: John S. Lawrence, 1912), 192–200.

3. Ibid., 200–209.

4. Thomas Dublin, "Women and the Early Industrial Revolution in the United States," *History Now: American History Online Journal* 10 (Dec. 2006). Available on-line at http://www.historynow.org/12_2006/historian4.html; accessed 13 June 2007.

5. Ibid.

6. Peter M. Molloy, *Homespun to Factory Made: Woolen Textiles in America, 1776–1876* (North Andover, Mass.: Merrimack Valley Textile Museum, 1977), 56.

7. Ibid., 82

8. "Wool Growing and Manufacturing," *Encyclopedia of American History*, ed. Richard B. Morris and Jeffrey B. Morris. Available on-line at http://www.answers.com/topic/wool-growing-and-manufacturing; accessed 13 June 2007.

9. Stone, *History of Massachusetts Industries*, 329–33.

10. See Jacqueline Field, Marjorie Senechal, and Madelyn Shaw, *American Silk: 1830–1930, Entrepreneurs and Artifacts* (Lubbock, Tex.: Texas Tech University Press, 2007), 20–29.

11. Ibid., 5–7.

12. Information courtesy of the quilt's current owner.

13. *Lowell—The Story of an Industrial City*, National Park Service Handbook #140 (Washington, D.C.: U.S. Government Printing Office, 1992), 32; and Richard D.

Brown and Jack Tager, *Massachusetts, A Concise History* (Amherst: University of Massachusetts Press, 2000), 124.

14. *Lowell—The Story of an Industrial City*, 39.

15. Brown and Tager, *Massachusetts*, 124.

16. Lowell Historical Society, *Lowell: The Mill City* (Dover, N.H.: Arcadia Publishing Co., 2005), 15.

17. Barbara Brackman, *Encyclopedia of Pieced Quilt Patterns* (Paducah, Ky.: American Quilter's Society, 1993), 72–73; pattern number 433c.

18. Diane L. Fagan Affleck, *Just New from the Mills: Printed Cottons in America* (North Andover, Mass.: The American Textile History Museum, 1987), 91; see plate #70.2.2, Hamilton 21995, July 1881–March 1882.

19. Ibid., 84–87.

20. For definitions of the Art Deco movement and discussions of its influence on fine and decorative arts see http://www.artlex.com/ArtLex/a/artdeco.html and http://www.freenet.buffalo.edu/bah/a/archsty/deco/index.html; accessed 3 July 2007.

21. Ibid.

22. A very similar butterfly template and grid organization can be seen in a butterfly quilt (#2000.09) in the collection of the New England Quilt Museum; however it contains a broderie perse floral medallion in the center box, rather than a single flower. The NEQM has another butterfly quilt (1991.12) created with Art Deco–inspired patterns published by Laura Wheeler, a well-known quilter who sold iron-on transfer patterns through the *Kansas City Star* in the 1930s.

23. Helen Glinos, conversation with author, February 2007.

24. Orra Stone, *History of Massachusetts Industries*, vol. 1 (Boston: S.J. Clarke, 1930), 329–30.

25. "AIM Salutes Its Member: This Month the Pacific Mills," *Industry* 1, no. 3 (December 1936): 11–13.

26. Brown and Tager, *Massachusetts*, 203–206.

27. Andrew E. Ford, *History of the Origin of the Town of Clinton Massachusetts 1653–1856* (Clinton, Mass.: Press of W. J. Coulter, 1876), 219–20.

28. Paul E. Rivard, *A New Order of Things: How the Textile Industry Transformed New England* (Hanover, N.H.: University Press of New England, 2002), 63–64.

29. Brown and Tager, *Massachusetts*, 216.

30. Ibid.

31. "The History of Clinton," available at http://www.clintonmass.com/history.shtml; accessed 25 May 2007.

32. U.S. Bureau of the Census, 1920. A "back boy," or "bobbin boy" (generally a child) replaced and re-

moved full and empty bobbins of yarn on the spinning frame of the mule-spinning machine.

33. U.S. Bureau of the Census, 1930; H. Anstey & T. Weston, *The Anstey Weston Guide to Textile Terms* (Frome & London: Weston Publishing Limited, 1997), 82. A "web drawer" readied the loom for weaving by drawing individual warp threads through various parts of the machine.

34. Brown and Tager, *Massachusetts*, 205–206.

35. "History of Monument Mill," available at http//eev.liu.edu/wall/millHistory.htm; accessed 24 February 2007.

36. Current quilt owner, email message to author, 19 February 2007.

37. The Ramsdell Public Library in the Village of Housatonic, Great Barrington, Mass., available at http://www.libraryautomation.com/gblibraries/ramsdellpichistory.html; accessed 10 September 2007.

38. U.S. Environmental Protection Agency, "The Ecological History of New Bedford Harbor," available at http://www.epa.gov/nbh/html/textile.html; accessed 7 May 2007.

39. Brown and Tager, *Massachusetts*, 207.

40. These variations include backgrounds for larger prints, overall mosaic patterns, floral patterns, diamond patterns, and more. See Brackman, *Encyclopedia of Pieced Quilt Patterns*, 27–31; Kathryn Berenson, *Quilts of Provence: The Art and Craft of French Quiltmaking* (New York: Henry Holt & Company, 1996), 88; Wendy Hefford, *The Victoria and Albert Museum's Textile Collection: Design for Printed Textiles in England from 1750–1850* (New York: Abbeville Press, 1992), 124–25, 139; Jen Jones, *Welsh Quilts: A Towy Guide* (Carmarthen, Wales: Towy Publishing, 1997), 12, 47; Linda Welters and Margaret T. Ordonez, eds., *Down by the Old Mill Stream: Quilts in Rhode Island* (Kent, Ohio: Kent State University Press, 2000), 22.

41. Barbara Brackman, *Clues in the Calico: A Guide to Identifying and Dating Antique Quilts* (McLean, Va.: EPM Publications, 1989), 97–99.

42. The history of Wyoma is told in a number of newspaper articles. In "Early Days When Wyoma Was Dyehouse Village," *Lynn Item* (14 July 1924), 195, this section of Lynn is referred to as Bacheller Parish or Bacheller Plains. By the early nineteenth century, the name "Dyehouse Village" was heard most often. The name was changed to Wyoma by the historian Alonzo Lewis in 1850 when Lynn was made a city.

43. Alfred Bacheller is listed as a silk dyer in the Lynn city records at the birth of his son George Henry in 1845. *Vital Records of Lynn, Massachusetts, to the End of the Year 1849*, volume 1, *Births* (Salem, Mass.: The Essex Institute, 1905), 46.

44. Pond lilies appear to have been plentiful. According to a newspaper article of unknown origin, now in the files of the Lynn Museum and Historical Society library, the local boys would gather the pond lilies and take them to the Lynn railway station to sell to the commuters.

45. The 1860 U.S. census lists Alfred and his family at 413 Broadway, where they lived with their eight children. Alfred is again listed as a dyer and his two oldest sons, Hartshorn, age eighteen, and Lindley, age sixteen, as silk finishers.

46. "Practical Patchwork: How to Arrange and Design Effective Articles," in *Weldon's Practical Needlework*, vol. 1 (London: Weldon & Co., 1885), 3.

47. The 1880 United States Census.

48. D. Farrar, "The Bacheller Family of North Lynn," unpublished manuscript in the files of the Lynn Historical Society and Museum library.

49. Alfred Bacheller's house was located at the intersection of Broadway and Springvale Street. The house later was purchased and renovated by Dr. Benjamin Percival. A picture of the house is included in the papers of Fred Gordon, now part of the collection of the Lynn Historical Society. "Bacheller's Plains, Dyehouse Village, Wyoma—Story of One of the Large Wards of the City," *Lynn Item*, 27 September 1913.

50. For an expanded discussion of the development and use of the sewing machine, see Anita B. Loscalzo, "The History of the Sewing Machine and Its Use in Quilting in the United States," *Uncoverings 1995*: 175–208.

51. Amy Boyce Osaki, "A 'Truly Feminine Employment'; Sewing and the Early Nineteenth-Century Woman," *Winterthur Portfolio* 23, no. 4 (1988): 225; Patricia Mainardi, "Quilts, the Great American Art," *Feminist Art Journal* 2, no. 1 (1973): 59; Laurel Thatcher Ulrich, *The Age of Homespun: Objects and Stories in the Creation of an American Myth* (New York: Alfred A. Knopf, 2001), 299–300.

52. Ibid, 58.

53. Rachel Maines, "Paradigms of Scarcity and Abundance: The Quilt as an Artifact of the Industrial Revolution," in *In the Heart of Pennsylvania*, ed. Jeannette Lasansky, 84–86 (Lewisburg, Penn.: Union County Historical Society, 1986).

54. Grace Rogers Cooper, *The Sewing Machine: Its In-*

vention and Development (Washington, D.C.: Smithsonian Institution Press, 1968), 11–15.

55. "Howe, Elias," *Encyclopedia Britannica Online Library Edition, Encyclopedia Britannica* 2007; accessed 27 January 2007; available from http://www.britannica.com.e2proxy.bpl.org/eb/article-9041238. Also, "Elias Howe," accessed 27 January 2007; available from http://www.todayinsci.com/H/Howe_Elias/HoweElias.htm.

56. Cooper, *The Sewing Machine*, 19–21.

57. Ruth Brandon, *A Capitalist Romance: Singer and the Sewing Machine* (Philadelphia: Lippincott, 1977): 43–51; Frank P. Godfrey, *An International History of the Sewing Machine* (London: Robert Hale, 1982): 64.

58. Cooper, *The Sewing Machine*, 65–76, 161–162.

59. Ibid., 41–42.

60. Nicholas Oddy, "A Beautiful Ornament in the Parlour or Boudoir: The Domestication of the Sewing Machine," in *The Culture of Sewing*, ed. Barbara Burman, 287 (New York: Berg, 1999).

61. William Ewers, *Sincere's History of the Sewing Machine* (Phoenix: Sincere Press, 1970), 93.

62. Sara Josepha Hale, "The Queen of Inventions— The Sewing Machine," *Godey's Lady's Book* 61, no. 1 (July 1860): 77.

9. Cooperative Quilting, 1770–1850 (pages 169–172)

1. Quoted in Marla R. Miller, "'My Daily Bread Depends Upon My Labor': Craftswomen, Community, and the Marketplace in Rural Massachusetts, 1740–1820," Ph.D. diss., University of North Carolina at Chapel Hill, 1997, 149. This essay is adapted from Lynne Zacek Bassett, "A Dull Business Alone: Cooperative Quilting in New England, 1750–1850," in *Textiles in New England II: Four Centuries of Material Life, The Dublin Seminar for New England Folklife Annual Proceedings 1999* (Boston: Boston University, 2001): 27–42.

2. Ruth Henshaw Bascom diary, Leicester, Massachusetts, 18 August 1803, American Antiquarian Society, Worcester, Mass.

3. Francis H. Underwood, *Quabbin, The Story of a Small Town with Outlooks Upon Puritan Life* (Boston: Lee and Shepard, 1893), 108–11.

4. Ibid., 108.

5. Ebenezer Parkman diary, 2–6 May 1757, 2–8 November 1768, American Antiquarian Society, Worcester, Mass., and 13–18 January 1781, Massachusetts Historical Society, Boston, Mass.

6. Ibid., 21 May 1771.

7. Ruth Henshaw Bascom diary, Leicester, Massachusetts, 6 October 1809, American Antiquarian Society, Worcester, Mass.

8. Ibid., 10 October 1803.

9. Ibid., 28 May and 18 June 1800.

10. Ibid., 15 and 16 November 1803.

11. Ibid., 7 October 1809.

12. Bassett, "A Dull Business Alone," 32.

13. James Parker diary, Shirley, Massachusetts, 9 June 1774 and 28 September 1780, ed. Ethel Stanwood Bolton, "Extracts from the Diary of James Parker of Shirley, Mass.," *The New England Historical and Genealogical Register* 70:138.

14. Bascom diary, 27 October 1802.

15. Rebecca Dickinson diary, Hatfield, Massachusetts, 23 September 1788, Flynt Library, Pocumtuck Valley Memorial Association, Deerfield, Mass. Transcription by Marla Miller.

16. Bassett, "A Dull Business Alone," 334–39.

17. George Davis, *A Historical Sketch of Sturbridge and Southbridge* (West Brookfield, Mass.: O.S. Cooke and Co., 1856), 176–77.

18. Marla R. Miller, "'And others of our own people': Needlework and Women of the Rural Gentry," in *What's New England About New England Quilts? Proceedings of a Symposium at Old Sturbridge Village* (Sturbridge, Mass.: Old Sturbridge Village, 1999), 19–33.

19. For more information, see Paula Bradstreet Richter, "Lucy Cleveland's 'Figures of Rags': Textile Arts and Social Commentary in Early-Nineteenth-Century New England," in *Textiles in Early New England: Design, Production, and Consumption, The Dublin Seminar for New England Folklife Annual Proceedings 1997* (Boston: Boston University, 1999), 48–63; Paula Bradstreet Richter, "Lucy Cleveland, Folk Artist," *Antiques* 158, no. 2 (August 2000): 204–13.

10. Anti-Slavery Quilts (pages 173–180)

1. Barbara Welter, "The Cult of True Womanhood 1820–1860," *American Quarterly* (1966): 151–74; and Catherine Clinton, *The Other Civil War: American Women in the Nineteenth Century* (New York: Hill & Wang, 1984), 42–45.

2. Historian Lori Ginzberg was the first to use the now common phrase "Benevolence Empire." See Lori D. Ginzberg, *Women and the Work of Benevolence: Morality,*

Politics, and Class in the Nineteenth Century United States (New Haven, Conn.: Yale University Press, 1990).

3. Barry Hankins, *The Second Great Awakening and the Transcendentalists* (Westport, Conn.: Greenwood Press, 2004), 109–10.

4. Carroll Smith-Rosenberg, "Bourgeois Discourse and the Age of Jackson: An Introduction," in *Disorderly Conduct* (New York: Oxford University Press, 1985), 79–89.

5. Quoted in Clinton, *Other Civil War*, 72. Italics appear in the original text.

6. James Brewer Stewart, "Boston, Abolition, and the Atlantic World, 1820–1861," in *Courage and Conscience: Black and White Abolitionists in Boston*, ed. Donald M. Jacobs, 107 (Bloomington, Ind.: University of Indiana Press, 1993); and Julie Roy Jeffrey, *The Great Silent Army of Abolition: Ordinary Women in the Antislavery Movement* (Chapel Hill: University of North Carolina Press, 1998), 25–26.

7. Jeffrey, *Great Silent Army*, 20.

8. Samuel J. May, Abby May Alcott's brother and Louisa May Alcott's uncle, was among the "agents" who spoke to such gatherings of women.

9. The Married Women's Property Acts began to be passed by state legislatures in the 1840s, but women with independent wealth were not common.

10. See Beverly Gordon, *Bazaars and Fair Ladies* (Knoxville: University of Tennessee Press, 1998), 42–46.

11. Pat Ferrero, Elaine Hedges, and Julie Silber, *Hearts and Hands: The Influence of Women and Quilts on American Society* (San Francisco: Quilt Digest Press, 1987), 72.

12. See especially Jacqueline L. Tobin and Raymond G. Dobard, *Hidden in Plain View: The Secret Story of Quilts and the Underground Railroad* (New York: Bantam Books, 1998).

13. Barbara Brackman, "Rocky Road to Analysis: Interpreting Quilt Patterns," *Uncoverings 2004*: 1–9. Lydia Maria Child's quilt was purchased by a family whose house was used by the Underground Railroad (see figure 133/MQ 4961). For more information on the underground railroad, see David Blight, *Passages to Freedom: The Underground Railroad in History and Memory* (Washington, D.C.: Smithsonian Books, 2004); Barbara Brackman, *Facts and Fabrications: Unraveling the History of Quilts and Slavery* (Concord, Calif.: C & T Publishing, 2006); Wilbur Henry Seibert, *The Underground Railroad: From Slavery to Freedom* (New York: The Macmillan Company, 1898), book online available from http://deila.dickinson.edu/theirownwords/title/0090.htm; accessed 30 May 2007;

William Still, *The Underground Rail Road; a Record of Facts, Authentic Narratives, Letters, &c. Narrating the Hardships Hair-breadth Escapes and Death Struggles of the Slaves in Their Efforts for Freedom, as Related by Themselves and Others, or Witnessed by the Author; Together with Sketches of Some of the Largest Stockholders, and Most Liberal Aiders and Advisers of the Road* (Philadelphia: Porter & Coates, 1872), book online available from http://www.gutenberg.org/ebooks/15263; accessed 30 May 2007; Giles R. Wright, "Critique: *Hidden in Plain View: The Secret Story of Quilts and the Underground Railroad*," distributed at a meeting of the Camden County (N.J.) Historical Society, 2 June 2001, available from http://historiccamdencounty.com/ccnews11_doc_01a.shtml, accessed 8 June 2007.

14. Nancy Carlisle, *Cherished Possessions: A New England Legacy* (Boston: Society for the Preservation of New England Antiquities, in association with Antique Collector's Club Ltd., 2003), 394–98. Jackson's family home was a stop on the Underground Railway, and is now open to the public as the Newton History Museum at the Jackson Homestead.

15. See Hildegard Hoeller, "A Quilt for Life: Lydia Maria Child's The American Frugal Housewife," *Transcendental Quarterly* (1 June 1999): 89–99; and Jean Fagan Yellin, *Women and Sisters: The Antislavery Feminists in American Culture* (New Haven, Conn.: Yale University Press, 1989).

16. Better known today with the words ". . . through the woods to Grandmother's house we go," the original version is available at http://www.hymnsandcarolsofchristmas.com/Hymns_and_Carols/over_the_river_grandfather.htm; accessed 15 August 2007.

17. Dorothy Sterling, *Ahead of Her Time: Abby Kelley and the Politics of Antislavery* (New York: W. W. Norton & Co., 1991), 36–38.

18. Ibid., 121–22.

19. Now called Liberty Farm, the home is a National Historic Landmark, but is not open to the public (see http://www.cr.nps.gov/nr/travel/pwwmh/ma42.htm). The Fosters housed runaway slaves there as a stop on the Underground Railroad.

11. Agricultural Fairs and Quilts (pages 181–193)

1. Mark A. Mastromarino, "Elkanah Watson and Early Agricultural Fairs, 1790–1860," *Historical Journal of Massachusetts* 17 (Summer 1989): 106–107.

2. Ibid., 106–107, 111–13; Catherine E. Kelly, "'The Consummation of Rural Prosperity and Happiness': New England Agricultural Fairs and the Construction of Class and Gender, 1810–1860," *American Quarterly* 49 (September 1997): 577.

3. Mastromarino, "Elkanah Watson," 109–10; Kelly, "Consummation of Rural Prosperity," 581.

4. Kelly, "Consummation of Rural Prosperity," 579.

5. Linda J. Borish, "'A Fair, Without *the* Fair, is No Fair at All': Women at the New England Agricultural Fair in the Mid-Nineteenth Century," *Journal of Sport History* 24 (1997): 162.

6. Kelly, "Consummation of Rural Prosperity," 586–587.

7. *New England Farmer,* 5 November 1834.

8. Cuesta Benberry, "Storrowton Village—Home of the First National Quilt Show," *Quilter's Newsletter Magazine* (September 1987): 36, 40. I am indebted to Helen Bardwell for alerting me to the existence of this article and to Jane Crutchfield for providing the exact citation.

9. Aimee E. Newell, "No Harvest of Oil: Nantucket's Agricultural Fairs, 1856–1890," in *New England Celebrates: Spectacle, Commemoration, and Festivity, The Dublin Seminar for New England Folklife Annual Proceedings 2000* (Boston: Boston University, 2002), 149.

10. *Transactions of the Nantucket Agricultural Society for 1856* (New York: Nantucket Agricultural Society, 1857), 6–10.

11. *Nantucket Inquirer,* 31 October 1856.

12. *Transactions,* 11–12, 64.

13. *The Weekly Mirror,* 1 November 1856.

14. *Transactions,* 47.

15. Barbara Brackman, *Encyclopedia of Pieced Quilt Patterns* (Paducah, Ky.: American Quilter's Society, 1993), 300.

16. *Transactions,* 63.

17. Coffin Family Research File, Nantucket Historical Association Research File.

18. *Inquirer and Mirror,* 3 October 1874.

19. *Barre Gazette,* 29 September 1899.

20. *Barre Gazette,* 6 October 1899. The older woman was Mrs. Mary Harrington of New Braintree, Massachusetts, who received a "gratuity" of 25 cents for her quilt.

21. James E. Sullivan, *American Town: Barre, Massachusetts 1774–1974* (Barre, Mass.: Barre Historical Society, 1974), 14, 17.

22. John Warner Barber, *Historical Collections . . . of Every Town in Massachusetts* (Worcester, Mass.: Dorr, Howland and Company, 1840), 554.

23. Helen Webber Connington, *History of Barre: Windows into the Past* (Barre, Mass.: The Barre Historical Commission, 1992), 111.

24. Sullivan, *American Town,* 46.

25. D. Hamilton Hurd, comp., *History of Worcester County, Massachusetts* (Philadelphia: J.W. Lewis and Company, 1889), 360.

26. *Barre Gazette,* 29 September 1899.

27. Sullivan, *American Town,* 46.

28. Connington, *History of Barre,* 79–80.

29. I am indebted to Bertyne R. Smith for sharing these details of Mollie's life with me.

30. Information on the history of the National Grange from the organization's website, www .nationalgrange.org; accessed 10 September 2007.

31. For information about the history of the Grange in Massachusetts and a list of local chapters, see www. massgrange.org; accessed 23 August 2007.

32. Ibid.

33. Membership Records, Massachusetts Grange Archives, Albert J. Thomas Library Museum, Rutland, Massachusetts. I am indebted to State Grange Historian Amber Vaill for her assistance in locating these membership records.

34. Eliza Leslie, *The House Book: or, A Manual of Domestic Economy* (Philadelphia: Carey and Hart, 1843), 311.

35. The medal is in the collection of Old Sturbridge Village (15.49.8) and is engraved, "The Mass Charitable Mechanic Association Award to Mrs. D. Baker for a quilted Counterpane exhibition of 1841."

36. Raymond J. Purdy, *The Quiet Philanthropy 1795–1995* (Boston: Massachusetts Charitable Mechanic Association, 1995), passim; *Annals of the Massachusetts Charitable Mechanic Association 1795–1892* (Boston: Rockwell and Churchill, 1892); *A Brief Historical Sketch of the Massachusetts Charitable Mechanic Association 1794–1930* (Boston: Massachusetts Charitable Mechanic Association, 1930), 1–7.

37. *Annals of the Massachusetts Charitable Mechanic Association 1795–1892,* 9.

38. Purdy, *Quiet Philanthropy,* 109.

39. Ibid., 110–11.

40. Exhibit pamphlet, Massachusetts Charitable Mechanic Association, 1841, p. 139, American Antiquarian Society, Worcester, Massachusetts.

41. Lynne Z. Bassett and Jack Larkin, *Northern Comfort: New England's Early Quilts 1780–1850* (Nashville, Tenn.: Rutledge Hill Press, 1998), 79, 85–86. For more information on whitework quilts, see Barbara Brackman,

Clues in the Calico: A Guide to Identifying and Dating Antique Quilts (McLean, Va.: EPM Publications, Inc., 1989), 112–14, 133–34.

42. *Boston Evening Transcript*, 29 September 1841.

43. M. V. Brewington, *The Peabody Museum Collection of Navigating Instruments* (Salem, Mass.: Peabody Museum, 1963), 118. I am indebted to Laura Pereira, assistant librarian at the New Bedford Whaling Museum, for bringing this reference to my attention.

12. *Politics and Patriotism in Quilts (pages 194–200)*

1. See G. Julie Powell, *The Fabric of Persuasion: Two Hundred Years of Political Quilts* (Chadds Ford, Penn.: Brandywine River Museum, 2000).

2. Mark Warda, *Two Hundred Years of Political Campaign Collectables* (Lake Wales, Fla.: Galt Press, 2004), 18–27.

3. Joan D. Hedrick, *Harriet Beecher Stowe: A Life* (Oxford: Oxford University Press, 1994), 383–84.

4. "Benjamin Harrison," available at www.whitehouse.gov/history/presidents/bh23.html, accessed 6 June 2007.

5. Dean Lahikainen, *In the American Spirit: Folk Art from the Collections* (Salem, Mass.: Peabody Essex Museum, 1994), 36.

6. Earl P. William, Jr., *What You Should Know about the American Flag* (Lanham, Md.: Maryland Historical Press, 1987), 25, 32–33.

7. U.S. Bureau of the Census, 1900. The silk mill is not identified by the census taker, but it was probably the Skinner Silk Mill, famous for its satins.

8. U.S. Bureau of the Census, 1910 and 1930.

13. *Lost Towns of the Quabbin (pages 201–211)*

1. J. R. Greene, *The Creation of the Quabbin Reservoir, The Death of the Swift River Valley* (Athol, Mass.: Transcript Press, 1981), 65.

2. Donald W. Howe, *Quabbin, The Lost Valley* (Ware, Mass.: The Quabbin Book House, 1951), 395–96.

3. Greene, *Creation of the Quabbin*, 89.

4. Ibid., 90.

5. Richard D. Brown and Jack Tager, *Massachusetts, A Concise History* (Amherst: University of Massachusetts Press, 2000), 267.

6. Thomas Conuel, *Quabbin, The Accidental Wilderness* (Amherst: University of Massachusetts Press, 1990), 2.

7. Ibid., 12–13.

8. Francis H. Underwood, *Quabbin, The Story of a Small Town with Outlooks on Puritan Life* (Boston: Northeastern University Press, 1986), 5. First published in 1893.

9. Ibid., 6.

10. Howe, *Quabbin, The Lost Valley*, 175–77.

11. Underwood, *Quabbin*, 107–109.

12. Ibid., 117.

13. Greene, *Creation of Quabbin Reservoir*, 106.

14. Quoted in Conuel, *Quabbin, The Accidental Wilderness*, 9.

15. Howe, *Quabbin, The Lost Valley*, 147–48.

16. Underwood, *Quabbin*, 108.

17. Howe, *Quabbin, The Lost Valley*, 147.

18. Ibid.

19. Howe, *Quabbin, The Lost Valley*, 465.

20. Ibid., 383.

21. Ibid., 382–83.

22. Quoted in ibid., 374.

23. Collection of the Swift River Valley Memorial Historical Society.

24. The author wishes to thank James and Anna Cullen for providing this information.

25. Information for this essay came from the U.S. Bureau of the Census records of 1880, 1900, 1910, 1920, and 1930, along with family history as remembered by Alice Lowell, granddaughter of Eva and Arthur Goodfield.

26. Brown and Tager, *Massachusetts*, 162.

14. *Family Quilts (pages 212–227)*

1. Over the course of the nineteenth century, various states passed laws providing a married woman or a woman abandoned by her husband certain rights, including the ability to write a will, to own property, or to keep her own wages. New York, in 1848, passed a Married Women's Property Act that became a model for other states. See http://memory.loc.gov/ammem/awhhtml/awlaw3/property_law.html; accessed 10 September 2007. By 1850, Massachusetts law assured a wife of property rights only if she had a prior marriage settlement with her husband—although courts often had shown sympathy for a wife's claims prior to this period. Marylynn Salmon, *Women and the Law of Property in Early America* (Chapel Hill: University of North Carolina Press, 1986), 138–40.

2. Laurel Horton, *Mary Black's Family Quilts: Memory and Meaning in Everyday Life* (Columbia, S.C.: University of South Carolina Press, 2005), 2.

3. Otis Olney Wright, *History of Swansea, Massachusetts 1667–1917* (Swansea, Mass.: Town of Swansea, 1917), 185; Vivian F. Chapin, "The Wilber Family Collection of Handwoven Textiles," unpublished research paper, 1984, curatorial files, Old Sturbridge Village, Sturbridge, Massachusetts, 8.

4. Chapin, "The Wilber Family," 9.

5. Ibid., 10.

6. Ibid., 16.

7. Ibid., 12–13.

8. For examples of the Colonial Revival understanding of quiltmaking, see Alice Morse Earle, *Home Life in Colonial Days* (New York: Macmillan, 1898), 270–76; and Ruth E. Finley, *Old Patchwork Quilts and the Women Who Made Them* (Philadelphia: J.B. Lippincott, 1929), 19–29, 48–54. For examples of 1970s work that perpetuated these myths, see Patsy Orlofsky and Myron Orlofsky, *Quilts in America* (New York: McGraw-Hill, 1974); Patricia Mainardi, *Quilts: The Great American Art* (San Pedro, Calif.: Miles and Weir, 1978); and Jonathan Holstein, *The Pieced Quilt: An American Design Tradition* (New York: Galahad Books, 1973).

9. Marla R. Miller, *The Needle's Eye: Women and Work in the Age of Revolution* (Amherst: University of Massachusetts Press, 2006), 92–94. See also Virginia Gunn, "From Myth to Maturity: The Evolution of Quilt Scholarship," *Uncoverings 1992*: 192–205.

10. Lynne Zacek Bassett, "'A Dull Business Alone': Cooperative Quilting in New England, 1750–1850," in *Textiles in New England II: Four Centuries of Material Life, The Dublin Seminar for New England Folklife Annual Proceedings 1999* (Boston: Boston University, 2001), 32.

11. One recent survey of over sixty quilts made by older women in America between 1820 and 1860 found thirty-two quilts with a provenance of being given as a gift; twelve of these were said to have been given by a mother to her daughter, often on the occasion of her marriage. In Aimee E. Newell, "A Stitch in Time: Needlework and Feminine Aging in Antebellum America," Ph.D. diss., University of Massachusetts–Amherst, forthcoming.

12. Laurel Thatcher Ulrich, *The Age of Homespun: Objects and Stories in the Creation of an American Myth* (New York: Alfred A. Knopf, 2001), 132–33; Barbara McLean Ward, "Women's Property and Family Continuity in Eighteenth-Century Connecticut," in *Early American Probate Inventories*, The Dublin Seminar for New England Folklife Annual Proceedings 1987 (Boston: Boston University, 1989) 76–77, 84; Toby L. Ditz, *Property and Kinship: Inheritance in Early Connecticut 1750–1820* (Princeton, N.J.: Princeton University Press, 1986), 79–80, 114.

13. Mary E. Gale and Margaret T. Ordonez, "Eighteenth-Century Indigo-Resist Fabrics: Their Use in Quilts and Bed Hangings," *Uncoverings 2004*: 157, 162.

14. Chapin, "The Wilber Family," 11, 48–50.

15. Ibid., 51–55.

16. Bassett, "A Dull Business," 28.

17. Chapin, "The Wilber Family," 15, 40.

18. Lynne Z. Bassett and Jack Larkin, *Northern Comfort: New England's Early Quilts 1780–1850* (Nashville, Tenn.: Rutledge Hill Press, 1998), 75.

19. John Warner Barber, *Historical Collections . . . of Every Town in Massachusetts* (Worcester, Mass.: Dorr, Howland and Company, 1840), 276.

20. Laurel Horton, *Mary Black's Family Quilts: Memory and Meaning in Everyday Life* (Columbia, S.C.: University of South Carolina Press, 2005), 115.

21. Information and statistics on 4-H history from a 4-H website, www.4hcentennial.org/history; accessed 10 September 2007.

22. Barber, *Historical Collections*, 260–61.

23. Ibid.

24. Mary Louise Kete, *Sentimental Collaborations: Mourning and Middle-Class Identity in Nineteenth-Century America* (Durham, N.C.: Duke University Press, 2000), 53, 82, 105.

25. These books were published throughout the 1800s; for one example, see Samuel J. Goodrich, *Peter Parley's Method of Teaching Arithmetic to Children* (Boston: Charles J. Hendee, 1833).

26. Marquetry, used to decorate furniture and household accessories, has been called "male quilting." Like quilting, it uses small pieces and scraps to make a whole, repeats patterns, and sometimes reuses materials. Quilt patterns in popular ladies' magazines from the late 1800s also may have inspired men's marquetry patterns. See Richard Muhlberger, *American Folk Marquetry: Masterpieces in Wood* (New York: Museum of American Folk Art, 1998), 85–111. More generally, all forms of woodworking require precise measurements and tight corners.

15. Immigrant and Ethnic Communities (pages 228–250)

1. Richard D. Brown and Jack Tager, *Massachusetts, A Concise History* (Amherst: University of Massachusetts Press, 2000), 173.

2. Ibid., 162.

3. Ibid., 178 and 180.

4. Elizabeth L. O'Leary, *At Beck and Call: The Representation of Domestic Servants in Nineteenth-Century American Painting* (Washington, D.C.: The Smithsonian Institution Press, 1996), 113.

5. Brown and Tager, *Massachusetts*, 179.

6. Lucy Larcom, *A New England Girlhood* (Boston: Northeastern University Press, 1986), 165. First published in 1889.

7. Brown and Tager, *Massachusetts*, 203.

8. MassQuilts #522 and 523. The quilts of Georgiana (Jondreau) Hall (1867–1964) currently are unlocated.

9. Brown and Tager, *Massachusetts*, 204.

10. Ibid., 243.

11. Louise Silk, *The Quilting Path: A Guide to Spiritual Discovery through Fabric, Thread, and Kabbalah* (Woodstock, Vt.: Skylight Paths Publishing, 2006), vii–viii.

12. Ronda McAllen, "Jewish Baltimore Album Quilts," *Uncoverings 2006*: 187–217.

13. Email from Martha Supnik to Lynne Bassett, 11 November 2006.

14. *Tercentenary Program Brookfield, Massachusetts 1673–1973* (Brookfield, Mass.: Brookfield Tercentenary Committee, 1973), 93.

15. Unless otherwise noted, all Clancy family history is credited to an interview with Barbara Clancy, 16 May 2007.

16. U.S. Bureau of the Census, 1910.

17. F. W. Beers, *Atlas of Worcester County Massachusetts* (New York: F.W. Beers & Co, 1870), 53.

18. U.S. Bureau of the Census, 1910, 1920, and 1930.

19. U.S. Bureau of the Census, 1930.

20. Brown and Tager, *Massachusetts*, 203.

21. Penny McMorris, *Crazy Quilts* (New York: E. P. Dutton, 1984), 16–17.

22. "The Sovereign Grand Lodge Independent Order of Odd Fellows Symbols," available at http://www.ioof.org/symbols.htm; accessed 4 September 2007.

23. One of the cotton foundation pieces is stamped with "Kings Road Fabrics." The maker of this fabric is unidentified.

24. Linda Welters and Margaret Ordonez, *Home from the Mill: French-Canadian Quiltmakers in Rhode Island* (Saint-Lambert, QC: Musée Marcil, 1996), 7.

25. Butterfly patterns first appeared as decoration for both apparel and quilts in the early 1900s. For additional references to published butterfly patterns from 1900–1930, see Dorothymae Groves "Free as a Butterfly," in *Butterfly Pattern Collections* (Berne, Ind.: House of White Birches, 1992), 4.

26. U.S. Bureau of the Census, 1910.

27. Personal information about Minnie Louison and her family comes from an interview with Donna Lee Dupras, 28 June 2007. The Federal Census records that Minnie was a weaver at the Berkshire Cotton Mill. Her 1979 obituary, however, noted that she was employed by the Berkshire Fine Spinning Corporation. (The obituary is a loose clipping provided by the quilt owner; source unknown.)

28. In Poland, a pierogi is a dumpling with a cabbage or fruit filling. The author is indebted to Julia's daughter, Justyna Carlson, for her generous assistance and detailed information about the Kruszyna and Steuer families.

29. Justyna Carlson, email to author, 15 March 2007.

30. Ibid.

31. Letter from Justyna Carlson to author, January 2007, and email to author 23 March 2007.

32. The author thanks Josephine Rossi Anzalone's granddaughter for sharing details of Josephine's life in interviews conducted in May and June, 2007.

33. Oscar Handlin, *The Uprooted: The Epic Story of the Great Migration that Made the American People* (Philadelphia: University of Pennsylvania Press, 2002), second edition, 204–205. See also Stephen Puelo, *The Boston Italians: A Story of Pride, Perseverance and Paesani, from the Years of the Great Immigration to the Present Day* (Boston: Beacon Press, 2007).

34. Puelo, *The Boston Italians*, 41–52.

35. Richard Gambino, *Vendetta: The True Story of the Largest Lynching in America, the Mass Murder of Italian-Americans in New Orleans in 1891, the Vicious Motivations Behind it, and the Tragic Repercussions That Linger to This Day* (New York: Doubleday, 1977), 135.

36. Puelo, *The Boston Italians*, 69–97.

37. For a complete discussion of the molasses flood and its political ramifications, see Stephen Puelo, *The Dark Tide: The Great Boston Molasses Flood of 1919* (Boston: Beacon Press, 2003).

38. Barbara Brackman, *Encyclopedia of Pieced Quilt Patterns* (Paducah, Ky.: American Quilter's Society, 1993), 213, pattern #1687b.

39. Bets Ramsey, "The Land of Cotton: Quiltmaking by African-American Women in Three Southern States," *Uncoverings 1988*: 9–28. Personal information regarding the Bailey family courtesy of Irma Bailey Foster interview, 15 March 2007.

40. Mary Elizabeth Johnson et al., *Mississippi Quilts* (Jackson: University Press of Mississippi, 2001), 125–47.

41. A more complete discussion of life in the mills of Lowell may be found in William Moran, *The Belles of New England: The Women of the Textile Mills and the Families Whose Wealth They Wove* (New York: St. Martin's Press, 2002).

42. Originally, their name was Oliviera, but they changed it to Oliver in their adopted country. Information courtesy of Anne M. Keating, granddaughter of Theresa Oliver Mello.

43. Biographical information is taken from an unpublished essay in the files of the New England Quilt Museum written by Anne M. Keating, and from "Theresa Mello: Mill Girl and Quiltmaker" in Jennifer Gilbert, *The New England Quilt Museum Quilts* (Lafayette, Calif.: C&T Publishing, 1999), 23–27.

44. All are illustrated in Gilbert, *New England Quilt Museum*, 27. Theresa's granddaughters believe that the "Z-Lightning" quilt, NEQM 2000.06 (MQ 1831) definitely was made by Theresa, while the "Hour Glass" quilt, NEQM 2000.05 (MQ 1830), may have been made by her daughter, Amelia.

45. For information on the Armenian genocide, see http://www.unitedhumanrights.org/Genocide/armenian_genocide.htm and http://www.umd.umich.edu/dept/armenian/facts/genocide.html; accessed 5 July 2007.

46. The author thanks Susan Lind-Sinanian of the Armenian Library and Museum of America, located in Watertown, Massachusetts, for her assistance in examining this quilt and for providing information about traditional Armenian needlework.

47. "A History of Hopedale," available at http://www.hopedale-ma.gov/Public_Documents/HopedaleMA_WebDocs/about; accessed 6 July 2007.

48. Email correspondence with Kaye Barsamian, 3 July 2007 and 8 July 2007. The author thanks Kaye for her generous assistance with rediscovering Antaram's history.

49. Kevork B. Barkakjian, *Hitler and the Armenian Genocide* (Cambridge, Mass.: The Zoryan Institute, 1985); excerpts available at http://www.armenian-genocide.org/hitler.html; accessed 6 July 2007.

50. "Dahlia" is the family name for this pattern; it is more generally known as "Sunflower." See Brackman, *Encyclopedia of Pieced Quilt Patterns*, no. 3473.

51. Brown and Tager, *Massachusetts*, 7.

52. All quotes and biographical material come from an interview with Ann's granddaughter, Kathy West, 15 March 2007. The author is grateful for her generous assistance.

16. Quilts in War Time (pages 251–265)

1. www.army.mil/cmh/books/RevWar/risch/chpt-1.htm, accessed 7 May 2007.

2. Charles J. Stille, *History of the United States Sanitary Commission, being the general report of its work during the war of the rebellion* (Philadelphia: J.P. Lippincott & Co., 1866), 53–56.

3. Virginia Gunn, "Quilts for Union Soldiers in the Civil War," *Uncoverings 1985*: 96.

4. William Schouler, *The History of Massachusetts During the Civil War*, vol. 2, *Massachusetts During the Rebellion* (Boston: E.P. Dutton, 1871), 422–77.

5. Thomas K. Woodard and Blanche Greenstein, *Twentieth Century Quilts, 1900–1950* (New York: E. P. Dutton, 1988), 8.

6. Excerpt from a letter written by James George to his wife Thomasine, presumably after the Battle of Gettysburg, from the East Chesnut St. Hospital, Harrisburg, Pennsylvania; in the possession of the family and printed here by permission.

7. A quilt in the collection of the Smithsonian Institution (Catalogue Number T. 7726) of similar construction (blocks quilted before assembly) and size (83¾" × 49¾"), with inked Bible quotations, jokes, words of advice, and recipes for medicines was completed in September of 1863 by Mrs. Gilbert Pullen's Sunday School class in Augusta, Maine. It was sent to Washington, D.C., to be used as entertainment for hospitalized Union soldiers from Maine, and returned to Mrs. Pullen about two years later.

8. MassQuilts documentation record #4026.

9. MassQuilts #4026, Row 5, Block 3.

10. United States census, 1860, 1870, 1880; available at www.ancestry.com; accessed 11 June 2007.

11. William Stephens, *In the Matter of Claim for Pension of Thomasine George, Widow of James George, Late Sergeant of Company "H" 76th Regiment New York Infantry Volunteers*, Kings County, New York, 4 November 1872; *Reg-*

ister of Departures of Federal Prisoners of War Confirmed at Andersonville, Ga., Feb. 1864–April 1865, 17.

12. Re-enlistment certificate of James George, Culpeper, Virginia, 2 January 1864.

13. Records privately held by the family.

14. Stephens, *In the Matter of Claim*, 17.

15. Quoted in the biography of Clara Barton, http://www.civilwarhome.com/bartonbio.htm; accessed 5 September 2007. See also Stephen B. Oates, *Woman of Valor: Clara Barton and the Civil War* (New York: Simon and Schuster, 1995).

16. It also has been postulated that the quilt was a fundraiser for the G.A.R. See Dawn C. Adiletta and Tora Sterregaard, *Unfolding History: Quilts from New England Collections* (Hartford, Conn.: Harriet Beecher Stowe Center, 2006), 15.

17. http://www.suvcw.org/gar.htm; accessed 5 September 2007.

18. Sylvia G. Buck, *Warren, A Town in the Making 1741–1991* (Warren, Mass.: Warren Arts Council, 1994), 130. As Dr. Cutter had died by the time the quilt was made, possibly his wife signed for him; Eunice Powers Cutter (1819–1893) was the daughter of Warren's first woolen manufacturer. The author wishes to thank Sylvia Buck for her dogged assistance with this essay, attempting to track down any surviving records of the Clara Barton Post and its ladies' auxiliary.

19. Buck, *Warren*, 130.

20. Ibid., 129, 148.

21. Beverly Gordon, *Bazaars and Fair Ladies* (Knoxville: University of Tennessee Press, 1998), 156–57.

22. Helen Frost and Pam Knight Stevenson, *Grand Endeavors: Vintage Arizona Quilts and their Makers* (Flagstaff: Northland Publishing, 1992), 78.

23. Interview, Dorothy Balise, April 2007. Unless otherwise noted, all Balise family information is derived from this source, with thanks.

24. Thomas K. Woodard and Blanche Greenstein, *Twentieth Century Quilts, 1900–1950* (New York: E. P. Dutton, 1988), 8.

25. Ibid., 24–25.

26. The author thanks Pam Collette for sharing her memories and her quilt.

17. Quilts as Memory (pages 269–291)

1. Barbara Brackman, "Signature Quilts: Nineteenth-Century Trends," *Uncoverings 1989: 25–37.*

2. See Linda Otto Lipsett, *Remember Me: Women and Their Friendship Quilts* (San Francisco: The Quilt Digest Press, 1985), 17–18. In fact, the best ink for use on paper or textiles was India ink, imported from China, which had been known and used throughout the world for centuries already. Even so, many women continued to make their own ink at home throughout the nineteenth century, as evidenced by instructions provided in household advice books. The poor condition of many inked blocks on surviving friendship quilts attests to the fact that acidic inks were used, even though stable ink was available commercially, and had been for generations. Furthermore, inking designs on cotton cloth was not new; inkwork was a fancywork technique practiced in the late eighteenth and early nineteenth centuries. Finely drawn and inscribed drawstring bags, called "reticules," were particularly popular to make; examples can be seen in many museum collections. For more information on ink, see Margaret Ordoñez, "Ink Damage on Nineteenth-Century Cotton Signature Quilts," *Uncoverings 1992: 148–68.*

3. The First Great Awakening happened in the late 1730s and 1740s, led by ministers including the Reverend Jonathan Edwards of Northampton, Massachusetts.

4. "Annette," "The Patchwork Quilt," in *A Patchwork of Pieces: An Anthology of Early Quilt Stories, 1845–1940*, ed. Cuesta Ray Benberry et al., 18 (Paducah, Ky.: American Quilter's Society, 1993).

5. Lynne Z. Bassett, "'A Dull Business Alone': Cooperative Quilting in New England, 1750–1850," in *Textiles in New England: Four Centuries of Material Life, The Dublin Seminar for New England Folklife Annual Proceedings 1999* (Boston: Boston University, 2001), 27–42.

6. Lynne Z. Bassett and Jack Larkin, *Northern Comfort: New England's Early Quilts, 1780–1850* (Nashville, Tenn.: Rutledge Hill Press, 1998), 112.

7. See Elizabeth Alden Green, *Mary Lyon and Mount Holyoke: Opening the Gates* (Hanover, N.H.: University Press of New England, 1979).

8. Anna E. Walker to her brother, Oct. 1, 1849, Mount Holyoke College Archives.

9. Ibid.

10. Charlotte B. Mead to "Miss Peck," May 19, 1850, Mount Holyoke College Archives.

11. Anna Benton to her "dear Aunt," Oct. 16, 1850, Mount Holyoke College Archives.

12. Mary Elizabeth Dewell, "I have no time," unpub. composition, 1847, Mount Holyoke College Archives.

13. Frances Harback to "Friend," Oct. 21, 1851, Mount Holyoke College Archives.

14. Information on students in Mount Holyoke College Alumnae Association, *One Hundred Year Biographical Directory of Mount Holyoke College, 1837–1937* (South Hadley, Mass.: Alumnae Association of Mount Holyoke College, 1937). The author thanks Patricia Albright of the Mount Holyoke College Archives for her assistance.

15. This essay is based on research prepared by Falmouth Historical Society volunteers Shirley and Bill Dunkle and Muriel Locklin. Their sources include U.S. census records; vital records of the towns of Falmouth and Sandwich; archives at the Falmouth Historical Society; the North Falmouth Congregational Church records; *American Nyes of English Origin* (The Nye Family of America Association); and Simeon L. Deyo, *The History of Barnstable County, Massachusetts* (New York: H. W. Blake, 1890). We are grateful to Mr. and Mrs. Dunkle and Ms. Locklin for their generosity in sharing their work.

16. AC2001-01, First Church Papers. Subgroup 5, Series 2. Membership List, n.d. Archives of the First Church in Salem, Unitarian. The author thanks Kris Kobialka, Archivist, First Church for assistance with this research.

17. "Soc. Met agreeably to adjournment for work preparatory to the Mass. A.S. Fair. Rev. Mr. Stone accepted the invitations extended to lecture." 15 September 1847, Record Book 1847–62, Papers of the Salem Female Anti-Slavery Society, Salem, Massachusetts. MSS 34, B1 V2 Phillips Library, Peabody Essex Museum; "Fourteenth National Anti-Slavery Bazaar, Faneuil Hall," *Boston Courier*, 27 December 1847.

18. "Arrest of a Fugitive Slave," *Salem Gazette* 5, no. 41, (5 April 1851): 2. On 3 April 1851, an African-American man, Thomas Sims, was arrested in Boston and arraigned for extradition under the Fugitive Slave Act. For several weeks, Boston and Salem newspapers recounted details of the trial and public demonstrations surrounding this event. Although Sims was represented by prominent lawyers, including Robert Rantoul, Jr., Charles G. Loring, Samuel E. Sewall, Richard H. Dana, and Charles Sumner, the judge eventually upheld the provisions of the Fugitive Slave Act and ordered Sims returned to Georgia and enslavement. In a sermon, "Unrighteous Decrees," delivered at First Church on 6 April 1851, Thomas T. Stone addressed this incident. See Thomas T. Stone, *Sermons* (Boston: Crosby, Nichols, and Company, 1854), 269–70.

19. *Sermon at the Installation of Rev. George W. Briggs as Pastor of The First Church in Salem with Notices of the First Church and its Ministers* (Salem, Mass.: Gazette Press, 1853), 59–60.

20. Ibid.; Thomas T. Stone, *Sermons*. See Sermon XIX, "Unrighteous Decrees" delivered at First Church, Salem, April 6, 1851, 269–283 and Sermon XXIII, "The Worship Called Heresy" delivered at First Church, Salem, February 22, 1852. "Man About Town," *Salem Evening News*, December 4, 1903, 3.

21. Martha E. Waite to Essex Institute, 27 July 1924. American Decorative Art department files, Peabody Essex Museum. The author thanks intern Jessica Zdeb of Harvard University for research assistance.

22. The 1880 United States Census lists James (born c. 1822), and Sarah Gallup as living with Sarah's mother, Hannah S. Colburn. They had married sometime since 1870; Sarah's marriage to James was apparently at least her second, as she had a daughter born in 1863. By 1900, Sarah was widowed and living with her daughter, Nellie, and son-in-law, Willis Upham, in Leominster. Sarah appears for the last time in the 1910 census, still living with Nellie and Willis, who is noted as having his "own income." Census records available at www.ancestry.com; accessed 10 September 2007.

23. Much of this essay is based on two articles about this quilt that appeared in *Quilt World* magazine. See Pat Flynn Kyser, "Pieces and Patches," *Quilt World* 8, no. 1 (January/February 1983): 52–54; and Pat Flynn Kyser, "Pieces and Patches," *Quilt World* 10, no. 4 (July/August 1985): 46–49. The author thanks Ms. Kyser for her generous assistance in preparing this essay.

24. Following the publication of this quilt in *Quilt World* magazine in 1983, a reader recognized that her family owned the second quilt top, along with Mrs. Gallup's scrapbook, in which she had kept the letters and business cards of the celebrities who answered her request for a signature. Unfortunately, this group of artifacts is now unlocated and may have been lost in a house fire. Some photographs of the scrapbook do survive.

25. Catalogue records for 68.49, Historic Northampton.

26. Obituary for Mrs. Jasper E. Lambie, *Daily Hampshire Gazette*, Northampton, Mass., 7 March 1932.

27. Lynne Zacek Bassett, *Textiles for Regency Clothing, 1800–1850* (Arlington, Va.: Q Graphics Production Co., 2001). See also Ellen Rollins, *New England Bygones* (Philadelphia: J. B. Lippincott & Co., 1883), 134. Rollins recalled in this memoir that in 1830s New Hampshire, women wore yellow-and-white gingham aprons in the summer.

28. "Blessed Be the Tie that Binds," words by John

Fawcett (1740–1817); available at http://www. igracemusic.com/hymnbook/hymns/b04.html; accessed 28 July 2007. The author thanks Deborah Kraak for alerting her to the source of this verse.

29. This verse, from a hymn of unknown origin, appears on a Worcester County gravestone from 1838; see http://ftp.rootsweb.com/pub/usgenweb/ma/worcester/towns/northbridge/cemeteries/Friends.txt; accessed 28 July 2007.

30. The author thanks Dennis R. Laurie of the American Antiquarian Society in Worcester, Mass., for this information.

31. Donald Spencer Smith, "Printers and Related Tradesmen of Rural Worcester County (1790–1840); A Look at Them as Printers and as People," unpublished research paper, 1989, Old Sturbridge Village research library, Sturbridge, Mass. Ebenezer Merriam's nephews, George and Charles Merriam, were also his apprentices. They became famous as the publishers of Noah Webster's unabridged dictionary, and their company, Merriam-Webster, Inc., continues in business to this day.

32. *Map of Worcester County* (Boston: Wm. E. Baker & Co., 1857). Collection of Old Sturbridge Village research library.

18. The Colonial Revival (pages 292–301)

1. Alan Axelrod, ed., *The Colonial Revival in America* (New York and London: W.W. Norton & Company for The Henry Francis du Pont Winterthur Museum, 1985); Beverly Gordon, "Stitching Together the American Home," in *The Arts and the American Home, 1890–1930*, ed. Jessica H. Foy and Karal Ann Marling, 135–140 (Knoxville: The University of Tennessee Press, 1994).

2. Alice Morse Earle, *Home Life in Colonial Days*, (New York: The Macmillan Company, 1899), 270–71.

3. Thomas Andrew Denenberg, *Wallace Nutting and the Invention of Old America* (New Haven, Conn.: Yale University Press in association with The Wadsworth Athenaeum Museum of Art, 2003), 57–78; Wallace Nutting, *Massachusetts Beautiful* (Framingham: Old American Company Publishers, 1923), 64, 75, 172, 260.

4. Beverly Gordon, "Spinning Wheels, Samplers, and the *Modern Priscilla*: The Images and Paradoxes of Colonial Revival Needlework," *Winterthur Portfolio* 33, nos. 2/3 (Summer/Autumn 1998): 169–71. See also Margery Burnham Howe, *Deerfield Embroidery* (New York: Charles Scribner's Sons, 1976).

5. Gordon, "Spinning Wheels," 179–94; Carol Shankel, ed., *American Quilt Renaissance: Three Women Who Influenced Quiltmaking in the Early Twentieth Century* (Tokyo, Japan: Kokusai Art, 1997), 17–20, 92–92.

6. Jennifer Gilbert, *The New England Quilt Museum Quilts: Featuring the Story of the Mill Girls* (Lafayette, Calif.: C&T Publishing for the New England Quilt Museum, 1999), 50–55.

7. Family genealogy available at www.ancestry.com; accessed 18 July 2007. Henry Appling's grandmother was Betsy Bradford, great-great-great-granddaughter of William Bradford.

8. Barbara Brackman, *Encyclopedia of Pieced Quilt Patterns* (Paducah, Ky.: American Quilter's Society, 1993), 30–31.

9. Merikay Waldvogel, *Soft Covers for Hard Times: Quiltmaking and the Great Depression* (Nashville, Tenn.: Rutledge Hill Press, 1990), 91.

10. Brackman, *Encyclopedia of Pieced Quilt Patterns*, 186–97.

11. Louise Parker Young, comp., *Biographical Dictionary of the Youngs (Born ca. 1600–1870)* (Bowie, Md.: Heritage Books, 1994), 66.

12. Quoted in Barbara Brackman, *Encyclopedia of Appliqué: An Illustrated, Numerical Index to Traditional and Modern Patterns* (McLean, Va.: EPM Publications, 1993), 32.

13. Barbara Brackman, *Clues in the Calico: A Guide to Identifying and Dating Antique Quilts* (McLean, Va.: EPM Publications, 1989), 29, 31.

14. Stella Rubin, *Treasure or Not? How to Compare and Value American Quilts* (London: Octopus Publishing Group., 2001), 93; Brackman, *Encyclopedia of Appliqué*, 30–32.

15. I am indebted to Betsy Giles, the quiltmaker's daughter, for sharing her mother's story and her family history with me.

16. Lenice Ingraham Bacon, *American Patchwork Quilts* (New York: Bonanza Books, 1973), 86–87.

17. Celia Y. Oliver, *Enduring Grace: Quilts from the Shelburne Museum Collection* (Lafayette, Calif.: C&T Publishing, 1997), 4–13; Linda Eaton, *Quilts in a Material World: Selections from the Winterthur Collection* (New York: Abrams, 2007), 164–87.

18. Exhibition brochure, *Preserving the Legacy: Quilts from the Collections of Annie S. Offen and the New England Quilt Museum* (Lowell, Mass.: New England Quilt Museum, 1990).

SELECTED MASSACHUSETTS QUILTS FEATURED IN OTHER PUBLICATIONS

Atkins, Jaqueline Marx. *Quilting Together—Past and Present*. New York: Viking Studio Books, in association with the Museum of American Folk Art, 1994. See pieced cotton quilt, "Patriotic," made in Florence, 1865, page 91; pieced cotton signature quilt, "Wheel of Mystery," made for the Boston Street Aid Society, Lynn, c. 1886, page 91.

Barron, Tracy W. "Mary Susan Rice and the Missionary Quilt." *Uncoverings 1998*. Lincoln, Neb.: American Quilt Study Group, 1998. Pieced cotton friendship quilt, made for Mary Susan Rice of Lincoln, 1847, pages 71–107.

Bassett, Lynne Z. and Jack Larkin. *Northern Comfort: New England's Early Quilts, 1780–1850*. Nashville, Tenn.: Rutledge Hill Press, 1998. See whitework quilt, made by Susanna Allen Anderson Howard of Ware, c. 1840, page 7; pieced wool quilt, from Wellfleet, c. 1800–1825, page 25; pieced cotton quilt, block-printed by John Waterman, South Scituate, c.1815, page 35; pieced and embroidered cotton quilt, made in Hadley, c. 1815–1830, page 46; pieced cotton quilt, "Star Variation," made by Lucretia Cogswell Rees of Stockbridge, c. 1822, page 48; pieced cotton quilt, "Nine Patch Variation," from Fitchburg, c. 1835, page 55; strip-pieced cotton quilt, from the Capen family of Stoughton, c. 1835, page 57; pieced cotton quilt, "Nine Patch Variation," from the Capen family of Stoughton, c. 1835, page 59; pieced cotton quilt, "Mariner's Compass," made by Emily Gordon of Springfield, c. 1840, page 62; pieced cotton quilt, "Orange Peel," made by Sophia Young of Athol, c. 1835–1840, page 63; pieced cotton friendship quilt, made in South Weymouth, c. 1845–1850, page 109–110.

Bassett, Lynne Z. *Telltale Textiles: Quilts from Historic Deerfield*. Deerfield, Mass.: Historic Deerfield, Inc., 2004. See strip-pieced cotton quilt, made by Eliza Howland of Nantucket, c. 1830, page 23; pieced silk cradle quilt, made by Deborah Ellis Shaw of Palmer, c. 1850–1859, page 25.

Crews, Patricia Cox and Richard C. Naugle. *Nebraska Quilts & Quiltmakers*. Lincoln, Neb.: University of Nebraska Press, 1991. See whole-cloth wool quilt, made by Nancy Clark Phelps of Northampton, c. 1800, page 13.

Eaton, Linda. *Quilts in a Material World: Selections from the Winterthur Collection*. New York: Abrams, in association with the Henry Francis du Pont Winterthur Museum, Inc., 2007. See pieced cotton quilt, hand-block printed by a member of the Waterman family of South Scituate, c. 1780–1815, pages 98–102.

Fox, Sandi. *For Purpose and Pleasure: Quilting Together in Nineteenth-Century America*. Nashville, Tenn.: Rutledge Hill Press, 1995. See pieced cotton friendship quilt, made for Hannah Woodman Coffin of Newbury, 1845, pages 20–26; pieced cotton signature quilt, made to commemorate the history of the Boston Street Aid Society, Lynn, 1886, pages 96–104.

———. *Small Endearments: Nineteenth-Century Quilts for Children and Dolls*. Nashville, Tenn.: Rutledge Hill Press, 1994. See pieced cotton cradle quilt, made to commemorate the birth of Alfred P. Sawyer of Lowell, 1856, pages 5–6; appliquéd cradle quilt, attributed to Mrs. L. G. Richardson of Woburn, mid-nineteenth century, page 42; appliquéd cradle quilt, Massachusetts, 1883, page 145.

Gilbert, Jennifer. *The New England Quilt Museum Quilts*. Lafayette, Calif.: C & T Publishing, 1999. See pieced cotton quilt, "Log Cabin," made by Sarah Bryant of Scituate, c. 1865, page 39; appliquéd cotton quilt, "Peony Quilt," made by either Abigail Bentley Larkin or Abigail's daughter, Sarah Ann Larkin, of Tolland, c. 1870, page 41; appliquéd cotton quilt, "Centennial Quilt," made by Mary Haddy of Cape Cod,

1876, page 42; silk crazy quilt, "Lowell Crazy Quilt," made by Blanche Wiggin Staples (Robinson) of Lowell, c. 1893–1904, page 46; silk crazy quilt, made by Mary Moody Lucy of Deerfield, 1875, page 47; silk crazy quilt, made by Carrie White Reed of Chelmsford, 1885, page 48; silk crazy quilt, made by members of the Ladies' Aid Society of North Egremont, 1886, page 49.

Houck, Carter, and Myron Miller. *American Quilts and How to Make Them.* New York: Charles Scribner's Sons, 1975. See pieced cotton quilt, "Checkerboard Paths," made by Josephine Merrill of Berkshire County, 1868, page 185; appliquéd cotton quilt, "Rose in a Wreath," owned by Eliza Ann Smith of Sheffield, c. 1850–1875, page 186; pieced cotton quilt, "Mystic Maze," from the family of Henry S. A. Black of Hancock, c. 1840–1850, page 188.

International Quilt Study Center, Lincoln, Nebraska, http://www.quiltstudy.org/index.html. As of 2007, this website includes thirty-eight quilts made in or attributed to Massachusetts.

Kort, Ellen. *Wisconsin Quilts: Stories in the Stitches.* Charlottesville, Va.: Howell Press, 2001. See pieced silk quilt, "Center Medallion Yankee Puzzle," made by Catharine Ann Penniman of Braintree (now Quincy), 1825, pages 2–4.

Kraak, Deborah. "Early American Silk Patchwork Quilts," *Textiles in Early New England: Design, Production, and Consumption, The Dublin Seminar for New England Folklife Annual Proceedings, 1997* (Boston: Boston University). See pieced silk quilt top, the "Abercrombie quilt," from the Abercrombie family of Massachusetts, c. 1775–1800, page 9.

McMorris, Penny. *Crazy Quilts.* New York: E. P. Dutton, 1984. See pieced silk crazy quilt, "My Crazy Dream," made by M. M. Hernandred Ricard of Boston and Haverhill, 1877–1912, pages 88–91.

Oliver, Celia. *Enduring Grace: Quilts from the Shelburne Museum.* Lafayette, Calif.: C & T Publishing, 1997.

See appliquéd cotton quilt, "Tree of Life," made by Jeriesha Kelsey, Boston, c. 1800–1825, page 10; pieced cotton quilt, "Hexagon Medallion," made by Jane Morton Cook of Scituate, c. 1820–1840, page 51; pieced cotton quilt, "Tumblers," made by a member of the Almy family of Fall River, c. 1880–1930, page 69.

Oliver, Celia. *Quilts from the Shelburne Museum.* Tokyo, Japan: Kokusai Art, 1996. See pieced cotton quilt, "Paisley Christian Cross," from the Morton family of East Freetown, 1890, pages 100–101; pieced and appliquéd cotton quilt, "Lily Flower," made by Mary Beaman Cummings of Princeton, 1850, pages 54–55.

Peck, Amelia. *American Quilts & Coverlets in the Metropolitan Museum of Art.* New York: Dutton Books for the Metropolitan Museum of Art, 1990. See quilted silk petticoat, worn by Susanna Saunders Hopkins of Salem, c. 1771, page 90.

Peck, Amelia, and Cynthia V. A. Schaffner. *American Quilts & Coverlets in the Metropolitan Museum of Art.* New York: MQ Publications USA, 2007. See template-pieced silk quilt, "Mosaic Quilt," made by Anne Record of Bristol County, begun in 1864, pages 74–75; silk whole cloth quilt, English, owned by Ann (Nancy) Maverick and Nathaniel Philips of Boston, 1747, pages 122–125.

Sullivan, Kathlyn F. *Gatherings: America's Quilt Heritage.* Paducah, Ky: American Quilter's Society, 1995. See pieced cotton quilt, "Postage Stamp," made by Frank Howard Taber of Medfield, c. 1890–1893, pages 68–69; pieced cotton quilt, "Blue and White Scrap Quilt," made by Azelie Maillet Girouard of New Bedford, c. 1925–1935, pages 102–103.

Woodard, Thomas K., and Blanche Greenstein. *Twentieth-Century Quilts, 1900–1950.* New York: E. P. Dutton, 1988. See appliquéd cotton quilt, "Funny Papers," made by the children of Augustine and Jane Savery, Middlefield, 1916, page 128.

CONTRIBUTORS

DAWN C. ADILETTA has been the Curator of the Harriet Beecher Stowe Center in Hartford, Connecticut, since 2000. A historian, author, and lecturer, Ms. Adiletta has an M.A. in American history from the University of Connecticut at Storrs and serves as a board member of the National Collaborative of Women's History Sites, the New England Bibliography, and the editorial board of *The Hog River Journal*, a Connecticut history journal.

LYNNE ZACEK BASSETT is an award-winning independent scholar who publishes and lectures widely on the subject of American costume and textile history. She has been a member of MassQuilts since it was founded in 1994. Ms. Bassett is a former Curator of Textiles and Fine Arts at Old Sturbridge Village, where she was responsible for the exhibition and accompanying book *Northern Comfort: New England's Early Quilts, 1790–1850*. She holds an M.A. in costume and textile history from the University of Connecticut at Storrs and is an Associate Fellow of the International Quilt Study Center in Lincoln, Nebraska.

MARJORIE CHILDERS grew up in Missouri, in a family that treasured quilts and sewed energetically. She studied sociology at Vassar College and at the New School for Social Research, where she earned a doctorate. Later, she earned several degrees in nursing with a specialty in mental health. After forty years of teaching in both areas, she is now Professor Emeritus at Elms College. In 2000, she joined MassQuilts, and in 2002 she became a certified quilt appraiser through the American Quilters Society.

HELEN EWER, who passed away in December of 2007, was a long-time resident of Boston; she had a master's

degree in Asian studies from Goddard College in Plainfield, Vermont, and was enrolled in the Master's degree program in historic textiles at the University of Nebraska at Lincoln at the time of her death. She researched, catalogued, and rehoused historic costumes, quilts, and sewing tools for the International Quilt Study Center, Falmouth Historical Society, and Historic New England. She also volunteered for the New England Quilt Museum, researching and writing about the museum's history for its twentieth-anniversary celebration in 2007.

AIMEE E. NEWELL is Curator of Collections at the National Heritage Museum in Lexington, Massachusetts. She is the former Curator of Textiles and Fine Arts at Old Sturbridge Village, as well as the former Curator of Collections at the Nantucket Historical Association. She currently is pursuing her Ph.D. in History at the University of Massachusetts, Amherst. A widely published scholar, Ms. Newell is an Associate Fellow of the International Quilt Study Center in Lincoln, Nebraska.

ANITA B. LOSCALZO, an independent quilt historian and exhibition curator, is the former Curator of the New England Quilt Museum. She received her B.A. in art history from the University of Pennsylvania, an M.S. in Library Science from Drexel University, and an M.A. in textiles, clothing, and design from the University of Nebraska. She is a member of the American Quilt Study Group and the Alliance for American Quilts.

MARLA MILLER of the University of Massachusetts at Amherst acted as the historical advisor for *Massachusetts Quilts: Our Common Wealth*. Her award-winning book,

The Needle's Eye: Women and Work in the Age of Revolution, appeared from the University of Massachusetts Press in 2006. She presently is completing a microhistory of women and work in Federal Massachusetts, and a scholarly biography of that most-misunderstood early American craftswoman, Betsy Ross.

PAMELA A. PARMAL, David and Roberta Logie Curator of Textile and Fashion Arts and Department Head, has been with the Museum of Fine Arts, Boston, since 1999. Ms. Parmal has curated and written on work as varied as contemporary fashion and Japanese Noh costume. She is now working on a series of exhibitions on Boston colonial embroidery.

PAULA BRADSTREET RICHTER is the Curator of Textiles and Costume in the American decorative arts department at the Peabody Essex Museum in Salem, Massachusetts. Ms. Richter has published exhibition catalogues and articles and she lectures regularly on American textiles and decorative arts of New England. Her articles have appeared in *The Magazine Antiques* and *PieceWork* magazines. Exhibitions she has curated have included *Painted with Thread: The Art of American Embroidery* (2001) and *Transforming Tradition: Arts of New England* (2003).

VIVIEN LEE SAYRE is an historian, lecturer, teacher, and appraiser certified by the American Quilter's Society, who consults extensively on the history of quilts, textiles, color, designs, and symbology. Mrs. Sayre is a member of the board of directors of the New England Quilt Museum. As the founder of the Massachusetts Quilt Documentation Project, which began in 1994, Mrs. Sayre has served continually on its steering committee as historian, documenter, and advisor.

LAUREN WHITLEY is Curator in the David and Roberta Logie Department of Textile and Fashion Arts at the Museum of Fine Arts, Boston. She holds an M.A. degree in Museum Studies from the Fashion Institute of Technology, State University of New York, and received her B.A. in art history from Trinity College in Hartford, Connecticut. Ms. Whitley joined the staff of the MFA Boston in 1992 and has curated several exhibitions, including *The Quilts of Gee's Bend* and *High Style and Hoop Skirts: 1850s Fashion*, and has written essays for museum publications.

INDEX